New Perspectives in Modern Korean Buddhism

New Perspectives in Modern Korean Buddhism

Institution, Gender, and Secular Society

Edited by

HWANSOO ILMEE KIM

and

JIN Y. PARK

Cover: Bongeunsa temple in spring with cherry blossoms, Seoul, South Korea. Shutterstock

Published by State University of New York Press, Albany

© 2022 State University of New York

All rights reserved

Printed in the United States of America

No part of this book may be used or reproduced in any manner whatsoever without written permission. No part of this book may be stored in a retrieval system or transmitted in any form or by any means including electronic, electrostatic, magnetic tape, mechanical, photocopying, recording, or otherwise without the prior permission in writing of the publisher.

For information, contact State University of New York Press, Albany, NY
www.sunypress.edu

Library of Congress Cataloging-in-Publication Data

Names: Kim, Hwansoo Ilmee, [date], editor. | Park, Jin Y., editor.
Title: New perspectives in modern Korean Buddhism : institution, gender, and secular society / Hwansoo Ilmee Kim and Jin Y. Park.
Description: Albany : State University of New York Press, 2022. | Includes bibliographical references and index.
Identifiers: LCCN 2022017001 | ISBN 9781438491318 (hardcover : alk. paper) | ISBN 9781438491332 (ebook) | ISBN 9781438491325 (pbk. : alk. paper)
Subjects: LCSH: Buddhism—Korea.
Classification: LCC BQ656 .N49 2022 | DDC 294.309519—dc23/eng/20220609
LC record available at https://lccn.loc.gov/2022017001

10 9 8 7 6 5 4 3 2 1

Contents

Acknowledgments — ix

Note on Translations and Conventions — xi

Abbreviations — xiii

Introduction — 1
 Hwansoo Kim

Part 1
Beyond the Grand Narratives in Zen Buddhism

Chapter 1
What Do Zen Masters Teach Us Today? The Case of Sŏn Master
Hyeam Sŏnggwan — 21
 Jin Y. Park

Chapter 2
Paek Yongsŏng and the Boundaries of Early Modern Korean
Buddhism: Historiographical Issues and the Question of Scale — 47
 Mark A. Nathan

Part 2
Nuns and Laywomen in Modern Korean Buddhism

Chapter 3
Lady Chŏn and Modern Korean Buddhism — 73
 Hwansoo Kim

Chapter 4
Experiencing a Different Buddhist Community: Nun Suok's Travel
to Japan and Her Contribution to the Korean Community of Nuns   101
   Eun-su Cho

Part 3
Clerical Celibacy, Marriage, Scandals, and Monastic Rules

Chapter 5
Rethinking Married *Bhikṣu*: An Examination of *Bhikṣu* Ordinations
and Clerical Marriage in 1920s Korean Buddhism   121
   Jeongeun Park

Chapter 6
Flesh in the Closet: The "Secret Wife" in Korean Buddhism   157
   Su Jung Kim

Chapter 7
Monastic Regulations in Contemporary Korea   181
   Uri Kaplan

Part 4
Secularity, Society, and Politics

Chapter 8
Han Yongun, Fukuzawa Yukichi, and Questions of Nationalism
and Colonialism   211
   Gregory N. Evon

Chapter 9
Kim Kugyŏng's Liminal Life: Between Nationalism and Scholarship   233
   Kim Cheonhak

Chapter 10
Praying in Kangnam and Longing for the Mountains: The Dilemma
of Centrality in Contemporary Korean Buddhism   251
   Florence Galmiche

Bibliography	277
Contributors	313
Index	317

Acknowledgments

This volume partly comes out of a conference titled "Identities and Identifications: Faces of Modern Korean Buddhism (1910–1945)," which was held in 2015 at Duke University in partnership with Dongguk University in Korea. We are glad that the current volume has come to fruition, adding much to the scholarship on modern Korean Buddhism. Our sincere gratitude first and foremost goes to Professor Jongwook Kim, director of the Humanities Korea (HK) Project at Dongguk University's Academy of Buddhist Studies. The Humanities Korea (HK) Project is sponsored by the South Korean government to promote humanities research in South Korea and beyond. As director, Professor Kim not only supported the conference but also encouraged us to turn the presented papers into an edited volume, which materialized thanks to his saintly patience and flexibility. We are also grateful to James Peltz, associate director and editor-in-chief at SUNY Press, for his advocacy of this book project throughout the process of bringing it to publication. Last but not least, a bow of gratitude to all the contributors who shared their excellent research, greatly expanding the current understanding of modern Korean Buddhism. It was our true honor and privilege to collaborate with them to produce a collective work that will advance the field.

This book was supported by the Ministry of Education of the Republic of Korea and the National Research Foundation of Korea (NRF-2021S1A6A3A01097807).

An earlier version of chapter 4 was previously published in *Religions* 10, no. 6 (2019): 385, https://doi.org/10.3390/rel10060385, under the title "Chŏng Suok's Tour of Imperial Japan and Its Impact on the Development of the Nuns' Order in Korea." An earlier version of chapter 5 was previously published in *Seoul Journal of Korean Studies* 30, no. 2 (December

2017): 131–63 under the title "Re-thinking Married Bhikṣu: Examination of Bhikṣu Ordinations and Clerical Marriage in 1920s Korean Buddhism." An earlier version of chapter 7 was previously published in *Contemporary Korea Contemporary Buddhism* 17, no. 2 (2016): 252–74 under the title "Updating the Vinaya: Formulating Buddhist Monastic Laws and Pure Rules." An earlier version of chapter 10 was previously published in *Sociology and Monasticism*, coedited by Jonveaux, Pace, and Palmisano (Leiden: Brill, 2014): 227–39, under the title "A Space of Mountain within a Forest of Buildings?: Urban Buddhist Monasteries in Contemporary Korea."

Note on Translations and Conventions

Transliterations of East Asian Languages in this volume follow McCune-Reischauer for Korean, revised Hepburn for Japanese, and pinyin for Chinese. As for Korean, the rule does not apply to proper names with established use of romanization and the names of the authors who have already published in English (e.g., Jogye Order instead of Chogye Order; Dongguk University, Tongguk University; Syngman Rhee, Sŭngman Yi; Jin Y. Park, Chin Y. Pak). However, for bibliographical information, with the exception of already published names, all other terms follow the McCune-Reischauer romanization system.

In addition, English translation, romanization, and sinographs preserve the following order: English translation succeeded by K./J./C. romanization and sinographs. For example, "Song of Enlightenment" (K. *odoga* 悟道歌); abbot (K. *chuji* 住持); "Admonitions for Beginning Students" (*Kyech'o simhak inmun* 誡初心學入文). Name of Korean temples and monasteries and mountains are written as follows: for example, "Pulguksa" to "Pulguk Monastery"; Odaesan, Mountain Odae. "Chan," "Sŏn," and "Zen" are used interchangeably, as are "monastery" and "temple." Last, Sanskrit terms are used with diacritics, for example, "Tuṣita"; "Bhikṣu."

Abbreviations

C	Chinese pronunciation
F	French
G	German
J	Japanese pronunciation
K	Korean pronunciation
HPC	*Han'guk Pulgyo chŏnsŏ* 韓國佛教全書
Skt	Sanskrit
T	*Taishō shinshū daizōkyō* 大正新脩大藏經

Introduction

HWANSOO KIM

A decade has passed since the publication of the first English-language edited volume on modern Korean Buddhism, *Makers of Modern Korean Buddhism*, edited by Jin Y. Park (2010). The book included thirteen articles by leading scholars of colonial and postcolonial Korean Buddhism on topics ranging from modernity, nationalism, and colonialism to Buddhist reform, Sŏn (Zen 禪) revivalism, gender, and politics. These articles problematized the tendentious interpretation of modern Korean Buddhism as divided between modernity and tradition and between nationalism and collaboration, thus enriching our understanding of modern Korean Buddhism.

Since the publication of *Makers of Modern Korean Buddhism*, six other monographs on modern Korean Buddhism have been published that, taken together, have furthered and finessed that volume's themes while also contributing new approaches and perspectives on the role and nature of Buddhism in modern Korea.[1] Numerous articles written over the past decade have also advanced the multifaceted aspects of modern Korean Buddhism. It is high time to gather some of this new research into a single volume, and the present one is a result of this need.

New Perspectives in Modern Korean Buddhism is composed of ten chapters divided into four parts. It continues to engage with the themes covered in *Makers of Modern Korean Buddhism*, namely colonialism, nationalism, and modernity, but it also emphasizes the lived experiences of individuals as well as the transnational and institutional dimensions of modern Korean Buddhism. The current volume also expands on four areas that, although mentioned in the first volume, have gained greater attention in recent years: perennial existential concerns and the persistent relevance of contemporary religious practice, gender issues, ethical concerns about clerical marriage and scandals, and engagement with secular society. These chapters reveal the limits of metanarratives, such as those of colonialism, nationalism, and modernity, in understanding the complexity of the individual's lived experience of religion: thus, they demand that we diversify the methods by which we articulate modern Korean Buddhism. Indeed, some of these issues have been sidelined *because* of the dominance of the nationalistic, modernist, and ethnocentric historiography of modern Korean Buddhism.

Spanning the period from the late nineteenth century to the present, *New Perspectives in Modern Korean Buddhism* addresses both ongoing and new themes to help the reader understand recent scholarly trends in the field and to rethink the role of religion in today's context. Is religious practice still relevant to modern, secular society? If so, which aspects of religion should scholars explore? What roles do gender and sexuality play in the evolution and understanding of a religion? Where do the religious and secular worlds meet, and what kind of revelations do we encounter at that juncture? What might these revelations tell us about the current situations of religion and Buddhism? These are some of the questions with which the ten chapters in this compilation are engaged.

Korean Buddhist Nationalism, Modernity, and Institutional Reform

Following the end of the Neo-Confucian Chosŏn dynasty (1392–1910), Korean Buddhism faced two distinctive forces during the colonial period: the West and Japan. Western culture flooded in as an imperialistic force that highlighted the differences in power and resources between East and West. Japan was a neighboring country, but in the process of modernization, it also exercised imperial power over Asian neighbors.

The fact that Korean Buddhists were governed by Japanese colonizers who were fellow Asians and Buddhists complicated their responses to colonialism and modernity. Unlike Chinese Buddhists and Buddhists in other Asian countries, who were responding primarily to Western imperialists and Christian missionaries, Korean Buddhists faced a contradictory, complex situation. They had been marginalized by their own Neo-Confucian government for centuries. Though they were resentful about Japanese political rule, monastic leaders saw an opportunity to elevate Korean Buddhism by drawing on the status, resources, and connections of Japanese Buddhist sects and the pro-Buddhist Japanese state. On the one hand, Korean Buddhists considered Japanese Buddhism to be a model for modernizing themselves in terms of building on institutional structure, developing propagation programs, and forming a symbiotic relationship with the state in much the way that Chinese Buddhists looked up to Japanese Buddhism for their own modernization initiatives.[2] On the other hand, Korean Buddhists felt threatened by Japanese Buddhist sects, which were significantly more powerful politically, institutionally, and financially, and they worried that Japanese Buddhism would eventually take control of Korean Buddhism. This conflicted relationship was further complicated by the rapid rise of Christianity in Korea. Korean Buddhists found themselves competing with both Japanese Buddhism and Western Christianity in the religious marketplace, not to mention that they also had to counter the threat posed by the rapid spread of numerous new religious movements.[3]

The influence of Christianity in Korean society intensified following Japan's defeat in the Pacific War, which ended its colonial rule and heralded the arrival of Western forces in postwar Korea. To meet the challenges posed by Japanese colonialism and Christian aggression, Korean Buddhists appropriated ideas from multiple sources that were both Western and non-Western, as did Japanese,[4] Chinese,[5] and other Asian Buddhists.[6] One could characterize this complex engagement of Korean Buddhists with two imperial powers—the West and Christianity as well as Japan and Japanese Buddhism—as a distinctive feature of *Korean Buddhist modernity*.

During the colonial period, lacking political and material resources, some Korean Buddhists came to depend on the Japanese colonial government to keep both Japanese Buddhism and Western Christianity at bay while also drawing on the state to revitalize Korean Buddhism and restore it to social and political prominence.[7] Under these circumstances, Korean Buddhism's modernization, creation of a national identity, and institutional reform efforts were deeply enmeshed in the governing apparatus of the Japanese empire.[8] Some Korean Buddhists engaged with the practices, ideologies, and platforms presented by the Japanese empire to assert their own national and religious identity. But Korean Buddhists tended to avoid outright political and ethnocentric nationalisms in developing a sense of identity: they articulated their own form of what might be called a *Buddhist* nationalism. Likewise, many Chinese Republican monastic and lay Buddhist leaders developed an "alternative notion of nationalism" that was rooted in Buddhist moral and ethical values.[9] In the case of Korean Buddhism, this form of nationalism was informed by its interaction with Japanese Buddhism and further facilitated by global knowledge and ideas.

Korean Buddhists' strategic engagement and negotiation with the colonial government bore fruit as Japanese imperialism advanced further into China and beyond, especially as Japan needed effective support from the leadership of Korean Buddhism through the propagation of state ideology. After decades of attempts to centralize Korean Buddhism institutionally, all of them futile because of factionalism, internal power struggles, and the lack of support from colonial authorities, a great head temple was founded in 1938 to function as the administrative headquarters for Korean Buddhism. Denominational bylaws that established governance over monastics and lay communities were written in 1941, and the colonial government quickly recognized and approved them. This new, centralized system put an end to the traditional independence of the thirty-one head temples, placing them all directly under the great head temple T'aegosa (太古寺; later, Jogye Monastery 曹溪寺), where the administrative central office was also located. Thus, the Jogye Order (曹溪宗) came into being upon its official recognition by the colonial government in 1941.

The centralization of Korean Buddhism turned out to be both a blessing and a curse for the Buddhist community. Like major Japanese Buddhist sects and the Catholic Church, Korean Buddhism had finally developed into a single, unified community under one administrative system. However, this modern institutional structure also centralized power into the hands of a small group of administrative monks, in particular the administrative head of the Jogye Order, which significantly changed the traditional model of sangha governance and leadership. Struggles over powerful administrative positions have plagued Korean Buddhism since then, and its leaders have continuously wrestled with how to mold the institution into a workable governing system to both preserve traditions and respond to the needs of contemporary society.

Beyond the Grand Narratives in Sŏn Buddhism

If nationalism as a dominant reference point hampers the creation of a multifaceted picture of modern Korean Buddhism, the concept of modernity as a linear trajectory has also confined Korean Buddhism's narrative.

As such, scholars have identified the events signifying Korean Buddhism's modernization as the fissures, disruptions, and transformations of Buddhist tradition occasioned by modern forces. Examples abound, such as the encounter of Korean and Japanese Buddhism following Japan's forced opening of Korea in 1876; the lifting of the prohibition on monks' access to the capital as part of the Kabo Reforms of 1897; the reopening of a temple in the capital in 1911, centuries after the last one there was disestablished; the creation of preaching halls in major cities; and the development of missionary work and education. As for individual cases, scholarship has focused on Han Yongun's radical reform to upend the institutional structure of Korean Buddhism;[10] Paek Yongsŏng's (白龍城, 1864–1940) founding of a new Buddhist religion, Taegakkyo (Great Enlightenment Teaching 大覺敎), and his project to translate Chinese Buddhist texts into Korean;[11] and the lay intellectual Yi Nŭnghwa's (李能和, 1869–1943) efforts toward objectivity in scholarship.[12] Even in postcolonial Buddhism, the Minjung Buddhist movement of the 1980s, the temple-stay programs of the past two decades,[13] and the most recent monastic[14] and lay education reforms have been showcased as unprecedented changes driven by modern forces.

Yet this near-exclusive focus on modernization has come at the expense of accounting for the ways in which these figures and efforts worked through personal, social, and political problems on the basis of tradition. For example, David Ownby and Vincent Gooseart look at Buddhists and Taoists in Republican China to show that their focus has not always been on radical change, but on finding tools and methods informed by tradition for dealing with the problems at hand.[15] Similarly, Justin Ritzinger's research on modern Chinese Buddhism challenges the dominant image of the reformer Taixu (太虛, 1890–1947) as a staunch modernizer. Ritzinger shows that Taixu constantly harkened back to his tradition, as is demonstrated in his unswerving faith in Maitreya and Tuṣita Heaven.[16] Likewise, Richard Jaffe revises our understanding of modern Japanese Buddhism as a product of Japan's encounter with European modernity. He argues that modernity did not derive solely from the West but came from multiple sources. Japanese Buddhist leaders in the modern period turned to South Asian and Southeast Asian Buddhisms as much as if not more than they looked to the West in a quest for an authentic, original Buddhism that could reorient and update their religion.[17]

Scholars of modern and contemporary Korean Buddhism are also aware of the limits of modernist and nationalist frameworks in explaining Korean Buddhism. As such, two chapters of Part I complement the modernity- and linear-centered narrative of Korean Buddhism by looking carefully at how traditional religious experiences, practices, and identities were resurrected and have persisted as ways of coping with recurring existential issues and social dilemmas.

In chapter 1, Jin Y. Park studies the nuanced legacy of one of the leading Sŏn masters of modern Korean Buddhism. Hyeam Sŏnggwan (慧菴性觀, 1920–2001) is widely known as an ardent and traditional Sŏn master who practiced strict asceticism, eating just one meal a day and never lying down to sleep. He later assumed a senior leadership position in the Jogye Order. He became deeply involved in political resistance to stop the order's administration from devolving into a monopoly in 1994 and 1998. A strong proponent of the Sŏn teaching of sudden enlightenment, Hyeam was sectarian in his approach to Sŏn practice, asserting that the teachers of gradual enlightenment descended from an illegitimate line of Korean Buddhism.

Park details Hyeam's dynamic life and contentious work in relationship to these institutional and sectarian identities in order to move away from prior hagiographical depictions of him. Her contribution in this chapter lies as much in her critical analysis of Hyeam's life as in her attention to his indefatigable commitment to awakening. In so doing, Park philosophizes Hyeam's life and argues that he struggled with existential questions. Specifically, his version of Sŏn Buddhism was an expression of his awareness of human reality and could create for readers, in Park's words, "a moment of rupture in the midst of the quotidian and the familiar." In a sense, his Sŏn experience and teaching were a response to religious and perennial realities that were not unique to his time.

Park avers that Hyeam's Buddhism is continuous with that of previous masters in Korea's history, such as the Buddhisms of Kyŏngho (鏡虛, 1849–1912), Iryŏp (一葉, 1896–1971), and Sŏngchŏl (性徹, 1912–1993) in their rigorous struggle in the midst of human suffering. On the basis of this understanding, she cautions against limiting Hyeam to the sectarian lineage of Sŏn. She proposes placing him in the larger philosophical dimensions of Korean Buddhism and concludes that Hyeam's religiosity, rather than his Sŏn sectarian identity, was what made him a modern Korean Buddhist through his insight into the nature of religiosity based on the awareness of human mortality.

In a similar way, in chapter 2, Mark Nathan critically examines the Sŏn monk and reformer Paek Yongsŏng as an example of a Buddhist figure who evades easy categorization. Yongsŏng endeavored to establish an ideal institutional form for Korean Buddhism. As part of this effort, Yongsŏng opened a temple in 1911 in the central part of Seoul, where Buddhist temples had been banned for centuries, and strove to centralize Korean Buddhism on the basis of his version of Sŏn Buddhism. When his efforts did not bear fruit, he founded his own school out of frustration, which later developed into the aforementioned Taegakkyo religion.

Conventional scholarship, Nathan argues, has colored Yongsŏng as either an ardent modernist or a staunch traditionalist, and one whose leitmotif only rested on nationalism and anticolonialism. By stepping away from these metanarratives and instead taking a microhistorical approach, Nathan makes the case that Yongsŏng is better understood through a fine-grained analysis of his various motivations, his fluid identity, and the complex network of relationships he employed in response to colonial and global forces. Building on Anne Blackburn's concept of "locative pluralism" and Thomas Tweed's "translocal" understanding of Buddhism, Nathan suggests that scholars must incorporate a "relational approach" to adequately account for the richness of figures in modern Korean Buddhism.

The two chapters in Part I that follow largely deploy this relational, existential, microhistorical, transnational approach, providing substantially more multiperspectival stories that reflect the real complexities of the era and its key figures.

Nuns and Laywomen in Modern Korean Buddhism

Scholarship that employs modernity, colonialism, and nationalism as dominant reference points for investigating modern Korean Buddhism has also muted the voices of female monastics and laywomen. A number of books on female Korean Buddhists have been published recently to rectify this absence. Martine Batchelor, a former Korean nun, wrote *Women in Korean Zen: Lives and Practices* (2006) in memory of her teacher, the eminent nun Sŏn'gyŏng (禪敬, 1903–1994), a Sŏn master at Naewŏn Monastery (內院寺). *Makers of Modern Korean Buddhism* also included two chapters on Korean nuns, Masters Daehang (大行, 1927–2012)[18] and Iryŏp, contributed by Chong Go and Jin Y. Park, respectively. In 2011, Eun-su Cho published an edited volume of seven articles on Buddhist women in Korean history, giving voice to Korean Buddhist women leaders. Six chapters were on figures from the premodern era; the last, by Pori Park, examined the establishment of nunneries in contemporary Korea.

In addition to this book, Jin Y. Park's research on Kim Iryŏp, an intellectual writer and influential master, has shown that Iryŏp was a seminal figure among the "New Women" in modern Korea and for colonial Korean Buddhism. She is the first female Korean Buddhist figure to receive extensive, in-depth scholarly examination.[19]

The two chapters of Part II join this ongoing effort to recover the marginalized voices of female Buddhists, one lay and one monastic. A number of nuns have been brought into the narratives of modern Korean Buddhism in recent works,[20] but the voices of lay Buddhist women have been less heard. This is vexing given that the vast majority of devotees of Korean Buddhism have been female and must have been working behind the scenes in large numbers to modernize Korean Buddhism. In the third chapter, Hwansoo Kim examines the work of a largely forgotten laywoman, Chŏn Ilchŏng (千一淸, 1848–1934?), one of the highest-ranking ladies in the court of the late Chosŏn dynasty.

Chŏn did not remain confined to a servant's role in the Yi royal household; rather, she became an influential figure in Chosŏn politics and diplomacy, especially with Japan. She also played a crucial role in modernizing Korean Buddhism during the precolonial and colonial eras, one possibly equal in significance to the roles of monastics such as Yi Hoegwang (李晦光, 1862–1932), with whom she worked. In this chapter, Kim draws on the fragments that are known about Chŏn to make the case that she contributed vitally to the incipient stages of modern Korean Buddhism. Chŏn drew on a wide network of relationships both inside and outside the court to establish the very first modern institution of Korean Buddhism, the first modern temple in central Seoul, and the first modern Buddhist clinic in Korea. Kim restores Chŏn's centrality as a Buddhist modernizer while also demonstrating that Chŏn was highly traditional. Kim uses Chŏn's story to bring some balance to a largely monastic-centered history and lengthen the lineage of lay female leadership.

In chapter 4, Eun-su Cho introduces us to a fascinating nun, Suok Sŭnim (守玉, 1902–1966), who made an indelible impact on the Korean Buddhist nuns' community. Suok was the rare Korean nun who went to Japan to study. For more than two years in the late 1930s, she formed close relationships with nuns in the Nichiren and Rinzai sects. After witnessing the vibrancy of the Japanese nuns' traditions, including meditation halls and modern education programs, Suok wrote a travelogue for a Korean Buddhist journal back home. In one section, she delivered a scathing and vociferous critique of Korean monks as culprits in the mistreatment of nuns. After returning to Korea, Suok became an influential leader in the nuns' community and worked strenuously as a dharma instructor and abbess. She was instrumental in generating a strong *bhikkhuni* consciousness and identity in Korean Buddhism. She also played a leading role in the movement to reinstate celibacy in the monastic community, which had become largely married under Japanese colonial rule. Cho argues that Suok was the foremost leader not only among Korean nuns in matters of education, practice, social engagement, and the establishment of feminist awareness, but more broadly in institutional reform and the modernization of Korean Buddhism.

Clerical Celibacy, Marriage, Scandals, and Monastic Rules

Like Japanese Buddhism,[21] clerical marriage has been a central issue in modern Korean Buddhism.[22] The conventional narrative says that the spread of clerical marriage was due to the influence of modern Japanese Buddhism and even that the Japanese colonial government actually imposed marriage on the celibate Korean monastic community. But recent scholarship reveals a more complicated story.

During the Chosŏn dynasty, the definition and status of monastics was fundamentally compromised as a result of policies regulating Buddhism. Monastics were assigned duties to the state as soldiers and corvée labors, which blurred their identities. By the end of the nineteenth century, it was common for monks in the countryside to take wives and even raise children.[23] Thus, in the first decade of the twentieth century, even before Japan's colonization of Korea, Buddhists and state officials petitioned the Korean government to legalize clerical marriage as part of the country's nation-building efforts. While modern Japanese Buddhism undoubtedly influenced this trend by decriminalizing clerical marriage and meat eating in 1871, these petitions also reflected the reality in Korea at the time.

Previous scholarship has tended to attribute clerical marriage to the colonial government's revision of the Temple Law of 1911 by eliminating the clause on celibacy, which had been a prerequisite for appointment to the abbacy of head temples. Recent scholars have stressed that the colonial government never clearly imposed clerical marriage on the monastic community, that there were public debates on the matter without state interference,[24] and that state authorities were, in a sense, responding to the demands of Korean monastic leaders who had already been practicing clerical marriage. The three chapters in Part III develop a new understanding of celibacy and marriage using case studies. They further examine the long-term consequences of policy decisions in contemporary Korean Buddhism.

In chapter 5, Jeongeun Park provides an analysis of how clerical marriage came to be dominant by delving into specific cases from the mid-1920s. Park points out that the Temple Law of 1911 standardized not only clerical rank, education, and the management of temple properties, but also the rules regarding ordination, the implementation of the Vinaya, and clerical celibacy. As mentioned above, it stipulated that *bhikṣu* (celibacy) was a prerequisite for abbacy of the head and local temples. As more monks began taking wives, including the abbots of head temples, it became imperative to change this provision. Otherwise, the *bhikṣu* status of these monks would be nullified; more importantly, those serving as abbots would be dismissed.

Park describes fascinating cases of the colonial government demanding family lineage registers for newly appointed abbots and rejecting some on the basis of their marriage. But the government faced a dilemma, as more monastic leaders than they expected were married. The authorities eventually agreed to eliminate the celibacy requirement for abbacies. However, neither married monastics nor the colonial government wanted the prestigious *bhikṣu* status to be eliminated, so they agreed that, as long as monastics faithfully followed the *ordination* rituals specified in the Temple Law, being married would not negate their *bhikṣu* status. For the colonial government, this was a compromise that minimized disruption. Park maintains that, as a result, the oxymoron "married *bhikṣu*" (K. *taechŏsŭng* 帶妻僧) became a common term, and Korean monks carried this dual identity of being ritually *bhikṣu* and in practice married for the remainder of the colonial period.

After the Japanese left, the married monks who had enjoyed prestige and power under colonial rule were ousted from their positions. A purification movement ensued: backed by the newly established South Korean government, celibate monks took over the major head temples and the leadership of the denomination. But the question of clerical marriage continued to plague Korean Buddhism, and this is the focus of the next chapter.

In chapter 6, Sujung Kim zooms in on a recent scandal involving the head monk of the celibate Jogye Order, who fathered a daughter with a nun but kept the matter secret. He denied the reports even as mounting evidence became public. By focusing on this and a slew of other sex scandals of recent years, Kim historicizes the prevalence of monks secretly taking wives. One of the many factors that led to the discourse of secrecy, she argues, was the way the Purification Movement was implemented. In an effort to drive married monks out of the temples, the celibate faction colored them as collaborators with Japanese colonialists who had adopted the practice of clerical marriage uncritically. In the postcolonial era, anyone daring to come out as married would automatically be stigmatized as a pro-Japanese collaborator.

The unmarried camp also hastily began ordaining untrained men in an effort to offset the numerical imbalance and to more forcefully oust the married monks. The rampant incorporation of these low-quality monks led to pervasive moral laxity. In addition, the unmarried camp enticed married monks to join their cause by asking them to divorce their wives on paper while what they did in private was overlooked.

Kim offers five angles for making better sense of this situation and understanding why the public shows considerable tolerance for violations of celibacy. For example, she writes that, although the present situation is partly the result of colonialism, Japanese Buddhists, and modernity, the Sŏn Buddhist tradition of antinomianism and the lionization of morally flexible Buddhist monastics such as Wŏnhyo and Kyŏnghŏ are equally responsible. Despite this internal contradiction, the Jogye Order, established by the unmarried camp, has continued to present itself as the preserver of the monastic tradition of celibacy. Kim concludes that it is the policies and rhetoric of the order itself that are responsible for the widespread secrecy, rather than the moral failings of individual monks.

Likewise, since the inception of the monastic community, the Buddhist sangha has been perpetually concerned with keeping its reputation in society intact. In chapter 7, Uri Kaplan examines the Jogye Order's reforms of its monastic rules following a series of scandals that culminated in an incident in 2012. A group of monks from the renowned Paegyang Monastery were caught drinking, smoking, and gambling on a hotel's hidden camera. Faced with a slew of such scandals, which sparked a public outcry against monastic corruption, the Jogye Order reined in its clergy by reeducating them on the Vinaya rules.

Kaplan points out that the Jogye Order was well aware that the traditional Indian and Chinese monastic rules would be difficult to enforce in the present, highly globalized, wired society. Therefore, the order created simplified, standardized, and updated Vinaya rules in the hopes that they could be realistically and effectively implemented. Called *The Pure Rules for the Sangha* (K. *Sŭngga chŏnggyu* 僧家清規) and instituted in 2015, they concern monastic etiquette and mindset as well as how to deal with money and property. Like the traditional rules that were written centuries ago, these new rules are very much in line with the secular government's legal system. Kaplan stresses that the new rules are a telling example of "the constant negotiation between reform and revival, modernization and traditionalism." Moreover, Kaplan reminds us in his conclusion that this negotiation and any other undertaking by the Jogye Order is intent primarily on "maintaining the favorable social reputation" of the Sangha, a central concern of the monastic community throughout history.

The strong attachments to these aspects of Buddhist practice and identity cannot be fully grasped in modernist terms because they are manifestations of traditional practices and ideas as ways of reckoning with contemporary concerns. These three chapters provide a clear reminder that scholars should account for the persistence of the tradition and perennial issues as much as the advent of change and transformation.

Secularity, Society, and Politics

The three chapters in Part IV of this volume bring to light the limitations of ethnocentric and binary interpretations of modern Korean Buddhism, such as nationalism versus collaboration, tradition versus modernity, or mountain Buddhism versus city Buddhism. To better understand the diverse players in modern Korean Buddhism and to better elicit the details of the agency they exercised in the colonial and secular context, transnational and relational perspectives are needed. The dichotomous, modernity-centric understanding of postcolonial Korean Buddhism also overlooks a dynamic interaction between tradition and modernity and between religion and secularization, in which traditional values and identities constantly reinforce themselves even amid the heightened discourse of modern Buddhist propagation advanced by the Jogye Order.

In chapter 8, Gregory Evon reevaluates Han Yongun's (韓龍雲, 1879–1944) nationalism by analyzing his fiction and reveals Han's indebtedness to

Japanese intellectual trends, particularly to the Buddhist scholar Fukuzawa Yukichi (福澤諭吉, 1835–1901). Han's 1910 treatise on the reformation of Korean Buddhism was informed by Fukuzawa's rendering of the difference between East and West.[25] Painfully aware of the wretched condition of his native Buddhism, Han accepted Fukuzawa's social Darwinism but articulated a way of repackaging his tradition to bring it up to date. But Evon maintains that not all of Han's writings should be considered signifiers of Korean nationalism, Japanese colonial aggression, and political liberation. Using the novel *Fate* (K. *Pangmyŏng* 薄明) as evidence, Evon argues that when Han wrote it in the 1920s, he had joined the intellectual milieu of his time in which popular culture was focused on the idea of "love." Driven by the commercial literary market and the mass publication industry, Han used print capitalism as an opportunity to disseminate his religion in vernacular language, making it more accessible to the populace.

Evon concludes that the tension between coloniality and modernity was not as acute as previously believed and that many Buddhist leaders, including Han, had other, equally pressing concerns and interests, as reflected in their writings and activities. One must look at colonial Korean Buddhism in the broader context in which multiple human concerns and motivations played out. This perspective is especially important for locating the agency of historical figures. Instead of being shackled by colonial aggression and manipulation, historical figures performed intelligent navigation to realize their goals.

One figure who exemplifies the agency of the colonized was Kim Kugyŏng (金九經, 1899–1950?), who traversed the Japanese empire while making significant contributions to transnational scholarly work. In chapter 9, Kim Cheonhak studies the life of Kim Kugyŏng, who was employed at Keijo Imperial University and worked as a researcher and librarian in Beijing and Manchuria during the colonial period. Working with prominent Chinese and Japanese scholars, Kim conducted extensive fieldwork to procure rubbings of historical memorials. Through articles that circulated among East Asian scholars, he took the role of a bridge between Chinese, Japanese, and Korean scholarship, which enabled him to make major contributions to contemporary East Asian history, religion, and cultural studies. His scholarly endeavors were also made possible by the platforms he was offered by the Japanese empire, not to mention the education he received in Japan and the network of relationships he cultivated.

However, Kim's relationship with Japan was not one-directional. He also influenced Japanese scholars such as Suzuki Taisetsu (鈴木大切,

1870–1966) and Seizan Yanagida (聖山 柳田, 1922–2006), who relied on Kim's research for their own works. His scholarship even had an impact on the compilation of the *Taishō shinshū daizōkyō* (大正新脩大藏經). Kim Cheonhak shows that Kim Kugyŏng cannot be placed in a binary framework. Even though Kim Kugyŏng later took a Japanese name, he was a transnational figure whose primary devotion was to Buddhist scholarship and who indirectly promoted the prestige of Korean Buddhism in scholarly circles. He was even thought of as a Buddhist nationalist in his own right, on a par with Han Yongun.

Although a primary concern of colonial and postcolonial Korean Buddhism has been to make Buddhism socially relevant and influential, traditional values and structures continue to assert themselves. In chapter 10, Florence Galmiche examines the tension between the need to modernize Buddhism and the idea of reviving the monastic tradition by defining monastic life in the mountains as the authentic form of Buddhist practice. In fact, this conflicting demand of maintaining the tradition while modernizing Buddhism has been a main phenomenon ever since Korean Buddhism encountered modernity, but recent years have witnessed new developments in this dual task. The Jogye Order, the largest Buddhist denomination in South Korea, recently launched programs to educate the laity, especially female devotees, and reemphasize propagation (K. *p'ogyo* 布敎). These programs were largely implemented in urban temples, where laity were trained to become Buddhists of the "highest quality" who understand and practice Buddhism correctly in the face of increasing secularization. To regulate lay practices and instill a Buddhist identity, the Jogye Order issued membership cards to the laity and organized communal educational programs.

Galmiche points out that this "churchification" of urban temples had both expected and unexpected consequences. On the one hand, it closed the gaps between the monastic and lay populations and between the mountain and city temples. On the other hand, she argues that the education programs in fact reinforced the supremacy of the monastic community over the laity and heightened the significance of the mountain temples over their city counterparts. She suggests that this reinforcement came about through the strengthening of monastic precepts and retreats, the reemphasis on monastic ethos, and the encouragement of pilgrimages to mountain temples by lay members. In making this case, Galmiche articulates the ongoing tension and negotiation between tradition and modernity that can be found in the policies and programs initiated by the Jogye Order.

Going Forward

Together, the ten chapters in this volume direct our attention to a set of new approaches meant to help us comprehend colonial and postcolonial Korean Buddhism in a more nuanced way. The chapters also reflect the need for a new direction in Buddhist scholarship in accordance with the changing landscape of religious life and the role of religion in modern times.

According to the most recent census data available from Statistics Korea (2015), South Korea has more Christians than followers of any other religion. Among the country's population of 51 million, 19.7 percent practice Protestantism, 15.5 percent practice Buddhism, and 7.9 percent practice Catholicism.[26] The two branches of Christianity together account for 27.6 percent of the population, making it the dominant religion in South Korea. The Christian paradigm, or as Vladimir Tikhonov calls it "the Christian monopoly,"[27] has been firmly established in Korean society on all fronts—cultural, economic, and political. This presents a serious challenge for Korean Buddhism.

Another pressing issue for Korean Buddhism is a rapid drop in new novices, especially among women.[28] The situation has become so dire that the Jogye Order recently launched an ad campaign to entice people to become monastics by emphasizing the benefits of monastic life.[29] This drop-off is not unique to Korean Buddhism, though; it has become a major problem for the Catholic Church as well. Nevertheless, Korean Buddhism was not prepared for the trend. The issue is only compounded by the increasingly aging population of monastics, largely in line with the general demographics of Korean society.

In addition, South Korea is becoming increasingly secular in the same pattern that many European countries have experienced.[30] Although Christianity has numerically surpassed Buddhism in South Korea, total religious affiliation in the Korean population fell to 43.9 percent in 2015,[31] and it is likely to fall further in the years to come.

Korean Buddhism has been hard-pressed to reckon with these challenges and with its diminishing relevance to Korean society. The prisms of sectarian discourse, ethnocentric nationalism, and male-centered modernity as well as the dualism of celibacy versus clerical marriage are no longer adequate interpretative tools for understanding Korean Buddhism in particular or the function of religion and the manifestation of religiosity in modern society more generally. This situation tells us that Buddhist scholarship cannot be satisfied with simply bringing more attention to the ways that modern and contemporary Korean Buddhism have continuously worked to resolve the tension between internal concerns (doctrine, ritual, and institution) and external forces (modernity, colonialism, and Christian missions). It demands that scholars, monastics, religious organizations, and followers address issues that are urgent today, such as gender, sexuality, race, secularization, and globalization. It also demands that we ask what forms of engagement the Buddhist community should use to address these issues, as lay practitioners or monastics and as individuals or institutions.

The diminishing number of people declaring religious affiliation does not mean that the role of religion in human life and society has completely lost its ground. The existential pain of human life has not changed. In what new ways does religion influence people's lives, implicitly and explicitly? What new scholarship and methods are needed to understand these new modes of religiosity? In lieu of the meta-narratives that dominated Korean Buddhist scholarship until recently, an understanding of the lived experiences of Buddhism, positive or negative, might bring us closer to understanding the multifaceted nature of modern Korean Buddhism from more critical and creative perspectives. The chapters in this volume are the results of this aspiration.

Notes

1. The six monographs are Mun, *Purification Buddhist Movement, 1954–1970* (2011); Kim, *Empire of the Dharma* (2013) and *The Korean Buddhist Empire* (2018); Park, *Women and Buddhist Philosophy* (2018); Nathan, *From the Mountains to the Cities* (2018); and Kaplan, *Monastic Education in Korea* (2020).

2. Cho, "Reconsidering the Historiography of Modern Korean Buddhism," 54–74.

3. Two representative new religions were Chŏndogyo and Pochŏngyo. See Young, *Eastern Learning and the Heavenly Way*; and Jorgenson, "Pochŏngyo and the Imperial State: Negotiations between the Spiritual and Secular Governments," 177–205.

4. For the most recent work on the transnationality of Japanese Buddhism, see Jaffe, *Seeking Sakyamuni*.

5. See Ritzinger, *Anarchy in the Pure Land*; and Hammerstrom, *The Science of Chinese Buddhism: Early Twentieth-Century Engagements*.

6. See Blackburn, *Locations of Buddhism*; and Turner, *Saving Buddhism*.

7. Evon, "Korean Buddhist Historiography and the Legacies of Japanese Colonialism (1910–1945)"; Kim, *The Korean Buddhist Empire*; and Nathan, *From the Mountains to the Cities*.

8. Kim, *The Korean Buddhist Empire*.

9. Kiely and Jessup, eds., *Recovering Buddhism in Modern China* (see "Introduction").

10. For example, see Tikhonov and Miller, trans., *Selected Writings of Han Yongun*.

11. See Han, "Yongsŏng Sŭnim ŭi chŏnbangi ŭi saengae" (The Early Part of Venerable Yongsŏng's Life) and "Yongsŏng Sŭnim ŭi hubangi ŭi saengae" (The Later Part of Venerable Yongsŏng's Life).

12. See Yi, *Yi Nŭnghwa wa kŭndae pulgyohak*.

13. See Kaplan, "Images of Monasticism."

14. A detailed analysis of the monastic education reforms appears in Uri Kaplan's monograph published in 2020.

15. See "Introduction," Ownby and Gooseart, *Making Saints in Modern China*.

16. Ritzinger, *Anarchy in the Pure Land*.

17. Jaffe, *Seeking Sakyamuni*.

18. Most recently, Pori Park published an article on Daehaeng Sunim titled "Uplifting Spiritual Cultivation for Lay People: Bhikṣuṇī Master Daehaeng (1927–2012) of the Hanmaum Seonwon (One Mind Sŏn Center) in South Korea" (2017).

19. See "Gendered Response to Modernity: Kim Iryŏp and Buddhism"; *Women and Buddhist Philosophy: Engaging Zen Master Kim Iryŏp*.

20. One nun who has recently gained increasing attention is Pongnyŏgwan (蓬廬觀, ?–1938), who revitalized precolonial and colonial Buddhism on Cheju Island by building and rebuilding all of the major temples standing today. See Kim, *Minjok Pulgyo ŭi isang kwa hyŏnsil*, 35; Pongnyŏgwan Sŏnyanghoe, *Hyeowŏldang Pongnyŏgwan sŭnim*.

21. See Jaffe, *Neither Monk nor Layman*.

22. For the most complete discussion of the movement, see Mun, *Purification Buddhist Movement, 1954–1970*.

23. Kim, "The Mystery of the Century."

24. Auerback, "Ch'inil Pulgyo yŏksahak ŭi chaego" (Rethinking the Historiography of Pro-Japanese Buddhism), 15–53.

25. Tikhonov and Miller, trans., *Selected Writings of Han Yongun*.

26. Statistics Korea, "2015 in'gu chut'aek ch'ongjosa p'yobon chipkye kyŏlgwa" (Results of the Sample Survey on the 2015 Population and Housing Census), 17.

27. Tikhonov, "South Korea's Christian Military Chaplaincy in the Korean War: Religion as Ideology?"

28. For example, the female novitiates numbered 137 in 2005 and decreased to 52 by 2018 (Kim, "Sutch'a ro ponŭn Pulgyo wa Chogyechong 2017" (Buddhism and Jogye Order of 2017 Seen through Numbers).

29. Pak, "Sŭnim kuin kwango sidae" (The Age of Advertisement for Recruiting Monastics).

30. See Chaves, *American Religion: Contemporary Trends*.

31. Statistics Korea, "2015 in'gu chut'aek ch'ongjosa," 17.

PART 1

BEYOND THE GRAND NARRATIVES IN ZEN BUDDHISM

Chapter 1

What Do Zen Masters Teach Us Today?
The Case of Sŏn Master Hyeam Sŏnggwan

JIN Y. PARK

Introduction

Korean Sŏn Master Hyeam Sŏnggwan (慧菴性觀, 1920–2001) is a relatively unknown figure within English-language scholarship.[1] However, among Korean Buddhists, his rigorous Zen practice has been well recognized. One-meal-per-day (K. *ilchongsik* 一種食), no-meal-in-the-afternoon (K. *ohu pulsik* 午後不食), and staying-sitting-in-meditation-without-lying-down (K. *changjwa purwa* 長坐不臥) are all well-known practices that frequently appear when describing Hyeam as a Zen master. What is less frequently asked is what these rigorous Zen practices might mean to us commoners who live in a secular world or to monastics whose practice might not be as rigorous as Hyeam's. Should Zen masters such as Hyeam who appear to exhibit superhuman capacity for religious practice be only an object of awe and admiration in our secular modern times? Even if so, what do the awe and admiration indicate? In this chapter, I try to bridge the gap between the rigorous practice typically seen in Korean Zen masters' lives and its meaning for people living in modern times. What questions does a Zen master like Hyeam raise for us, and how should scholars address these issues? These are the inquiries with which I hope to engage.

Hyeam's Life and Sŏn Thought

Hyeam was born in 1920 in the South-Chŏlla Province in the southern part of South Korea. After completing high school, he went to Japan in 1936 to continue his education, studying both Eastern and Western philosophies. It is said that a passage he encountered during this time opened his eyes and inspired him to follow the path of Buddhism. He returned to Korea in October 1946 at the age of twenty-seven and received precepts at Hyein Monastery, earning the dharma name Sŏnggwan.[2] After that, Hyeam's life was a series of rigorous practices at various meditation halls, hermitages, and caves in Korea in addition to Korean monastics' seasonal retreats. He practiced at most of the well-known meditation venues in Korea and with major figures in modern Korean Buddhism, such as Han'am (漢巖, 1876–1951), Chŏngdam (靑潭, 1902–1971), and Sŏngchŏl (性徹, 1912–1993), all of whom served as Supreme Patriarch (K. Chongjŏng 宗正) of the Jogye Order, the largest order in contemporary Korean Buddhism. In 1999, Hyeam himself became the tenth Supreme Patriarch of the order and maintained the position until he passed away in 2001.

This simple outline of Hyeam's life does not show much about the extraordinary rigor with which he practiced Buddhism, but publications on Hyeam are full of stories of the superhuman level of Hyeam's practice. Just to give an idea of this, I offer a story set at Sago Hermitage (史庫庵) on Odae Mountain, currently Yŏnggam Monastery (靈鑑寺). Early in the winter of 1957, Hyeam was determined to enhance his practice and went to the hermitage. Journalist Chŏng Ch'anju describes Hyeam's practice at the time as follows:

> The hermitage was nothing other than four walls made of soil and a roof covered with dry grasses. In the cold winter when Hyeam was under practice, the inside temperature of the hermitage was around minus twenty degrees Celsius [minus four degrees Fahrenheit]. Everything inside the room and kitchen was frozen. For each meal, all Hyeam ate was uncooked leaves of Korean pine trees and ten beans. He never warmed up his room. He loathed wasting his time making firewood, and since he worried that he would feel drowsy if the room got warm, he never even tried to light the firewood. In order not to lose his concentration on the *hwadu* meditation, he cut off anything and everything unnecessary for the meditation practice. As he

remained seated without lying down, he felt his mind became clearer as if he were doing seated meditation on the ice, and sleep vanished.³

After four months of such demanding practice, the practitioner found that sleepiness completely vanished. Once he had overcome bodily obstacles such as sleepiness, other obstacles to his meditation gradually gave way, his vision becoming clearer. With this experience, Hyeam realized that sleepiness did not exist. It is said that he never lay down to sleep from that point until he passed away.⁴

Hyeam's life was a continuation of the rigorous practice as described above. How would normal people who do not possess such an exceptional capacity respond to his life story? What lesson does one gain from a story like the above of Hyeam's practice? In fact, in modern Korean Sŏn Buddhism, Hyeam was not an exception. Kyŏnghŏ Sŏngu (鏡虛惺牛, 1849–1912), frequently credited as the revivalist of Sŏn Buddhism in modern Korea, is known for practicing with a sharpened knife under his chin so that he would be warned if he fell asleep. Another Sŏn master, Sŏngchŏl, put up a barbed wire fence around his hermitage and did not go out for ten years in addition to not-eating-in-the-afternoon and performing staying-sitting-in-meditation-without-lying-down.

One might say that such severe practices are possible because Zen masters are special people and their rigor is not related to us, normal people. If so, why do we want to read about them? And what do we expect to learn from their lives, if we desire to learn anything at all? I begin with a short episode that might bridge the wide gap between Hyeam's life as a practitioner and our own lives in the secular world.

In explaining the meaning of Zen practice, Hyeam tells us a story about a rabbit. While a rabbit was relishing her daytime nap, she was hit by an acorn falling from a tree. The poor rabbit was startled and jumped to dash away. Seeing the rabbit speeding away, deer and roe started hopping, and the rest of the animals in the forest followed suit. A lion asked one of them why they were dashing away, and the creature answered that he did not know the reason, because he was only following others who were running. Although simple and funny, this fable seems to mirror our lives in modern times. People are getting busier and busier, working from early in the morning until late at night, eating sandwiches in front of their laptops for lunch, covering dinner with fast delivery food. If asked why we work so hard, one might answer that we don't have the time to think about it, so we should run faster first and think about its meaning later. After telling us the fable, Hyeam says that "to know why one should run is Sŏn."[5]

To continue the simile of running, most of us might not spend much time thinking about the meaning of why we run. One might ask why it is a problem if we do not know the exact meaning of each of our actions; at least people know what they want, such as to complete college, to get a job, to give children a comfortable life, and so on. Hyeam asks us to think deeper and tells us that the life we live without knowing the meaning of "running" is like a dream. Hyeam observes that Buddhist teaching is about "attaining the Buddhahood by waking up one's mind" and that attaining the Buddhahood is like waking from a dream.[6] "One can compare the waking of one's mind with waking from a dream. In a dream, there are moments when we feel like we do everything freely and of our own will without obstruction, but we are not aware that we are dreaming. Once awake, we say, 'Oh, I was dreaming.' . . . Sentient beings are not aware that their lives are like dreams."[7]

The comparison is understandable, because people wouldn't want to think that their lives are not rooted in reality and thus are nothing but a fantasy. But still, some might ask why life-as-a-dream should be a problem if that dream looks as solid as reality, because people usually think that their lives are rock-solid. Hyeam connects dreaming with the issue of freedom. He observes, "Before one attains the Buddhahood, one is not only dreaming in this life but also is not free. The freedom of sentient beings is freedom in a dream, and the freedom of those who attain the Buddhahood is freedom after one awakens from the dream."[8]

Freedom is an important issue in Western philosophical tradition, especially in modern times, because modernity began with a promise of freedom at various levels. Gaining freedom from monarchy introduced democracy, a political system controlled by the people; gaining freedom from the transcendental or divine power is the foundation of the anthropocentric worldview. The latter is also called "secularization," the etymology of which emphasizes being related to this world instead of to anything religious. In his discussion of religion, the twentieth-century French philosopher Jacques Derrida (1930–2004) once defined secularization as "the transition from heteronomy to autonomy."[9] In modern times, the authority or legitimacy of values and judgments lies not with a transcendental power but in the autonomous power of human beings. Freedom is the foundation of one's autonomy because, if a decision is made not out of free choice but through a command or a coercion by an external force, the subject who makes the decision is subject to the control of the author of that command.

A representative figure in European modern philosophy, Immanuel Kant (1724–1804), hence took autonomy as the foundation of moral action. For Kant, moral action should be what one performs based on one's own free choice in relation to the values of the actions themselves, uninfluenced by external forces. This also means that, to Kant, morality is equal to freedom.

Freedom is also not an alien topic to modern Korean Buddhism. Kim Iryŏp (金一葉, 1896–1971), a leading figure in the Korean nuns' community in the twentieth century, wrote about her realization of the loss of autonomy and freedom in our existence. She observed:

> After I joined the monastery, three things greatly astounded me. First, I was shocked when I realized that I had lost my own self. Second, I was astonished to realize that the entire world consists of people who have lost their selves. And third, I was stunned to realize that, even though the entire world is populated by people who have lost their selves, they are not aware of it and instead delude themselves that they are smart and pretend to know everything. People act, but they do not even try to think about what it is that makes them act. This last point shocked me even more.[10]

Iryŏp states that even though people pretend to be the owners of themselves, their actions are always constrained by external influences instead of being autonomous free actions, which to Iryŏp is equal to losing oneself, because one is not the owner of oneself if one's actions are a result of external constraints. It is not difficult to notice similar concerns in Iryŏp's realization and Hyeam's teaching of the delusion of being free in a dream. How does one attain freedom, then? Hyeam says that the method to attain freedom is *hwadu* (話頭) practice.[11]

Hwadu meditation, observing the critical phrase, or Kanhwa Sŏn (看話禪), is one of the major practices in Korean Sŏn Buddhism. Introduced by Pojo Chinul (普照知訥, 1158–1210) during the thirteenth century, *hwadu* meditation uses internally oriented questioning on the existential reality of the practitioner as a way to awaken the practitioner from the taken-for-granted attitude of the quotidian.

Hyeam proposed *hwadu* meditation as a weapon to earn freedom. In a commonsense fight, the enemy is outside the subject, who must fight to earn a goal by defeating the enemy. Religious wars take a form somewhat different from this traditional warfare. Religions have engaged in regular warfare, but one of the values of religious teaching is to help us rethink what is commonly taken for granted and, by doing so, facilitate environments in which a radical transformation takes place in the practitioner's way of understanding themselves and their relation to others. How does the transformation occur? Zen Buddhism tells us that it should come from inside instead of outside the individual. The battle then becomes one's struggle against oneself with one's mind as the battlefield.

One characteristic feature of *hwadu* meditation is its emphasis on the function of doubt. Hyeam identifies doubt as a major element of this battle, observing, "The very life of *hwadu* meditation is to have doubts. Practicing *hwadu* meditation without doubt leads one to the dead word (K. *sagu* 死句)."[12]

Doubt has an ambiguous, to say the least, position in the modern world, which began with a confirmation of the human capacity to make right decisions through the exercise of reason. When doubt was invoked in modern philosophy, it had more to do with methodological questions to confirm the certainty of human knowledge, as in the case of the famous doubt by Rene Descartes (1596–1650). In religious tradition, doubts can also mean a lack of faith or a weakness in religious confidence. Iryŏp recalled how her father, a faithful pastor of evangelical Christianity, chided her when she was about to express her doubts about some of the Christian doctrines. Her father interpreted Iryŏp's doubts as a symptom of her wavering faith and advised her to pray, which her father saw as the only medicine to cure doubt.

Against such a tradition that requires certitude of faith and knowledge, *hwadu* meditation calls for doubts as a pillar of meditation practice. The fundamental goal is to change the direction of questioning so that the practitioner can face their own existential reality. In Korean tradition, doubts are usually indicated with the expression "What is this?" (K. *yi muŏtggo* 이 뭣꼬?). Hyeam explains how he practiced the *hwadu* meditation of doubts as follows:

> When I practice the [*hwadu*] of "Zhaozhou's No" (趙州無字), instead of asking why Zhaozhou said no, I practice by asking,

"What is this thing that is asking this question?" Since I was focusing on "Zhaozhou's No," the answer "no" got stuck in me, so I practiced by asking, "What is this thing that is 'no'?"[13]

Why is asking a question, or doubting, so important in Zen practice, and what does this tell us about the nature of Zen practice? As shown in what Hyeam said above, the purpose of asking a question in Zen practice is not to find an answer to that question. The question functions to destabilize the practitioner's understanding of things and eventually of the self. This seemingly counterintuitive practice is also contrary to what one usually pursues in practice or education. The purpose of learning is to earn knowledge, and Zen Buddhist practice facilitates moments of rupture in this process. The goal is not to reject learning or the accumulation of knowledge in its entirety but rather to reconsider the relationship between the subject and knowledge acquisition, be it academic knowledge that is learned through formal education, knowledge of the norms of society one acquires through socialization, or the views that one has developed over time. Hyeam even says, "With small doubt, one attains small awakening; with great doubt, one attains great awakening; with no doubts, there is no awakening."[14] Doubt in the process of Zen practice, then, is not limited to an existential inquiry performed by an individual but instead has a heavy social impact.

When we say that one should not be attached to views, we can easily interpret this to mean that we should find good views and reject wrong views. However, Buddhism teaches that even a right view is not a right view. The Vietnamese Buddhist monk/thinker Thich Nhat Hanh, the founder of engaged Buddhism, thus observes, "We should not be attached to any view; we have to transcend all views. . . . When you consider something to be the truth and you are attached to it, you must release it in order to go higher. Right view, first of all, means the absence of all views. . . . Wisdom is not views. Insight is not views."[15]

Rejecting views or being attached to them involves both good and bad views. Even good views and ideas, if one is attached to them, will have harmful effects on the person who holds the views. This is an idea that does not attract our attention as much as it should. What one considers negative should be avoided. That is not difficult to understand. However, one should be just as mindful of one's approach to what one considers positive.

This Buddhist position is comparable to Derrida's teaching on religious practice. Derrida claims that prayer should be practiced with *epoché*, or suspension. When we pray, Derrida asks, "To whom do we pray?" We probably would respond without hesitation that we pray to God or to the Buddha. But if we were certain that God, the Buddha, or any other divine beings would listen to our prayers exactly as they were made, Derrida says that these would not be prayers: each one would be an "order."[16] Hence, according to Derrida, a prayer requires "suspension of certainty, not of belief," and "suspension must take place in order for prayer to be authentic."[17] Even though Derrida's discussion is located in the context of the Judeo-Christian tradition, it is not difficult to see the similar problematics that are addressed in Zen Buddhism's emphasis on doubt and Derrida's claim of *epoché* as a foundational feature of religious practice in order for that practice to be authentic. After all, religion is finite beings' efforts to reach out to the infinite. The different ontological levels that are assumed in this practice are often forgotten, risking the danger of reifying the ideas constructed by the finite as the revelation by the infinite. Religion is also a practice of aspiring to the incalculable through calculable measurements. When this aspiration is combined with the desire to influence the secular domain, the calculable disguised as the incalculable comes to function as the legitimizing power, as we have witnessed in the recent history of religion's involvement with politics.

Self-Reflection, Social-Reflection

The idea of doubt in Zen practice is deeply connected with the Buddhist concepts of self, time, and practice. Hyeam explains the practice and attainment through *hwadu* meditation by using the temporal, or rather nontemporal, concept of "suddenness" (K. *ton* 頓). Hyeam observes, "Suddenness means a fleeting moment in terms of temporality. Delusion does not disappear through a step-by-step process. Rather, one needs to learn about the right teaching and completely eliminate fundamental ignorance in a fleeting moment to attain ultimate awakening. It is called 'sudden' because there is no temporal duration in getting rid of the entirety of delusion. Instead, it occurs in the blink of an eye."[18]

The suddenness of awakening is a well-known position of Zen Buddhism with regard to Buddhist awakening. All the same, the puzzling nature of this position must remain unmitigated for many people. If awakening occurs in a fleeting moment without a temporal duration, why did Hyeam and all of the other Zen masters and practitioners go through such rigorous practice? Reflecting on this question, one comes to realize that "suddenness" is not in fact related to the concept of time—or, at least, it is not related to time in the way that we commonly understand it.

In explaining his practice of *hwadu*, Hyeam observes:

> A week passed by [without resulting in awakening]. Then, I restarted the practice as if [the next one] were the first week. I was told that awakening can be attained in a week, so I thought about only "in a week." After a week [without result], I erased the week and restarted the [next] week as week one instead of counting the next week as the second week. I practiced each week as if it were the first week, and a year passed by, and [while practicing] I would not know whether it was night or day. There is no morning or evening when you practice. Buddhism says that everything depends on one's mind. My mind was all about practicing.[19]

The issues of subitism and gradualism were hot topics in the world of Korean Buddhism in the late twentieth century. Whether enlightenment happens through sudden practice and sudden awakening or through gradual practice and sudden awakening was at the core of that debate. What would it mean that practice is sudden? The Buddha himself practiced for six years before he attained awakening. Hyeam's description above gives us a glimpse of how to approach this idea. The suddenness of practice does not mean "sudden" in the physical sense of the time taken. Instead, it means that practice should be done anytime and all the time. Each moment is a new moment, as each week was the first week for Hyeam.

The suddenness of practice and awakening goes hand in hand with another Zen Buddhist adage: that sentient beings are buddhas. Like the proposal that practice is sudden, the idea that sentient beings are buddhas sounds illogical, because it emphasizes the equal status of the two opposite concepts of the unenlightened being and the enlightened being. But this is so only when we understand these ideas in a literal sense.

About the idea that unenlightened people are enlightened, Hyeam says that each and every moment and event in our daily lives is the buddha. Awakening is not some special event, but one that occurs and should occur in the midst of our daily lives. This has been the claim of Zen Buddhism for a long time. A well-known *gongan* (公案) in the *Gateless Gate* (*Wumen guan* 無門關), a major text in Zen Buddhism, tells the story of a newly arrived novice monk who asked for guidance from Master Zhaozhou (趙州, 778–897). Case 7 of the *Gateless Gate* records the story as follows:

> A monk said to Zhaozhou: "I have just entered this monastery. Please teach me."
>
> Zhaozhou responded, "Have you eaten your rice porridge?"
>
> The monk said, "Yes, I have."
>
> Zhaozhou said, "Wash your bowl, then." The monk attained awakening.[20]

One should notice the seriousness of the novice monk's question and the dailiness of the Chan master's response. The monk must have left behind all of the desires and wishes of the secular world to practice Buddhism. He must have expected a great teaching by the great Chan master of the time. The master's response, however, couldn't have been more mundane: eat breakfast and do the dishes.

Eihei Dōgen (永平道元, 1200–1253), the founder of Japanese Sōtō Zen, whose *Treasury of the True Dharma Eye* (*Shōbōgenzō* 正法眼藏) Hyeam is said to have admired,[21] teaches that awakening occurs with our daily work. Dōgen's encounter with a Chinese master is a good example: during his stay in China, the Japanese Zen master was visited by an old monk who ended their encounter quickly because he had to return to the monastery to attend to his work as a cook. Dōgen wanted the Chinese master to stay longer and told him that someone of his status should be released from such a duty, to which the master replied that his monastic duty of cooking "was indeed the 'practice of the way' [*bendō*], something to be eagerly pursued and by no means to be avoided."[22]

Steven Heine, a scholar of Japanese Zen Buddhism, elaborates on Dōgen's understanding of this encounter: "Dōgen realized that enlightenment is not a matter of waiting, anticipation, or expectation, but is to be actualized right here and now through continuing practice."[23] Heine's interpretation ties together the two sides of our discussion: the nontemporality and the dailiness of awakening. With these examples from Chan/Zen masters, one cannot but wonder whether the idea that dailiness is the very venue of awakening works for everybody. Why do some people attain awakening while cooking, while for others cooking is just cooking? Why am "I" still a sentient unenlightened being, when Zen Buddhism teaches that everybody is already a buddha?

Chinul received a question of exactly this nature from a student. The core of Chinul's teaching is in the phrase "Mind is the Buddha" (K. *sim chŭk Pul* 心卽佛). Because each of us has a mind all the time, Chinul's discussant asks why, then, is he not aware of his own Buddha-nature and how to realize and practice this teaching. Chinul advises him as follows:

> Chinul: "Do you hear the sounds of that crow cawing and that magpie calling?"
>
> Student: "Yes."
>
> Chinul: "Trace them back and listen to your hearing-nature."[24]

The very fact that one is capable of experiencing the sound of a bird is, Chinul tells us, evidence that one's existence is always already related to the combined effects of multiple elements. People have a fragmented understanding of self and others, subject and object, and interpret their situations as such: "I am listening to the bird singing." Buddhism says that one does not exist in total separation from the bird and its singing, but rather that a person's existence at that moment is the combination of the person themselves with a physical body, the sounds of the bird, the capacity to recognize the sound as birdsong, and so on. Buddhism claims that what enables turning a fragmented understanding of one's relation to others into an interconnected worldview is the mind. Hyeam observes, "Buddhism has a lot of scriptures, as the expression 'eighty thousand scriptures' shows. But if we roll them all into one, that is 'the mind' [K. *sim* 心]. Once one opens the mind's eye, all of the problems will be understood and all of the teachings will be attained."[25]

One of the best known of Hyeam's teachings is his advice "Practice until you die" or "Face death while practicing" (K. *Kongbu hada chugŏra* 공부하다 죽어라). It's not easy to render this expression in English, but the above translation should at least reveal the urgency and rigor of Hyeam's demands and teachings. To some people, this phrase might sound petrifying in revealing the firmness of Hyeam's attitude toward meditation practice. Hyeam's intention, however, was not to promote a die-hard attitude toward Zen practice.

Death can arrive anytime. For most of us, except some Zen masters or spiritual people, it is not possible to know when we will face death. The only way to face death while practicing is to practice consistently and constantly. Understood in this manner, Hyeam's *hwadu* "Practice until you die" is another way of saying that each and every moment of life should be an occasion for practice.

At the bottom of that practice, one finds the absolute necessity of finding one's self, for which self-reflection and inner transformation are a must in Zen Buddhism. An episode from early in his career reveals the importance of this ultimatum: a lay practitioner asked Hyeam where he was going, and the monk responded that he was on his way to Sangwŏn Monastery. The practitioner asked whom he was going to meet at the monastery, and Hyeam responded, "The Great Sŏn Master Hanam is there. But I am not going there to meet him. I am going there to meet myself. To meet oneself is Buddhism. The goal of Buddhism is not to find a founder or teacher of Buddhism."[26]

The novelist Chŏng Ch'anju, who published two books on Hyeam, observed in an essay, "It seems that Buddhist awakening is a synonym of awakening of meaning."[27] Buddhist practice demands that the practitioner take a renewed view of the taken-for-granted approach to being and the world, and this change begins with the individual's understanding of themselves. For this change to take place, internal transformation is inevitable. Hyeam's following statements clarify the importance of finding one's mind:

> The core of Buddhism demands that we get rid of the mode of thinking we have maintained for the past two thousand and five hundred years and transform our way of thinking . . . by seeing things as they are. . . . The *hwadu* for humanity in the twenty-first century is change and renovation. Real change and renovation require, as their premises, changes in the way of thinking, that is, a revolution of consciousness. Zen Buddhism emphasizes revolutionary change that transforms one's way of thinking and at the same time simplicity that looks into the nature of things.[28]

As an example of the revolutionary nature of Zen training and Buddhism's relevance today, Hyeam connects Buddhist teaching with the ecological problem that the world now faces. Buddhism teaches that all beings—not only humans, but nonhuman animals and even inanimate beings like rocks and stones—have the Buddha-nature, and Hyeam emphasizes that such a teaching should be the foundation for building a nature-friendly, environment-friendly civilization.

Hyeam did not offer details about how Buddhism could actually be involved with social issues beyond the broad strokes I mentioned above. Hyeam's engagement with worldly affairs outside meditation on mountains mostly involved issues directly related to the Jogye Order. In that context, Hyeam earned credit for his leadership at the time when the organization faced institutional crises.

In 1994 and 1998, the Jogye Order faced what was considered its gravest crisis since the persecution of Buddhism in 1980. The 1980 persecution was caused by external forces: the then military government of South Korea, under martial law, raided Buddhist monasteries and hermitages around the country on October 27 and 30, mobilizing combat police and soldiers. More than 1,500 people connected to Buddhism, including Song Wŏlchu, the then executive director of administration (K. *ch'ongmuwŏnjang* 總務院長) of the Jogye Order,[29] were arrested in the name of purification and subjected to threats, torture, and various forms of violence.[30] Monks were humiliated and brutalized; some were forced to disrobe, and Song Wŏlchu was forced to resign. The incident came to be known as the October 27 Buddhist Persecution (K. *Sibich'il pŏmnan* 10.27 法難).

The crises of 1994 and 1998, by contrast, occurred through an internal power struggle ignited by incumbent executive directors of administration who attempted to run for reelection even though the constitution and bylaws of the order limited the position to two terms. In 1994, Sŏ Ŭihyŏn tried to run again after eight years.[31] In 1998, Song Wŏlchu, who had been reelected after his forced resignation, tried to run for another term and faced objections.[32] It is ironic that someone who went through such hardship as the leader of the organization in the October 27 Persecution and who was elected to replace Sŏ after the 1994 crisis allowed himself to be the cause of another power struggle in the organization.

In both crises, amid the conflicts between factions of the order, organized gang members were called in, police were deployed, monks fought with batons and stones, and images of the chaos spread through the national and international media. The picture of violent monks in a Buddhist tradition that emphasizes nonviolence disappointed believers, shocked many others, and caused serious damage to the order's reputation. It also gave the impression to people outside Korea that Korean Buddhism was violent.[33]

Hyeam earned credit for his role in settling the crises and leading monastics to the purification and reformation of the order. A number of leaders of the Jogye Order testified to Hyeam's activities at the time: Master Muyŏ stated that "in 1994, Master Hyeam was able to successfully lead the order to reformation, which was possible because he is someone who acts when he considers the action inevitable."[34] Master Wŏlsong recalled, "Both in 1994 and 1998, Master Hyeam could not just stand aside when he witnessed wrongdoings, even though he might face sanctions later for his actions."[35] Wŏlsong further observed, "I haven't seen many masters in modern Korean Buddhism who were capable of handling both principle [K. *li* 理] and worldly affairs [K. *sa* 事]. Great Master was a teacher equipped with the capacity for both."[36]

Korean Buddhism uses the expressions "monks for principle" (K. *ip'ansŭng* 理判僧) and "monks for worldly affairs" (K. *sap'an sŭng* 事判僧). The former focus mostly on meditation practice, whereas the latter deal with the administrative work of the monastery. The separation of meditation and worldly affairs might look odd if we consider that in Zen Buddhism, awakening occurs in daily events, and daily affairs like cooking or washing dishes should be the moments of awakening. The above expressions and the division of labor between the two groups of monastics originated in the history of Korean Buddhism during the Chosŏn dynasty, which we do not go into here. But Yi Nŭnghwa, a scholar of the intellectual history of Korea, says, "Without the monks of principle, the wisdom of the Buddha cannot be maintained, and without the monks of worldly affairs, the monastery cannot be sustained."[37] Such harmonious cooperation of the two groups was not always the case, and further consolidation of this division caused a number of conflicts in the order.[38]

In the 1994 incident, Hyeam led the handling of the situation as vice chair of the Elders Council (K. *Wŏllo hoeŭi* 원로회의), the highest decision-making unit in the order. Buddhist scholar Cho Kiryong gives great credit to Hyeam in an article on the 1994 incident, claiming that Hyeam's leadership led to the then incumbent executive director of administration of the order Sŏ Ŭihyŏn receiving a no-confidence vote and a call for resignation from the Elders Council, which settled the core issue of the feud.[39]

Following the resignation of Sŏ, a new election was held. Song Wŏlchu won, and the Elders Council confirmed the result. Four years later, however, Song's attempt to rerun again divided the order into pro- and anti-Song factions, and, as in 1994, violence erupted again. This time, even the senior leadership was divided. In less than two months, Song Wŏlchu withdrew, but the division ignited by his candidacy did not end. After considerable drama between his supporters and opponents, during which external force was again called in, a new executive director of administration was confirmed on December 30, 1998, by the Elders Council, for which Hyeam was now the chair.

The 1994 and 1998 incidents were caused by the incumbent executive directors of administration attempting to rerun despite the term limit articulated in the order's law. However, those who became involved in the conflicts were not limited to the executive directors of administration and their followers. The supreme patriarchs of the order were also part of the feud. In both cases, the supreme patriarchs received no-confidence votes from the Elders Council because they were complicit in causing the problems and had to resign from the position. It was Hyeam who confirmed the no-confidence votes in both cases as the chairperson of the Elders Council. In theory, as the famous passage from Rinzi states, Zen Buddhism touts the idea, "When you encounter the buddha, kill the buddha. When you encounter the patriarch, kill the patriarch."[40] Challenging any form of reification to the degree of rejecting the founder of the tradition and of the school has been proposed as the spirit of Zen. On the other hand, in reality, a religious organization is an institution in which the practitioners' capacities for religious practice create strongly hierarchical relationships in both positive and negative terms. To pass a no-confidence ruling for the supreme patriarch of the order not once but twice would not be an easy task.

In his account of Hyeam's role in the 1994 and 1998 crises, Cho Kiryong observes that the following two factors must have been the most agonizing for Hyeam to deal with: leading no-confidence votes of two supreme patriarchs of the order and the division of the sangha caused by the conflicts.[41] However difficult the decision might have been, Cho Kiryong tells us that Hyeam strongly held on to two principles for his actions: a determination to "follow the teaching of the Buddha" and his conviction "to sustain the constitution and bylaws of the order."⁴² Cho considers that the division of the sangha must have been the more difficult of the two for Hyeam to accept.

In April 1995, in his dharma talk marking the one-year anniversary of the reform of the sangha after the 1994 incident, Hyeam wrote,

> Who is an authentic person? . . .
> Buddhist teaching from the beginning pervades in this world.
> One should attain awakening in daily life.
> Trying to find awakening outside of the quotidian
> Is like trying to find a rabbit-fire.
>
> Good and evil, right and wrong, are originally empty.
> Māra and the Buddha are from the beginning one body.
>
> The moon of the original mind brightly shed lights on everything; this secular world is nirvāṇa.
>
> One should get rid of [the ideas of] advantages, disadvantages, gain or loss, and find true happiness by making oneself the owner of oneself following the context.

The message contains a conventional Zen Buddhist idea of emptiness of absolute value judgment and interconnectedness of all things. If Hyeam had demanded what he said in this poem, without engaging himself with practical efforts to resolve the 1994 incident, Hyeam's poem might have sounded void, a mere rhetoric, because in the reality world, good and bad, right and wrong always conflict one another. However, hearing this poem after what he had done with his leadership to resolve the problem should reveal another type of leadership: he was a religious leader in this poem, asking for the application of Buddhism in real life. However, Hyeam's appeal for unity unfortunately became futile when the order once again faced a conflict three years later in 1998.

From the general public's perspective, the 1994 and 1998 incidents might be remembered only through the devastating images of monks throwing stones and engaging in physical fights against one another and the Buddhist temple surrounded by combat police. From the Jogye Order's perspective, however, the crises were also the time to renovate and reform the order. Hence, the former calls the 1994 incident "Conflicts in the Jogye

Order," while the latter calls it "Reformation of the Order." The issues that led to the 1994 incident were not limited to the problems of Sŏ Ŭihyŏn but instead were caused by accumulated structural flaws within the order that had to do with the evolution of modern Korean Buddhism over the several decades before the conflict took place. The order's dependency on political power and the division of labor or consolidation of power between supreme patriarchs and the executive directors of administration were all catalysts for the events. The perspective of "Reformation of the Order" reveals an important turning point in the history of the Jogye Order.

The sociologist Pak Suho evaluates the incident in the context of social movements. On the surface, the reformation of the Jogye Order of 1994 was meaningful in the sense that Buddhism established its autonomy and also its function in society by freeing itself from political power.[43] Pak even further credits the reformation movement of the Jogye Order as a big step toward the creation of a Buddhist civil society, which he identifies in two aspects: "One is securing a realm of Buddhism within civil society; and the other is the creation of a realm of civil society within the Buddhist order."[44]

Pak's interpretation of the 1994 reformation movement places the event in the broader context of Korean Buddhism's engagement with the democratization of Korean society, which can be traced back to at least the 1970s–1980s Minjung Buddhism or Buddhism for the Masses movement. In the process of the democratization of Korean society in the second half of the twentieth century, Christianity was the religion that mainly contributed to the movement, and Buddhism seriously felt its lack of engagement. Minjung Buddhism was one of the major efforts through which Korean Buddhism presented itself as having a religion's capacity to participate in the issues of society.[45] Cho credits the 1994 reformation for the emergence of various forms of engaged Buddhism in Korea, which expanded the horizon of civil society both inside and outside the order.

However, the voices that pointed out the limitations of the 1994 reform were not quiet. The fact that the order faced another crisis of a similar nature within four years of the reform evidenced that the 1994 reform was far from perfect. Commonly mentioned in this regard is the negation of the work of Buddhist nuns. Buddhist nuns fought together with the monks in the reformation, but they were not allowed positions in the order's new leadership.[46]

In an article on the October 27, 1980, Buddhist Persecution, the sociologist Yi Han-meh examined sociopolitical dimensions of the Korean

Buddhist community's attitude toward the persecution and the future of Korean Buddhism. Yi observed that whether the Korean Buddhist community would understand the incident only as the government's persecution of Buddhism or was capable of responding to the event in the context of the broader issues of state violence and the violation of human rights could be critical for the future of Korean Buddhism.[47] Yi's evaluation is worth remembering in considering Buddhism's relevance to modern times. The same can be said about the 1994 and 1998 crises of the Jogye Order, as the incidents are evaluated as part of the democratization of the Buddhist community. Details of Hyeam's involvement in this context and the degree of Hyeam's influence on these issues have yet to be further explored, but accounts have testified to his leadership during this period and his support for the young monastics during the 1994 event.

Hyeam was not free from sectarian discourse, however. In the 1981 publication *The Orthodox Path of the Sŏn School* (*Sŏnmun chŏngno* 禪門正路), Sŏngchŏl claimed that Chinul was a heretic in Sŏn Buddhism and could not be the founding patriarch of Korean Sŏn school.[48] Sŏngchŏl was one of the most well-known Sŏn masters in the second half of the twentieth century in Korea and the leader of a 1947 movement to reform Sŏn Buddhism in which Hyeam took part. Hyeam repeated Sŏngchŏl's position on the issue of the Sŏn lineage and claimed that Chinul should be removed from the dharma lineage of Korean Sŏn Buddhism as the founding patriarch of the tradition and that T'aego Pou (太古普愚, 1301–1382) should be given the position instead. Hyeam observed: "In order to clarify the authenticity of Korean Buddhism and enliven its future, a change of the dharma lineage of the school is essential. From the perspective of the orthodox dharma lineage, National Master Pojo is an outsider, not a member of our family. He never received *bhikṣu* precepts (K. *pigugye* 比丘戒), nor did he receive full precepts (K. *kujokkye* 具足戒). He never said that he had received the dharma transmission, nor is there a record that any such evidence was claimed."[49]

Hyeam asserted that this change was needed because, with Chinul recognized as the founding patriarch, foreign scholars would misjudge Korean Sŏn Buddhism because of its lack of an orthodox dharma lineage: "I have always made it crystal clear that Sŏn Master T'aego Pou should be the authentic founding patriarch of Korean Sŏn Buddhism. If we consider the international context, when foreign scholars study Korean Buddhism, the first thing they would examine would be whether the orthodox dharma lineage is still alive or not, and since no lineage has been established, the constitution of the order regarding the founding patriarch of the school is all messed up."⁵⁰

Who might these foreign scholars be? And what is the basis of the claim that the sectarian discourse of the founding patriarch of the school would be their main concern in evaluating Korean Sŏn Buddhism? Hyeam didn't say. Still, during the 1994 reformation of the Jogye Order, Hyeam proposed to change the clause in the order's constitution regarding the founding patriarch of the school. In the end, Hyeam had to compromise because not everybody was on the same page regarding the question of the founding patriarch, and the committee in charge of the reformation of the constitution and bylaws was busy with other, more urgent issues.⁵¹

Didn't Hyeam contradict himself by claiming that Chinul was not qualified for the founding patriarch's position? In his teaching about Buddhist practice, Hyeam repeatedly emphasized that "Whether one is a monastic or a lay practitioner does not count in practice. The teaching happens wherever one sits or wherever one goes. Finding one's own mind is the core of the teaching, so one should practice how to find one's mind."⁵² If even the distinction between monastic and laity does not matter in practicing Buddhism, why should Chinul be considered as not "a member of our family" and excluded from the dharma lineage of Korean Sŏn Buddhism? Why was such a distinction of inside and outside, the cause of most forms of discrimination, so important to him?⁵³ The Sŏn master's reference to the concerns of foreign scholars does not answer these questions because the claim itself is misleading.

What Do Zen Masters Teach Us Today?

Religious traditions have often created hagiographies of major figures in the tradition. A hagiography is a gesture to glorify and legitimize a person's life events for the benefit of and to justify a religious tradition. Moralizing one's life and narrowly applying moral imperatives to an individual's conduct could be considered the opposite of a hagiography. In modern Korean Buddhism, Kyŏnghŏ was subjected to both. Hagiographical approaches to his life claim that Kyŏnghŏ's behavior of violating precepts, such as getting drunk, was an expression of the liberated spirit of an enlightened Zen master. Scholars call such a life story in East Asian Zen Buddhism a "hippie monk tradition." The opposite evaluation of his life, as performed by his disciple Hanam, moralizes his liberal lifestyle and warns the reader that "practitioners should learn from Master Kyŏnghŏ's embodiment of dharma, but not his behavior."[54] What is missing with these two opposite evaluations is Kyŏnghŏ as a human being. Before being a Zen master or the revivalist of a religious school, Kyŏnghŏ was a human being who faced existential reality, searching for the meaning of being alive. At bottom, religion is human beings' reflection on and efforts to deal with the existential conditions of human existence. Buddhist scholar Park Jae-Hyun thus points out that Hanam's moralist evaluation of Kyŏnghŏ's life contributed to the situation in which "Korean Buddhism comes to pay more attention to the external and formalistic aspects of Kanhwa Sŏn instead of the original nature of Kanhwa meditation, which is the rigor that comes from the awareness of the existential reality of human beings."[55]

I propose to consider the legacy of Hyeam's Buddhism in a similar context. Hyeam was a great Sŏn Master with a superhuman capacity for practice, a supreme patriarch of the largest Buddhist order in modern Korea who was also an efficient leader at times when the organization faced crises. These are accomplishments that one can look up to; he also had shortcomings, one of which I would count to be his sectarian approach to Buddhism. In the end, however, his life itself is what might attract people's attention most.

As someone learns about Hyeam's theory of soteriology, his activities as the leader of the Jogye Order, his teachings for lay practitioners, and even his sectarian discourse, they might wonder, as I did, what made this practitioner Hyeam so rigorous in his practice? What was it that he was looking for in this life as the meaning of existence? For most of us who have not tried any practice, not to mention doing so with such rigor as Hyeam, Hyeam's life itself is a *hwadu* that raises questions inside us about the meaning of existence; his life story creates space in us through which we reflect on the meaning and values that we adhere to in various activities in our existence. The point, then, might not be whether or not one should follow or accept what Hyeam did. Nor is it a question of whether he was a great master or not. It is rather the rigor, passion, and even severity with which Hyeam practiced that becomes an existential question for the reader of his life.

This proposal to see Hyeam's life itself as a *hwadu*, or an existential question, does not negate Hyeam's achievements; instead, it invites the reader to place them in a different context. In another of my publications, I proposed a "narrative philosophy" based on "lived experience" in interpreting the life and thoughts of Kim Iryŏp, whom I mentioned earlier.[56]

One of the goals of this effort was to find a space to understand philosophy from a perspective and practice that are different from the familiar and dominant forms of male-centered Western philosophy. At stake in this approach was not only Iryŏp's Buddhist philosophy but also the lived experiences of women as well as the participants of non-Western thought traditions. As a feminist, Zen master, and Buddhist thinker, Iryŏp lived life in her own way and left behind records of her life that are a mixture of personal life stories, Buddhist doctrines, teachings, and feminist agendas. The style of her writing and life might not be considered a "philosophy" if we apply the still-dominant concept of philosophy. But if we conceive of philosophy as human beings' efforts to understand existence and its various corollaries, diverse expressions of life can serve as different modes of philosophizing. This approach calls for understanding one's life and events through their lived experiences instead of getting them ready to be subject to existing measurements and judgments. After all, standards tend to be created by those who have power to create them, and those who are not in that position and therefore whose lived experiences and values might be fairly different from the lived experiences and values of the rule makers come to be subjugated to those rules.

Hyeam's life story can be approached in a similar manner. Unlike Iryŏp, a woman who had to live within a patriarchal society, Hyeam might not have experienced being marginalized. In the broad spectrum of the ontological scale, however, human beings are all at the margin, and religion is a story of finite beings' aspiration to overcome their marginality. If a hagiography works to justify a religious figure's life and demands us to take it as a legitimate form of life for a religious practitioner, an "existential approach" to one's life should disturb us, creating a moment of rupture in the midst of the quotidian and the familiar. In such a situation, one's life itself becomes a *hwadu*, a question to reflect on. Hyeam's life could be such a *hwadu* to readers.[57] Whether one would make a hagiography, a justification for a sectarian discourse, or a *hwadu* out of Hyeam's life—and in that sense out of the lives of any other religious figures in Korean Buddhism—is up to the readers, scholars, and followers of Hyeam.

Notes

1. In this article, I use "Chan," "Sŏn," and "Zen" interchangeably.
2. Hyeam Taejongsa mundohoe, "Hyeam Taejongsa Haengjang" (Short Biography of Great Master Hyeam), 15–16.

3. Chŏng, *Kayasan chŏngjin Pul* (The Buddha in Practice on the Mountain), vol. 1, 216–17. The description of this practice also appears in Yŏ Yŏn, "Kayasan ŭi taejjok: Hyeam Sŏnggwan ŭi saengae wa sasang" (A Piece of Bamboo on Mountain Kaya: The Life and Thoughts of Great Master Hyeam Songgwan), 27.

4. Yi, "Hyeam Chongjŏng yeha haengjang" (Life of the Eminent Supreme Patriarch Hyeam).

5. Chŏng, *Kongbu hada chugŏra* (Practice until Die), 57.

6. Hyeam mundohoe, ed., *Hyeam Taejongsa pŏbŏ jip* (Collection of the Dharma Talks by Great Master Hyeam), vol. II, 14.

7. Hyeam mundohoe, ed., *Hyeam Taejongsa pŏbŏjip*, vol. II, 14.

8. Hyeam mundohoe, ed., *Hyeam Taejongsa pŏbŏjip*, vol. II, 15.

9. Derrida, "Faith and Epoché," 35.

10. Kim, *Ŏnŭ sudoin ŭi hoesang* (Reflections of a Zen Buddhist Nun), 1. English translation, Park, *Reflections of a Zen Buddhist Nun*, 29.

11. Hyeam mundohoe, ed., *Hyeam Taejongsa pŏbŏjip*, vol. II, 73.

12. Hyeam mundohoe, ed., *Hyeam Taejongsa pŏbŏjip*, vol. II, 74.

13. Hyeam mundohoe, ed., *Hyeam Taejongsa pŏbŏjip*, vol. II, 226. For Hyeam's Kanhwa Sŏn, see Mun Kwang, "Hyeam Sŏnsa ŭi chasŏng samhak ŭi Sŏn suhaeng koch'al" (Studies on Sŏn Master Hyeam's Sŏn Practice of Three Disciplines of Self Nature), and O, "Hyeam Sŏnsa ŭi Kanhwa Sŏn e daehan koch'al" (Studies on Sŏn Master Hyeam's Kanhwa Sŏn).

14. Hyeam mundohoe, ed., *Hyeam Taejongsa pŏbŏjip*, vol. I, 80.

15. Thich Nhat Hanh, "Dharma Talk: History of Engaged Buddhism," 8.

16. Derrida, "Faith and Epoché," 31.

17. Derrida, "Faith and Epoché," 31.

18. Sin, *Kongbu hada chugŏra: Hyeam Taejongsa sangdang pŏpŏ jip* (Practice until Die: Collection of Great Master Hyeam's Dharma Talks), 58.

19. Chŏng, *Kayasan chŏngjin Pul*, vol. 1, 88.

20. Wumen, *Wumen guan* (Gateless Gate), 293c.

21. Mun Kwang, "Hyeam Sŏnsa ŭi sasŏng samhak ŭi Sŏn suhaeng koch'al," 46–47.

22. Heine, *Existential and Ontological Dimensions of Time in Dōgen and Heidegger*, 26.

23. Heine, *Existential and Ontological Dimensions of Time in Dōgen and Heidegger*, 26.

24. Chinul, *Susim kyŏl* (Secrets on Cultivating the Mind), 4.710b. English translation, Buswell, "Secrets on Cultivating the Mind," 104.

25. Hyeam mundohoe, ed., *Hyeam Taejongsa pŏbŏjip*, vol. II, 22.

26. Chŏng, *Kayasan chŏngjin Pul*, vol. 1, 142.

27. Chŏng, *Kongbu hada chugŏra*, 86.

28. Hyeam mundohoe, ed., *Hyeam Taejongsa pŏbŏjip*, vol. II, 270.

29. The English website of the Jogye Order translates this position as "President of the Jogye Order."

30. Yun, *Yu wŏl hangjaeng kwa Pulgyo* (The June Resistance and Buddhism), 16; Yi, "10/27 pŏmnan kwa kŭ ch'ŏngsan kwajŏng e taehan hoego wa sŏngch'al" (Recollection and Examination of the 10.27 Buddhist Persecution and its Settlement Process), 318. The Korean Buddhist community claims that the October 27 Persecution was one of the worst such incidents in its history. The military government justified its action as purifying Korean society, including the Jogye Order and Korean Buddhism, organizations that needed governmental intervention to eliminate corruption and resolve internal conflicts. It has been claimed that purifying the Jogye Order was only a pretense for the incident, however, and that the Korean government wanted to divert attention from the aftermath of the Kwangju Democratization Movement that took place that spring. In May 1980, in the city of Kwangju in the southern part of the Korean peninsula, the government had mobilized air forces in response to democratization protests, and more than 200 people were killed. The investigation of the incident and the trauma and healing of its aftermath continue today.

31. His running for a third term, against policy, was only the immediate catalyst of the events. While Sŏ was executive director of administration, the Jogye Order supported the candidates of a specific political party in the 1987 and 1992 presidential elections, violating the principle of the separation of church and state and implying the order's subservience to the party. There was also the issue of corruption, as it had been revealed that Buddhism had become a money-laundering venue for a political party. See Pak, "Chogyejong chongdan kaehyŏk pulsa" (Reformation of the Jogye Order), 40–41; Kim, "1994 Taehan Pulgyo Chogyejong kaehyŏk chongdan ŭi sŏngnip kwa ŭiŭi" (Process and Meaning of the 1994 Reformation of the Korean Jogye Order), 332–35.

32. Song claimed that because his first term was halted after only six months by external forces during the October 27 Persecution, it should not count toward his term limit and he was still eligible to run.

33. For example, see Kirk, "Monk Factions Vie to Control Korea's Biggest Sect: Buddhist Temple Tug-of-War."

34. Hyeam Sŏnsa Munhwa Chinhŭng hoe, ed., *Sŭsŭng Hyeam* (Teacher Hyeam), 113.

35. Hyeam Sŏnsa Munhwa Chinhŭng hoe, ed., *Sŭsŭng Hyeam*, 31.

36. Hyeam Sŏnsa Munhwa Chinhŭng hoe, ed., *Sŭsŭng Hyeam*, 32.

37. Yi, *Chosŏn Pulgyo T'ongsa* (Comprehensive History of Korean Buddhism 1918), 930. According to Yi, the division started during the Chosŏn dynasty, when one group of monks focused on meditation, sutra reading, and propagation, while another focused on the management of the monastery. The former were called monks of principle; the latter, monks of worldly affairs.

38. For example, see Park, "Han'guk kŭndae Pulgyo ŭi t'ajadŭl: sap'ansŭng kwa taech'ŏsŭng ŭi t'oejo" (The Others in Modern Korean Buddhism: The Decline of the Administrative Monks and Married Monks).

39. Cho, "Chogyejong ŭi chongdan kaehyŏk kwa Hyeam Sŏnggwan ŭi hwaldong" (The Reformation of the Jogye Order and the Activities of Hyeam Sŏnggwan), 74.

40. Linji, *Linji lu* (Recorded Sayings of Linji), 500b.

41. Cho, "Chogye chong ŭi chongdan kaehyŏk kwa Hyeam Sŏnggwan ŭi hwaldong," 79.

42. Cho, "Chogye chong ŭi chongdan kaehyŏk kwa Hyeam Sŏnggwan ŭi hwaldong," 82–83.

43. Cho, "Chogyejong ŭi chongdan kaehyŏk kwa Hyeam Sŏnggwan ŭi hwaldong," 59.

44. Cho, "Chogyejong ŭi chongdan kaehyŏk kwa Hyeam Sŏnggwan ŭi hwaldong," 87.

45. On Minjung Buddhism, see Jorgensen, "Minjung Buddhism: A Buddhist Critique of the Status Quo—Its History, Philosophy and Critique."

46. Kim, "1994 Taehan Pulgyo Chogyejong kaehyŏk chongdan ŭi sŏngnip kwa ŭiŭi," 54; Pak, "Sahoe undong ŭrosŏŭi Chogyejong chongdan kaehŏk" (The Reformation of the Jogye Order as a Social Movement), 86.

47. Yi, "10/27 pŏmnan kwa kŭ ch'ŏngsan kwajŏng e taehan hoego wa sŏngch'al," 319.

48. Sŏngch'ŏl, *Sŏnmun chŏngno* (The Orthodox Path of the Sŏn School), 209.

49. Hyeam mundohoe, ed., *Hyeam Taejongsa pŏbŏjip*, vol. II, 221.

50. Hyeam mundohoe, ed., *Hyeam Taejongsa pŏbŏjip*, vol. II, 221.

51. Cho, "Chogyejong ŭi chongdan kaehyŏk kwa Hyeam Sŏnggwan ŭi hwaldong," 74.

52. Hyeam mundohoe, ed., *Hyeam Taejongsa Pŏbŏjip*, vol. II, 224.

53. Dharma lineage has been a topic of dispute in Korean Buddhism, and several different theories of the founding patriarch and dharma lineage have been proposed over time. In his article "Formation of the Dharma Lineage Discourses of the Jogye Order and Their Problems" (Chogyejong pŏpt'ongsŏl ŭi hyŏngsŏng kwajŏng kwa munjejŏm), Pak Hyedang, a scholar of Korean Buddhism, surveys different proposals on the orthodox dharma lineage of Korean Buddhism and their limitations. He points out that, except for the proposal by Hyujŏng (休靜, 1520–1604) in the sixteenth century, all other claims of the orthodox dharma lineage are historically groundless, and therefore debates on the dharma lineage are futile. A main reason that the debates have taken center stage in Korean Buddhism is because of the nature of Zen Buddhism, which maintains the tradition that a recognition (K. *in'ga* 認可) of one's awakening occurs through one's teacher; what is called "mind-to-mind-transmission" made it necessary for Korean monks

during the Chosŏn dynasty to develop a dharma lineage as a way to demonstrate the authenticity of their practice and awakening. The tradition continues today.

54. Han'am Chungwŏn, "Sŏnsa Kyŏnghŏ hwasang haengjang" (A Record of the Deceased Teacher Master Kyŏnghŏ), 405, 420. English translation, Park "'A Crazy Drunken Monk': Kyŏnghŏ and Modern Buddhist Meditation Practice," 143.

55. Park, "Sŏngin chŏn iron kwa Han'guk Pulgyo ŭi kŭn sŭnim mandŭlgi e taehan goch'al" (Theory of Hagiography and Studies on Korean Buddhism's Creation of Great Masters), 164. On the existentialist approach to Kyŏnghŏ's life and Sŏn Buddhism, see Park, "Kyŏnghŏ Sŏngu and the Existential Dimensions of Modern Korean Buddhism."

56. Park, *Women and Buddhist Philosophy*. See especially "Introduction" and "Chapter Seven," "A Life Lived: Women and Buddhist Philosophy."

57. What I call an existential approach here has some similarities with the idea of "lived religion" that was proposed by David Hall, a religious scholar. See Hall, *Lived Religion in America: Toward a History of Practice*. Hall's point is to examine how religion is practiced in various contexts, with the distinctions of high and low fading. For example, see my colleague Onaje Woodbine's *Black Gods of the Asphalt*, in which the author discusses how street basketball play is pervaded with religious function and how the players find religious meaning in playing street basketball in racist America. The existential approach, however, focuses more on the existential questions that arise from the disturbance caused by the life story of a religious practitioner, which is also a way that *hwadu* meditation functions.

Chapter 2

Paek Yongsŏng and the Boundaries of Early Modern Korean Buddhism
Historiographical Issues and the Question of Scale

Mark A. Nathan

Introduction

Paek Yongsŏng (白龍城, 1864–1940) is one of the most fascinating figures in the history of early modern Korean Buddhism. His life spanned a period of momentous change in Korean society. Born in the first year of the reign of King Kojong (高宗, 1864–1907), the last monarch to effectively rule the Chosŏn dynasty (1392–1910), Yongsŏng lived through the demise of a political and social order that had held sway for 500 years. He also experienced life under Japanese colonial control, passing away just five years before Korea's eventual liberation. Shortly after the turn of the twentieth century, when he was reaching the middle point of his life, Yongsŏng began to dedicate himself to preserving and strengthening the Korean Buddhist tradition in the face of grave new challenges, guiding his fellow Buddhist monks, nuns, and countless laypeople through tumultuous times. He is probably best remembered in Korean history as one of the thirty-three signers of the Korean Declaration of Independence from Japanese colonial rule, which played a crucial role in sparking the historic March First movement (K. *samil undong* 3.1 運動) in 1919. In the context of modern Korean Buddhist history, however, one of his most enduring contributions was the development of new methods and strategies for popularizing and propagating Buddhism in Korean society. His painstaking and pioneering work, such as translating Buddhist scriptures from literary Chinese into vernacular Korean, created a lasting legacy that produced many followers who shared his belief that Buddhist teachings should be made both widely available and easily accessible to ordinary people.

Primarily because of his participation in the March First movement, Yongsŏng is frequently depicted as a staunch nationalist who actively resisted the Japanese takeover of Korea. His vociferous opposition to certain colonial policies, especially those that he viewed as detrimental to the traditions on which Korean Buddhism had stood for centuries, further buttressed not only his nationalist image, but also his perceived conservatism. One of the decisions he strongly opposed was the Japanese governor-general's approval of changes to the Temple Laws (K. *Sabŏp* 寺法) that allowed Korean monks, and even the abbots of temples, to marry and eat meat, much as Japanese Buddhist priests and clerics were permitted to do. His principled stance on this matter, which he expressed in a strongly worded petition sent to the governor-general in 1926 as the decision loomed, earned him a reputation as a traditionalist. Yongsŏng has been called "perhaps the most important, and certainly the most traditional, of the conservative reformers" during the colonial period.[1] Moreover, he was also the first Korean Buddhist monk to mount a detailed doctrinal defense of Buddhism in the face of Christian and Confucian polemical attacks, arguing for the superiority of Buddhist teachings over rival religious ideas and doctrines.[2] In all of these various guises, Yongsŏng is cast as an ardent defender of Korean Buddhism and its ancient traditions.

At the same time, Yongsŏng was clearly willing to depart from prevailing customs and traditions whenever he saw fit in his role as a committed reformer. This was especially true if doing so would help to accomplish his ultimate goal of increasing ordinary people's exposure to Buddhist teachings and encouraging their participation in Buddhist religious practices. The various activities he undertook in pursuit of this goal are collectively known as *p'ogyo* (布教) in Korean. This term is sometimes translated as proselytizing or missionizing, but it is more accurately translated as the propagation of Buddhist teachings and practices in society.[3] Although this was not necessarily viewed as an entirely novel practice in the history of Buddhism, the methods that Yongsŏng developed to reach ordinary people were certainly innovative, and they broke with tradition during his lifetime. In addition to his scriptural translation work, which sought to make the word of the Buddha readily available to people who could not read literary Chinese, he also used vernacular Korean for Buddhist rituals and liturgies. He started numerous "Sunday schools" at temples for young children and introduced Buddhist hymns that he composed for use in Buddhist services.[4] Yongsŏng's efforts to establish Buddhist religious spaces in the capital led him to found an independently operated urban temple that he named Taegaksa (大覺寺, Great Awakening Temple) in the heart of the city.[5] He attempted to launch what he termed the Great Awakening Religion (Taegakkyo 大覺教) or the Religion of Great Awakening, but he faced financial difficulties and relentless pressure from the Japanese authorities. Nevertheless, Yongsŏng was clearly willing to chart a new course by introducing novel practices borrowed from rival religions, altering inherited traditions, and even renaming the religion itself to help spread Buddhism more widely in society.

Even this brief description of Yongsŏng's life suggests that he defies easy categorization. From one perspective, he was a conservative traditionalist and staunch nationalist; from another, he was a progressive reformer who implemented modern changes to Buddhist practice that often broke with tradition. A number of scholars have adopted a relational approach to deal with these dual and seemingly contradictory aspects of his place in the history of modern Korean Buddhism. Yongsŏng is most often compared with his younger contemporary Han Yongun (韓龍雲, 1879–1944), popularly known by his sobriquet, Manhae (萬海), with the former considered to be, in the words of one scholar, "less revolutionary and less political than Manhae."[6] The two men knew each other well and worked closely together in the years immediately following Japan's annexation of Korea in 1910. When Manhae became involved in the independence movement spearheaded by leaders in the Chŏndogyo (天道教) and Protestant religious communities toward the end of the first decade of colonial rule, he turned to Yongsŏng with the hope of enlisting additional support from the Korean Buddhist community. The two monks subsequently became the only Buddhist representatives to sign the Korean Declaration of Independence that incited the March First movement.

In his role as both a nationalist hero and conservative upholder of the Buddhist traditions of his country, Yongsŏng is typically viewed as having guarded the core identity of Korean Buddhism from a variety of contaminating and pernicious influences, the foremost of which were Japanese colonial control, Japanese Buddhist propagators, and Christian missionaries. However, the presumed boundaries and identities ascribed to the different historical entities and actors were not nearly as sharply defined as this view suggests. For instance, how do we account for the fact that Yongsŏng apparently was not averse to forging alliances with prominent Japanese Buddhists when doing so might advance his cause or provide political cover for the organizations he created or supported?[7] Similarly, his selective borrowing of Christian missionary methods and techniques to propagate Buddhism seems incongruent with his strong doctrinal defense of Buddhism from Christian polemical attacks. Part of the problem here is that Yongsŏng and his contemporaries moved within an intricate web of interconnecting and intersecting religious, social, and political networks, all of which were subject to legal and economic pressures under Japanese colonialism. The complexity of these relationships makes it difficult to apply distinct categories, fixed identities, and rigid boundaries to the historical actors whom we seek to understand, particularly individuals like Yongsŏng who defy easy categorization and appear to cross certain impenetrable boundaries.

This effort to define Yongsŏng and to situate him historically creates a productive tension, however, that can be useful for exploring some of the larger methodological and historiographical issues involved in our study of Buddhism in colonial-era Korea. After delving a little deeper into his background and major activities, this chapter shifts to an examination of the prevailing scholarly perspectives on Yongsŏng, paying particular attention to the way in which his place in the history of early twentieth-century Korean Buddhism has been portrayed. Most of the analytical approaches have adhered to a binary conceptualization of the relevant historical categories, identities, and boundaries, and thus they appear to have difficulty dealing with the totality of Yongsŏng's life and work. More recent and highly nuanced analyses of the diverse motivations, fluid identities, and interconnected networks of historical actors like Yongsŏng call into question such simple categorizations of complex individuals. Anne Blackburn's study of Sri Lankan Buddhism under British colonialism provides a useful methodological model here, and her ideas are considered alongside others as possible ways to overcome the limitations of prior approaches. In particular, her call for greater use of microhistories and her pointed criticism of the analytical frameworks used by earlier theorists who attempted to explain the modernization of Buddhism under colonial rule are worth exploring in the context of Korean Buddhism during the Japanese occupation period.

This chapter argues, however, that the microhistorical approach has its limitations when applied to the effort to understand the ways in which the religion as a whole was changing and being adapted to this newly emerging environment. In many ways, this comes down to a problem of scale. A close examination of Paek's life, activities, thoughts, struggles, and personal relationships certainly helps to dismantle some of the simple binaries that have characterized the historical narratives of early modern Korean Buddhism. Such an approach necessarily problematizes the nationalist narratives that tend to reify a pure, unadulterated, and uniquely Korean Buddhist essence stretching back through time and standing in opposition to supposedly external, colonial, and transnational influences. Nevertheless, it does not readily furnish counternarratives that can adequately explain how Korean Buddhism as a religious tradition was changing and being adapted to fit the new environment in the first few decades of the twentieth century. The challenge is to find a way to incorporate the insights drawn from microhistorical studies into macroscopic analyses of the changes that have taken place within Korean Buddhism over the previous century and a half.

Other potentially useful approaches for understanding the broader patterns and trends that characterize this historical period should also be explored, and the final section briefly addresses a few of these models. Rather than viewing Korean Buddhism as an enduring and essentialized entity, perhaps we should consider it as something similar to a complex adaptive system. Doing so would allow the processes of boundary formation and boundary crossing that are apparent in Yongsŏng's thought and activities to be understood as resulting from interactions between Korean Buddhism and other religious, social, political, and legal systems. Moreover, shifting the scale of analysis would also allow us to capture some of the emergent patterns in the evolution of modern Korean Buddhism that might otherwise remain unexplained or unnoticed at the microhistorical level. Ultimately, these considerations are not meant to settle the matter by solving the problem of scale in our historical investigations, but rather to stimulate further methodological and historiographical discussions in the field.

Paek Yongsŏng's Background and Major Activities

Yongsŏng was born in Namwŏn County (present-day Changsu County) in North Chŏlla Province. His father, Paek Namhyŏn, was a member of the

Suwŏn Paek lineage, while his mother was part of the Miryang Son clan. One of his ancestors, Paek Changgong, was apparently a high-ranking official in the late Koryŏ dynasty (918–1392) during the reign of King Kongmin (r. 1351–1374), who failed in his attempts to reform and revive the dynasty in its final decades. His allegiance to the Koryŏ royal house and his refusal to join the newly established Chosŏn dynasty (1392–1910) resulted in the family's relocation. Yongsŏng's mother died not long after giving birth to him, and his father later remarried. He was the oldest son, with five younger half siblings, and his given name was Sanggyu (相奎). He is said to have excelled in his studies as a young boy. He left home for the first time in 1877 when he was just thirteen years old, taking up residence at a small hermitage not far from his hometown in the nearby city of Namwŏn. It was here that he received his Dharma names Chinjong (震鍾) and Yongsŏng (龍城) from the monk who oversaw the hermitage. Having left home without his parents' approval, however, he was soon forced to return after they discovered his whereabouts. Yongsŏng left home again two years later in 1879 and was formally admitted into the sangha as a novice (K. *sami* 沙彌, Skt. *śrāmaṇera*) at the famous Haein Monastery. Five years later, at the age of twenty, he was fully ordained in a ceremony at T'ongdo Monastery, another famous monastery that was well-known for its ordination platform.

The details of Yongsŏng's early life do not set him apart in any significant way from most of his contemporaries who joined the monastic community around the same time. After 1905, however, as the political conditions in Korea worsened and the country was forced to become a protectorate of Japan, Yongsŏng's activities started to show an increasing concern with the social issues of his day. Han Pogwang, one of the foremost scholars on Paek Yongsŏng, has suggested that his life can be broadly divided into two halves: a period of monastic training, intense meditation, and spiritual cultivation that lasted until he was thirty-nine years old, followed by a period of teaching and leading others.[8] Han categorizes these two halves in terms of the formulaic phrase applied to bodhisattvas within the Mahāyāna Buddhist tradition: a focus on the pursuit of one's own enlightenment (K. *sanggu pori* 上求菩提) combined with a commitment to teaching and saving others (K. *hahwa chungsaeng* 下化衆生).[9] The evidence that Yongsŏng's life took a new direction at this time lies in his establishment of a *sŏnhoe* (禪會), or a gathering for the purpose of practicing Sŏn meditation, on Mountain Chiri. Over the next several years, Yongsŏng formed a meditation gathering at a different mountain monastery at least once a year. Eventually, he brought his teaching and guidance in Sŏn meditation as well as other Buddhist devotional practices such as chanting (K. *yŏmbul* 念佛) to the city center so that he could more easily involve laypeople in Buddhist practice.

Although Yongsŏng traveled quite often in the years leading up to 1910, he spent most of his winter and summer retreats at monasteries in the southern part of the Peninsula. After relocating to the capital in 1905, he embarked just two years later on a trip to China, returning to Korea the following year. Upon his return in 1908, it seems that Paek again spent some time in the environs of the capital, and he would later recount his astonishment upon seeing so many churches and Christian followers when there were still no Korean Buddhist temples within the capital's walls. He left Seoul the following year and departed for the southern provinces once again. Then, in 1910, reportedly at the behest of two elder monks, Paek wrote his first treatise, *The True Doctrines that Return to the Source* (*Kwiwŏn chŏngjong* 歸源正宗), at the Ch'ilbul Hermitage on Mountain Chiri.[10] Written in a style that was prevalent at the time, combining vernacular Korean and literary Chinese, the text seeks to counter Confucian and Christian polemical attacks on Buddhism from a doctrinal standpoint. This represents the first time a Korean Buddhist text engaged directly with Christian doctrines, and it offered a vigorous defense of Buddhist teachings and argued for their superiority over the teachings of other religions.

The same year that Yongsŏng wrote his treatise in defense of Buddhist doctrines, Manhae Han Yongun laid out his ideas for reforming Korean Buddhism in his seminal work, *On the Restoration of Korean Buddhism* (*Chosŏn Pulgyo yusillon* 朝鮮佛教維新論).[11] The two monks then worked side by side just two years later, running the Central Propagation Temple of the Imje Order (*Imjejong chung'ang p'ogyodang* 臨濟宗中央布教堂), which opened its doors in May 1912, making it one of the earliest Buddhist religious spaces in the capital after centuries of legal exclusion from the city. This temple served as the headquarters of the Imje Order, a monastic organization formed in response to the slightly earlier efforts of Yi Hoegwang (李晦光, 1862–1932) to use his role as Patriarch of the newly created Wŏn Order (Wŏnjong 圓宗) to bring about a merger with the Sōtō Sect of Japan.[12] Yongsŏng was put in charge of propagation activities at the temple, which was soon forced to change its name because of pressure from the Japanese colonial authorities.[13] Additionally, both monks were frequent contributors to the Korean Buddhist journals that began to appear at this time. Most famously, though, as previously mentioned, when Manhae joined with other religious leaders to declare Korea's independence from Japan in March 1919, he enlisted Yongsŏng's support. These two monks thus became the only representatives from the Buddhist community whose names appear among the thirty-three signers of the document that sparked the March First movement.

Yongsŏng was incarcerated for his participation in the March First movement. Following his release from prison in 1921, he devoted himself to translating and publishing Buddhist scriptures to make Buddhist teachings more readily accessible and available to ordinary people.[14] He founded the Tripitaka Translation Association (*Samjang yŏkhoe* 三藏譯會) just a month after gaining his freedom, and he worked tirelessly for rest of his life to translate as many sūtras and important Buddhist texts as possible into vernacular Korean. He produced approximately twenty translations of major Buddhist scriptures and texts in the 1920s and 1930s and also published original texts.[15]

In the early 1920s, Yongsŏng also became involved with the creation of the Seminary for the Study of Sŏn (*Sŏnhagwŏn* 禪學院), a monastic organization designed to preserve Korean meditation practices and monastic training, including the strict observance of the precepts, particularly those concerning celibacy. He famously petitioned the colonial government-general a few years later in an effort to prevent a proposed change in Temple Laws that would relax the restrictions against marriage and meat-eating within the Korean monastic community, even for its presumptive leaders, the abbots of the main temples. He believed firmly that Imje Sŏn (臨濟禪) represented the orthodox lineage of teaching and transmission of the Korean Buddhist tradition, and he sought to preserve and uphold that lineage.

As a result of his various independent organizational endeavors, however, Yongsŏng quickly faced a number of financial problems. Adding to his fiscal burden was the purchase of a sizeable plot of land at the base of a mountain in South Kyŏngsang Province that he turned into an orchard to carry out his vision of the combined practice of Sŏn meditation and agriculture. He believed in self-sufficiency in the monastic community and tried, but ultimately failed, to operate a gold mine in the northern part of the country. Around the same time that he began his translation work, he also established the Taegak Kyodang (大覺教堂), an independent urban Buddhist temple located in the heart of downtown Seoul, which reflected his efforts to rebrand Buddhist teachings and tailor Buddhist practices and propagation methods to the needs of people living in a rapidly changing world. He also founded a temple in the city of Rongjin, Manchuria, as part of his Great Awakening Religion movement. The temple catered mainly to expatriate Koreans, lay Buddhists, and exiled monastics. The Japanese takeover of Manchuria, however, doomed the project at great cost to both Yongsŏng and those who had invested in the venture.[16]

This synopsis of Yongsŏng's life, especially his activities during the Japanese colonial occupation, indicates the extent to which he was willing to alter certain Buddhist practices to meet the needs of ordinary people in a changing world. He was eager to modify prevailing traditions and customs when he thought it would facilitate people's access to Buddhist teachings, such as by using vernacular Korean in the liturgy and introducing hymns aimed at laypeople into Buddhist religious services. At the same time, however, Yongsŏng strongly defended the monastic traditions and precepts that he saw as vital to the continuation of Imje Sŏn in Korea. His staunch opposition to the relaxation of traditional monastic proscriptions against marriage and meat-eating, which many others favored or simply ignored, is often cited as an example of his conservatism and defense of tradition.

In the final analysis, Yongsŏng appeared willing to accommodate changes to the mediums through which ordinary people understood and accessed Buddhist teachings and practices, but he held fast to that which he considered the core content of those teachings as passed down through history. However, the types of labels that are often used to describe historical figures from this period, such as "traditionalist" or "progressive reformer," can only be applied to Yongsŏng in some combination with one another. For that reason, certain scholars have adopted a novel strategy for dealing with this problem: a relational approach that compares Yongsŏng with other historical figures (or organizations) that represent various paradigmatic attitudes and/or ideologies.

Relational Approaches in the Study of Yongsŏng

In contrast with the relatively few studies of Yongsŏng available in English, a great deal has been written about him in Korean scholarship. He is second only to Manhae in terms of the sheer volume of work on colonial-era Korean Buddhist historical figures dedicated to him.[17] Kim Kwangsik, one of the foremost experts in the field, published his assessment of the scholarly output on Yongsŏng through the first decade of the twenty-first century and offered suggestions for the direction of future research based on his findings.[18] Interestingly, he noted that the circle of scholars working on Yongsŏng had up to that point been far too small, with the bulk of the scholarship produced by Kim himself and the aforementioned Han Pogwang, a state of affairs that Kim said resulted in a rather narrow perspective.[19] Moreover, the research has been focused mainly on confirming basic facts about Yongsŏng's life and his ideas on Buddhist reform, leaving scholars unable to meaningfully move beyond either nationalist or Jogye Order–based perspectives. Yi Tŏkchin notes that, despite exhaustive research into his biography and ideas on reform, virtually no work has been done on Yongsŏng's Sŏn teachings and practice methods.[20] This is, of course, an important area for scholars to explore, and there is still much about Yongsŏng's life and thought that remains to be investigated. However, the remainder of this chapter focuses on the question of methodology in the study of Yongsŏng and what it reveals about our understanding of colonial-era Korean Buddhism more generally.

An example of the difficulties that scholars of colonial-era Korean Buddhism have encountered when trying to situate Yongsŏng historically in this period can be found in Henrik Sørensen's examination of Buddhist journals produced during the colonial period.[21] Sørensen suggests at the outset of his study that scholars of Korean Buddhism should move beyond the bifurcating perspective of postcolonial nationalist scholarship. And yet, at the same time, he seems to inadvertently employ the very categories that inform such nationalist views when discussing Yongsŏng. His focus on Korean Buddhist journals as potential transmitters of political propaganda for the colonial regime causes him to ponder how it was possible for certain Buddhist intellectuals and monks with impeccable nationalist credentials, like Yongsŏng, to contribute so heavily to these journals. For Sørensen, this meant having to reconcile their political views with their participation in what he claims were endeavors that enjoyed the full backing as well as the possible financial support of the colonial occupiers.[22] Sørensen notes that Yongsŏng was one of the most frequent contributors to Buddhist journals throughout the colonial period, while adding that he "is generally considered a genuine patriot and staunch anti-Japanese monk who was imprisoned after the Independence Declaration together with Han Yongun."[23] However, he then addresses what he takes to be a basic contradiction, or at the very least a conundrum, between these two aspects of Yongsŏng's life and work: "His contributions, however, appear in the very first issue of *Korean Buddhism Monthly* (*Chosŏn Pulgyo wŏlbo*

朝鮮佛教月報) under the editorship of Yi Hoegwang, which means that even he wrote for a journal which served as a vehicle for the government's political propaganda."[24]

Yi Hoegwang, briefly mentioned above, was an influential leader of the monastic community in the early twentieth century who has been consistently reviled in postcolonial Korean Buddhist scholarship for being the epitome of a Buddhist collaborator with the Japanese regime. Like Yongsŏng, however, Yi was fully committed to the reform of Buddhism and especially to the propagation of its teachings. Hence, the fact that these two individuals worked together on a Buddhist periodical that sought to convey a variety of Buddhist-related material and information to its readership, an activity known as written or textual propagation (K. *munsŏ p'ogyo* 文書布教), should be seen as an expression of the importance of print media to propagation in the context of the reform efforts of the time. As Sørensen himself points out, the editors and contributors to these journals included nearly all of the most prominent monastic and lay Buddhist figures of the colonial period, and their participation can also be understood as an expression of their commitment to Buddhist propagation rather than any kind of political statement or endorsement of colonialist rhetoric. Yongsŏng's tireless work to compose vernacular translations of important Buddhist scriptures, for example, had less to do with nationalist sentiment about championing the vernacular Korean script than with the desire to make Buddhist teachings available to a wider audience for the purpose of propagation.

One way that scholars have tried to make sense of the ambiguity of Yongsŏng's place in the history of this period is through a relational approach. At the end of his study on Yongsŏng, for example, Woosung Huh, a scholar of Korean Buddhism, asks, "Where should we place Yongsŏng's life and thoughts in the history of modern Korean Buddhism?"[25] The way he chooses to answer this question is very much in keeping with other efforts to situate Yongsŏng in the history of colonial Korean Buddhism. Relying on a comparison with Manhae as well as Sŏngch'ŏl (性徹, 1912–1993), who was not really his contemporary but who was nonetheless in the same dharma lineage, Huh determines that Yongsŏng lies somewhere on the continuum between these two men. He was not as socially or politically engaged as Manhae, whom Huh places on the far left of his spectrum for his advocacy of what would later be termed as *minjung* Buddhism, nor was he as much of an "elitist" or "purist" as Sŏngch'ŏl, who represents the far right of Huh's spectrum for his doctrinal and monastic conservatism.[26]

Although he employs a similar type of comparative or relational approach, Chanju Mun applies a slightly different metric to his analysis of Yongsŏng's place in Korean Buddhist history. Mun evaluates Buddhist figures in this period according to their ecumenical as opposed to sectarian leanings, and he concludes that Yongsŏng should be characterized as a moderate Imje Sŏn sectarian, as opposed to Sŏngchŏl, whom he labels an "extreme" Sŏn sectarian.[27] Given his interest in plotting historical actors along a continuum based on their perceived ecumenical or sectarian traits, such comparisons are inevitable in Mun's doctrinal analysis, but it nonetheless demonstrates the ubiquity and utility of this analytical strategy.

This type of relational approach also underlies Kim Kwangsik's effort to categorize a wide array of twentieth-century Buddhist individuals, organizations, texts, events, and ideas on the basis of their conservative or progressive orientation toward Buddhist reform. For colonial period categorization, he identifies three basic orientations, represented by Han Yongun's *On the Restoration of Korean Buddhism*, the founding of the Seminary for the Study of Sŏn, and Yongsŏng's Great Awakening Religion movement.[28] Interestingly, this tripartite taxonomy departs from the binary analytic categories of conservative and progressive that Kim uses; not surprisingly, Yongsŏng and his Great Awakening Religion movement comprise a discrete category in this more nuanced system. Kim explains that both the Seminary for the Study of Sŏn and the Great Awakening Religion represent a conservative orientation regarding Buddhist reform under Japanese colonialism, but these conservative reformist agendas are further subdivided along conservative and progressive lines, with Yongsŏng representing the progressive wing of conservative reform efforts.[29]

Kim's typology largely agrees with other relational approaches that assign Yongsŏng a somewhat liminal place in this historical period, but none of these other approaches can match the comprehensiveness and range of Kim's method in terms of the sheer number of organizations, events, ideas, texts, and positions that he includes. Moreover, until quite recently, these types of categorizations often betrayed a nationalist bias by excluding those figures identified as pro-Japanese collaborators or sympathizers from the ranks of reformers, which Kim recognizes and tries to avoid in his typology.[30] Nonetheless, Hwansoo Kim has questioned whether a "nation-centered paradigm" can even be applied to Yongsŏng or indeed to any of his contemporaries without distorting various aspects of their lives.[31] His approach to understanding Yongsŏng is similar to the method he employed in his earlier work, offering a more nuanced view of Yongsŏng's identity and vision based on previously unpublished letters and other archival material. This approach gives greater agency to the historical actors themselves by treating them as complex individuals with concerns and goals that may not fit neatly within the binaries of nationalist historiography.[32]

More importantly, though, Kim's approach demonstrates what Anne Blackburn calls "locative pluralism," meaning that the historical actors whose lives we seek to explain exhibit "plural and shifting collectives of belonging to which they feel a sense of responsibility and emotional investment."[33] This kind of approach emphasizes the fluid identities and complex networks through which individuals moved and mobilized resources, which do not always align with the nationalist or even religious paradigms that we invariably assign to the historical realities under scrutiny. In much the same way that Blackburn focuses on networks in her approach to understanding Hikkaḍuvē,[34] Kim points to the importance of networks in examining colonial-era individuals like Yongsŏng:

> Paek's case attests to the complex colonial realities that prompted Koreans and Japanese alike to employ multiple visions and identities, including religious affiliation, around which they could successfully built personal and group networks, however perilous and short-lived these networks might have been.[35]

Adopting a networks-based approach, or at least using the building blocks of that approach, to create a framework for understanding the larger-scale changes taking place in Korean Buddhism in the early twentieth century is one way around the methodological problems that have allowed nationalist and/or modernizing narratives to overly influence our analyses of modern Korean Buddhism.

Microhistorical Studies and the Question of Scale

In the concluding chapter of her book *Locations of Buddhism*, Ann Blackburn declares, "The promise of a first generation of scholarship on the character of—and relationships among—Buddhism, colonialism, and modernity has yet to be fully realized."[36] The frameworks proposed to study these relationships in Sri Lanka, developed mainly from the 1960s to the 1980s, introduced three categories for understanding the changes that

Buddhism experienced under British colonial rule: Buddhist modernism, Buddhist Revival, and Protestant Buddhism.[37] Blackburn observes that, despite some readily apparent flaws and shortcomings, these approaches have had remarkable longevity. They have also had astonishing reach and can be found in studies of Buddhism spanning a variety of contexts outside South Asia, including Buddhism in colonial Korea during the early twentieth century. Although the arguments put forward possess an "attractive simplicity," they have, according to Blackburn, failed to provide a sufficiently rich historical understanding of "the intellectual, social, and institutional lives and practices of the Buddhists in Laṅkā during the period of intensive British colonial presence."[38] Blackburn suggests that the problem may be a question of scale, and she argues for reducing the scale to the level of the individual, calling for more microhistorical studies. In fact, her examination of the late nineteenth-century monk Hikkaḍuvē Sumaṅ gala, which comprises the bulk of her study, serves as a methodological example of this approach.[39]

Although Blackburn's critique of earlier approaches is directed mainly at the scholarship on the history of Buddhism in Sri Lanka during the British colonial period, the theoretical and methodological concerns she raises are also relevant to the study of modern Korean Buddhism. One reason is that the nexus of Buddhism, colonialism, and modernity was indisputably influential in the early history of modern Korean Buddhism. Japanese colonial rule in Korea certainly differed from British rule in Sri Lanka in significant ways, starting with the dominant religion of the colonizer, but we find many of the same general conditions, patterns, and collective responses to the changing environment in Korea that we do in Sri Lanka. Buddhist communities in different parts of Asia were aware of the developments elsewhere through the transnational networks and global exchange of knowledge that characterized this period and influenced local developments in ways that scholars still seek to understand. Blackburn's concerns are also relevant because the same or similar frameworks that were developed to make sense of the historical experiences of Sri Lankan Buddhists under British colonial rule have been used to explain the changes that occurred in Korean Buddhism under Japanese colonialism.

Blackburn rightly highlights the issue of scale as central to some of the problems here. Microhistories are certainly needed to gain a better understanding of the various challenges and practical realities that historical actors faced in their lives and the different avenues and opportunities open to them in their communities. They can be particularly useful for uncovering flaws in the metanarratives and macrohistorical perspectives that scholars have previously put forward. A careful study of Yongsŏng's life—one that fully considers his activities, thoughts, struggles, personal relationships, and social networks—can certainly help, for example, to dispel some of the simple binaries that have characterized past studies of early modern Korean Buddhism. Such an approach would ideally problematize the nationalist paradigms that tend to reify a pure, unadulterated, and uniquely Korean Buddhist essence stretching back through history and standing in opposition to the external, colonial, and transnational influences of the early twentieth century. However, this type of microhistory does not readily furnish a counternarrative capable of explaining how Korean Buddhism as a whole was evolving and transforming in the first few decades of the twentieth century.

It is problematic to focus on a single individual or a select number of people to make sense of the complex processes that exerted a wide range of influences and pressures on the tradition as a whole. The pervasive emphasis on representative individuals is clearly apparent in repeated attempts to divide Buddhist reformers into certain analytic categories, which may or may not be commensurate with the actual organizational affiliations of the individuals themselves. The problem, however, may not be the specific categories that are being used, but rather the methodological approach that tacitly locates the effects of modernization, colonialism, and competing religious groups solely in the minds and actions of individual Korean Buddhist figures. The perceptions and motivations of only a handful of interest-driven Buddhist historical actors selected by a researcher thus become the lens through which the transformative processes shaping the development of the religion in the early modern period are viewed. The crucial organizational matrix within which these individuals operated and the diverse networks that connected them must also be carefully examined to begin to understand some of the larger forces shaping their lives.

Within the shifting social, political, legal, economic, and religious environments of early-twentieth-century Korea, a certain amount of change and adaptation on the part of Buddhist historical actors and the tradition as a whole was inevitable. Nonetheless, how we understand this type of change is largely determined by the analytic categories we employ in our approaches to studying this history. A conspicuous feature of Korean Buddhism since the early twentieth century, for instance, has been the emphasis placed on propagation or proselytizing as a method to reform, revitalize, and modernize the tradition. In fact, this was one of Yongsŏng's major contributions to the development of modern Korean Buddhism, and the various studies of his life and work almost invariably highlight these activities. The influence of Protestant Christian and Japanese Buddhist missionaries on this emphasis has long been recognized, but existing studies of modern Korean Buddhism have been hampered by the tendency to view these different religions as enduring entities with stable boundaries. A networks perspective can help to overcome these limitations by shedding light on the dynamic, relational, and spatial aspects of Buddhist propagation in Korea since the early twentieth century.

This approach is particularly useful for dealing with three salient aspects of Buddhist propagation: boundaries, movement, and change or adaptation. The presence of transnational religious representatives produced both boundary formation (through the discursive sharpening of religious differences) and boundary crossing (through the mimetic appropriation of propagation methods). Moreover, in line with insights gained from the work of Thomas Tweed and Manuel Vásquez, we should pay attention to the dynamic and kinetic aspects of religious propagation as a practice that propelled individuals and organizations through space. A networks approach in combination with complex adaptive systems theories could provide an alternative framework for dealing with the interplay of continuity and change in modern Korean Buddhism by allowing us to view something like propagation—its concepts, practices, and activities—as an adaptive mechanism for dealing with structural changes in the environment through the interactions of independent elements and the flow of information between them.

Following the Flows: Networks and Systems Theories

One of Blackburn's main concerns with existing theories of the relationship between Buddhism and colonial modernity is the presumption that colonialism and the advent of modernity marked a radical break in the lives of colonial-era Buddhist monks, whose thoughts and actions can then be read as responses to this new totalizing reality. Blackburn suggests a different perspective, one that considers the colonial and Christian presence but does not assume the precedence of either in shaping the thoughts and behaviors of the historical subjects under scrutiny. As she says, "We can choose to examine spheres of intellectual and social activity in a historical context *emphatically marked by* the presence of colonial rule instead of looking at intellectual and social *responses* to colonialism."[40] Assuming that this can be done for a large enough number of Buddhist figures from the colonial period, and provided that scholars are able to produce sufficiently rich accounts of complex individuals with multiple identities and collectives of belonging, we might optimistically hope to arrive at a more nuanced, complete, and historically accurate picture of early-modern Korean Buddhism.

I remain skeptical, however, that this will furnish us with new theoretical insights about the changes that the tradition as a whole underwent during this period of history. First, researchers have to make choices about who or what to study as well as the type of information to include and exclude in their studies, and these choices are typically determined by the preexisting theories and methodological assumptions that guide their work. The type of "thick description," to use Clifford Geertz's well-worn phrase, that Blackburn seems to be advocating will certainly tell us more about the lived realities of the historical subjects that scholars choose to study, but it will not necessarily produce new theories capable of explaining the material gathered. Blackburn was acutely aware of the inadequacies of existing theories concerning Buddhism under British colonialism before she began her work, and this conviction ostensibly led her to write about Hikkaḍuvē in the first place. Second, it is a fallacy to think that we can fully explain the many transformations and continuities that characterized Buddhism in colonial Korea by assembling as many descriptions of Buddhist individuals and their spheres of activity as possible. Again, the choice of individuals to study is constrained, not simply because of researchers' bias about which historical figures were important or influential, but also because there are not that many to choose from; the historical record has sufficient information about only a small number of individuals in relative terms.

On a more basic level, however, the whole cannot be explained simply as the sum of its parts. To understand system-wide changes, in other words, we may need to fundamentally alter our view of Buddhism. Thomas Tweed has proposed what he calls a "translocative analysis" of Buddhism.[41] Building on his own unique theory of religion, which relied on spatial metaphors (*dwelling* and *crossing*) and aquatic metaphors (*confluence* and *flows*) to analyze religion, Tweed maintains that scholars of Buddhism should "trace the flow of people, rituals, artifacts, beliefs, and institutions across spatial and temporal boundaries."[42] To follow the flows to wherever they may lead, as Tweed recommends, scholars must avoid ascribing an "essence" to the religious traditions that they study. As Tweed explains, "There is no pure substratum, no static and independent core called 'Buddhism'—in the founder's day or in later generations. What we have come to call 'Buddhism' was always becoming, being made and remade over and over again in contact and exchange, as it was carried along in the flow of things."[43]

Although most scholars are acutely aware of the dangers that come with ascribing an enduring and unchanging essence to their object of study (and would emphatically deny doing so in most cases), we can find abundant traces of this essentialist viewpoint in much of the work being done on modern Korean Buddhism. Tweed's perspective on religion as expressed through the aquatic metaphor, as he explains in an earlier book, "avoids essentializing religious traditions as static, isolated, and immutable substances."[44] Tweed argues for the mutual intercausality of religion, economy, society, and politics, writing that "[t]he transfluence of religious and non-religious streams propels religious flows."[45] In his later article addressing certain methodological and theoretical matters in his work, Tweed acknowledges the feedback he received from colleagues and students, and he admits that more consideration should be given to institutional power, which prevents these organic-cultural flows from moving unimpeded in all directions.[46] Thus, he points out, "the kinetics of dwelling and crossing are always mediated not only by transportation and communication technology but also by institutional structures . . . [that] channel and regulate religious flows."[47] To this, I would add the importance of legal structures, which also "channel and regulate" these same cultural and religious flows and shape the institutional structures themselves.

Manuel Vásquez has offered constructive criticism of Tweed's theories. Like Tweed, Vásquez focuses on immigrant communities and diasporic religions in his studies, and he finds much to admire in Tweed's theory of religion. However, the emphasis on aquatic or hydraulic metaphors runs the risk of becoming "excessively anti-structural, blinding it to powerful and proliferating processes of spatially mediated control, surveillance, and exclusion."[48] As a corrective, Vásquez adds models of relationality and connectivity, such as networks, webs, and pathways, to the spatial and hydraulic metaphors or tropes that Tweed employs. As he states, "Networks mark relatively stable but always contested differentials of power, of inclusion and exclusion, of cooperation and conflict, of boundary-crossing and boundary-making."[49] These differentials of power are important to consider, especially when trying to make sense of Buddhism under colonial control and surveillance or when analyzing the networks that formed between and among Korean and Japanese Buddhist groups and individuals.

A systems approach can help us to avoid the pitfalls of essentialism while still allowing us to talk about the tradition as a whole and the way it was changing in the early twentieth century under Japanese colonialism. A microhistorical study of a single, complex individual is no less susceptible to generalizations or simplifications than are macrohistorical studies of the Korean Buddhist tradition. The fact remains, however, that we need to find a way to reconcile the different scales or levels of analysis without imputing an abstracted essence to Korean Buddhism in the process. For this purpose, it might be helpful to think of Buddhism as a complex system, which would entail viewing "Buddhism as a system embodied collectively in individual humans. The varying Buddhism of each individual is a subsystem coexisting with other systems, such as local and personal contacts. These individual subsystems communicate with others across individuals, forming a distributed whole."[50] Because complex systems are open, their boundaries are fluid and responsive to feedback from the environment, particularly from other systems with which they come into contact. The individual elements of the system all present opportunities for small-scale analysis; however, in a complex system, the whole cannot be understood as merely the sum of its parts.

If we imagine early twentieth-century Korean Buddhism as something more akin to a complex adaptive system than an enduring entity with fixed boundaries, then we may find it easier to deal with the seemingly contradictory elements, attributes, and actions of a figure like Yongsŏng. Whether this proves to be a valuable or even viable approach for analyzing specific individuals or explaining changes to the religion as a whole during this period remains to be seen. But even skeptics who question its value or validity will surely recognize the need to find some new approaches that can offer fresh insights to a few long-standing theoretical and methodological issues at the core of our study of Korean Buddhism in the early twentieth century. If this chapter helps to initiate some broader discussions on these matters within the field, then it will have served its main purpose.

Concluding Reflections

Returning once again to the place where this inquiry began, it may be useful to briefly reflect on the ways in which the perspective outlined above might influence our understanding of Yongsŏng's life and his place in the history of this period. The first thing to note is that it effectively eliminates the need for the relational approach that has characterized so many previous studies by rendering the categories being used either irrelevant or significantly altered in terms of their meaning. Was Yongsŏng a conservative traditionalist and a nationalist who defended Korean Buddhism against external influences? Or was he a progressive reformer who introduced modern practices and ideas, some of which he appropriated or creatively adapted from those very same external influences? To say that he was both and neither carries little meaning but somehow rings true, which suggests that the basic categories on which these questions rest are suspect. Put another way, if Yongsŏng does not fit neatly within the conceptual frames that are commonly used to analyze the important events and individuals from this period of Korean Buddhist history, then perhaps the fault lies in our conceptualizations and the use of terms like internal, external, traditional, modern, conservative, and reformist.

If we take seriously Tweed's statement quoted earlier that Buddhism "was always becoming, being made and remade over and over again in contact and exchange," then, in the broadest sense, Yongsŏng's historical role was to help remake Buddhism in Korea at this time. The same is true for many of his contemporaries, of course, who all saw themselves as part of a line of Buddhist transmission stretching back over a thousand years in Korea and extending beyond its shores and were committed to ensuring the continuation of the religion in some form in their country far into the future. The countless individuals who played greater or lesser roles in Korean Buddhist organizational and social activities at this time did not entirely agree on the specific contents of that transmission or on the exact boundaries of the group (or its subgroups), or on the direction that the religion needed to go to respond to the changing times. Collectively, however, they gave shape and form to what we recognize as Korean Buddhism in the early twentieth century through their aggregate actions and decisions, which were influenced not only by well-connected thought leaders like Yongsŏng, but also by the colonial state, its legal constraints, rival religious groups, cultural norms, transnational Buddhist communities, and so on. This reshaping of that which had been handed down from the past would persist, meaning that Korean Buddhism was continually being remade in large and small ways through the constant incorporation of new individuals and ideas as well as sustained interactions with other societal systems.

From this perspective, Yongsŏng's contributions placed him at the forefront of the effort to grow the boundaries of Korean Buddhism by spreading the religious doctrines and practices to greater numbers of lay people. These endeavors involved networks of individuals and organizations with whom he associated or worked. His connectedness exposed him to a variety of ideas and influences, and his efforts to deploy the resources at his disposal to spread the religion were a major feature of the final decades of his life. At the same time, his principled opposition to relaxing the precepts to allow monks to marry, together with his advocacy of Imje Sŏn, led to his involvement in still more networks of monastics and organizations, sometimes overlapping, that shared similar views and concerns, such as the Sŏnhagwŏn. Both of these spheres of activity and influence (Buddhist propagation and adherence to the precepts on celibacy) became central to the historical trends in the second half of the twentieth century, which helped to ensure that Yongsŏng would naturally come to occupy an important place in the historical narratives concerning early twentieth-century Korean Buddhism. His network of monastic disciples and dharma heirs further guaranteed that his historical contributions and accomplishments would receive the attention that they deserved and not be forgotten. These endeavors did not place him on simultaneously opposing sides of a constructed divide between traditional and modern or nationalist resistance and colonialist acquiescence or even grant him some liminal status between them. Instead, they signal his commitment to the continuation of Korean Buddhism, including both its spread among the laity and its continued viability as an orthodox line of monastic transmission from one generation to the next.

Notes

1. Buswell, "Buddhist Reform Movements in Korea During the Japanese Colonial Period: Precepts and the Challenge of Modernity," 144.
2. Paek, *Kwiwŏn chŏngjong* (Correct Doctrines That Return to the Source).
3. Nathan, *From the Mountains to the Cities: A History of Buddhist Propagation in Modern Korea*, 21–23.
4. Han, *Yongsŏng sŏnsa yŏn'gu* (A Study of the Sŏn Master Yongsŏng), 104–5.
5. There are questions surrounding the actual date of this temple's construction. Despite the fact that most scholars have accepted 1911 as the year that Yongsŏng opened his temple, Han Pogwang has argued that 1916 appears to be a more accurate date based on the available evidence. See Han, "Taegaksa

ch'anggŏn sijŏm e kwanhan chemunje" (Problems Regarding the Timing of Taegaksa's Founding), 269.

6. Huh, "Individual Salvation and Compassionate Action: The Life and Thoughts of Paek Yongsŏng," 38.

7. Kim, "Seeking the Colonizer's Favors for a Buddhist Vision: The Korean Buddhist Nationalist Paek Yongsŏng's (1864–1940) Imje Sŏn Movement and His Relationship with the Japanese Colonizer Abe Mitsuie (1862–1936)."

8. Han, "Yongsŏng sŭnim ŭi chŏnban'gi ŭi saeng'ae" (The Early Part of Master Yongsŏng's Life), 27–50. Han added two more in-depth articles on the life of Paek Yongsŏng in subsequent issues of *Taegak sasang* (1999 and 2001), which can be accessed at www.taegak.or.kr. These built on and in some cases updated Han's previously published work on Yongsŏng.

9. Woosung Huh follows this same line of thought in his English-language publications on Paek Yongsŏng. See the aforementioned Huh, "Individual Salvation and Compassionate Action," as well as Huh, "A Monk of Mukti and Karma: The Life and Thought of Baek Yongseong."

10. Yongsŏng wrote *Kwiwŏn chŏngjong* (The Correct Doctrines That Return to the Source) in 1910, the same year that Korea was formally annexed by Japan, but it was not published until 1913.

11. As was the case with Yongsŏng's text, Manhae's treatise had to wait several years before being published because of the circumstances following Japanese annexation.

12. Among the complaints about such a merger, aside from the nationalistic concerns, was the fact that the Korean tradition traced its lineage through the Imje (C. *Linji*; J. *Rinzai*) line, whereas the Sōtō sect represented a separate branch of Sŏn (C. *Chan*; J. *Zen*) altogether.

13. The governor-general refused to recognize either the Imje or Wŏn orders, creating instead the Sŏn and Kyo Dual Orders of Korean Buddhism (*Chosŏn Pulgyo Sŏn-Kyo yangjong* 朝鮮佛教禪教兩宗). The propagation temple where Yongsŏng and Manhae had previously worked faced unrelenting pressure as a result and was eventually absorbed into the newly created Japanese organizational structure of head-branch temples.

14. Han, *Yongsŏng sŏnsa yŏn'gu*, 60–61.

15. For a complete list of these translations, their dates, and their places of publication as well as other details about them, see Han, *Yongsŏng sŏnsa yŏn'gu*, 72–73.

16. Hwansoo Kim notes that some members felt cheated and requested compensation, even attempting to involve the police in their cause. See Kim, "Seeking the Colonizer's Favors," 190.

17. Yi, "Yongsŏng Chinjong Sŏn sasang e kwanhan ilgoch'al" (A Study of Yongsŏng Chinjong's Sŏn Thought), 483.

18. Kim, "Paek Yongsŏng yŏn'gu ŭi hoego wa chŏnmang" (A Retrospective and Prospective Look at Research on Paek Yongsŏng).
19. Kim, "Paek Yongsŏng yŏn'gu ŭi hoego wa chŏnmang," 49–50.
20. Yi, "Yongsŏng Chinjong ŭi Sŏn sasang" (A Study of Yongsŏng Chinjong's Sŏn Thought), 483–84.
21. Sørensen, "Korean Buddhist Journals During Early Japanese Colonial Rule."
22. Although Sørensen does not provide any evidence for these claims of financial support, the difficulty that these journals encountered in staying afloat for very long certainly suggests a precarious economic outlook.
23. Sørensen, "Korean Buddhist Journals," 23.
24. Sørensen, "Korean Buddhist Journals," 23. Sørensen's identification of Yi Hoegwang as the editor of this journal is somewhat puzzling. Not only does it contradict the widely accepted fact that Kwŏn Sangno edited the *Chosŏn Pulgyo wŏlbo*, but he actually acknowledged on the previous page that Kwŏn was indeed the "formal editor." Sørensen, "Korean Buddhist Journals," 22.
25. Huh, "Individual Salvation and Compassionate Action," 35.
26. Huh, "Individual Salvation and Compassionate Action," 35.
27. Mun, *Ha Dongsan and Colonial Korean Buddhism: Balancing Sectarianism and Ecumenism*, 32.
28. Kim, *Pulgyo kŭndaehwa ŭi yisang kwa hyŏnsil* (The Ideal and Reality of Buddhist Modernization), 352.
29. Kim, *Pulgyo kŭndaehwa ŭi yisang kwa hyŏnsil*, 354–55. For a more in-depth discussion of Kim's reasoning behind Yongsŏng's placement within this typology, see 437–51.
30. Kim, *Pulgyo kŭndaehwa ŭi yisang kwa hyŏnsil*, 354.
31. Kim, "Seeking the Colonizer's Favors," 172.
32. See, for instance, Kim, *Empire of the Dharma: Korean and Japanese Buddhism, 1877–1912*.
33. Blackburn, *Locations of Buddhism: Colonialism and Modernity in Sri Lanka*.
34. Blackburn, *Locations of Buddhism*, 215–216.
35. Kim, "Seeking the Colonizer's Favors," 172–73.
36. Blackburn, *Locations of Buddhism*, 200.
37. Blackburn, *Locations of Buddhism*, 197.
38. Blackburn, *Locations of Buddhism*, 200.
39. Blackburn, *Locations of Buddhism*, 203.
40. Blackburn, *Locations of Buddhism*, 201. Emphasis in the original text.
41. Tweed, "Theory and Method in the Study of Buddhism: Toward 'Translocative' Analysis."
42. Tweed, "Theory and Method in the Study of Buddhism," 23.

43. Tweed, "Theory and Method in the Study of Buddhism," 23.
44. Tweed, *Crossing and Dwelling: A Theory of Religion*, 60.
45. Tweed, *Crossing and Dwelling: A Theory of Religion*, 61.
46. Tweed, "Theory and Method in the Study of Buddhism," 26.
47. Tweed, "Theory and Method in the Study of Buddhism," 25–26.
48. Vásquez, *More Than Belief: A Materialist Theory of Religion*, 290.
49. Vásquez, *More Than Belief: A Materialist Theory of Religion*, 298.
50. Cho and Squier, "Religion as a Complex and Dynamic System," 370.

PART 2

NUNS AND LAYWOMEN IN MODERN KOREAN BUDDHISM

Chapter 3

Lady Ch'ŏn and Modern Korean Buddhism

Hwansoo Kim

Introduction

This chapter examines the work of a largely forgotten Korean Buddhist laywoman, Court Lady Chŏn Ilchŏng (千一淸, 1848–1934?), who served as one of the highest-ranking ladies in the court of the late Chosŏn dynasty.[1] I show that Chŏn, driven by the vicissitudes of the times, did not remain confined to being a mere servant of the Yi Royal Household.[2] Rather, she was an influential figure in Chosŏn politics and diplomacy. She also played a crucial role in modernizing Korean Buddhism during the precolonial and colonial eras, equal in significance to the roles played by the Korean Buddhist monastics with whom she worked.

Stretching from the second half of the nineteenth century to the first third of the twentieth, Chŏn's life spanned a period of massive upheaval in Korea. She was born in 1848 and brought to the court at the age of four.[3] Queen Dowager Hyojŏng (孝定, 1831–1904), the second wife of King Hŏnjong (r. 1834–1849), was childless and took Chŏn to raise her as if she were her own daughter.[4] During her lifetime, Chŏn served the Chosŏn dynasty's final two kings, Kojong (r. 1897–1907) and Sunjong (r. 1907–1910),[5] Queen Ŏm (1854–1911), and Prince Yi (1897–1970). Chŏn was a firsthand witness to the dramatic events of her time, including the opening of Korea in 1876, the Sino-Japanese War in 1895, Japan's taking of Korea as a protectorate in 1905, Japan's colonization of Korea in 1910, and the March First movement in 1919. She also witnessed the end of the Yi royal court lineage with the death of King Kojong in 1919 followed by King Sunjong's passing in 1926, which marked the end of the court lady (K. *sanggung* 尙宮) tradition.

There recently has been an increase of scholarship on court ladies, inspired partly by the popularity of historical TV dramas, especially *Dae Jang Geum* (Jewel in the Palace [2003–2004]). Scholars have examined topics ranging from the dynamics of their lives to the political, economic, and cultural influence they exerted in and beyond the palace.[6] Although attention has been given to a number of notable court ladies, no work has been done on Chŏn. This is perplexing given her political and diplomatic influence at the time. She is also absent in the scholarship of Korean Buddhism, which is even more mysterious, particularly when considering her remarkable contributions toward modernizing the tradition. Scholarship on Korean Buddhism has mainly focused on the "new women" of the 1920s who, educated in Japan and Europe, challenged traditional values with modern ideas. A well-known example is Kim Wŏnju (金元周, 1896–1971), who, as Hyaeweol Choi describes her, "literally and symbolically started the New Women's Movement" in colonial Korea in the 1920s.[7] Educated in Japan, Kim was also a devout Buddhist who was later ordained as a Buddhist nun and continued to use her pen name, Iryŏp. As Jin Y. Park characterizes her, Iryŏp was also a philosopher who deeply engaged with philosophical issues through a Buddhist lens.[8] Another example is the Buddhist nun Chŏng Suok (1902–1966), who also studied in Japan in the 1930s. She was critical of the misogynist nature of Korean Buddhism and became known as one of the three most respected lecturer nuns.[9] Chŏn, by contrast, remains a footnote in historiography despite the fact that a writer for the Korean journal *Kaebyŏk* (Creation 開闢) as early as 1934 named Chŏn as one of the figures who deserved a biography.[10]

However, Chŏn's obscurity can be attributed to several factors. First, as mentioned, Chŏn did not fit the profile of other modern women such as Kim Wŏnju, "the symbol of modern womanhood," as Hyaeweol Choi characterizes her.[11] Court ladies were a relic of an oppressive traditional Confucian-oriented society, a system that confined women to the court for the entirety of their lives. Second, unlike Iryŏp and Chŏng Suok, about whom one can find ample primary materials, sources on Chŏn's life are scattered and fragmentary, making it challenging to draw a full picture of her legacy. Third, Chŏn's reputation is sullied by her association with the Korean monk Yi Hoegwang (李晦光, 1862–1932). Because Yi has been condemned by historiographers as the worst of Buddhists who collaborated with Korea's colonizer,[12] Chŏn's leadership and legacy are likewise sidelined.

In this chapter, I draw on the known bits and pieces of information on Chŏn to make a case that she played a seminal role in the incipient stage of modern Korean Buddhism. Chŏn, working primarily with Yi, drew on a wide network of relationships both inside and outside the court to help Yi establish the first modern institution of Korean Buddhism, build the first modern temple in central Seoul, and open the first modern Buddhist clinic in Korea. This chapter seeks to restore Chŏn's centrality as a Buddhist modernizer, thereby ultimately bringing balance to a largely male-centered and nationalist history and lengthening the lineage of lay female leadership in the transformation of Korean Buddhism in the beginning of the twentieth century.

Court Lady Buddhism

Chŏn's Buddhism and Buddhist work are not unique. Rather, they reflect a long tradition of "court Buddhism" (K. *kungjung pulgyo* 宮中佛敎). The tradition begins perhaps with the Buddha's aunt, who was also a queen, and the hundreds of court ladies who joined her as they all took robes in the women's sangha. Throughout the history of Buddhism, rulers, courtesans, royal women, and court ladies were a driving force in the spread, prosperity, and preservation of Buddhism in the lands where it developed. Korea was not an exception: throughout the Koryŏ dynasty (918–1392), the royal family sponsored numerous projects to build and repair temples, print and disseminate sutras, and commission various rituals.

However, the court Buddhism in Chosŏn Korea had a distinctive significance for Korean Buddhism, far more than for the Buddhisms of the preceding Korean dynasties and in other countries. From the beginning of the Chosŏn dynasty, Neo-Confucian ideologies intensified their challenge to Buddhism, which gradually led to the closing of many urban temples and the presence of monastics in the capital and other major cities. Anti-Buddhist sentiment made the visible support of Buddhism by the royal families increasingly challenging as it came under scrutiny. Neo-Confucian officials and scholars persistently problematized the lavish spending of royal women and court ladies on Buddhist projects. They demanded that the royal women and court ladies cut ties with Buddhist monastics, whom the Neo-Confucians characterized as evaders of taxes and military duties. As the majority of the Chosŏn kings caved to these requests, albeit often reluctantly, "Buddhism," as John Jorgenson points out, "at least in public, was almost extinct."[13] Gone were the days when the royal families freely communicated with monastics in the capital and countryside and directed funds to sponsor religious projects and rituals. Their financial support of temples had to be carefully and even secretively conducted because of the harsh criticism from the Confucian elites.

As male monastics' visits to the capital city became a rarity, nuns emerged as a conduit through which funds were funneled out of the palace to support various temples. Two centers within the palace that operated like nunneries, Insuwŏn (仁壽院) and Chasuwŏn (慈壽院), played an essential role in this collaboration. These quarters were where retired royal women and court ladies lived like nuns, even with shaved heads. These court semi-nuns communicated with Buddhist monastics outside the court, providing the last avenue through which the court could quietly satisfy its religious needs and support Buddhism. Because of the women's royal status, Neo-Confucian officials initially were unsuccessful in persuading kings to disestablish these quasi-nunneries. However, in 1661, King Hyŏngjong capitulated and closed the nunneries completely.[14] The women in the palace thereby lost one remaining bastion of their religion and a secure connection through which they could communicate with monastics outside the palace.

Under these circumstances, the court ladies, who were allowed to travel outside the palace, began to take on the role of providing contact between royal women and the temples. Thus, Chosŏn Buddhism was sustained by the footwork of the court ladies alone, to the extent that Chosŏn Buddhism has been called "Court lady Buddhism" (K. *sanggung Pulgyo* 尙宮佛敎). As a contemporary Buddhist newspaper declares, "It was the Chosŏn court ladies who protected [Chosŏn] Buddhism."[15] There are long lists of court ladies' names written and carved on temple buildings, drawings, and other Buddhist artifacts that they patronized.[16] Court lady Buddhism became even more prominent toward the end of the Chosŏn era as the court ladies gained increasing influence beyond the bounds of the royal court and the country. Chŏn emerged as an important figure in modernizing Korean Buddhism during this overall rise in the influence of colonialism.

Ch'ŏn as a Powerful Court Lady

Court ladies, as well as eunuchs (K. *naesi* 內侍), had been an indispensable part of the royal court and court politics throughout Korea's history. Court ladies served the royal families in early Korean kingdoms, and the Chosŏn dynasty inherited much of the court lady system from its predecessor, the Koryŏ dynasty. During the Chosŏn period, court ladies were legally and systematically incorporated into the state bureaucracy with designated salaries for the first time.[17] Since the beginning of their service, regulations on their role were detailed in the *Great Code for Managing the State* (*Kyŏngguk taejŏn* 經國大典), the legal codes for the Chosŏn dynasty, completed in 1485. Such incorporation did not mean that they had the same stature as other state officials. Nonetheless, Hong Sunmin asserts that they were perceived in reality as "half public and half private" (K. *pangong pansa* 半公半私), meaning that often court ladies did wield political influence.[18] The number of court ladies varied throughout the Chosŏn period from 200 to 600 at its peak.[19] They were overseen by the Affairs of the Internal Court (K. *naemyŏngbu* 內命婦) and divided into nine ranks. The highest ranks—the first to the fourth ranks—were those who were directly chosen by the king as his consorts. The lower ranks—from the fifth to the ninth—were structured according to seniority and merit. The fifth-ranked court lady, called the head administrator court lady (K. *chejo sanggung* 提調尚宮), was the highest position of this second tier to which a court lady could climb. The head administrator court lady was the head administrator of the Affairs of the Internal Palace, supervising all the court ladies beneath her. Ch'ŏn held this position beginning in the 1910s, working at Kyŏngbok Palace, while Sŏ Hŭisun, another senior court lady, assumed the same rank at Ch'angdŏk Palace at the time.[20] The sixth rank of the second tier was the court lady who managed the royals' intimate life (K. *chimil sanggung* 至密尚宮); like the head administrator court lady, she served the king and queen and the royal family most closely. The court ladies of the other ranks, the seventh to the ninth, undertook a variety of tasks, including cooking, medical care, laundering, sewing, and other chores.[21]

Ch'ŏn's closeness to and influence on the royal family was noticed early on by the Japanese, who were eager to curry favor with the king and queen. The Japanese had discerned the importance of court ladies in the political sphere. For example, Ko Taesu (顧大嫂, 1843–?), a court lady and member of a reform party, participated in a coup in 1884 by setting off an explosive at a location close to the sleeping quarters of King Kojong. She was brutally executed in public for this.[22] In 1896, court ladies disguised the king and secretly took him to the Russian consul, catching the Japanese by surprise, for they had been striving to bring him under the protection of their legation. King Kojong's second wife, the former court lady Ŏm, was the mastermind behind the Russian legation incident. After King Kojong's first wife, Queen Myŏngsŏng (明成, 1851–1895), was assassinated in 1895, Ŏm bore a son and later rose to prominence to become his official queen in 1901.[23] Fully cognizant of the level of the court ladies' influence, the Japanese resident-general Itō Hirobumi strategically lavished them with gifts, such as clothes, watches, and necklaces, whenever he returned from Japan.[24]

However, decreasing the number of court ladies was inevitable. The 1894 Kabo Reforms reshuffled the court lady system, reducing them to 200. After Japan made Korea its protectorate in 1905, Itō, who previously had tried to impress these court ladies but regarded them as getting in his way, further reduced their number to fewer than 100 to weaken their clout. In 1919, scores of court ladies who had worked at Kyŏngbok Palace were dismissed following the death of King Kojong, who had resided there.[25] The number fell further after the passing of the final king, Sunjong, in 1926, and diminished to roughly seventy in 1930.[26] In 1936, not long after Chŏn passed away, it is believed that only fifty remained. Because of financial challenges, the Yi Royal Household decided to sell several palace buildings. As a result, twenty-four court ladies who were very old were let go, leaving just twenty-six.[27] At the end of the colonial period, there were fewer than ten court ladies remaining, and they became civilians. The last court lady, Sŏng Ogyŏm (成玉艷, 1920–2001), who was brought to the court at age fifteen and worked as a seamstress, passed away in 2001, ending the court lady lineage altogether.[28] Thus, Chŏn was one of the few remaining senior court ladies at the sunset of Korea's monarchical era.

Travel to Japan, 1909

The Japanese viewed Chŏn as an ideal figure to approach to influence the Korean court. And, as it turned out, they needed to draw on her proximity to the king and queen to resolve a small but significant problem. When Japan made Korea its protectorate in 1905, the Japanese government sent King Kojong's third son and Prince Sunjong's half-brother,[29]

Prince Yi, born from the king's second wife, Queen Ŏm, to Japan on the pretext of providing him with modern education. The King and Queen viewed it differently: they believed that Prince Yi was taken as a hostage. Gondō Shirōsuke (權藤四郎介, 1875–?), who had served at the palace for fifteen years as an advisor and worked closely with the court ladies, later recalled in 1925 that a rumor had quickly spread that Japan was holding the prince hostage. To rebuff this rumor and calm the king and queen, in 1908 Itō organized a diplomatic visit composed of Envoy Min Pyŏngsŏk (1858–1940) and nine other officials.[30] This group included three court ladies,[31] one of whom was Chŏn. To the public, it was announced that the court ladies would accompany Envoy Min to observe a state visit of the Philippine royal family to Japan so that they could learn and be prepared for the family's visit to Korea the following year.[32]

Upon their arrival on February 16, 1909, for the official monthlong visit, Japanese daily newspapers took extra interest in them and regularly reported their movements as well as featuring essays on the history and status of the court ladies in Korea. According to *Asahi shinbun*, Envoy Min was reported to have said that Chŏn was the most influential senior court lady in Korea and that her status and power paralleled or even exceeded those of a minister.[33] The newspaper also presented the Korean court ladies as the most diplomatically savvy, intelligent women "in the entire world" and asserted that Chinese and Japanese women should learn from them.[34] During their stay, the court ladies visited Prince Yi and observed firsthand how well he had been taken care of by the Japanese government.

When they returned on March 17, Itō and the Japanese Residence-General Office arranged a special meeting, in which Chŏn was asked to report on the safety of Prince Yi and provide her impressions of Japan. She also had an audience with the king and queen in person and assured them that Prince Yi was in good hands and enjoying his studies. The Japanese official present for these meetings wrote that the king and queen were relieved to hear the report and expressed appreciation for the Japanese government's excellent treatment of Prince Yi.[35] In gratitude, Queen Ŏm awarded a royal medal to Chŏn along with Envoy Min and the two other court ladies.[36] In the written report, Chŏn summed up her personal impression of Japan by saying, "I am a Buddhist who wants to be reborn in the Pure Land, but Japan is the Pure Land on earth."[37]

In 1920, Chŏn made another trip to Japan for the wedding of Prince Yi to the Japanese Princess Masako of Nashimoto (Yi Pangja, 1901–1989), which was supposed to be held in 1919 but was postponed on account of the passing of King Kojong. After a year of mourning, the wedding finally took place at the Kasumigaseki Detached Palace in Tokyo on April 24, 1920. At the wedding, Chŏn and two other court ladies sat with other Korean and Japanese dignitaries, thus signifying her stature.[38] Taken together, Chŏn's diplomatic role between the Korean court and the Japanese government makes it clear that she had risen to prominence as an important figure.

Chŏn's Connection to the Buddhist Monk Yi Hoegwang (1862–1933)

In addition to Chŏn's role as a court ombudsman, Chŏn was also a primary conduit between the court and Korean Buddhism. Japanese officials wrote in a government document:

> The person [Chŏn] is naturally gifted with cleverness and delivers the [Korean] Emperor's secret instructions in the court [to the outside world]. In addition, it is believed that when various prayers at local temples are secretly arranged, most of these events commonly go through the hands of this court lady. At present, she is a court lady with [great] clout: thus, one should be on one's best behavior when interacting with her.[39]

By 1909, Chŏn was in charge of the court's funds for Buddhist prayer rituals and building projects, working in close consultation with Queen Ŏm, who was a former court lady and a devout Buddhist herself.[40] But she did not simply distribute funds: instead, she traveled around the country, making donations and attending rituals in person. At one prayer event commissioned by the court, Chŏn met an ambitious monk for whom she developed deep respect; in time, they shared a lifelong companionship.

Chŏn met Yi for the first time at Mangwŏl Temple, located roughly twenty miles north of the palace in 1906. Chŏn and another court lady, Im, visited the temple for a ritual. According to the daily newspaper, *Tonga ilbo*, which featured a series of articles on Yi, Chŏn was impressed by his appearance, breadth of knowledge, and charisma, and subsequently frequented this temple for other rituals.[41] Born in 1850 in Kangwŏn Province in northeast Korea, Yi was ordained at the age of sixteen at Sinhŭng Temple. He studied sutras and practiced meditation at various monasteries, later teaching as a lecturer at Kŏnbong Temple. He had already become well-known among Korean monastics as a scholar and Zen master, and young monks lined up to learn from and practice under him.[42] However, unsatisfied with serving as an educator in remote temples, Yi had a bigger vision: to bring Buddhism out of its centuries-long exile and restore its presence in the capital city. He came to Seoul and took up residence in Mangwŏl Temple, where he came to meet Chŏn and other court ladies who had heard of his fame.

Yi was among the many Korean monks who flowed into the capital city as the Neo-Confucian dynasty was disintegrating. Monks had been prohibited from entering into the four gates of inner Seoul for centuries, but this law was lifted in 1895 because of pressure from Japanese Buddhist missionaries. Consequently, Korean monks sought to reintroduce Buddhism to Seoul. However, as a result of the peripheralization of Chosŏn Buddhism, they lacked political power. They were in desperate need of connections to government officials. Although Japanese Buddhist missionaries helped introduce Korean Buddhists to Japanese officials, they likewise had limited access to Korean officials (because of language barriers and other issues). As had been the custom throughout the proceeding Chosŏn period, court ladies were Korean Buddhists' best allies. Thus, Yi, who was ambitious, approached Chŏn to draw on her political and financial clout. For Chŏn, Yi was a great master who could guide her spiritually. In the years after their initial meeting, Chŏn became an ardent supporter of Yi's visions for Korean Buddhism. He sought to establish a modern Korean Buddhist institution and construct a temple in the center of Seoul to symbolize the end of the anti-Buddhist policies of the Chosŏn dynasty. Chŏn shared Yi's vision and saw that he had the potential to revitalize Buddhism. As an indication of how closely the two worked together, whenever Yi came to do business in Seoul, he stayed at her residence outside the palace.[43]

Yi's Appointment as Abbot of Haein Monastery

Two years after meeting Chŏn, Yi was appointed as the de facto abbot of one of the most prominent monasteries in Korea, Haein Monastery—even though he had had no strong affiliation with the monastery. If anything, the appointment should have gone to the monk Paek Yongsŏng (白龍城, 1864–1940), who would later become Yi's opponent surrounding institutional visions for Korean Buddhism. Paek had been ordained at the temple and rose to become the head teacher and master of Haein Monastery. Yi's becoming the abbot of the monastery over Paek likely had to do with Lady Chŏn's influence. Here is the backstory.

In 1906, Paek was in residence at Mangwŏl Temple where Yi was teaching. One day, Paek received a visit from Court Lady Im (Chŏn's close colleague), who became moved by Paek's teachings. Paek complained to Im about the dilapidated condition of the Canon Hall (K. *Changgyŏng-gak* 藏經閣) at Haein Monastery, which contained the extremely valuable woodblocks for printing the Koryŏ Canon. Im donated 6,000 won of her own money and later persuaded King Kojong and Queen Ŏm to provide an additional 20,000 won to fix the building.[44] If anything, Paek was the natural successor for the abbacy of the temple. However, very likely Yi became the abbot because of Chŏn's influence and financial support of Haein Monastery.

One clue to this speculation is the fact that Chŏn donated her own money to build a residential hall for monks at Haein Monastery called Kwanŭmjŏn (觀音殿), which was completed sometime in 1908.[45] (Although Chŏn was paid generously by the court, it is unclear how she amassed sufficient wealth to give away such high sums of money. It is possible that because of her proximity to the center of power, she might have received bribes or payments for connections.) Chŏn made a number of trips to Haein Monastery along with Im and other court ladies.[46] Staying for several days to attend rituals, her funding and presence must have raised Yi's profile at the monastery. Signifying her prominence, the monastery later built a memorial stone in honor of Chŏn on which her dharma name, Chŏn Chŏngongsim (千 淨空心), was inscribed. Chŏn also accompanied Yi to temples in other provinces, donating funds to support them and meeting prominent monastics.[47] Thus, by late 1908, Chŏn was so well connected and well-known in the Buddhist monastic world that if she requested someone be considered for an abbot position, it would have happened. The abbacy of the most powerful monastery at the time, Haein Monastery, gave Yi a solid purchase from which he could pursue such grand ambitions as unifying Korean Buddhism.

Laying Groundwork for the Wŏnjong

The Korean government was reluctant to reintroduce Buddhist establishments inside the four gates of Seoul. Yet it feared that Japanese Buddhist missionaries would overtake Korean Buddhism. Thus, in 1910, the Korean government constructed Wŏn'gak Monastery outside the eastern gate of Seoul. In 1908, monks selected Yi to lead the organization housed at the temple and, along with other Korean Buddhist leaders, establish a modern institutional body, the Wŏnjong (Complete School 圓宗). Yi had two ambitions: to build the Wŏnjong into a centralized administrative office for all of Korean Buddhism and to build a new temple inside the four gates of Seoul.

In addition to his connection to Chŏn, Yi was able to move projects forward through the highly influential Sōtōshū (曹洞宗) priest Takeda Hanshi (武田範之, 1864–1911). As early as 1907, Yi's own disciple Kim Yŏnggi introduced Yi to Takeda, a pan-Asianist who was deeply involved in paving the way for Japan's colonization of Korea. Takeda was equally interested in revitalizing Korean Buddhism: he believed that the Sōtōshū was the best Japanese Buddhist sect to make it happen and that Yi was the ideal ally to work with from the Korean side. Well connected to Japanese politicians, including Itō Hirobumi, Takeda began to work closely with Yi for their shared Buddhist cause.

How and when Chŏn came to meet Takeda is not known, but Takeda had previously noticed Chŏn's influence at the court. In a report on Korean Buddhism to the Sōtōshū headquarters in 1908, Takeda wrote that there were two key figures at the court who were supportive of Buddhism: Empress Ŏm and Court Lady Chŏn.[48] In early 1910, Yi and Kim arranged a meeting between Takeda and Chŏn. In addition to sharing their views about Buddhism, Takeda and Chŏn also promised to collaborate with each other for the sake of Korean Buddhism. After their meeting, Chŏn sent Takeda a thank-you note in Korean,[49] which was translated by Kim into Japanese: "I will never forget that I was able to have an audience with you in person. According to Kim Yŏnggi, you have done your utmost on behalf of the central office [of the Wŏnjong] and Korean Buddhism. A mere lay Buddhist like myself cannot truly thank you more. I deeply wish that, with the immense power of the original vow, you can revitalize Korean Buddhism and fulfill the task of opening the mountain of the first generation [the central office of Korean Buddhism] without obstruction."[50]

Thus, it is clear that Chŏn did her best to work the levers of power to advance Yi's goals for Korean Buddhism. Yi and Takeda submitted a petition to the Resident-General Office and the Korean government to recognize the new Korean Buddhist institution, Wŏnjong, as the legitimate administrative center for Korean Buddhism. A lack of response from the authorities led Yi to make a dramatic move. He decided to seek the Sōtōshū's institutional power to push forward the petition by forming an institutional alliance between the Wŏnjong and the Sōtōshū. In collaboration with Takeda, Yi submitted a joint petition not long after Japan's annexation of Korea.

Chŏn and Yi also worked on building a temple in central Seoul, the first inside the four gates of Seoul since the seventeenth century. Yi received an outpouring of support from monastics and lay followers across the country for this project, but securing a property on which a temple could be built was a difficult matter. It was Chŏn who resolved this obstacle, as Kyŏnghun Pak maintains that sometime in late 1908, Chŏn influenced the royal family to donate a piece of land that belonged to the palace for this purpose, located just a ten-minute walk from the Kyŏngbuk Royal Palace.[51] Kim Kwangsik disagrees with Park: he questions whether Chŏn had such direct influence. Nonetheless, he acknowledges that she helped Yi purchase the property, though rather indirectly. Given the status of Chŏn and her connections, I would argue that she must have been *directly* involved in securing the site.

With 80,000 wŏn donated by Buddhists around the country as well as 2,000 bass of white rice,[52] construction commenced using the wood of an old palace building. In October 1910, the Kakhwang Temple was completed. Built in the style of a Sōtōshū temple, it reflected both Takeda's influence and Yi's anticipation that an alliance between the Wŏnjong and the Sōtōshū would be approved. He hosted an opening ceremony in which dozens of Japanese Buddhist missionaries from different sects were invited to witness the historic event. In an interview for a Japanese Buddhist newspaper, Yi declared that the temple was built "purely for the purpose of propagation, and it is the first one built in central Seoul."[53] Yi's comment was directly addressed to the newly established colonial government, communicating that his institutional plan with the construction of the temple was religiously rather than politically motivated and thus was in full compliance with the government's policy on religion. Chŏn donated money and rice for the opening ceremony and attended it as a VIP.[54] Between securing a property and fully providing her political and social clout, Chŏn helped orchestrate a defining moment for modern Korean Buddhism: building a temple from which Korean Buddhism could be freely disseminated within the four gates of Seoul.[55]

While Chŏn and Yi were successful in restoring a physical presence for Korean Buddhism to central Seoul, their plan to have the Wŏnjong recognized failed despite the desperate push to do so through an alliance with the Sōtōshū. Worse, this proposed alliance instigated Yi's opponents to counter the Wŏnjong by forming a Korean Buddhist-only sect. This was spearheaded by Paek Yongsŏng, who had been pushed away from Haein Monastery back in 1908 by Yi. Paek set up a counterinstitution in 1911, Imjejong (臨濟宗), or Imje Order, thereby challenging Yi's leadership. As mentioned earlier, Paek was likewise supported by court ladies. When he came to Seoul in 1908, two court ladies, Ch'oe and Ko, helped him establish residence at a house, which later turned into a small temple called Taegaksa (大覺寺). In a sense, the two rivals of Korean Buddhism in 1911, namely Yi and Paek, were supported by the same group of court ladies.

While the Wŏnjong and Imjejong vied with each other for institutional control of Korean Buddhism, Chŏn continued to support Yi with her financial and political resources. When Yi began publishing the first Buddhist journal of Korean Buddhism, *Journal of Korean Buddhism* (*Chosŏn Pulgyo Ch'ongbo* 朝鮮佛教叢報), he allocated a vernacular Korean script (K. *han'gŭl* 한글) section that was dedicated to female readers to promote a more active role for women Buddhists. Chŏn, unsurprisingly, contributed the very first *han'gŭl* article to the journal. The article is titled "A Word of Warning for [Buddhist] Female Believers" (*Sin'gyo puin'gye ae irŏn ŭro kyŏngoham*) (discussed below). Chŏn was a learned person and was expert at a special penmanship style called Palace style (K. *kungch'e* 宮體), a *hangul* penmanship distinctively used in the palace. Very unusually for her time, she often wrote letters for the royal family,[56] a service most often performed by a male royal scribe. She also wrote in *hangul* "Namo Amit'abul" ("Homage to the Buddha Amitābha," see below), which was carved into the rock by a monk in Haein Monastery in 1907.[57]

Chŏn as an Ideal Lay Buddhist

As was the case for other court ladies, Chŏn was a philanthropist who supported a number of schools and donated to those in need. In particular, two private schools, Hodong Hakkyo (壺洞學校) and Yangjŏng Yŏhakkyo (養貞女學校), received patronage from Chŏn, to the extent that she was called the owner (K. *kyoju* 校主) of the latter. By virtue of Chŏn's close relationship with Yi, these two schools became affiliated with Kakhwang Temple. The schools regularly sent students to attend public events held at the temple. For example, a group of students participated in the Buddha's birthday ceremony in 1912, singing celebratory songs and joining the ceremony to light lanterns. For the event, Chŏn spent considerable funds and donated two large, horizontal embroidered flags. One flag had sixteen letters on it that were painted in pure gold, reading "The Ceremony in Celebration of the 2939th Birth of the Buddha." Another sixteen letters in pure gold were written on the other one, praising the virtuous qualities of the Buddha.[58]

Chŏn also sponsored a sightseeing trip for the staff at Kakhwang Temple, including Yi, the journal staff, and the students of Hodong School. They visited various scenic sites for two days in late May at Kaesŏng, roughly thirty-five miles north of Seoul.[59] During the trip, she donated supplies such as pencils and notebooks to the local schools in Kaesŏng. She took a group of students to Mangwŏl Monastery, where Yi and Paek used to live.[60] She became well-known for her generosity to Buddhism, thereby elevating the public image of Kakhwang Temple and thus Yi. Acknowledging her work, she was recognized as an exemplary Buddhist. The widely read national daily newspaper *Maeil sinbo* lauded her:

> Buddhism has an extremely long history and thus boasts a lot of followers. In recent years, Buddhist work has gradually advanced, and the number of followers increases day by day. There are not a small number whose faiths are sincere. Most prominently among them is Lady Chŏn Ilchŏng, who is a model for other followers and who is determined. From what I hear about her background, she began to deeply follow Buddhist teachings from an early age and, for the past five or six decades, has praised the Buddha's teachings whole-heartedly. On more than several occasions has she helped and saved many people with her money and materials. Since entering into the palace at age seven, she has been consistent in the way she lived, and her disposition is astute and honest. Everybody praises her and says that Chŏn is renowned as a woman of faith in the world of Buddhism.[61]

Given that the *Maeil sinbo* was not a Buddhist publication, clearly Chŏn's philanthropy was widely recognized beyond Buddhist circles.

Unswerving Dedication to Yi's Visions

Chŏn continued to back Yi's aspirations. The initial rivalry between Yi and Paek, which peaked in 1912, ended up being Yi's victory. More amicable toward Japan than Paek was, Yi received preferential treatment from the colonial government. Although the authorities disestablished both the Wŏnjong and Imjejong, they recognized Yi as the first head monk of a new, state-recognized institution, the Office of the Coalition of the Thirty Head Temples (K. *Samsip ponsan yŏnhap samuso* 三十本山聯合事務所). Paek and his protégé, Han Yongun, failed to undermine Yi's leadership, and for several years Yi was more or less the head of Korean Buddhism. With increasing challenges from his opponents, Yi was voted out of his position in 1915. His battle to regain power commenced. Yi established a lay organization called Promotion of Buddhism (*Pulgyo Chinhŭnghoe* 佛教振興會) that was not successful in providing sufficient support for him to regain the position. He then turned to the Rinzaishū (臨済宗) as a possible ally in the effort to shuffle the Korean Buddhist institutional structure. The Rinzaishū missionary Godō Zuigan (後藤瑞г, 1879–1965) considered Yi the best candidate to work with to bridge Japanese and Korean Buddhism. He invited Yi to his temple in Seoul, Myōshinji, for a series of dharma talks. Chŏn also accompanied Yi as a representative of a new female Buddhist group that Japanese Buddhists had organized to bring Korean and Japanese female Buddhists together.[62]

When the March First Independence Movement shook colonial Korea in 1919, the effectiveness of the colonial government's restrictive policies was thrown into question. The new governor-general took a more conciliatory approach called the "cultural policy" that allowed for a greater degree of native voices and representation. Capitalizing on this chaos and transition in policy to reshuffle the Korean Buddhist institutional body, Yi, in 1920, collaborated with several other Korean monks to form an alliance with the Rinzaishū. He visited Japan to meet state officials and Rinzaishū leaders to garner support for his plan. He returned to Korea feeling optimistic and stayed at Chŏn's house to further develop a plan. However, when his plan was leaked prematurely, he was again criticized by Korean monks for, as they saw it, "annexing" Korean Buddhism so that it became a mere sect of Buddhism in Japan. The two sides traded threats of lawsuits, but Yi's plan was effectively dead.

Yi did not give up. When Korean Buddhism became mired in factional infighting in the early 1920s, Yi hatched another scheme to retake power. He boldly decided to build a great head temple that could represent all of Korean Buddhism. This would supersede Kakhwang Temple, which he himself had built to achieve the same goal. Because a great head temple would go against the temple laws promulgated by the colonial government, he called it a "preaching hall." When he shared his vision with Chŏn, she again backed him. Using her connections to the Yi Royal Household, Chŏn again made available a piece of property that belonged to the royal palace so that Yi could purchase it for 300,000 wŏn. Without having sufficient funds, he, out of desperation, used his status as the abbot of Haein Monastery to collect funds. Taking a mortgage on Haein Monastery, he borrowed 60,000 wŏn from the bank and used the money to found the Central Propagation Hall (*Chungang p'ogyoso* 中央布教所) in 1924. In addition to the main building, he also opened a clinic called Mass Saving Buddhist Clinic (*Pulgyo chejungwŏn* 佛敎濟衆院). At this time, Buddhists who wished to modernize followed the template of Christian missionaries. It was thought that such clinics would establish Buddhism's usefulness to society. To equip the facility properly, Yi and his lay partner, Chang Il, purchased and imported medical devices from a defunct Red Cross hospital in Vladivostok. However, Yi was unable to remit the first payment due on the land he purchased from the Yi Royal household. To make matters worse, he was already in deep debt by several tens of thousands of wŏn. He further failed to raise enough donations from Buddhists because the construction of the clinic and the Central Propagation Hall was perceived to be Yi's personal project rather than one that would benefit the entire Korean Buddhist community. On top of this, Chang Il, who worked as the manager of the clinic, embezzled 30,000 wŏn of Chŏn's money. These complications and reckless spending forced Yi to resign from his position as the abbot of Haein Monastery in 1924. As such, the temple and clinic were also forced to close down in 1925.[63]

This time, Chŏn could not tolerate Yi's missteps. She had to bear his financial burdens as well as the fraud perpetrated by some of Yi's people, which jeopardized her very own assets. Another lay Buddhist working for Yi, Song Yongp'il, took away a rental facility that Chŏn had temporarily allowed the Central Propagation Hall to use. As a newspaper lamented, "Yi, who broke the precepts and humiliated himself with his greed," eventually "caused blameless Chŏn to lose her house."[64] According to the Korean daily newspaper *Tonga ilbo*, Chŏn allegedly filed a lawsuit against Yi in 1925[65] as well as against Yi's lay partners, Song[66] and Chang Il.[67] However, it is questionable whether Chŏn sued Yi in reality. Another source reports that both Chŏn and Yi sued Chang together,[68] indicating that Chŏn did not believe that Yi was responsible for the messes.

Unfortunately, the lawsuits were futile. Chŏn's influence waned rapidly with the death of the last king, Sunjong, in 1926. Two years after the passing of the king, the royal family office laid off dozens of staff who worked for the Ch'angdŏk Palace where King Sunjong had resided. The office deemed them unnecessary because Prince Yi, the only heir, lived in Japan. Court ladies were allowed to volunteer to retire. However, Chŏn, a high-ranking court lady, was not laid off because of her decades-long tenure with the Yi Royal Household Office.[69] One piece of evidence that verifies this claim is that, following King Sunjong's passing, Chŏn and another court lady, Kim Ch'ungyŏn (1848–1936),[70] conducted a three-year period of mourning, which would have been completed in 1929.[71] It is most likely that Chŏn kept her position to the end of her life. However, in 1926, now age eighty, Chŏn was old, tired, and frail and could not do much about the damage Yi had done. No matter what, it is clear that Chŏn unreservedly supported Yi to the end in spite of Yi's futile forays into grand projects on Korean Buddhism, his overreliance on Japanese Buddhists, and his lack of organizational skills. Likewise, Yi continued to rely on Chŏn even as her influence was ebbing.

Chŏn's Buddhism

A question arises as to what it was in Chŏn's faith in Buddhism that led her to dedicate massive amounts of energy, time, and money to assist Yi and his vision, despite setbacks and recurring fiascos. One article she wrote provides a glimpse of her religiosity and understanding of Korean Buddhism as well as her vision for it. It is a 1912 article written in *han'gŭl* that was featured in the Buddhist journal *Korean Buddhism Monthly* (*Chosŏn Pulgyo Wŏlbo* 朝鮮佛教月報).[72] Titled "A Word of Warning for [Buddhist] Female Believers," Chŏn addresses all female Buddhists in Korea with advice on the best practices of new, modern female Buddhists. This short article reflects the ways she had lived as a Buddhist and how she would live for the remainder of her life as a socially engaged and modern Buddhist woman.

Reflective of rhetoric that was pervasive among intellectuals at the time, Chŏn starts her article with a lamentation of the poor conditions faced by Korean women in general. "When we, women, think of our lives," she writes, "they clearly reveal the [unwholesome] karma of our previous lives, and our next lives will also be full of unparalleled illness too difficult to cure." She writes, "Even though it is a relief to be reborn as a human being rather than as an animal, if one thinks of women's lives . . . it is rather shameful." She enumerates a number of hardships that Korean women are subjected to, "albeit too many to express in words properly." She writes that there are women who cannot freely exit their own houses; in terms of skills, they cannot move beyond sewing; in terms of study, more than half of them are illiterate; in terms of manners, they have to behave like those in prison; if they don't bear children, they are accused of terminating the family line; and women put up with the abuses of their husbands and mothers-in-law. Chŏn ascribes all of these conditions to the fact that "the right way" (K. *chŏngdo*, written in *han'gŭl*) "is still immature." "How infuriating it is!" she exclaims.[73]

This emotional detailing of the oppression inflicted on women was common among those who envisioned creating a new identity for women. Often, this argument was made for the purpose of involving women in nation-building movements. But Chŏn's description of women's poor circumstances during the Chosŏn period is a way of arguing that Buddhism could provide women with, as Ji-Young Jung points out, "an alternative space outside of Confucian social norms."[74] The highly male-dominated Neo-Confucian Chosŏn society compelled women to remain chaste and be confined to the home as well as prohibited them from remarrying after their husbands died.[75] In addition, Confucian ideology, which consisted primarily of patriarchal, sociopolitical rituals, did not sufficiently address questions of suffering, sorrow, death, and afterlife. As such, many ordinary people turned to Buddhism to fill in the gap between these real-world challenges and the teachings and rituals needed to support them in times of loss.[76]

Chŏn acknowledges then that Buddhism had been prejudiced against women. She admits that the Buddha taught that, for men, relationships with women are a hindrance to enlightenment. Praising the virtues of the Buddha and his teachings as unrivaled, she nonetheless defends the Buddha's seeming discrimination against women by reasoning that he was primarily concerned with curtailing the five desires[77] of human beings rather than with ostracizing women. She defends that the Buddha's teaching did not contain any gender differences and that there were great masters who often took on women's bodies out of compassion. She notes that many Buddhas and Bodhisattvas (Avalokiteśvara being most representative) had female forms as counterparts to their male manifestations. Thus, she declares that there is no difference between the genders in the unparalleled religion, namely, Buddhism.[78] Chŏn then addresses what had happened to this unrivaled religion in Chosŏn Korea over the previous hundreds of years. She claimed that, in theory, there should be no rises and declines for this peerless religion. But because they were living in the latter days of the world, Buddhists experienced both prosperity and stagnation.

Regarding the stagnation of Buddhism during the Chosŏn era, she asserts that there were nearly none who understood the Buddhist teachings correctly. She then specifically criticized that they did not possess the right set of religious thoughts, charging that monastics, having dwelt deep in the mountains, were overboisterous in their meditation practices alone and did not have the capability to save people. This explains why Chŏn was vigorously supportive of Yi, who endeavored to bring Buddhism from mountains to cities. Regarding women, Chŏn blamed them for not knowing that Buddhism was a religion and accused them of merely seeking apotropaic benefits through prayers and rituals rather than taking care of themselves.[79]

Chŏn also fully embraced the movement of civilization and enlightenment (K. *munmyŏng kaehwa* 文明開化), which was translated, for women, into the discourse of "wise mother and good wife" (K. *hyŏnmo yangchŏ* 賢母良妻). This discourse was pervasive at the time among intellectuals and nation-builders. Although Chŏn did not exhibit a sense of nationalism or focus on women's role in nation-building, she understood educated and socially engaged women as essential to a modern Buddhism. "At the age of enlightenment when Buddhism has come back," Chŏn begs of female Buddhists to "abandon old, corrupt habits and customs, encourage new knowledge and ideas . . . and be diligent in good works [philanthropic activities]." Otherwise, she warns that, no matter how much one prays and seeks good fortune from the Buddha, no good results or blessing will be forthcoming. She makes this point clear to her female readers by adding, "[However], if you, on Sundays, come to the teaching halls [preaching halls or temples], listen carefully to all of the teachers' dharma talks and all of the laymen's speeches, study them in detail . . . do charity works, tend to the household, and pay homage to the Buddha with faith, you will be full of fortune and blessings."[80]

Among other benefits, Chŏn includes some that are fairly traditional, thus contradicting her own admonition. She writes, "[If one does so], one will naturally see her descendants fill up the house. If one exerts oneself this way, one should think that one will enter into the supreme lineage [or path] [of Buddhism] and go to the Internal Hall of Tuṣita Heaven [where the Buddha Maitreya resides] at one's will. It won't be difficult for one to turn one's female body into a male body for eons."[81] Familiar with the parable in the *Lotus Sūtra* of the daughter of the Dragon King who transforms herself into a man to prove she could attain enlightenment,[82] Chŏn retains the traditional view that one must shed the female body and be reborn as a male to gain final nirvāṇa, reflective of the androcentric and misogynistic features in Buddhism that even women held as true.[83] It seems that Yi also held this belief of the inferiority of the female body, which might have influenced Chŏn's understanding of Buddhism. Not long after Chŏn's article came out, he published and distributed *The Sūtra on the Descent of Maitreya* (*Mirŭk sangsaeng kyŏng* 彌勒上生經), which also contains two additional short sutras: *The Sūtra of Maitreya Bodhisattva's Attainment of Buddhahood* (*Mirŭk sŏngbul kyŏng* 彌勒成佛經) and *Dhāraṇī of the Bodhisattva Merciful One's Promise* (*Chassi posal sŏwŏn tarani kyŏng* 慈氏菩薩誓願陀羅尼經). *The Sūtra of Maitreya Bodhisattva's Attainment of Buddhahood* teaches that if one keeps, reads, and chants the sutra as well as worships the Buddha and respects teachers, one will eliminate all bad karma and afflictions, and "one will not receive a woman's body [in the next life]."[84] Chŏn concludes by reiterating her earlier point, "Dear female fellows, if you follow the religion [of Buddhism], please be diligent in cultivating your mind and body!"[85]

As reflected in this article, Chŏn was both modern and traditional. Overall, she leaned toward the modern, encouraging other Buddhist women to join her in promoting a new Buddhism with a heightened female role. Her own life reflected this traditional configuration that harkened back to the old to generate something new.

Chŏn's Death

Chŏn's public activities from 1926 on rapidly dwindled. Other than giving small donations for natural disasters, she retired from the public scene. Yi Hoegwang died on February 3, 1932, at the age of seventy.[86] It is believed that Chŏn took pity on Yi when he did not have any place to go, purchased a small straw house for him near the Han River in Seoul, and continued to take care of Yi until his death.[87] She most likely attended the funeral held four days after his death at Kakhwang Temple, which they had built together in late 1910. In 1934, elderly, sick, and sensing that her death was near, Chŏn sent a letter to the department head of the Yi Royal Household Office, Yi Songmuk (served, 1931–1935) and the treasurer of the department, Yi Ŭngun. In her letter to Yi Sŭngmuk, she beseeches him to take care of several matters after her death.

I am extremely ill, and it seems likely that I am going to leave this world soon. Could you, the Head of the Department [of the Yi Royal Household], be kind enough to think of me? I will have to ask you a favor. Please take pity on this old body. I beg you to arrange all of the matters [the funeral] and help me with care after I die. Please forgive me for sending you a letter without inquiring after you in person. After I die, I rely only on your highness, the head of the department.[88]

In a separate letter to Yi Ŭngun, Chŏn similarly asks, "I hope you can help my soul rest in peace after I die."[89] With Yi Hoegwang not in this world anymore, there was nobody who could tend to her funeral other than the official Yi Ŭngun.

The exact date of her death is unknown, but it is unlikely that she did not endure long after sending these letters. However, in the absence of Yi's reciprocal care, it is unclear whether Chŏn's funeral was held at the same temple. Given her two letters requesting that the officials take care of her body and other matters, this might not have been the case.

Conclusion

Was Chŏn's loss of a place in history a causality of Yi's failure and pro-Japanese tendencies? Yi's reputation in historiography for trying to sell out Korean Buddhism to Japanese Buddhism might have buried Chŏn's significance to modern Korean Buddhism, not to mention a male- and monastic-centered interpretation of Korean Buddhism. However, her place in history should not be undermined.

Chŏn had an indelible impact on Korean Buddhism as a female Buddhist leader. With her political connections, she enabled Yi's institutional visions by introducing him to government and court officials, both Japanese and Korean. She poured significant personal assets as well as funds from the court into pushing forward their shared goals. In a sense, it was Chŏn who made Yi a prominent leader of Korean Buddhism. It was Chŏn who influenced Yi to become the leader of the first modern Korean Buddhist institution, the Wŏnjong, and to be appointed the abbot of Haein Monastery. She was indispensable in building the first modern temple in central Seoul, Kakhwang Temple, thereby symbolically ending the anti-Buddhist policies of the Chosŏn dynasty. Kakhwang Temple later morphed into Jogye Temple, which today is the great head temple of South Korea's dominant order. Her charity work and philanthropy raised Yi's profile. As she had done with Kakhwang Temple, she was deeply involved in founding the Central Preaching Hall to function as the headquarters for Korean Buddhism, and she contributed to the establishment of the first modern Buddhist clinic, however short-lived it proved to be. It could be true that Yi ruined Chŏn's sincere intentions with his futile ambitions. Yet Yi's damaging legacy should not undermine her contributions, which are significant in the context of modern Korean Buddhism. She is a key shaper of modern Korean Buddhism, on par with the monastics who swarmed into Seoul to bring a new era to the religion.

One might wonder about the nature of the relationship between Yi and Chŏn. Undoubtedly, given the extent and duration of Yi and Chŏn's collaboration, it could be speculated that their relationship was more than that between a master and a devotee. However, Chŏn was fourteen years older than Yi. In that regard, it is most likely that Chŏn felt like Yi was a son—perhaps even a companion whose work could give her life meaning and assurance of future salvation. For Yi, Chŏn was perhaps like a mother or even a partner to rely on in good times and bad ones. Given that Yi and Chŏn spent time together at her house and took numerous trips in the country, their close relationship could be seen as a violation of the rules governing their status as court lady and monk. However, the understanding that both of them had taken vows of celibacy might have rendered their closeness less suspicious in the eyes of the public. It is also possible that the visible presence of an increasing number of married monks as well as the waning oversight of the Chosŏn government might have enabled them to be close without worrying too much. As such, it appears that their relationship did not create any scandalous stories. Besides, in extant sources, Yi never endorsed clerical marriage, unlike many of his fellow monks who took wives themselves, including Han Yongun. Yi died as an unmarried monk.

By the 1910s, the connection between court ladies and monks became widespread as monastics began to come back to Seoul. As such, Chŏn was just one of many court ladies who helped monastic leaders establish a foothold in Seoul. In fact, there were hardly any monastic leaders in the late nineteenth and early twentieth centuries who moved to Seoul to propagate Buddhism who were untouched by court ladies. Monastics were eager to make connections with court ladies. As mentioned, when Paek came to Seoul, the court lady Ch'oe found him a place to stay.[90] His close relationships with court ladies, especially Ko, who later built the temple Taegaksa for Paek, were responsible for rumors of sex scandals.[91] Several other court ladies were essential in the establishment of a new Buddhist religion called Teachings of Great Awakening (Taegakkyo 大覺敎) and later initiatives, including cooperative farm communities in Korea and Manchuria.[92] The very last court lady of the Yi Royal Household, Sŏng, was also a member of the Teachings of Great Awakening.[93]

Han Yongun, who was a protégé of Paek in the early 1910s, was close to the same court ladies who supported Paek. Han also worked with the court lady Ch'oe Songsŏltang (崔松雪堂, 1855–1939),[94] who was well-known for her philanthropy, particularly her promotion of education.[95] Other leading masters such as Song Man'gong (1871–1946), Park Hanyŏng (1870–1948),[96] and Pang Hanam (1876–1951),[97] to name just a few, received support from court ladies in one way or another. Without court ladies, Korean monastics almost certainly would have had a hard time reestablishing Buddhism in the cities, especially in Seoul.

In prior centuries, court ladies went to the mountains to support monks; at the turn of the twentieth century, the monks came to them from the mountains. Thus, "Court Lady Buddhism" is to a great extent responsible for modern Korean Buddhism. Contemporary Korean Buddhism is often dubbed as nothing more than female Buddhism (K. *posal Pulgyo* 菩薩佛敎). *Posal* means bodhisattva, but in this case it refers to female Buddhists. It has also been called "skirt Buddhism" (K. *ch'ima Pulgyo* 치마불교). Both terms are pejorative, because they imply that Korean Buddhism is composed of predominantly women and that the primary concern of these women in following Buddhism is merely to receive good fortune (K. *kibok* 祈福).[98] The terms "female Buddhism" and "skirt Buddhism" are, in a way, an accurate description of modern Korean Buddhism, but the implied meaning is incorrect. In the absence of monastics in the cities, it was female Buddhists who made Buddhism known wherever they went. They were essential agents in transmitting Buddhism. Thus, it behooves us to rectify the monastic/male-centered understanding of modern Korean Buddhism—"a flawed vision of the complex history of Buddhism,"[99] as Eun-su Cho points out—and give due attention to the significance of court ladies among many other Buddhist women in the making of modern Korean Buddhism.

Notes

1. This article was supported by a generous grant from the Academy of Korean Studies through the collaborative project called the "Laboratory for the Globalization of Korean Studies" (AKS-2013-LAB-2250001).

2. Because the Chosŏn dynasty was founded by Yi Sŏnggye (李成桂, r. 1392–1398) and his descendants ruled the kingdom until 1910, it was often called the Yi Royal Household.

3. Based on her interview with a reporter of *Maeil sinbo* (March 24, 1921), "Ch'anggyŏnggung yang chŏngha" (Two Highnesses of Ch'anggyŏng Place). Cho Hasŏ (趙霞棲, 1880–1965) was another girl who was brought to the court at the age of four. See Sin, *Kungnyŏ: Kunggwŏl ŭi kkott* (Court Ladies: Flowers of the Palace), 115–16.

4. Sin, *Kungnyŏ*, 116–18.

5. Ch'ŏn's boss, Kim Ch'ungyŏn, also served the two kings closely ("Yunghŭi Hwangche rŭl mosi nŭn saramdŭl" [Those Serving Emperor Yunghŭi]), *Maeil sinbo*, May 8, 1926.

6. Sin, *Kungnyŏ*; Pak, *Kungnyŏ ŭi haru: Yŏindŭl i ssŭn sumgyŏjin sillok* (Court Ladies' Day: True Hidden Stories Written by Women); Pak, *Hwan'gwan kwa kungnyŏ* (Eunuch and Court Lady); Kim, *Chōsen chōkyuchū fuzoku no kenkyū* (A Study on the Court Customs of the Chosŏn Dynasty), 9.

7. Choi, *Gender and Mission Encounters in Korea: New Women, Old Ways*, 166.

8. Jin Y. Park has published two excellent books on Kim. See *Reflections of a Zen Buddhist Nun: Essays by Zen Master Kim Iryŏp* (2014) and *Women and Buddhist Philosophy: Engaging Zen Master Kim Iryŏp* (2017).

9. An, "Suok sunim" (Nun Suok).

10. "Paegin paekhwa" (100 People and 100 Stories), 117.

11. Choi, *Gender and Mission Encounters in Korea: New Women, Old Ways*, 7.

12. Im, *Ch'inil sŭngnyŏ 108-in: Kkŭnnaji anŭn yŏksa ŭi murŭm* (108 Pro-Japanese Korean Monks: Unfinished Questions of History), 48–49.

13. Jorgensen, "Marginalized and Silenced Buddhist Nuns of the Chosŏn Period," 123.

14. For more detail on nunneries in the palace, see Yi, "Chosŏn sidae wangsil ŭi piguniwon sŏlch'i wa sinhaeng" (The Establishment of the Bhksuni Temple by the Chosŏn Royal Family and Buddhist Belief).

15. Yŏ, "Chosŏn sanggung tŭri Pulgyo chik'yŏ watta" (The Court Ladies of Chosŏn Preserved Buddhism). This claim supported the depictions of the prominence of Buddhist faith in their court lives in the drama *Dae Jang Geum*.

16. T'ak, "Chosŏn sidae wangsil yŏin tŭrŭn sach'al ŭi 'taehwaju' yŏtta" (Royal Women of the Chosŏn Dynasty Were the Great Financial Resources for Buddhist Temples).

17. Kim, *Chōsen chōkyuchū fuzoku no kenkyū*, 9.

18. Hong, "Chosŏn sidae ŭi kungnyŏ ŭi wisin" (The Status of the Court Ladies during the Chosŏn Dynasty), 243.

19. Kim, *Chōsen chōkyuchū fuzoku*, 29.

20. Kim, *Chōsen chōkyuchū fuzoku*, 21.
21. Kim, *Chōsen chōkyuchū fuzoku*, 15–20.
22. Sin, *Kungnyŏ*, 53–59.
23. Han, "KuHanmal Sunhŏnhwangbi Ŏmbi ŭi saengae wa hwaltong" (Empress Um's Life and Activities in the Last Chosŏn Dynasty).
24. Shirōsuke, *Ri Ōkyū hishi* (A Secret History of the Yi Royal Palace), 15.
25. Kim, "KuHanmal ŭi kungjung p'ungsok."
26. "Ch'unsaek tŭngjin kokung e yŏgwan tot'aesŏl taedu" (Rumors of the Disestablishment of the Court Lady System Come to the Fore to the Old Palace against Spring).
27. "Sirŏp sŏnp'ung un 'Nain' egedo, Andong Pyŏlgung to hŏllyŏ" (A Sweeping Unemployment Hits the Court Ladies, and Even the Andong Royal Palace Faces Demolition).
28. Kim, "Chosŏn-jo majimak Sangung Ttŏnada" (The Last Court Lady of Chosŏn Korea Passes Away). She served the last wife of King Sunjong, Queen Yun (1894–1966), and she was demoted to a civilian after the colonial period.
29. King Sunjong was the only son born between King Kojong and Queen Min (1851–1895).
30. Gondō, *Ri Ōkyū hishi*, 16–17.
31. The other two are Lady Ko and Lady Cho.
32. "Naeji hŭibo" (Miscellaneous News from Japan), *Taehan hyŏphoe hoebo*, February 25, 1909. In *Yomiuri shinbun*, it was reported that one of the reasons for their trip was to study the rites and etiquette of the Japanese imperial court ("Kankoku Shaonsi to jokan" [Korea's Gratitude Delegates and the Court Ladies]).
33. "Sō Naishō no kien" (Internal Minister Song's Spirit). When she arrived in Shimonoseki, Chŏn was visited by her nephew, Chŏn Kyŏngsik (千璟植, 1883–?), who had been studying law at Meiji University in Tokyo since 1905 ("Raichō no Kankoku san jōkan" [Three Korean Court Ladies Visiting Japan], and "Chorŏpsaeng illan" [List of Graduates]).
34. "Kankoku no jokan seikatsu" (The Life of Korean Court Ladies).
35. "Rainichi jokan no danppen (196)" (A Short Story of a Court Lady Who Visited Japan 196).
36. *Sunjong sillok* 4 3/38/B (August 21, 1910).
37. "Rainichi jokan no danppen (196)."
38. "Karye ch'amgaja ch'uga" (Additional Participants in the Royal Wedding). She was accompanied by two other court ladies, Kim Myŏnggil and Oh Yŏngson. Gondō, *Ri Ōkyū hishi*, 208–9.
39. "Rainichi jokan no danppen (196)."
40. For Queen Ŏm's faith in Buddhism, see Yu, "Kojongdae Sunhŏnhwanggŭibi Ŏmssi parwŏn pulhwa" (Buddhist Paintings Sponsored by Empress Ŏm during the Reign of King Gojong).

41. "Chonggyo paengnyŏn 14: Ch'inilsŭng Yi Hoegwang" (The Recent Hundred Years of Religion: Pro-Japanese Monk Yi Hoegwang).

42. Im, *Ch'inil sŭngnyŏ 108-in*, 48–49; Kagan, *Tongsa yŏlchŏn* (Biographies of Korean Monks), 325–26.

43. Yi, *Chosŏn Pulygo t'ongsa: kŭndae* (A Comprehensive History of Korean Buddhism: Modern), 119.

44. Han, "Paek Yongsŏng ŭi Haeinsa mit Koam sŭnim kwa ŭi inyŏn (Paek Yongsŏng and Haein Monastery and His Affinity with Koam Sŭnim), 26–27.

45. Yi, "Haeinsa kihaeng" (A Trip to Haein Monastery).

46. "Chonggyo paengnyŏn 15: Ch'inilsŭng Yi Hoegwang" (The Recent Hundred Years of Religion: Pro-Japanese Monk Yi Hoegwang).

47. Im, *Kisan munjip* (Collection of the Writings). For example, she accompanied Yi to Songgwang Monastery and donated 400 wŏn.

48. Takeda, *Kochū iseki*, reel 3 (Collection of Takeda's Writings), 3–9.

49. Kawakami, *Takeda hanshi den* (A Biography of Takeda Hanshi), 511. Kawakami Zenbe (1868–1944), who was a lay Buddhist and a patron of Takeda, wrote a biography of Takeda that contains Chŏn's letter. In it, he uses her Buddhist name, Chŏn'gongsim (千空心).

50. Kawakami, *Takeda hanshi den*, 511–12.

51. Kang and Park, *Kŭnsae Pulgyo paengnyŏn* (Recent Hundred Years of Buddhism), 46.

52. "Chongmuwŏn mit Pulygodang" (The Administrative Office and Buddhist Hall).

53. Shimada, "Kakunōji no nyūbusshiki" (Kakhwang Temple and the Enshrinement Ceremony of the Buddha).

54. "Chappo: Kakhwangsa pulsang pongansik" (Miscellaneous: The Enshrinement Ceremony of the Buddha Statue).

55. Yi, *Chosŏn Pulgyo t'ongsa: kŭndae*, 21.

56. Yi, "Hangŭl py'ŏnji ae nat'anan Sunwŏn Wanghu ŭi ilsang kwa kajok (Queen Sunwŏn's Daily Life and Family on Hangul Letters), 3.

57. Chonghyŏn, "Sobang chŏngt'o rŭl hyanghayŏ-Namu amit'abul kwa pŏmsŏ" (Toward the Western Pure Land—Paying Homage to the Amida Buddha and Sanskrit Writing).

58. "Jappo: paril sŏnghwang" (Miscellaneous: A Great Success of [April] Eight), 67–69.

59. "Jappo: Chŏnssi kwŏnhak" (Miscellaneous: Chŏn's Recommendation of Education), 73.

60. "Samgyo ilhaeng" (Three Schools' Trip), 65.

61. "Mobŏmjŏk Pulgyo sinja: yumyŏnghan Chŏn Ilchŏng yŏsa" (An Exemplary Buddhist: Famous Madame Chŏn Ilchŏng).

62. "Che ilhoe kaech'oe toen Chosŏn puinhoe" (The First Meeting of the Association of Chosŏn Women).

63. "Chŏnsanggung sogigo sammanwŏn kich'ŭihan Chang'il Kŏmsaguk haeng" (Chang'il Arrested in Charge of Deceptively Extorting 30,000 Wŏn from Court Lady Chŏn).
64. "Ujadong e paekgŭisu" (A Foolish Person Moves, Numerous Ghosts Follow).
65. "Hyujit'ong" (Wastebasket).
66. "Chŏnsanggung ŭi karyŏnhan p'alja" (Court Lady Chŏn's Pitiful Fate).
67. "Chang Il susongguk" (Chang'il Finally Sent to the Prosecutor's Office).
68. "Ujadong e paekgŭisu."
69. "Sangsisawŏn yŏgwan dŭng samsip'yŏmyŏng ch'ong haejik" (Dismissal of Thirty High-Ranking Court Ladies and Others).
70. Kim Ch'ungyŏn (1848–1946) and Chŏn, who were the same age, worked closely together. Kim became a chief administrative court lady in 1932 but passed away in 1936 at Kyŏngsŏng Nursing Home (*Kyŏngsŏng yoyangso*) ("Insa sosik" [Personal News]).
71. "Ch'ojo uryŏ ro pargun oilya ŭi Ch'anggyŏnggung" (Fifth Night of Ch'anggyŏng Palace Dawning with Restlessness and Worry).
72. "Singyo puingye e iron ŭro kyŏngoham," 44–47. In fact, the journal titled *The Complete School* (Wŏnjong 圓宗) was the very first journal of Korean Buddhism, but it was discontinued after just a few issues, and there are no extant copies of them.
73. "Singyo puingye e iron ŭro kyŏngoham," 44–45.
74. Jung, "Buddhist Nuns and Alternative Space in Confucian Chosŏn Society," 158.
75. Han, "Women's Life during the Chosŏn Dynasty."
76. Lee, "The Exemplar Wife: The Life of Lady Chang of Andong in Historical Context," 43.
77. The five desires are for wealth, sex, fame, food, and sleep.
78. "Singyo puingye e iron ŭro kyŏngoham," 45–46.
79. "Singyo puingye e iron ŭro kyŏngoham," 46.
80. "Singyo puingye e iron ŭro kyŏngoham," 46.
81. "Singyo puingye e iron ŭro kyŏngoham," 47.
82. For the detailed story, see Watson, trans., *The Lotus Sutra*, 188–89.
83. For more detail on Buddhism's multivocal attitudes toward women, see Sponberg, "Attitudes toward Women and the Feminine in Early Buddhism," 3–36.
84. Yi, *Mirŭk sangsaenggyŏng* (Sutra on Maitreya's Previous and Future Lives), 63.
85. "Singyo puingye e iron ŭro kyŏngoham," 47.
86. "Yi Hoegwang Sŏnsa changsŏ" (Zen Master Yi Hoegwang Passes Away).
87. "Chonggyo paengnyŏn (final): Ch'ininsŭng Yi Hoegwang" (The Recent Hundred Years of Religion: Pro-Japanese Monk Yi Hoegwang).

88. Chŏn Ilchŏng, "*Sanggung Chŏn Ilchŏng t'anwŏnsŏ*" (Court Lady Chŏn Ilchŏng's Petition).

89. Chŏn Ilchŏng, "*Sanggung Chŏn Ilchŏng t'anwŏnsŏ.*"

90. Cho, "Paek Yongsŏng ŭi ch'amsŏn taejunghwa undong kwa puinsŏnwŏn" (Paek Yongsong's Movement of the Popularization of Son and the Women Medication Center).

91. An editorial titled "Sexual Scandals of the So-Called Buddhist Masters, the Exemplars of the Itinerant" was featured in *Maeil sinbo* on July 26, 1914.

92. Kim, "Hwagwawŏn ŭi yŏksa wa sŏngkkyŏk" (History and Characteristics of Hwagwawŏn).

93. *Pulgyo sinmun*, May 22, 2001, quoted from Kim, "Hwagwawŏn ŭi yŏksa" (2017), 38.

94. "Sŭt'ori t'elling inmul yŏlchŏn" (Storytelling Biographies).

95. Kim, ed., *Han'guk yugyŏng saŏp ŭi ŏmŏni Ch'oe Songsŏltang* (The Mother of Korea's Educational Work).

96. Court Lady Ch'oe often supported him. See Sŏ, "Sŏkchŏn Pak Hanyŏng sŭnim 4."

97. Court Lady Kim was a patron of Hanam. See Hong, "Hanam sunim kasa" (Master Hanam's Robes).

98. Yi, "Ch'ima Pulgyo poda sangŏpjuŭi ka pip'andoeya" (Commercialized Buddhism Should be Criticized More Than Skirt Buddhism).

99. Cho, *Korean Buddhist Nuns and Laywomen*, 1.

Chapter 4

Experiencing a Different Buddhist Community

Nun Suok's Travel to Japan and Her Contribution to the Korean Community of Nuns

Eun-su Cho

Introduction

In the past decade, various theories have been shared about the nature and characteristics of modern Korean Buddhism in the twentieth century. Korean Buddhist scholarship, however, has revolved almost entirely around men, focusing on monks (Skt. *bhikkhus*) in particular. Little attention has been paid to either lay or monastic women, despite the important role they played in the Korean Buddhism of the modern period. During this period, nuns emerged as notable meditation practitioners and community leaders, and laywomen provided significant material support that shaped the fabric of Buddhism at the time.

This chapter deals with the life and teachings of the nun Chŏng Suok (鄭守玉, 1902–1966).[1] Suok studied in Japan as a young nun from 1937–1939 and became an educator and scholar after coming back to Korea. While in Japan, Suok published a travelogue in a Buddhist magazine in Korea that remains a valuable cross-cultural testimony of a colonial subject and religious aspirant traversing the material and cultural boundaries of the empire and the colony.[2] With a particular emphasis on the state of nuns, her travelogue is a unique record of a Korean Buddhist nun who employed her observational skills during her stay in Japan to develop a keen analysis of Korean Buddhism in transition. Despite her contribution to the evolution of the Korean nuns' community, Suok's position in Korean Buddhism has been obscure, and this chapter hopes to demonstrate the important role she played in modern Korean Buddhism as a scholar-monastic.

Suok's Early Life

Suok was born in 1902 in Chinhae in the southern part of South Korea. According to her epitaph, "she was gifted and held no stock in secular life from an early age."[3] She had no desire to lead a secular life, aspiring instead to the life of a practitioner in the mountains. One late autumn day in 1917, she left home unbeknownst to her parents and traveled to Haein Monastery (海印寺). She was fifteen. When she arrived at the monastery, she expressed her desire to join it and was immediately rejected. She was told that the monastery only accepted men. She had to turn around and go to Kyŏnsŏng Hermitage (見性庵) at Sudŏk Monastery (修德寺), a well-known place for nuns practicing meditation. There, she became a student of Myori Pŏphŭi (妙理 法喜, 1887–1975), the Sŏn master who is credited with reviving the nuns' lineage in modern Korea.

Suok could not have found a better teacher than Pŏphŭi, who practiced under Sŏn master Man'gong (滿空, 1871–1946). A renowned figure in Korean Buddhism during the colonial period, Man'gong was also recognized for his willingness to provide nuns with Sŏn training. Pŏphŭi was his first female disciple, receiving a dharma transmission from Man'gong in 1916. Suok entered the sangha only a year after Pŏphŭi had been recognized as a Sŏn master and started teaching at Kyŏnsŏng Hermitage. Pŏphŭi became a pioneer who almost singlehandedly restored nuns' practice after the tradition had fallen into disarray.

After some years of practicing Sŏn meditation and serving her master Pŏphŭi, Suok decided to study Buddhist scriptures and left Kyŏnsŏng Hermitage for a seminary at Haein Monastery. She was nineteen. She completed the first, or elementary, course (K. *samigwa* 沙彌科, Skt. *śramaṇera*) and the second, or intermediate, study (K. *sajipgwa* 四集科) of novice training in two years under the tutelage of a nun named Kogyŏng. She then finished the third-year course on four Mahāyāna texts (K. *sagyogwa* 四教科) and the advanced and final year course (K. *taegyogwa* 大教科) in

Seoul at Unsŏng Hermitage under the scholar monk Taeŭn Kim T'aehŭp (大隱 金泰洽, 1899–1989), who would play an important role in the direction of her future studies of Buddhism.⁴

Suok was twenty-eight by the time she finished her studies in March 1929. In April, she received full *bhikṣuṇī* precepts from Yongsŏng (龍城, 1864–1940), a precept master at Haein Monastery renowned for his reform work in Korean Buddhism during the Japanese colonial period. For the next two years, Suok studied Vinaya, or monastic rules (K. *yul* 律), under Yongsŏng and returned to Kyŏnsŏng Hermitage to complete five summer retreats.⁵ Mastering all three sections of Buddhist practice—Sŏn (meditation), Kyo (doctrine), and Vinaya (precept) studies—was a rare achievement for a practitioner of the time.

Suok in Japan and Her Cross-Cultural Observations

Suok still wanted to further her studies at that point and decided to go to Japan. There are some discrepancies in the sources about her time there, but Suok's own travelogue states that she left for Japan in 1937 and returned to Korea in 1939. In 1939, while still in Japan, she published a travelogue titled "Observations from a Tour of Japanese Buddhism" (Naeji Pulgyo Kyŏnhakki 內地佛教見學記) in the July and August 1939 issues of *Buddhist Times* (*Pulgyo Sibo* 佛教時報),⁶ which will serve as our main source material for examining what Suok learned on her trip to Japan.

The first essay begins by capturing her motivation to study abroad: "In Korea, I'd always heard that Japan was a Buddha land. So, I was hoping that I would have an opportunity to visit Japan to study Japanese Buddhism."⁷ By the time she left Korea, she had been a nun for more than two decades and had already been trained in the sangha and studying Buddhist doctrine under notable monks for many years. She was probably already a notable figure in the community of Korean nuns. As an elite nun with the highest degree of education who had talent as well as devotion, she stood well above her contemporaries.

Although it is understandable that a talented thirty-six-year-old nun such as Suok would have a passionate desire to go to Japan, there are no records of how she was able to get there. It was not unusual for Korean monks to study abroad during the Japanese colonial period, but I was not able to find any record of Korean nuns other than Suok studying in Japan at that time.

As for her motivations to go to Japan, we can reasonably assume that her teacher, Kim T'aehŭp, might have encouraged her to study in Japan. Kim was a leading intellectual during the colonial period and had studied in Japan himself. In 1920, he had supported himself through college at Toyo University while studying Indian philosophy and at Nihon University, where he studied religion. In 1928, after spending nine years in Japan, he returned to Korea and became active in promoting Buddhism as a lay dharma teacher, publishing a number of articles in the leading Buddhist journal *Buddhism* (*Pulgyo* 佛教), giving speeches on the street, and broadcasting radio programs. He also organized Buddhist choirs and theater troupes, composed hymns, and wrote and directed plays. For the seven years from 1928 to 1935, he actively engaged with Korean Buddhism. *Buddhism* went out of circulation in July 1933, and he started a new monthly periodical called *Buddhist Times* in August 1935. Given that Suok studied under Kim right after his return from Japan, there is a good possibility that Suok was stimulated by him to study in Japan and to look for a new approach to Buddhism for the new era. It hardly seems a coincidence that her travelogues were published in two parts in Kim's *Buddhist Times*.

Suok arrived in Japan in 1937. She wrote, "Two years ago, during the twelfth year of Showa [1937], I crossed the Korea Strait and landed in Japan. Upon my arrival, I went on a pilgrimage to Buddhist temples in Osaka, Kyoto, Nara, and Kobe. Since last year, I have studied at a Nichiren temple for more than a year, and this spring I moved to the Training School for Nuns [Nishugakurin 尼衆學林], a Rinzai temple in Mino Prefecture."[8]

As someone who was familiar with the situation of Korean Buddhism at the time, her attention was rightly directed to noticeable differences between Korean and Japanese Buddhism. The sectarian nature of Japanese Buddhism was one of the aspects that attracted her attention. Suok observed:

> I feel that an introduction to the situation of Buddhism here is in order. It is said that Korea had different Buddhist schools in the past, but for the present, the Sŏn school dominates; we study sūtras and we chant, but we do it in the context of the Sŏn school. Japanese Buddhism is different from Korean Buddhism in this regard. Thirteen schools and fifty-six branches of Buddhism exist. What's more, regardless of the identity of the school, the temples revere the founding patriarchs of the school and of the branches more than the Buddha himself.[9]

Experiencing a Different Buddhist Community | 105

In Korea, the Chosŏn dynasty government had integrated different Buddhist schools into the two categories of the meditational (K. Sŏn 禪) and the doctrinal (K. *kyo* 敎) schools. During the Japanese colonial period, these two schools were merged into the Sŏn school, and the Wŏn Order (圓宗)—the predecessor of today's Jogye Order of Korean Buddhism—was established. Suok wrote,

> In Japan, if you visit a large temple, more attention is paid to the Hall of the Patriarch, in which the founding patriarch of the school is enshrined, than the Buddha Hall, where the Buddha is located. Lay followers are the same in this regard. If you visit the sacred temples on Koya Mountain of Shingon Buddhism [眞言宗], you will see that they respect the statue of Kūkai [空海] more than that of Mahāvairocana Buddha. In the Pure Land Sect, they revere the founder Shinran [親鸞] above Amitābha Buddha; and the Nichiren sect, Nichiren [一連]. . . .
>
> In a small temple, the statue of the Buddha is in the rear, and the statue of the patriarch is situated in front. As a result, sometimes it is hard to see the Buddha, situating itself behind the patriarch. I think this is a distinctive feature of Japanese Buddhism. In our temples at home, it is the complete opposite. A portrait of the patriarch or the founding master can only be found hung in the corner of a small shrine, covered with dust; monastics might pay attention to the patriarchs once a year, such as in a tea ceremony, but no devotees pray to them, nor is there any great ceremony on their anniversaries. It truly seems that the founding patriarchs of schools or branches in Korean Buddhism chose wrong disciples. There exist almost 1,300 temples in Korea. Among them, how many venerate their founding masters? Most of the old temples in Korea claim that they were founded by Ado [阿道] or Wŏnhyo [元曉] or Ŭisang [義湘], but where are the temples that clearly venerate these masters?[10]

Following this, Suok suggests, "In order to advance Korean Buddhism, there must be a faith that reveres the founders and seeks to venerate the patriarchs." Given that Korea was a Japanese colony at the time, Suok's criticism of Korean Buddhism seems to mean more than just pointing out Korean Buddhism's lack of awareness of its traditions and how it had neglected them along with its founders and ancestors. It is as if she demands that the reader see the difference between a tradition that preserves its history and one that does not and how that has resulted in different realities in the present.

Still, Suok does not uncritically praise the sectarian nature of Japanese Buddhism. She also pays attention to its weaknesses:

> Although there are fine advantages [in focusing on sectarian identity], there are also limitations. [Japanese Buddhism] focuses too narrowly on their foundational suūtras and doctrines and disparages other schools. For example, the temples of the Pure Land School [淨土宗] or the Shin School [眞宗] display only *Three Principal Texts of the Pure Land Tradition* [淨土三部經], which is all they read. In Nichiren Shū [日蓮宗] anything other than the *Lotus Sutra* and in Shingon Shū [眞言宗] anything but the *Bore liqu jing* [般若理趣經] is considered a heretical teaching.[11]

Korea has a long tradition of Mahāyāna Buddhist practice, beginning when Buddhism arrived in the Korean peninsula in the fourth century. It has been claimed that an ecumenical attitude to Buddhism developed in Korea soon after the introduction of Buddhism to Korea. Questions remain regarding the philosophical or religious efficacy of the syncretic approach and whether Korean Buddhism had really put such syncretism into practice. But still, there has been a tradition in Korean Buddhist scholarship that views this synchronizing attitude as a superiority of Korean Buddhism. A defense of this ecumenical ideology coming from Suok would have been especially acute. Since the beginning of the Chosŏn dynasty, Buddhist training had been organized into the two tracks of meditation and doctrinal study; by the end of the Chosŏn dynasty, Sŏn practice had become more prevalent.

With this ecumenical approach in her background, Suok was not too impressed by the sectarian and devotional nature of the Nichiren or Pure Land sects. She was, after all, an educated nun who studied Buddhist doctrines and practiced meditation. She tells us that she moved from a Nichiren temple to a Rinzai Zen temple "because of boredom": "I am now at a temple of the Rinzai Zen school, the same school as the Korean Sŏn school. From what I can see, whether it is in doctrine, as an institution, or in practice, Rinzai Zen is the exemplar of Japanese Buddhism."[12]

Suok seems to suggest by analogy that the Sŏn school is superior and that the mainstream of Korean Buddhism was and ought to be Sŏn. In this, she reflects the attitude of contemporary Koreans who, although fearing Japan as a powerful nation, still considered Japanese culture as rather provincial.

Buddhist Nuns in Korea and Japan

Suok expressed her preference for Korean Buddhism's emphasis on Sŏn training in comparison to the existence of diverse sectarian schools in Japanese Buddhism. As a nun, however, she could not help noticing the different statuses of Buddhist women in Korea and Japan. One by one, she examined the qualifications and social realities of Japanese nuns:

> In Japanese Buddhism, monks cannot earn the trust of their devotees until they are considerably educated. Starting when they are young, they go through elementary school, middle school, vocational school, and university, and then they enter the monastery, where they practice Zen meditation for two to three years and then become abbots and dharma propagators. And the same is the case for Buddhist nuns [尼僧]. The Training School for Nuns [尼衆學林], where I am now, was founded a long time ago by Myoshin Monastery [妙心寺], a major branch headquarters of Rinzai Buddhism in Kyoto. It is a place for the cultivation of nuns and provides substantial scholarships of several thousand yen a year for the education of nuns. The nuns of Myoshin Monastery and its branch hermitages always come here for five years of middle school education, and then they enter a separate meditation hall to practice Zen meditation for a few years. After that, they go on to be abbesses, propagators, or even Zen masters of meditation halls. Because the nuns here have so much education and clearly marked levels of practice, they receive honorific titles such as Great Venerable [大和尙], Great Zen Master [大禪師], and Venerable Elder [老師] and are treated with the highest respect.[13]

Looking at the high qualifications and status of Japanese nuns, who were even given honorific titles, it would have been hard for Suok not to compare this to the wretched status of nuns in Korea. Many Korean nuns could not even read or write; far from being able to engage in religious practice, they were struggling simply to feed themselves like ordinary laypeople. Suok continues:

> What are the circumstances in Korea? Of course, there are temples where only nuns live and where nuns can aspire to become abbesses, but how many nuns in Korea even have an education? Aren't they mostly illiterate and barely able to read a letter of even the Korean alphabet? The situation being like that, they live as if they were still in the secular world, busy just making ends meet. And because this is the case, monks look down on the nuns, and lay followers regard them as nothing more than people to chat with when they come to the temple to pray. Although I am just a woman and a nun myself, after seeing the position of nuns here in Japan, I cannot help but sigh at the pathetic state of Korean nuns back home.[14]

Suok's criticism about the status of Korean nuns in her time is rather severe, but it is hard to tell exactly what the state of affairs was for Korean nuns during the early twentieth century. After receiving state support for more than a millennium until the end of the Koryŏ dynasty (918–1392), the fate of Buddhism waxed and waned throughout the Chosŏn period, as the dynasty held an anti-Buddhist policy. Although the effects of this policy depended heavily on particular kings and shifting social milieus as well as having different intensities and characteristics in affecting men and women, rich and poor, and centers and margins, we can say in general that, by the eighteenth century, Buddhist society in Korea had declined and lost its vigor. Only a handful of sources give more detailed hints of this. The description of the pitiful situation of a Korean woman in an 1803 poem by Tasan Chŏng Yagyong (茶山丁若鏞, 1762–1836) shows that, while temples functioned as shelters for women who left home,[15] conditions there were severely deprived, and no systematic training courses or programs for meditative practice were offered. We can only guess that, by the time of Suok's trip in the late 1930s, the material conditions of Korean nuns' lives were still rather deplorable.

Suok asks another pointed question: Whose fault is this? She adamantly insists that the blame lies not with the ignorance of the women, but instead with the men who had belittled and mistreated them:

> Of course, some may say that the fundamental cause [of the deplorable situation of Korean nuns] is the ignorance of nuns. In my view, however, the blame lies mostly with the men, the *bhikkhu*s [monks] in the Korean temples, and their sin is

grave. Monks are supposed to take responsibility for guiding nuns. If only they had worked to improve the status of nuns since ancient times, created seminaries, and built meditation halls for them so that they could have improved themselves through learning and practice! Even when Buddhism was ostracized in the secular world during the Chosŏn dynasty, nuns were able to mingle freely with most of the households and therefore were in a good position to edify and sway the common people, which could have become a huge source of strength for Korean Buddhism, enabling it to prosper. It is my hope that at least now the monks in Korea will stop oppressing, neglecting, and despising nuns and start to work to improve the status and dignity of nuns.[16]

Her criticism of Korean monks is harsh. That they should have taken "responsibility for guiding nuns" is a reference to the stipulations in the Eight Chief Rules (K. p'algyŏnggye 八敬戒) in the Vinaya, a corpus of monastic regulations. These rules apply exclusively to nuns, and nuns must accept them along with other rules to become fully ordained (Skt. bhikṣuṇī). These eight rules serve to subordinate nuns to monks in perpetuity, stipulating not only that all monks are superior to all nuns and requiring nuns to prostrate themselves accordingly, but also that nuns must be in the care of and educated by monks. This responsibility for supporting and controlling nuns is also stipulated in the Vinaya. This is why Suok claims that the responsibility should lie with monks, whose duty it is to supervise the nuns and whose privilege it is to receive their forced respect; monks, she argues, should reciprocate that respect instead of treating nuns with "oppression, neglect, and disdain." Suok continues, "There are almost a thousand nuns in Korea, but not a single seminary or educational institution exists for them, nor is there a meditation hall of any respectable size for them. Isn't this a disgrace to Korean Buddhism? I urge Korean temples to make efforts to educate nuns as soon as possible. I hope that, with such efforts, nuns will improve their quality and eventually become female doctrinal masters and Sŏn masters whom the lay followers would respect like the Buddha himself."[17]

It is unknown how the readers of Suok's article responded when it was published in *Buddhist Times* in July 1939. In the second installment of her travelogue that appeared in the August issue in 1939, Suok described the practices at Japanese Rinzai Zen temples and Japanese nuns' intense, strict, but simple lifestyle. Of particular interest is her description of the procedure of admission to a meditation hall, which captures well the ambience of Japanese Buddhism.

> With alms bowl in hand and clothed in monastic robes, I entered the temple grounds and prostrated in front of the garden. I pled with a long, thin voice, saying, "I plead your indulgence" [J. *otanomi itashimasu*]. Then, an officer inside the temple replied in a long voice, "Greetings" [J. *tōrei*]. Even after this, I was not immediately admitted to the monastery. They left me in the prostrate position for the whole day. They gave me lunch, as if I were begging. . . .
>
> In this monastery, people sit in the order not of age but of seniority of admission to the monastery. The eldest sits at the head of the table. While studying sutras and practice meditations, we take turns doing all of the chores instead of employing someone for them, whether that means cooking rice, making other dishes, or chopping wood and setting fires. Periodically, we go to town and beg for alms. In that way, students in this monastery manage to live for ourselves. It does not matter whether the students' masters are rich or poor. . . .
>
> Life in this monastery is truly simple; for breakfast and dinner, we eat porridge made of rice and barley. For lunch, it's just a bowl of cooked barley together with miso soup. . . . With my distaste for cooked barley, eating it without a single side dish is like taking medicine. I cannot eat more than half a bowl or maybe a bowl of barley, which leaves me living with constant hunger.[18]

Education was one of Suok's main interests. She marveled at the pedagogical curriculum in the Japanese seminary and its systematic organization, not only in meditation and doctrinal study, but also in character development and the cultivation of humility, endurance, and frugality. And despite its being a seminary, Zen meditation was also part of the curriculum. The intense and strict meditation regimen and the disciplined and modest way of life earned her praise. She exclaimed that the nuns there were true models for others and that the lay followers respected the nuns as if they were their own mothers. She ended her travelogue thus:

So, when will these seminaries and schools and meditation halls for nuns ever appear in our Chosŏn Korea? Whenever I think about this, I shed silent tears; whenever I see the marvelous facilities here in Japan, I get upset without even realizing it."[19]

The First Modern Dharma Instructor at a Seminary for Nuns

Suok returned to Korea in 1939 after more than two years in Japan, including her studies at the Training School for Nuns. One can imagine the thoughts that were going through her mind on her journey back to Korea. As luck would have it, a position for a dharma instructor had opened up at Kwanŭm Seminary (觀音講院) at Namjang Monastery (南長寺), and Suok's career as an educator was about to begin. Her experiences and keen observations in Japan paid off immensely in her work in Korea. For an account of the status quo that Suok was trying to overturn, we can reference an interview conducted around 2007 with the nun Kwangu (光雨, 1925–2019), Suok's first disciple.[20] Here, Kwangu offers her own account of the first time she met her teacher:

> At that time [1940], the first seminary for nuns was established at Namjang Monastery. Although Namjang Monastery was originally a place for monks to practice, Master Hyebong opened a seminary for nuns there when he was an abbot. It was solely through the support of Master Hyebong that the seminary became a reality. When I was at a meditation hall at Pudo Hermitage in Tonghwa Monastery, Master Suok was also there, after coming back from her studies in Japan. Whenever she had free time, she taught me the *Lotus Sutra*, and I proudly wrote this in a letter to the Master [her father, Hyebong]. When I went to Namjang Monastery to see him after my retreat ended, he handed me a letter and said I should deliver it to Venerable Suok. As it turned out, the letter said he was willing to give away the Kwanŭm Meditation Hall if she accepted the invitation to establish a seminary and serve as a dharma instructor. When Venerable Suok read the letter, her face lit up! Of course, she packed up her things

right there and went to be a dharma instructor at Namjang Monastery.[21]

Suok thus became the dharma instructor of the Buddhist vocational seminary at Namjang Monastery, where she trained disciples for three years. The seminary did not just rely on word of mouth to recruit nuns; it ran advertisements in the newspapers and brought in students from all over the country. Having a nun as a dharma instructor would certainly have garnered attention. Although there were more applicants, because of the limited space, only twenty nun students were accepted to study at the Kwanŭm Seminary. The curriculum was the same as that of the traditional seminaries for monks.

Kwangu noted that this was not only the first time a meditation hall became a seminary, it was also the first time that a seminary for nuns was officially established in Korea. She recollects, "Venerable Suok was very considerate when she taught her students, but she could be very strict when she needed to be. It was my great fortune to be able to spend my youth studying under someone like her."[22]

Although there is little evidence attesting to the attitude of contemporary monks to nuns' receiving such an education, one certainty was that there were male instructors who thought it worthwhile to educate nuns, though they were rare. Unhŏ (耘虛, 1892–1980), a leading scholar known for his modern thinking, was one such figure. He recognized that providing education to Korean Buddhist nuns was long overdue and made a vow to help educate nuns, a pioneering action to take at the time. However, Buddhist scriptures were written in classical Chinese and contained highly complex contents, and not all monks at the time agreed to teach that to nuns. To do so, he had to receive approval from a number of influential monks, including Masters Chŏngdam (青潭, 1902–1971), Sŏngchŏl (性徹, 1912–1993), and Hyanggok (香谷, 1912–1978).

Unfortunately, the seminary at Namjang Monastery did not last long. After the first graduating class in 1943, consisting of five nuns and including Kwangu,[23] the seminary closed in 1944. The last stage of the Pacific War posed a particularly horrible threat to single young women in Korea, who became the targets of brokers seeking "comfort women" for the Japanese Imperial Army. With the realities of the secular world crashing down in this tragic fashion, the flow of new students stopped. Suok returned to Kyŏnsŏng Hermitage in 1943 and devoted herself to her own practice.

Participation in the Purification Movement

In 1945, Korea was liberated from Japanese rule. In March 1947, at the age of forty-six, Suok began teaching at Pomun Monastery (普門寺) in Seoul, which she continued to do until the start of the Korean War. In 1951, she became the abbess of Podŏk Monastery (報德寺) in Tŏksan, South Ch'ungchŏng Province. The social upheavals of liberation and the war brought changes to the status of women, including nuns. After the war, orphaned girls were adopted by nuns' monasteries, and the number of nuns grew quickly. The nuns also had to rebuild their monasteries that had been destroyed during the war. These hardships in the early 1950s opened up new opportunities for Korean Buddhist nuns.

Another monumental shift in Korean Buddhism was the purification movement, which pitted celibate monks and nuns against married ones. A 1954 rally saw 30 nuns and 116 monks gathered at Sŏn Meditation Center (Sŏnhagwŏn 禪學院) in Seoul, and though the individuals' names were not recorded, Suok's name appears in various other records. Soon after the rally, on November 3, 1954, ten representatives of nuns, including Suok, were named within the Assembly of the Jogye Order,[24] marking the first time that nuns held any high positions in that order. Then, in December, a bloody confrontation between the married monks and the celibate Jogye clerics, including nuns, was followed by a series of violent demonstrations. A newspaper recorded it thus:

> A crowd of bald-headed, grey-robed monks and nuns marched in downtown Seoul on this snowy day. They were Buddhist monks and nuns who held the firm belief that Korean Buddhist society can be purified only when married monks are removed from temple grounds. It was the third day of their national meeting. At two o'clock on December 13, about 500 monks and nuns gathered from all over the country and, displaying their spirit and will for purification, departed from T'aego Temple [太古寺] and marched to the Blue House to meet with the president. A few hundred nuns also participated in this march, with senior nuns like Kang Chaho and Chŏng Suok at their head.[25]

The role of nuns in the purification movement was formidable. However, several years later, when the celibate monastics won the conflict and the redistribution of the seized monasteries began, nuns were denied their request to have even one of the twenty-five head temples (K. *ponsa* 本寺) run by monks designated as a headquarters for nuns. In recognition of the nuns' efforts, the Jogye Order transferred only a few branch monasteries to nuns, such as Naewŏn Monastery (內院寺), Taewŏn Monastery (大源寺), and Unmun Monastery (雲門寺). Given that there were as many nuns as monks at that point, space to match their numbers was desperately needed.[26]

Ultimately, however, the fundamental weakness of the leadership of the Korean nuns' community was a major reason that nuns failed to take their fair share after fighting on the streets alongside monks or after they outnumbered the monks. Most well-known nuns of the time dedicated their whole lives to practice and preferred staying in their mountain retreats to getting involved with secular affairs. Although Suok was a negotiator who could talk face-to-face with monks, this was not a war that could be won by a single person.[27] At this point, the realization set in among Korean nuns that they needed to politicize themselves and build their influence.

In March 1955, Suok was appointed abbess of Naewŏn Monastery on Chŏnsŏng Mountain in South Kyŏngsang Province. Like other deep mountain monasteries, this one had been burned to the ground during the Korean War. Three senior nuns were handed the task of rebuilding these monasteries, most of which had only their foundations remaining. The three were close dharma friends, and they resolved to secure a space where nuns could practice in peace.

Suok was fifty-four at the time. From this point onward, she worked to expand her horizons both as an individual and as a member of the nuns' community. Preserving and expanding her own lineage, she worked to build nuns' institutions and organizations, and she did so in accordance with the ongoing changes in Korean society, which was on the path to modernization. In her disciple's words, she put "every last drop of devotion and effort into rebuilding and organizing this space."[28]

Through all manner of personal sacrifice and hardship, the nuns were able to claim a space for themselves to live and practice. By actively carving out this space, they developed a communal awareness that enabled them to make visible their identities as practitioners. On a personal level, by securing space for themselves, they were able to build pride in their identities as nuns and create opportunities to find their own voices and gain recognition from society at large. For her work in rebuilding her temple, Suok received an award of merit from the governor of her province in 1959 and a similar award from the president of the Jogye Order. These commendations brought great esteem not only to Suok but to all nuns in Korea.

Honoring the Nuns' Doctrinal Dharma Lineage

The reconstruction effort was also an opportunity for Suok to perfect her leadership skills. Her influence did not stop at organizing and building the physical environment of Naewŏn Monastery,[29] because she also influenced Korean nuns as they gradually learned to manage their monasteries independently. The nuns also started codifying comprehensive standards for education in general and seminary education in particular, an effort that is now considered by many to be the greatest force for raising the status of nuns in contemporary Korean Buddhism.

Suok's life also became something more than her personal achievements, and her legacy lives on through nuns' dharma lineage, as was evidenced in a case involving the great scholar Myŏngsŏng (b. 1930).[30] Although she had already received dharma transmission from her own master, Myŏngsŏng performed a formal dharma transmission ceremony in which she pledged herself a disciple of the late Suok in front of her ancestral tablet in 1983. This kind of posthumous dedication ceremony was rare and showed Myŏngsŏng's strong desire to join Suok's lineage and continue the nun's dharma tradition through transmission from nun to nun, instead of from monks. She composed this dedication during the ceremony:

Before the spirit of my master:

I reflect on how I am living my own life right now while savoring these words you left behind. I had endless respect for you while you were alive, but I was not able to express it properly. Now it is the eighteenth anniversary of your passing, and my feelings of emptiness and regret are measureless as I pledge myself your disciple in front of your spirit. I am deeply ashamed and sorry that I, less significant than a firefly, should dare to carry on the dharma of one such as you, as lofty as Chŏnsŏng Mountain. Nevertheless, you gave me your clear permission. I intend to understand and carry out your will and to devote my body and soul to the spread of the Buddha's sea of teachings. As a small gesture of my heart, I have republished a collection of your valuable words, and I will share it with others who miss you, praying with palms together that you will soon be reborn as an eternal light for all sentient beings. (July 27, 1983)[31]

That women recognize other women as sources of authority and seek to inherit the dharma lineage through them demonstrates how much the Korean nuns' community had advanced since when Suok joined the monastery at the beginning of the twentieth century.

Closing Reflections

Suok worked to earn proper respect for nuns from the public and equal treatment from monks. The detailed account of monastic life in Japan that appeared in her travelogue displayed the sharp contrast with the social conditions of Korean nuns that spurred her work. In the end, what is most clearly revealed is a firm resolution to better Korean nuns' status, rooted in her self-awareness as a Korean nun. Upon her return to Korea, Suok's top priority was to establish a firm community for the nuns of Korea so that they could live and practice as "real" nuns. On the other hand, her harsh critique of the lack of support from the Korean Buddhist monks reflected the Buddhist milieu of the time, in which monks often despised nuns and ignored their educational needs.

Suok knew that it was time for nuns themselves to revive their traditions of education, practice, learning, and training and that it was only through institutions dedicated to this purpose—seminaries and meditation halls—that they could do so. Her critique of monks, whom she claimed bore responsibility for the inferior status of Korean nuns, addressed a persistent problem that has yet to be fully resolved even fifty years after her death. However, even today other nuns are continuing the efforts Suok made throughout her life to achieve religious self-realization in spite of hardship and adversity.

Experiencing a Different Buddhist Community | 117

Notes

1. An earlier version of this chapter appeaered in *Religion* 10, no. 6 (October 2019) as "Chŏng Suok's Tour of Imperial Japan and Its Impact on the Development of the Nuns' Order in Korea." The current chapter is a revised and refined version of this article.
2. On the delicate relationship of late Chosŏn Buddhist figures with Imperial Japan during the colonial period, see Kim, *Empire of the Dharma: Korean and Japanese Buddhism, 1877–1912*.
3. Ha, *Kkaedarŭm ŭi kkot* (Flowers of Enlightenment), 212.
4. For general information about Kim T'aehŭp's life, refer to Kim, "Kim T'aehŭp—Pulgyo taejunghwa e saengae rŭl hŏnsin hada" (Kim T'aehŭp, Devoting His Life to the Popularization of Buddhism).
5. Her biography is based on two sources: Yi, "Yangsan Naewŏnsa biguni Hwansandang Suok hwasang Pimun" (Epitaph of Master Bhikṣuṇī Hwansandang Suok of Yangsan Naewŏn Monastery), 1197–98; and Ha, *Kkaedarŭm ŭi kkot*, 207–20.
6. Chŏng, "Naeji Pulgyo kyŏnhakki (sang)" (Observations from a Tour of Japanese Buddhism: Part 1) and "Naeji Pulgyo kyŏnhakki (ha)" (Observations from a Tour of Japanese Buddhism: Part 2).
7. Chŏng, "Naeji Pulgyo kyŏnhakki (sang)," 6.
8. Chŏng, "Naeji Pulgyo kyŏnhakki (sang)," 6.
9. Chŏng, "Naeji Pulgyo kyŏnhakki (sang)," 6.
10. Chŏng, "Naeji Pulgyo kyŏnhakki (sang)," 6.
11. Chŏng, "Naeji Pulgyo kyŏnhakki (sang)," 6.
12. Chŏng, "Naeji Pulgyo kyŏnhakki (sang)," 6.
13. Chŏng, "Naeji Pulgyo kyŏnhakki (sang)," 6.
14. Chŏng, "Naeji Pulgyo kyŏnhakki (sang)," 6–7.
15. Cho, "The Religious Life of Buddhist Women in Chosŏn Korea," 81.
16. Chŏng, "Naeji Pulgyo kyŏnhakki (sang)," 7.
17. Chŏng, "Naeji Pulgyo kyŏnhakki (sang)," 7.
18. Chŏng, "Naeji Pulgyo kyŏnhakki (ha)," 6.
19. Chŏng, "Naeji Pulgyo kyŏnhakki (ha)," 6.
20. After her father Hyebong (1874–1956) joined the monastery, Kwangu followed suit and joined the sangha at Chikchi Monastery in 1939 together with her mother; she was fifteen years old. Kwangu later became a leader of the Korean Buddhist nuns' society. She served two terms as the president of the National Bhiksūnī Association, in 1995 and 2004. Her memories of her teacher are recorded in Ch'oe Chŏnghŭi, *Puchŏnim pŏpdaero sarara—Kwangu Sŭnim kwaŭi taedam* (Live by the Buddha's Dharma—The Interviews with Kwangu Sunim). Kwangu characterizes the nuns' community at the time as follows: "When I first joined the sangha [in 1939], there were no separate seminaries for nuns the way

it is now. Nuns had to study while moving between tiny hermitages and large monasteries. To put it in modern terms, they just had to pick it up from other people instead of officially enrolling at a school. Naturally, there were very few nuns who would really study sūtras. This became a vicious cycle, so that there were few nuns who were well-versed in the sūtras and nuns always had to rely on monks at large monasteries to teach them. That is also how I started." Ch'oe, *Puch'ŏnim pŏptaero sarara*, 48–49.

21. Ch'oe, *Puch'ŏnim pŏptaero sarara*, 49.

22. Ch'oe, *Puch'ŏnim pŏptaero sarara*, 49.

23. "Namjangsa Kwanŭm kangwŏn ŭi nisŭng kangwŏnsaeng suryosik" (Bhiksūni Students' Graduation Ceremony of Kwanŭm Seminary at Namjang Monastery).

24. Accounts by Tŏksu and Chŏnghwa, in Sŏnudoryang Han'guk Pulgyo kŭnhyŏndaesa yŏn'guhoe, ed., *Isibiin ŭi chŭngŏn ŭl t'onghae pon kŭnhyŏndae Pulgyosa* (Modern and Contemporary Buddhist History through the Testimonies of 22 People), 180–88.

25. *Kyŏnghyang Daily*, December 15, 1954, quoted in Hwang, "Kŭnhyŏndae piguni wa Pulgyo chŏnghwa undong" ("Modern Bhiksunis and the Buddhist Purification Movement"), 283.

26. On the purification movement of Korean Buddhist society, see Park, *Trial and Error in Modernist Reforms*, 8–9, 125–26.

27. Accounts by Tŏksu and Chŏnghwa, from Sŏnudoryang Han'guk Pulgyo kŭnhyŏndaesa yŏn'guhoe, *Yisip-yi-in ŭi chŭngŏn ŭl t'onghae pon kŭnhyŏndae Pulgyosa*, 180–88.

28. Ha, *Kkaedarŭm ŭi kkot*, 215.

29. The Naewŏn Monastery meditation hall soon grew in renown and continued to do so after her death in 1966, becoming one of the centers of Sŏn meditation practice. This was also where Martine Batchelor, a Frenchwoman who has written about Korean Buddhist nuns, lived and wrote. See Batchelor, *Women in Korean Zen: Lives and Practices*, 101.

30. Myŏngsŏng is now regarded as among the most influential Korean *bhiksūni*. She served as abbess and dean of the Unmun Monastery *bhiksūni* seminary, the largest educational institution for Buddhist nuns in Korea, from 1977 to 2011. In the traditional Korean separation of Buddhist practice into scholarship and meditation, she represents the former tradition.

31. Kim, *Pŏpkye Myŏngsŏng ŭi Pulgyogwan kwa piguni sŭngga kyoyukkwan yŏn'gu* (A Study of Pŏpkye Myŏngsŏng's Buddhist Thought and Her Perspectives on Bhikṣuṇī Sangha Education), 47–48.

PART 3

CLERICAL CELIBACY, MARRIAGE, SCANDALS, AND MONASTIC RULES

Chapter 5

Rethinking Married *Bhikṣu*

An Examination of *Bhikṣu* Ordinations and Clerical Marriage in 1920s Korean Buddhism

Jeongeun Park

Introduction

It is well-known that the monastic rules of Korean Buddhism—including those that govern monastic marriage—underwent a tremendous transformation during the colonial period, especially when the Japanese colonial government removed the distinct disadvantages to married monks from the head-branch temple laws (K. *ponmal sabŏp* 本末寺法) in 1926. However, little research has been conducted on the *bhikṣu* ordination practices of Korean monks and the connection between *bhikṣu* ordination and the rise of clerical marriage during the colonial period. Any attempt to understand how monastic rules—including the rule of celibacy—changed during the colonial period requires a consideration of the ways in which Korean monks' thoughts on the importance of those precepts, which encompassed approximately 250 *bhikṣu* precepts, altered between the late nineteenth century and the mid-colonial period.[1]

Many scholars associate the change in monastic rules with Japanese colonial policy, thereby characterizing monks' marriage as a serious deviation from the Korean Buddhist tradition. For example, in his book *The Zen Monastic Experience* (1992), Robert Buswell describes clerical marriage as a threat to the ethics of Korean Buddhism.[2] Henrik Sørensen associates pro-Japanese clerics with married clerics, whom he further distinguishes from traditional Korean monks.[3] On the other hand, Pori Park argues that we should avoid the reductionist rhetoric that defines married monks as Japanese collaborators just because clerical marriage was prevalent in Japanese Buddhist sects.[4]

Many Korean scholars agree with Buswell and Sørensen. Ko Yŏngsŏp points out that the Office of the Governor-General of Korea implicitly fostered the spread of monastic marriage and a meat diet through the revision of the temple laws.[5] Kim Sunsŏk claims that the Japanese colonial policy was a decisive factor in the rise of clerical marriage among Korean monks and that this policy was initially intended to assimilate Korean Buddhism into Japanese Buddhism.[6] On the other hand, Kim Kwangsik maintains that the practices of monastic marriage and meat eating should be interpreted instead as an autonomous movement among Korean monks who wished to give priority to the popularization of Buddhism to bridge the gap between Buddhist clerics and laypersons.[7]

Most scholars in the field of Korean Buddhism relate the issue of clerical marriage to Japanese colonial policy and Buddhist modernization, but I argue that the core rules concerning the prohibition of sexual conduct found in the *bhikṣu* precepts deserve a closer look to draw more finely tuned conclusions regarding the link between *bhikṣu* ordination and clerical marriage. An examination of *bhikṣu* voters in head-monk elections at T'ongdo Monastery (通度寺) and Magok Monastery (麻谷寺) around 1925 and 1926 is the key to a true understanding of the reasons behind the increase of *bhikṣu* ordination and its synchronization with the rise of clerical marriage as well as an exploration of the ways in which Korean monks applied and appropriated monastic rules as a living tradition.

Monastic Rules Revisited in Context

Monastic rules, including those concerning ordination and the ideal deportment of Buddhist clerics, were inseparable from the existing social norms. Therefore, as Charles Prebish noted at the Conference on World Buddhism in North America held in Michigan in 1987, the interpretation and the application of monastic rules changed in different times and places: "[Vinaya] is not a static thing because it concerns a living group of persons."⁸ Even if Vinaya literature such as the *Four-Part Vinaya* (*Dharmaguptaka Vinaya* or C. *Sifen lu* 四分律) did not change, monastic rules were selected and modified in harmony with secular laws. To understand monastic rules in various contexts, recent Buddhist scholars have realized the necessity of classifying Vinaya literature. Although this classification was made in the field of Theravāda Buddhism, for example in Prebish's research, this method is also applicable to Korean Buddhism because it provides a useful framework in which to rethink monastic rules in the late Chosŏn and Japanese colonial periods.

Charles Prebish defines the meaning of Vinaya as the established and institutional norms of the sangha and classifies Vinaya literature into three categories: paracanonical Vinaya literature (including *prātimokṣa*), canonical Vinaya literature, and non-canonical Vinaya literature.⁹ In Korean Buddhism, *prātimokṣa* is related to the *Four-Part Vinaya*, while the *Brahmā Net Sūtra* and various commentaries on Vinayas are classified as non-canonical Vinaya literature. Anne Blackburn also classifies the Buddhist canon by placing it into two categories, the formal canon and the practical canon, to explore how Buddhists set up "a set of textual strategies" that enabled novice monks to gain knowledge of the monastic rules and discipline.¹⁰ According to Blackburn, canonical Vinaya literature was not available to most ordinary monks because it demanded a higher understanding and greater knowledge; thus, they learned monastic rules from excerpts or commentaries on canonical Vinaya during their novice training.

With regard to the practical canon in the case of Korean Buddhism, Uri Kaplan mentions that Korean Buddhism also retains the historical Vinayas in practice. According to Kaplan, "admonitions" collections served as practical Vinaya texts, presenting a sole source from which monks were able to shape their own monastic codes.¹¹ Admonitions collections were composed of four Buddhist texts, three written by Korean monks and one by a Chinese monk, which were used in training courses for novice monks beginning in the mid-Chosŏn period.¹² These are "Awaken Your Mind and Practice" (*Palsim suhaeng chang* 發心修行章) by the eminent Silla monk Wŏnhyo (元曉, 617–686), "Self-Admonitions" (*Chagyŏngmun* 自警文) by the monk Yaun (野雲, d.u.) who lived in the late Koryŏ period, "Admonitions for Beginning Students" (*Kyecho simhak inmun* 誡初心學入文) by the renowned Koryŏ monk Chinul (知訥, 1158–1210), and the

Admonitions to the Gray-Robed Monks (*Zimen jingxun* 緇門警訓) compiled by the Chinese monk Rujin (如卺, 1425–?) in the fifteenth century. Because the first three texts were of short length, they were assembled and circulated into one volume named the *Self-Admonitions for Beginning Practitioners* (*Ch'obalsim chagyŏngmun* 初發心自警文). These texts were incorporated into the head-branch temple laws (hereafter referred to as the temple laws), a set of monastic laws of the thirty-one Buddhist parishes during the Japanese colonial period,[13] and they are still used as part of the curriculum in contemporary Korean Buddhist monasteries.

During the colonial period, each Buddhist parish had its own temple laws that were unilaterally instituted by the colonial government. The temple laws became the guidelines for all aspects of monastic life, including sexual conduct and meals. The temple laws described the ideal deportment of Buddhist clerics, and these laws were commonly circulated among ordinary monks. By putting monks who were married and meat eaters at a distinct disadvantage, the temple laws brought the issue of monastic marriage and meat diet to the foreground.[14] In a sense, the legitimacy of monks' deportment regarding sexual conduct and meals rested on the temple laws, which placed a strong emphasis on *bhikṣu* precepts and bodhisattva precepts. In other words, while admonitions collections were used as a guideline for novice monks to the overall monastic code at the time, the temple laws were begrudgingly embraced by the entire Korean monastic community as a crucial means of pointing Buddhist clerics in the right direction for the most delicate of matters: namely, sexual conduct and meals. In this sense, the temple laws partially took on the role of practical Vinaya.

The issue of clerical marriage and meat eating was inevitably connected to two different kinds of Buddhist ordinations, namely, *bhikṣu* and bodhisattva ordinations. Furthermore, the examination of this topic needs to be traced back to the late Chosŏn period to gain a clear and comprehensive picture of just how the monastic rules had changed. In the rest of this chapter, I attempt to answer two simple but previously unexamined questions. First, did Korean monks take *bhikṣu* precepts and bodhisattva precepts in the late Chosŏn period and the colonial period? And if so, in what way did they interpret clerical marriage, which was prohibited in the *bhikṣu* precepts, that allowed this practice to become widespread in 1920s colonial Korea? A contemporaneous understanding of Buddhist precepts and ordinations stands at the core of this chapter.

Bhikṣu Precepts and Bodhisattva Precepts in the Late Nineteenth Century

The *Biographies of Korean Masters* (*Tongsa yŏlchŏn* 東師列傳), written by the monk Pŏmhae (梵海, also known as Kagan 覺岸, 1820–1896) in 1894, describes the lives of monks who lived on the Korean Peninsula from 357 CE to 1894. It consists of six fascicles and includes portrayals of 194 Korean monks, two Chinese monks,[15] one Korean nun, and two Korean laypeople. Despite the author Pŏmhae's narrow understanding of dharma lineage[16] and the fact that most entries were confined to dealing with monks at Taedun Monastery (大芚寺), a temple with which Pŏmhae was affiliated, the *Biographies of Korean Masters* is important not only because it describes the lives of the largest number of Korean monks among those few existing hagiographies in Korean Buddhism, but also because it reveals the ways in which Buddhist clerics struggled to define their clerical identity in the late Chosŏn period, a period during which the government abandoned its supervision of institutional Buddhism after abolishing the monk examination and certification system in the mid-Chosŏn period.

To maintain clerical identity, late Chosŏn Buddhist clerics shaped and developed two different ordination lineages, which were launched respectively by the monk Taeŭn (大隱, also known as Nango 朗旿, 1780–1841) and the monk Manha (萬下, also known as Sŭngnim 勝林) in the 1890s. Regarding Taeŭn, it is said that he was self-ordained through a mysterious experience. Taeŭn and his master monk Kŭmdam (金潭, 1765–1848) prayed together in a small temple named Ch'ilbul Hermitage (七佛庵) on Mountain Chiri over the course of several days; on the seventh day, a ray of auspicious light suddenly penetrated Taeŭn's forehead. This kind of ordination was called a self-ordination (K. *chasŏ sugye* 自誓受戒) or a visionary ordination (K. *sŏsang sugye* 瑞祥受戒), which is mentioned in the *Brahmā Net Sūtra*.

There is still debate over the nature of Taeŭn's self-ordination. Because his ordination rested on the words in the *Brahmā Net Sūtra*, it can definitely be seen as a bodhisattva ordination, though perhaps not a *bhikṣu* ordination.[17] Regardless of the origin of the self-ordination, Taeŭn's ordination lineage was accepted in major Korean monasteries as a form of *bhikṣu* ordination. Modern Korean Buddhist monasteries, such as Haein Monastery, Songgwang Monastery (松廣寺), and Hwaŏm Monastery (華嚴

寺), saw Taeŭn as a forefather of ordination lineages, thereby establishing and accepting the transmission of a *bhikṣu* ordination lineage from Taeŭn through Kŭmdam[18] to Ch'oŭi (草衣, also known as Ŭisun 意恂, 1786–1866)[19] and Ch'oŭi to Pŏmhae.[20] In this way, Korean monasteries established the legitimacy of their own *bhikṣu* ordination tradition.

Along with Taeŭn, Manha was regarded as one of the forefathers of the ordination lineage in some monasteries, such as T'ongdo Monastery, Pŏmŏ Monastery, and Wŏlchŏng Monastery. On his trip to China in 1892, Manha took *bhikṣu* precepts at Fayuan Monastery (法源寺) in Beijing from a Chinese preceptor named Hanpai (漢派). Upon his return to Chosŏn Korea, he bestowed *bhikṣu* precepts to monks from major monasteries.[21] For example, Kim Kuha (金九河, 1872–1965), the first head monk of T'ongdo Monastery during the colonial period, received his *bhikṣu* precepts from the preceptor Manha at P'yoch'ung Monastery (表忠寺) in Miryang in 1896.[22]

Although Pŏmhae did not write about Taeŭn's ordination event in the *Biographies of Korean Masters*, he recognized Taeŭn's role as a preceptor because he associated Taeŭn with the Chinese monk Daoxuan (道宣, 596–667), the founder of the Vinaya School of China.[23] On the other hand, Pŏmhae did not mention the preceptor Manha at all in his book. It can perhaps be surmised that, at the completion of his book in 1894, Pŏmhae was unaware of Manha's ordination event of 1892 owing to the slow transmission of information at the time.

Although the *Biographies of Korean Masters* takes a typical hagiographical form in most of its accounts, it departs from the usual in its descriptions of the lives of Pŏmhae's contemporary monks, which are more vivid and critical than might be expected. It deals not only with the lives of eminent monks such as Wŏnhyo or Hyujŏng (休靜, 1520–1604) in ancient and medieval times, but also with the lives of ordinary monks who were coeval with Pŏmhae himself and affiliated with Taedun Monastery or neighboring temples. In other words, among the six fascicles, the entries in the fourth, fifth, and sixth ones depict the lives of nineteenth-century Chosŏn monks and examine their ordination records; thus, they can be considered reliable because these monks were people that Pŏmhae had actually met, heard of, studied with, been taught by, shared his dharma lineage with, and bestowed precepts on.

It is clear from the *Biographies of Korean Masters* that the author Pŏmhae understood the importance of *bhikṣu* and bodhisattva ordinations well because he himself was a preceptor who transmitted ordination lineage from the preceptor and Sŏn master Ch'oŭi. Although not all ordination records were written down, Pŏmhae tried to write ordination records for his contemporaries as often as possible. Thus, the true value of the *Biographies of Korean Masters* lies in its eyewitness account of the construction of the tradition of *bhikṣu* and bodhisattva ordinations among monks who lived in the late Chosŏn period.

In the *Biographies of Korean Masters*, the terms *sugu* (受具) and *su bigugye* (受比丘戒) were used when referring to taking bhikṣu precepts, and the terms *su taesŭnggye* (受大乘戒) and *su posalgye* (受菩薩戒) were used when referring to taking bodhisattva precepts. As seen in table 5.1, monks' *bhikṣu* ordinations records are found in ten of the sixty-four entries in the first three fascicles, but there is no record of bodhisattva ordination. Extrapolating from the increase in the number of *bhikṣu* and bodhisattva ordinations in the latter three fascicles, it can be easily argued that the importance of taking *bhikṣu* precepts and bodhisattva precepts increased among Korean monks in the nineteenth century. In short, a salient feature of nineteenth-century Buddhism is the increase in the taking of *bhikṣu* and bodhisattva precepts.

Table 5.2 tells us that monks at Taedun Monastery had specialized preceptors with the role of bestowing *bhikṣu* precepts or bodhisattva precepts. The preceptors were Wanho, Yŏnha, Ch'oŭi, and Pŏmhae. Wanho (玩虎, 1758–1826) became a monk under the guidance of the monk Sŏil (瑞日) in 1770 and received *bhikṣu* precepts from an unknown monk

Table 5.1. Ordination records in the biographies of Korean Monks, *Biographies of Korean Monks*

Fascicle no.	Number of entries	Monks whose *bhikṣu* ordinations were recorded	Monks whose bodhisattva ordinations were recorded	Period
Fasc. 1	20	6	0	357–1405
Fasc. 2	21	1	0	1301–1675
Fasc. 3	23	3	0	17th and 18th centuries
Fasc. 4	53	12	3	1720–1890
Fasc. 5	48	21	9	19th century
Fasc. 6	34	14	12	19th century through 1894

Table 5.2. Preceptors whose ordinands numbered more than two in fascicles 4, 5, and 6 of the *Biographies of Korean Monks, Biographies of Korean Monks*

Preceptor	Affiliated temple	Number of ordinands in bhikṣu ordinations	Number of ordinands in bodhisattva ordinations
Ch'oŭi (草衣, 1786–1866)	Taedunsa	3	10
Pŏmhae (梵海, 1820–1896)	Taedunsa	8	10
Wanho (玩虎, 1758–1826)	Taedunsa	2	n/a
Yŏnha (緣何, ?–?)	Taedunsa	2	n/a

in 1774.[24] Later, he conferred *bhikṣu* precepts on the monks Haŭi (荷衣, 1779–1852) and Chahaeng (慈行, 1781–1862).[25] The monk Yŏnha (緣何, d.u.) also conferred *bhikṣu* precepts on two monks, Pyŏkp'a (碧波, 1807–1887) and P'oun (浦雲, 1806–1867).[26] As the roles of Ch'oŭi and Pŏmhae expanded, they conferred bodhisattva precepts and *bhikṣu* precepts on monks not only at Taedun Monastery, but also at nearby temples. In addition, as seen in table 5.3, some monks such as Ch'wiun (翠雲, 1866–?),[27] Kŭmhŏ (錦虛, 1824–?), and Kŭmp'a (金波, 1833–?) took their *bhikṣu* precepts from Pŏmhae, even though they had already taken *bhikṣu* precepts from other monks, presumably to secure their positions by taking precepts from an authorized preceptor such as Pŏmhae.

Tables 5.2 and 5.3 show that a prevailing trend in late nineteenth-century Korean Buddhism had monks seeking to receive *bhikṣu* and bodhisattva precepts from specialized preceptors such as Ch'oŭi and Pŏmhae.

The final point that deserves attention is the increase in the number of bodhisattva ordinations that appear in the fifth and sixth fascicles of the *Biographies of Korean Masters*. Although bodhisattva precepts were created by early Chinese Buddhists as additional monastic rules because Indian Vinaya traditions did not quite fit the practices of Chinese society,[28] Korean monks in the nineteenth century appear to have recognized the importance of bodhisattva precepts as requirements rather than supplements. The renowned preceptor Ch'oŭi emphasized bodhisattva precepts as much as he did *bhikṣu* precepts, writing, "When taking 250 precepts, you will free yourselves from attachment and suffering and will attain

Table 5.3. Monks among the 134 monks in fascicles 4, 5, and 6 of the *Biographies of Korean Monks* whose preceptors were recorded, *Biographies of Korean Monks*

Monk	Affiliated temple	Original teacher	Bhikṣu preceptor	Bodhisattva preceptor	Fascicle no.
Chahaeng (慈行, 1782–1862)	Taedunsa	n/a	Wanho (玩虎)	n/a	Fasc. 4
Ch'immyŏng (枕溟, 1801–76)	Nŭnggasa	Kwŏnmin (權敏)	Ch'unp'a (春坡)	n/a	Fasc. 4
Chŏngbong (清峯, 1855–?)	Taedunsa	Chŏnge (千偈)	Sŏrhŏ (雪虛)	n/a	Fasc. 6
Ch'wiun (翠雲, 1866–?)	Taedunsa	Ŭnghŏ (應虛)	Pogam (褔庵), Pŏmhae (梵海)	Pŏmhae (梵海)	Fasc. 6
Hammyŏng (涵溟, 1824–1902)	Paengnyŏnsa	P'unggok (豐谷)	Toam (道菴)	n/a	Fasc. 5
Haŭi (荷衣, 1779–1852)	Taedunsa	Paengnyŏn (白蓮)	Wanho (玩虎)	n/a	Fasc. 4
Hoeam (梅庵, 1808–1887)	Nŭnggasa	P'yŏngchŏl (平哲)	Haŭi (荷衣)	Chŏŭi (草衣)	Fasc. 5
Honhŏ (渾虛, 1826–?)	Mihwangsa	Chinhak (眞學)	n/a	Chŏŭi (草衣)	Fasc. 6
Hoŭi (縞衣, 1778–1868)	Taedunsa	Kyŏnggwan (慶冠)	Paengnyŏn (白蓮)	n/a	Fasc. 4
Howŏl (湖月, ?–?)	Taedunsa	Pohae (普海)	Pŏmhae (梵海)	Pŏmhae (梵海)	Fasc. 5
Hwasŏn (華先, 1827–?)	n/a	Mirhong (蜜弘)	Ch'immyŏng (枕溟)	Chŏŭi (草衣)	Fasc. 5
Hwaun (化運, ?–1864)	Taedunsa	Ongok (溫谷)	n/a	n/a	Fasc. 4
Hwawŏl (化月, 1820–1886)	Taedunsa	Sŏju (犀舟)	Chŏlsŏn (鐵船)	n/a	Fasc. 5
Hyebong (惠峰, 1816–1881)	Mihwangsa	Hogi (好奇)	Ssangnyŏn (雙蓮)	n/a	Fasc. 5
Kibong (騎峯, ?–?)	Togapsa	n/a	Ch'imsong (枕松)	n/a	Fasc. 5
Kŭmhŏ (錦虛, 1824–?)	Taedunsa	Haŭi (荷衣)	Hwaun (化運), Pŏmhae (梵海)	Pŏmhae (梵海)	Fasc. 5
Kŭmp'a (金波, 1833–?)	Taedunsa	Sŏkho (石虎)	Chihŏ (正虛), Pŏmhae (梵海)	Pŏmhae (梵海)	Fasc. 6
Kŭmsŏng (錦城, 1825–1893)	Taedunsa	Kyŏnhyang (見香)	Pŏmhae (梵海)	Pŏmhae (梵海)	Fasc. 6
Kŭmwŏl (錦月, 1811–1888)	Taedunsa	Sŏngmuk (聖默)	Manhŏ (萬虛)	n/a	Fasc. 5
Kyŏngwŏl (鏡月, 1775–1857)	Taedunsa	n/a	n/a	Chŏŭi (草衣)	Fasc. 4

continued on next page

Table 5.3. Continued.

Monk	Affiliated temple	Original teacher	*Bhikṣu* preceptor	Bodhisattva preceptor	Fascicle no.
Pomun (普門, 1816–1892)	Mihwangsa	n/a	Chŏŭi (草衣)	Chŏŭi (草衣)	Fasc. 5
Muwi (無爲, 1826–1886)	Taedunsa	Hoŭi (縞衣)	Wanhae (阮海)	Chŏŭi (草衣)	Fasc. 5
Paegnyŏn (白蓮, 1737–1807)	Taedunsa	Ch'ongo (聰悟)	Manhwa (萬化)	n/a	Fasc. 4
Poje (普濟, 1828–1875)	Taedunsa	Hŭimun (禧文)	n/a	Chŏŭi (草衣)	Fasc. 6
Pŏmhae (梵海, 1820–1896)	Taedunsa	Hoŭi (縞衣)	Chŏŭi (草衣)	Chŏŭi (草衣)	Fasc. 4
P'oun (浦雲, 1806–1867)	Taedunsa	Ŭnam (銀岩)	Yŏnha (緣何)	n/a	Fasc. 5
Pyŏkp'a (碧波, 1807–1887)	Taedunsa	Chŏpcham (涉岑)	Yŏnha (緣何)	n/a	Fasc. 4
Sangun (祥雲, 1827–?)	Taedunsa	Sŭngil (勝日)	Pŏmhae (梵海)	Pŏmhae (梵海)	Fasc. 5
Sŏam (恕庵, 1812–1876)	Unhŭungsa	Taeŭn (大隱)	Taeŭn (大隱)	Taeŭn (大隱)	Fasc. 5
Sŏldu (雪竇, 1824–1889)	Paegyangsa	Chŏnggwan (正觀)	Paegam (白岩)	n/a	Fasc. 5
Sŏru (雪耰, 1830–1868)	Togapsa	Ch'imsong (枕松)	Pŏmhae (梵海)	Pŏmhae (梵海)	Fasc. 6
Susŏng (壽星, ?–1885)	Taedunsa	Ch'wiam (鷲岩)	n/a	Chŏŭi (草衣)	Fasc. 6
Ŭngam (鷹庵, 1829–1886)	Taedunsa	Chahaeng (慈行)	Sŏju (涇舟)	Pŏmhae (梵海)	Fasc. 6
Wŏrhwa (月華, 1836–?)	Mihwangsa	Ch'udam (秋潭)	Yŏngdam (靈潭)	n/a	Fasc. 6
Wŏryŏ (月如, 1824–?)	Taedunsa	Yangak (羊岳)	Chŏŭi (草衣)	Chŏŭi (草衣)	Fasc. 5
Wŏnhae (圓海, ?–?)	Songgwangsa	Susan (守山)	Pŏmhae (梵海)	Pŏmhae (梵海)	Fasc. 6
Wŏnŭng (圓膺, 1855–?)	n/a	Tonghwa (東化)	Yŏngho (靈湖)	Poje (普濟)	Fasc. 6
Yeam (艶庵, 1834–1894)	Taedunsa	P'oun (浦雲)	Manhyu (萬休)	Pŏmhae (梵海)	Fasc. 6
Yongun (龍雲, 1813–1888)	Songgwangsa	Namil (南日)	Kibong (奇峯)	n/a	Fasc. 4
Yŏnju (蓮舟, 1827–?)	Taedunsa	Sinwŏl (信月)	Muha (無何)	n/a	Fasc. 5
Yŏnp'a (蓮坡, 1772–1811)	Taedunsa	n/a	Wŏlsong (月松)	n/a	Fasc. 4

arhatship. On the other hand, taking bodhisattva precepts makes you achieve a stage of Buddhahood. . . . According to the *Brahmā Net Sūtra*, all sentient beings can be elevated to the status of the buddhas if they receive the Buddha's precepts. *Kyeyul* (precepts and Vinayas) becomes the foundation of enlightenment. It plays the role of a boat or raft that sails one across the sea of suffering."²⁹

In another text, when comparing Mahāyāna and Hīnayāna precepts, Ch'oŭi put a strong emphasis on bodhisattva precepts rather than *bhikṣu* precepts: "Precepts are divided into those of two vehicles [*yāna*], namely Mahāyāna and Hīnayāna. Hīnayāna deals with outer phenomena based on substances, and therefore it has precepts of outer phenomena. Mahāyāna treats inherent nature based on universal principle, and therefore it has precepts of inherent nature. It is myself who observes the precepts of outer phenomena and the precepts of inherent nature. If you must choose one of them, discard the precepts of outer phenomena and keep the precepts of inherent nature."³⁰ In this instance, Ch'oŭi suggests to his readers that bodhisattva precepts are more significant in that they deal with inherent nature, that is, Buddhahood.

In addition, the importance of bodhisattva precepts lies in the fact that not only Buddhist clerics but also laypeople are able to take these precepts. The *Biographies of Korean Masters* shows a notable example of this. Yi Tonghwan (李東煥, 1827–?), whose ordination name was Ch'imsan (枕山), was a lay Buddhist who received bodhisattva precepts from the monk Haemyŏng (海溟) at a temple at Mountain Kŭmgang.³¹ This same Yi Tonghwan is also found in an entry by the monk Honsŏng (混性) in the *Biographies of Korean Masters*. This entry says that the monk Honsŏng had two laymen as disciples whose names were Yi Tonghwan and An Hyangrang.³² From these records, it can be surmised that laypeople received bodhisattva precepts and played a vigorous role as members of the monastic community.

Despite the necessity of having three preceptors and seven witnesses for full ordination, it seems likely that most ordinations did not fulfill this requirement. Extrapolating from the ordination records in the *Biographies of Korean Masters*, among other documents of the period, it can be surmised that not all monks received *bhikṣu* precepts in the traditional procedure consisting of three preceptors and seven witnesses during the Chosŏn period. For example, according to the *Biographies of Korean Masters*, a monk named Sŏam (恕庵) received not only dharma but also the precepts of *bhikṣu* and bodhisattva from his original teacher, not, as might be expected, from the preceptor monks.³³ In this sense, it can be concluded that Chosŏn Buddhism had a weak ordination tradition. The orthodox ordination lineage had been broken because of a lack of preceptors until two kinds of ordination lineages appeared in the nineteenth century.

Considering all accounts, it is clear that Korean monks in the nineteenth century strove to overcome a weak ordination tradition and secure their clerical identity by taking *bhikṣu* and bodhisattva precepts. Their understanding of monastic rules, including *bhikṣu* and bodhisattva ordinations, lies in the basic concept that precepts and Vinayas (K. *kyeyul* 戒律) were fundamental to awakening and to the attainment of Buddhahood.

The Continuous Rise of *Bhikṣu* and Bodhisattva Ordinations under the Japanese Colonial Regime

Just how did the *bhikṣu* and bodhisattva ordinations change during the Japanese colonial period, a period that saw the emergence of a newly coined term, "clerical marriage and meat eating" (K. *taechŏ sigyuk* 帶妻食肉)? Did Korean monks discard *bhikṣu* and bodhisattva ordinations during this time of occupation? Quite the opposite, in fact: during the colonial period, *bhikṣu* and bodhisattva ordinations became more prevalent in Korean Buddhism despite the popular practice of clerical marriage and meat eating. This dichotomy can be attributed to a newly minted regulation in the temple laws enacted by the Japanese colonial government. Korean monks' perception of the status enjoyed by a *bhikṣu* also changed according to the colonial government's Buddhist regulations.

During the colonial period from 1910 to 1945, the autonomy of Korean Buddhism was circumscribed by the Japanese colonial government; at the same time, Korean Buddhism experienced a revival of rights with regard to the protection of temple property and a rise in the status of Buddhist clerics. The main tools in achieving this dual outcome were the promulgation of the Temple Ordinance (K. *Sach'allyŏng* 寺刹令) of 1911 and the creation of the head-branch temple laws. Korean Buddhist monasteries came under strong governmental supervision hundreds of years after the government of the mid-Chosŏn period abandoned its systematic supervision, which included monastic examination and ordination certificates. Through their Temple Ordinance, the Japanese colonial government divided Korean Buddhist temples into thirty parishes for more effective control. As a result, a hierarchical relationship between a head temple and branch temples in a Buddhist parish—a relationship that bestowed a tremendous amount of power on the head monk of each parish—was put in place.

In addition, the Temple Ordinance decreed that head temples should create temple laws to stipulate the names of affiliated branch temples and to establish monastic rules regarding ordination, education, rituals, and punishment.[34] Although in theory it might appear that the thirty head temples had the autonomy they needed to compose their own temple laws, the reality was different. The main content of the temple laws was drafted by the Japanese colonial government based on information about Korean Buddhist monasteries that had been collected in 1909 and 1910.[35] Although some clauses were clearly associated with Japanese Buddhist practice, such as the system of head-branch temples, the Japanese emperor's birthday ceremony (J. *Tenchōsetsu* 天長節), and the memorial ritual of Emperor Kōmei (孝明天皇, 1831–1867),[36] it is likely that other clauses were drawn from traditional Korean Buddhist practice. For example, the temple laws incorporated dharma lineage, the Sŏn/Kyo preference, an education curriculum, and the clerical ranking system, all of which were features of Korean Buddhism. Owing to a clever blend of Korean Buddhist practices and Japanese Buddhist customs in the temple laws, the colonial government minimized resistance among Korean Buddhists and stabilized the entire Korean Buddhist monastic community on the heels of the Japanese annexation of Korea.

Furthermore, the colonial government created rigid qualifications for head monks and branch temple abbots and had the authority to approve their final appointments. According to the temple laws, the head monk of each parish was elected for a three-year term through public election by monks who had achieved *bhikṣu* status and enrolled in the head temple. In addition, branch temple abbots were selected through traditional means: (1) by recommendation from a master monk, (2) by selection among dharma relatives by those same dharma relatives, or (3) by invitation from other temples.[37]

The temple law stated that monks who wished to run in the head-monk election were required to be older than forty, to have received *bhikṣu* and bodhisattva precepts, to have completed summer meditation retreats no fewer than ten times, and to have finished the highest training course (K. *taegyokwa* 大教科). Branch temple abbots were required to be older than twenty-five, to have received *bhikṣu* and bodhisattva precepts, to have finished a minimum of five summer retreats, and to have finished the intermediate training course (K. *sagyokwa* 四教科 or *sajipkwa* 四集科).[38]

As can be seen, the most notable requirement for head monks and branch temple abbots was that they had to have received *bhikṣu* and bodhisattva ordinations. The emphasis on *bhikṣu* ordination was also found among the qualifications for other official duties at the monasteries. Voters in the head-monk election and Sŏn practitioners who wished to join a summer or winter retreat had to have received *bhikṣu* precepts. Monks who wished to take an examination to attain a higher clerical rank had to submit certificates of *bhikṣu* and bodhisattva ordinations to the head temple.[39] In other words, without *bhikṣu* precepts, there was no way for a monk to participate in Sŏn retreats or climb to a higher rung on the clerical ladder.

It is more than conceivable that the Japanese colonial government incorporated *bhikṣu* and bodhisattva ordinations into the temple laws because they were existing practices in major Korean Buddhist monasteries. It is likely that *bhikṣu* and bodhisattva ordinations increased in frequency not only in the southwestern area, including Taehŭng Monastery, which had renowned preceptors, but also in other southern areas, in which the preceptor Manha began to confer *bhikṣu* precepts on monks in the late 1890s.[40] In short, the *bhikṣu* and bodhisattva ordination requirements in the temple laws resulted in an increase in *bhikṣu* and bodhisattva ordination ceremonies in the early colonial period.

Table 5.4 indicates that major Korean temples installed ordination platforms for bestowing *bhikṣu* and *bhikṣuṇī* precepts on monks and nuns early in the colonial period. The first ordination ceremonies took place in January of 1912 at Wŏnhŭng Monastery, a temple that was used as the temporary office of the Wŏnjong, the first modern Buddhist institution in Korea. With the head monk of Haein Monastery Yi Hoegwang as the preceptor, the monk of Chŏngnyong Monastery Yonghŏ as the reciting preceptor, and the head monk of Kŏnbong Monastery Unp'a as the instructional preceptor, more than 300 Buddhists—including sixty-six *bhikṣu*—took precepts.[41] The Buddhist magazine *Korean Buddhism Monthly* reported that it was an exceptional event for that time.[42] In addition, major head temples such as Sŏgwang Monastery and Kwiju Monastery in South Hamgyŏng Province established ordination platforms not just for Buddhist monks and nuns but also for laymen and laywomen. Taking into consideration all of the accounts, it can be seen that Korean Buddhism embraced the temple laws that made *bhikṣu* and bodhisattva ordinations mandatory for head monks and abbots, as evidenced by the frequent installation of ordination platforms. In addition, through these magnificent ordination ceremonies,

Table 5.4. Installation of ordination platforms during the early colonial period, *Chosŏn pulgyo wŏlbo*

Date[1]	Place	Preceptor	Source
January 4, 1912	Wŏnhŭngsa (元興寺)	Yi Hoegwang (李晦光)	*Chosŏn pulgyo wŏlbo* 1 (February 1912)
April 1, 1912	Hŭngguksa (興國寺)	Pak Manha (朴万下)	*Chosŏn pulgyo wŏlbo* 3 (April 1912)
September 27, 1912	Wŏnhŭngsa (元興寺)	Yi Hoegwang (李晦光)	*Chosŏn pulgyo wŏlbo* 9 (October 1912)
January 30, 1913	Sŏnamsa (仙巖寺)	Yi Kyŏngun (金擎雲)	*Chosŏn pulgyo wŏlbo* 14 (March 1913)
March 4–5, 1913	Hwaŏmsa (華嚴寺)	Pak Hŏŭn (朴虎隱)	*Chosŏn pulgyo wŏlbo* 17 (June 1913)
March 27, 1913	Paegyangsa (白羊寺)	Kim Hwanŭng (金幻應)	*Chosŏn pulgyo wŏlbo* 17 (June 1913)
March 1913	Hwanhuisa (歡喜寺)	n/a	*Chosŏn pulgyo wŏlbo* 17 (June 1913)
April 1, 1913	Sŏkwangsa (釋王寺)	Sŏ Wŏrhwa (徐月華)	*Chosŏn pulgyo wŏlbo* 17 (June 1913)
April 16, 1913	Hwajangsa (華藏寺)	n/a	*Chosŏn pulgyo wŏlbo* 17 (June 1913)
April 20, 1913	Yongjusa (龍珠寺)	n/a	*Chosŏn pulgyo wŏlbo* 15 (April 1913)
April 1913	Yujŏmsa (楡岾寺)	Yŏngbong (靈峰)	*Chosŏn pulgyo wŏlbo* 17 (June 1913)
May 1913	Kwijusa (歸州寺)	Sŏ Wŏrhwa (徐月華)	*Chosŏn pulgyo wŏlbo* 16 (May 1913)
May 13, 1913	Kŏnbongsa (乾鳳寺)	So Sego (趙世杲)	*Chosŏn pulgyo wŏlbo* 17 (June 1913)
May 13, 1913	T'ongdosa (通度寺)	Sŏ Haedam (徐海曇)	*Chosŏn pulgyo wŏlbo* 17 (June 1913)
May 30, 1913	Songgwangsa (松廣寺)	Kim Hobok (金浩鵬)	*Chosŏn pulgyo wŏlbo* 17 (June 1913)
May 5, 1914	Kabsa (甲寺)	Chang Pomyŏng (張普明)	*Haedong pulbo* 8 (June 1914)
May 13, 1914	Hŭngguksa (興國寺)	Cho Rangŭng (趙郎應)	*Haedong pulbo* 8 (June 1914)

[1] I converted some dates from the lunar calendar into the solar calendar.

the Korean Buddhist monastic community displayed its elevated status openly and was able to recruit young monks.

The most popular preceptor in the early colonial period was Yi Hoegwang, the first supreme patriarch of the Wŏnjong and head monk of Haein Monastery. He was one of the most renowned Korean monks of the time, to the extent that Pŏmhae described young Hoegwang as "the awakened one" and added Hoegwang's biography as the last entry in the *Biographies of Korean Masters*.[43] However, his reputation was undermined when he attempted to merge the Korean Buddhist sect Wŏnjong with the Japanese Buddhist sect Sōtōshū in 1910.

In table 5.4, we also find Pak Manha, who conferred precepts at Hŭngguk Monastery in 1912. The preceptor Manha, you will remember, traveled to Beijing to take *bhikṣu* precepts from a Chinese preceptor in 1892. The Buddhist magazine *Korean Buddhism Monthly* noted that Pak Manha was abbot of Yongyŏn Monastery (龍淵寺), a branch temple of the Tonghwa Monastery parish.[44] Although Pak Manha was the Yongyŏn Monastery abbot from December 1911 to August 1912[45] and occupied the role of preceptor during the early colonial period, no information about him after his resignation from the abbacy survives. Along with Yi Hoegwang and Pak Manha, other preceptors can be found in table 5.4. It is assumed that they were all recognized as renowned preceptors at that time, given that major monasteries invited them to their first ordination ceremonies during the Japanese occupation.

While the increase of *bhikṣu* and bodhisattva ordinations in the late nineteenth century can be attributed to Korean monks' desire to secure their clerical identity, the number of *bhikṣu* and bodhisattva ordinations peaked in the early colonial period when they were written into the temple laws as regulatory requirements for a higher clerical career. These frequent ordination ceremonies (table 5.4) resulted in an increase in the number of Buddhist clerics. There were 5,501 Buddhist clerics in Korea in 1909,[46] which climbed to 6,915 by 1914.[47]

The requirements for *bhikṣu* and bodhisattva ordinations, as written in the temple laws, resulted in two effects. First, *bhikṣu* and bodhisattva ordinations served as criteria to divide elite monks from rank-and-file monks. Without *bhikṣu* and bodhisattva ordinations, monks were unable to advance their monastic careers. Second, the term "clerical marriage and meat eating" moved to the foreground of Korean Buddhism, as the temple laws specified that *bhikṣu* ordination was not permitted for "one who has a wife and eats meat" (J. *taisai jikiniku o nasu mono* 帶妻食肉ヲ爲ス者).[48]

The policy of the Meiji government in Japan regarding monastic marriage and meat dishes was totally different from that of the Japanese colonial government in Korea. In 1872, official permission for clerical marriage and meat eating in Japanese Buddhism was clearly associated with the Japanese Meiji governmental policy to move forward in the process of modernization, a move that was intended at least in part to redefine Buddhist priests as citizens.[49] For this reason, ordination ceremonies were relegated to the "no-longer-mandatory" category in Japanese Buddhism according to the "eating meat and having a wife" (J. *nikujiki saitai* 肉食妻帶) law.[50]

In Japan, the government officially permitted the practice of monastic marriage and meat eating among Buddhist priests as one of its modernization initiatives. In Korea, however, the colonial government imposed strong restrictions on clerical marriage and meat eating and specified them in the temple laws. An explanation for these differing positions could be that the Japanese colonial government did not wish to carry out policies related to modernization within Korean Buddhism because the Japanese colonial regime knew that the best way to control the entire Korean Buddhist monastic community was to maintain the status quo of Korean Buddhism.

When the Japanese created a draft of the temple laws for Korean temples, their first goal was to seize and stabilize the entire Korean Buddhist sangha. However, when it came to the issue of clerical marriage and meat eating, Korean monks cleverly reinterpreted the status of *bhikṣu*, as discussed below using the cases of T'ongdo Monastery and Magok Monastery.

The Status of *Bhikṣu* and Clerical Marriage at T'ongdo Monastery and Magok Monastery in 1925 and 1926

In 1925, the head temple T'ongdo Monastery underwent serious internal strife, with its head monk Kim Kuha being the main cause of conflict. To ameliorate the situation, the Department of Religion in the Bureau of Education of the Governor-General of Korea decided to persuade Kim Kuha to resign from his position. To carry this out, it dispatched Watanabe Akira (渡邊彰), the hands-on official in the Korean Buddhism division, to do so. Watanabe arrived at T'ongdo Monastery in South Kyŏngsang Province in August 1925.

During his two-day visit, Watanabe uncovered Kim Kuha's clerical marriage using a copy of Kim's household register he had brought from the county office. Kim, who had been head monk of the T'ongdo Monastery parish since 1911, now had to step down because his marriage violated the temple laws of the T'ongdo Monastery parish. Watanabe recorded not only Kim Kuha's covert marriage, but also revealed seventy-seven other "married *bhikṣu*" (J. *bugusō nisite taisaisuru mono* 比丘僧ニシテ帶妻スル者) in his investigation report titled "Report on T'ongdo Monastery's Head Monk Kim Kuha's Movement after the Declaration of his Resignation and Transferring of the Duties of Temple Administration" (J. *Tsūdoji jūji Kim Kuha jishoku seimei ato no kōdō nami ni jimu hikitsugi kansuru shisatsu fukumeisho* 通度寺住持金九河辭職聲明後ノ行動竝ニ寺務引繼ニ關スル視察復命書).[51]

As can be seen in table 5.5, according to Kim's resume, which was submitted to the colonial government to gain approval for his installation as head monk in 1924, he had received *bhikṣu* and bodhisattva ordinations from the renowned preceptor Manha in 1896.[52] Despite this, he married a woman on June 20, 1923, and listed her as his wife in his household register. This was in clear violation of the temple laws of the T'ongdo Monastery parish, which prohibited head monks from marrying until its revision in December 1926.[53]

The modern household register system was introduced by the Japanese in 1909, through which one's marital status was legally confirmed by one's household register. Because the household register was not a document that needed to be submitted to the government by a head monk for approval until 1925, it was possible for monks to conceal their marriages as long as their household registers were not revealed. However, when the colonial government came to question the marital status of some monks, it collected these household registers to look into the situation. In this way, Kim Kuha's secret marriage was discovered.

During his visit to T'ongdo Monastery, Watanabe also discovered that Kim Kuha had ordered the deletion of a condition specifying that monks who were married and ate meat not be permitted to take *bhikṣu* precepts from the temple laws of T'ongdo Monastery parish when Kim circulated copies to monks in 1918. Because Watanabe doubted the veracity of the T'ongdo Monastery monks' claims of their marital status in 1925, he also suggested that the household registers of all *bhikṣu* enrolled at T'ongdo Monastery be collected as well.[54] He ultimately uncovered seventy-seven covert *bhikṣu* marriages, as seen in table 5.6.

Table 5.5. Ordination and marriage records of head monks at T'ongdosa around 1925 and 1926, *Sōtokufu kanpō*

Monk	*Bhikṣu* ordination		Bodhisattva ordination		Marital status	Source
	Year	Preceptor	Year	Preceptor		
Kim Kuha (金九河, 1872–1965)	1896	Manha (萬下)	1896	Manha (萬下)	Married (1923)	"通度寺住持再任就職認可申請ノ件" (March 5, 1924); "通度寺住持就職認可申請ノ件" (August 9, 1926)
Song Sŏru (宋雪牛, 1871–?)	1896	Cho Podam (曺普曇)	1896	Cho Podam (曺普曇)	Unmarried	"通度寺住持就職認可申請ノ件" (August 9, 1926)

Table 5.6. Marital status of *"bhikṣu"* at T'ongdo Monastery around 1925 and 1926, *Sōtokufu kanpō*

Year	Married bhikṣu	Unmarried bhikṣu	Source
1925	77	n/a	通度寺僧侶中帶妻者氏名記錄 (August 21, 1925)
1926	n/a	70	通度寺住持候補者ノ投票數調查ニ關スル件 (May 28, 1926)

The term "married *bhikṣu*" is contradictory because one of the key precepts among the 250 *bhikṣu* precepts is the vow of celibacy. Despite the contradiction, colonial Korea contained many "married *bhikṣu*" because monks who took *bhikṣu* precepts in their early twenties often married secretly in middle or old age and did not renounce their *bhikṣu* status afterward, as seen in the cases of Kim Kuha and the other seventy-seven monks at T'ongdo Monastery. The names of these "married *bhikṣu*" at T'ongdo Monastery were listed in a document called "List of Married Monks Among T'ongdo Monastery Monks" (J. *Tsūdoji sōryo chū saitaisha shimei kiroku* 通度寺僧侶中帶妻者氏名記錄) written by Watanabe Akira.[55]

How many unmarried *bhikṣu* were at T'ongdo Monastery, compared with the seventy-seven "married *bhikṣu*"? We cannot answer this question without examining the head-monk election of May 1926. After Kim Kuha's resignation, T'ongdo Monastery held an election that resulted in a win for Song Sŏru. The monk Song Sŏru, as can be seen in table 5.5, had taken *bhikṣu* and bodhisattva precepts in 1896 from the monk Chang Podam at Wŏnjŏk Hermitage in Mun'gyŏng. According to Song's household register, he was unmarried. However, the government nullified the outcome, claiming that the election had been illegal because of the discovery that, of 108 "*bhikṣu*" who had participated in the election, thirty-eight were "married *bhikṣu*."[56] Although information regarding the number of unmarried *bhikṣu* in 1925 and the number of married *bhikṣu* in 1926 does not survive, along with seventy-seven married *bhikṣu* in 1925 at T'ongdo Monastery, it can be extrapolated that, in 1926, T'ongdo Monastery had about seventy unmarried *bhikṣu*.

When the head-monk election was held again in July 1926 at T'ongdo Monastery, Song Sŏru was elected again. In this reelection, for unknown reasons, only forty-seven voters participated, quite a small number when compared with the 108 monks who had voted in the previous election in May 1926. After thoroughly examining the list of voters, the colonial government confirmed that the married *bhikṣu* whose names were on Watanabe's list had not voted in this reelection and finally approved the installation of Song as head monk.[57]

Another document that was created by the local government reveals that T'ongdo Monastery itself made an internal probe on the marital status of monks after the previous election was invalidated, requesting that unqualified monks—that is, married ones—abstain from this reelection. In addition, T'ongdo Monastery made voters who participated in the election take an oath stating that they had never been married and promising that they would never raise any question about the election's outcome.[58] It is conceivable that the small voter turnout arose from the internal investigation within T'ongdo Monastery regarding the marital status of *bhikṣu*.

From this T'ongdo Monastery case, at least two significant questions arise. First, why did married monks claim that they were still *bhikṣu*? Second, what was the definition of *bhikṣu* in their minds? We can find answers to these questions in the case of Magok Monastery's head-monk election in 1927.

In the colonial era, Magok Monastery was the head temple of South Ch'ungch'ŏng Province. As in the case of T'ongdo Monastery, the Magok Monastery situation also involved two head-monk elections held between 1925 and 1926. The August 1925 election was held because Yu Inmyŏng (兪寅明, d.u.), the head monk of the Magok Monastery parish, had been accused of embezzling temple property and had to step down.[59] In this election, the Magok Monastery parish elected Yi Sŏnghae as head monk-elect. Unfortunately, when the colonial government requested his household register in the process of approving his appointment, it was discovered that he was not eligible owing to his marriage.

The government demanded the submission of a household register not only from Yi Sŏnghae, but also from the head monks-elect of three other head temples: Kwiju Monastery, Pŏpchu Monastery, and Pohyŏn Monastery. This meant that when the government decided to revise the temple laws in 1925, the elections of the head monks of four head temples came under scrutiny that year.[60] It seems likely that the government had two purposes in collecting household registers: verification of monks' legal names and verification of their marital status.[61] In this way, Yi Sŏnghae's marriage was uncovered, thus preventing him from becoming the head monk of his temple.

Furthermore, the government doubted Yi Sŏnghae's clerical career as it was presented in his resume, which was submitted for approval of his appointment. For example, Yi's claim that he had achieved the highest clerical rank was thrown in doubt because he did not actually satisfy the requirement of a dharma age of at least twenty for this rank.[62] Their skepticism regarding the veracity of his claims caused the colonial government to summon Yi to Seoul for further investigation. In this face-to-face investigation, Watanabe Akira, acting as the official of the Department of Religion, asked questions and Yi provided the answers. As such, Watanabe discovered that Yi's knowledge of Buddhism was insufficiently profound to confirm that his clerical education and career were as extensive as he claimed in his resume. When Watanabe asked questions related to the highest training course (K. *taegyokwa* 大教科), the highest clerical teacher (K. *taegyosa* 大教師), and the highest clerical rank in existence, Yi failed to answer any of them. Instead, Yi admitted that he had not, in fact, completed the highest training course and that his master monk had promoted him to the rank of highest clerical teacher at the master monk's discretion in spite of his lack of qualifications.[63]

In addition, because Yi's other career claims had proven false, Watanabe doubted Yi's ordination record as well. Yi noted that he had received *bhikṣu* ordination from the preceptor Chang Pomyŏng in his resume. Watanabe quizzed Yi on the essential elements of *bhikṣu* precepts, and, as expected, Yi could not answer. Because Chang Pomyŏng was deceased at the time of this interview, there was no way to prove the veracity of Yi's *bhikṣu* ordination. Watanabe ultimately concluded that Yi's *bhikṣu* ordination record was unreliable.[64]

Because of these doubts and Yi's marital status, the Magok Monastery parish held a second head-monk election in November 1926. Because the temple laws of the Magok Monastery parish had been revised in August of that year, this election allowed married monks to run legally.[65] However, this head-monk election was embroiled in internal dispute because of the ironic situation underlying the revised temple laws.

In 1926, the colonial government revised some clauses in the temple laws, thereby lifting the former disadvantages for monks who did not follow the rules of celibacy and a vegetarian diet. Although the revised clauses stated that head monks, abbots, and Sŏn practitioners were no longer required to attain *bhikṣu* ordinations, some clauses related to *bhikṣu* ordination remained unaltered. A remarkable example of an unchanged law was a clause dealing with the qualifications for electors in head-monk elections. Despite the revised temple laws' lifting of the *bhikṣu* ordination requirement for the actual head-monk candidates, electors in head-monk elections were still required to have received *bhikṣu* ordination unless those electors held abbot positions.

The original temple laws specified that voters in head-monk elections were required to be (1) *bhikṣu* who were enrolled in the head temple, or (2) abbots of major branch temples.[66] These qualifications for voters were modified in the revision of the temple laws in 1926 as follows: (1) *bhikṣu* who were enrolled in the head temple or in the major branch temples, (2) those who were qualified to be branch temple abbots based on the revised temple laws, or (3) branch temple abbots.[67] According to the revision, even if monks did not take up an abbacy, those who met the branch temple abbot qualifications were now able to vote in a head-monk election regardless of their marital status. At the same time, monks who did not satisfy the qualifications of the abbacy still needed to have *bhikṣu* ordination to participate in elections.

It is ironic that, according to the revision in the temple laws, married monks were able to run for the position of head monk, while the government still insisted that those who wished to vote in a head-monk election should be *bhikṣu* and hence unmarried. It is conceivable that there was a hidden intention regarding the *bhikṣu* ordination requirement in the revision of the temple laws. The colonial government, wishing to avoid responsibility for the spread of monastic marriage, left the *bhikṣu* requirement in effect in some clauses in the revised temple laws.[68]

In this November 1926 election at Magok Monastery, the three candidates who received the most votes from among the total of seven candidates were all married monks and had all been either head monk or head monk-elect at Magok Monastery: Yu Inmyŏng, who had been head monk in 1923 but saw his appointment canceled in 1925 because of misappropriation of temple property, won twenty-five votes of seventy-two; An Hyangdŏk, who had occupied the head-monk position from 1919 to 1923, received twenty-four votes; and Yi Sŏnghae, who had become head-monk elect in 1925 but failed to attain final approval from the government on account of his clerical marriage, gained fifteen votes.[69] The household registers of Yi Sŏnghae and An Hyangdŏk indicate that they were married in 1917 and 1924, respectively (table 5.7). Although Yu Inmyŏng's household register does not survive, his marital status was confirmed because he was listed as married in the list of electors that classified monks as married or unmarried.[70]

Table 5.7. Ordination and marriage records of head monks-elect at Magok Monastery around 1925 and 1926, *Sōtokufu kanpō*

Monk	Bhikṣu ordination		Bodhisattva ordination		Marital status	Source
	Year	Preceptor	Year	Preceptor		
Yi Sŏnghae (李性海, 1874–?)	1914	Chang Pomyŏng (張普命)	n/a	n/a	Married (1917)[1]	"麻谷寺住持候補者李性海ニ關ス ル件" (March 2, 1926)
An Hyangdŏk (安香德, 1869–?)	1907	Yi Hoegwang (李晦光)	1907	Yi Hoegwang (李晦光)	Married (1924)	"麻谷寺住持就任認可申請ニ關ス ル件" (June 20, 1927); "麻谷寺住持 就職認可申請ノ件" (July 2, 1930)

Yi Sŏnghae's household register did not indicate the date of his marriage, but it is assumed that he married around 1917, given that his first child was born that year.

Although Yu Inmyŏng won the election, this outcome resulted in internal conflicts among the monks. The monks fell into two opposing camps: those who condemned Yu's appointment because of his misappropriation of temple property when he was head monk and those who thought this irrelevant because he had been found not guilty in the court.[71] The strife culminated in a petition that 110 monks sent to the colonial government, stating that this election was illegal because "married bhikṣu" had voted.[72] These monks argued that Magok Monastery monks did not properly understand the meaning of bhikṣu after the temple law had been revised:

> We did not hear a proper explanation of the qualifications of electors based on the revised temple laws, neither from the head temple nor from the local government administrations. As a result, regardless of their different marital status, both married monks and unmarried monks were considered bhikṣu who qualified as electors. We think this election was rigged because it violated Article 21 in the Magok Monastery head-branch temple laws. That is why we presented this petition.[73]

In short, the issue of the head-monk election of Magok Monastery morphed from a dispute about the election of Yu himself into a reexamination of the very definition of bhikṣu. To clarify the issue, the monks of Magok Monastery sent a written inquiry to the government:

1. Are married bhikṣu considered bhikṣu and thus qualified to vote in a head-monk election or not?[74]

2. If married monks receive bhikṣu ordination, are they acknowledged as bhikṣu or not?[75]

3. If monks marry after they have received bhikṣu ordination, is their bhikṣu ordination annulled or not?[76]

This is one of the most interesting moments in the Korean Buddhism of the colonial period. Although it is considered common knowledge that monks would comprehend the relationship between bhikṣu precepts and the vow of celibacy, Korean monks still felt it necessary to inquire about this matter with the colonial government. As stated earlier, the inquiry became necessary because their understanding of the monastic rules was based on the temple laws rather than on traditional Vinaya texts such as the *Four-Part Vinaya*. Through the temple laws, the colonial government replaced the Vinaya and became the final word on *bhikṣu* status and the vow of celibacy. In this way, monks became dependent on the government for understanding and clarification. This represented quite a shift.

The Japanese colonial government sent written answers to the Magok Monastery questions as follows:

1. There has never been a Buddhist rule permitting *bhikṣu* to marry. Therefore, married monks cannot be called *bhikṣu* (比丘僧ハ妻帶スヘキ佛制ナシ從テ妻帶者ハ比丘僧ト稱スヘキモノニアラス).

2. If married monks ask to receive *bhikṣu* precepts, this should not be permitted (妻帶ノ僧侶カ比丘戒ヲ受ケタシト申立ルモ之ヲ許容スヘキモノニアラス).

3. If monks marry after having received *bhikṣu* precepts, they should know that their *bhikṣu* ordination will no longer be valid because they have violated the precepts (比丘戒ヲ受ケタル後ニ娶妻スル者ハ卽チ破戒僧ナレハ比丘戒護持ノ實ナキモノト會得スヘシ).[77]

These answers made the colonial government's position regarding the issue of clerical marriage perfectly clear. The Japanese colonial government did not want to take responsibility for the spread of clerical marriage when it revised the temple laws and therefore held fast to the basic principles in the *Four-Part Vinaya*. It is likely that Watanabe Akira assisted in the composition of these answers: remember that it was he who interrogated Yi Sŏnghae about the *Four-Part Vinaya* and *bhikṣu* precepts at the time of Yi's election.

Based on the government's interpretation of *bhikṣu*, Magok Monastery classified voters in its head-monk election in November 1926 by marital status. Magok Monastery discovered that, of the eighty-nine electors, thirty-two among the forty-five monks who claimed *bhikṣu* status and voted in the election were married monks and were, therefore, not true *bhikṣu* based on the clarification from the government. The other forty-four monks qualified as branch temple abbots.[78] Following the government's redefinition of *bhikṣu* status, it distinguished these thirty-two married *bhikṣu* as a group of "non-*bhikṣu* due to clerical marriage" (K. *taechŏ e kwanhaya pibigu* 帶妻에 關하야 非比丘) and the remaining thirteen, who were unmarried, as "*bhikṣu* based on temple laws" (K. *sabŏp e ŭihan pigu* 寺法에 依한 比丘) (table 5.8). This classification reveals that monks were dependent on the temple laws as a guide to monastic conduct.

The internal conflict in the Magok Monastery parish was resolved without further struggle when the head monk-elect Yu Inmyŏng resigned due to unknown causes.[79] An Hyangdŏk, who had come in second, was appointed as head monk-elect and was ultimately approved by the government.

As seen in table 5.7, An Hyangdŏk received *bhikṣu* precepts from Yi Hoegwang at Pongŭn Monastery in 1907. According to his resume, he received novice precepts in 1883; however, for reasons that were not recorded, he did not receive *bhikṣu* precepts until 1907. He was head monk of the Magok Monastery parish from 1919 to 1923, and, according to his household register, he married in 1924 and had a son.

According to the government's definition of *bhikṣu*, his *bhikṣu* ordination should have been nullified because of his marriage. However, An Hyangdŏk did not remove his *bhikṣu* ordination record from his clerical resume when he submitted it to the government. The government chose not to care about his *bhikṣu* ordination because it realized that his appointment as head monk would be the best way to resolve the internal strife in the Magok Monastery parish owing to his neutral position regarding conflicts. Given that Magok Monastery conflicts were caused by Yu Inmyŏng's winning the election, which intensified the conflict between the two opposing factions of Yu's supporters and opponents, An Hyangdŏk, who took no one's side, was considered a perfect fit for the head monk position.[80]

These two cases of T'ongdo Monastery and Magok Monastery give us considerable insight into the ways in which Korean monks thought about *bhikṣu* ordination at the time. At the time of the occupation, Korean monks relied on the temple laws specifying that *bhikṣu* ordination was

Table 5.8. Marital status of *bhikṣu* at Magok Monastery in 1926, *Sōtokufu kanpō*

Marital status	Number	Sources
Married	32	"忠南 大本山 麻谷寺 第五世 住持選舉會 選舉錄" (February 5, 1927)
Unmarried	13	

the requirement for a higher clerical career. They regarded it as a necessary step toward the attainment of more powerful positions, such as that of head monk or branch temple abbot. The *bhikṣu* ordination became a way of securing their position as elite monks even after the revision in the temple laws. Despite this, many of them disregarded the temple laws and married after receiving *bhikṣu* ordination. In other words, although Korean monks regarded the temple laws as a kind of Vinaya text whose authority rested in the hands of the colonial government, they still found a clever way to evade those laws in order to marry.

The ethical paradox enabled an increase in *bhikṣu* ordinations and the proliferation of clerical marriage during the colonial period. When the colonial government revised the temple laws, lifting these restrictions for monks who wished to run for the position of head monk while at the same time still requiring *bhikṣu* ordination for voters in head-monk elections, Korean Buddhist monks found themselves in quite a paradoxical situation, one in which married monks were allowed to be candidates in elections while their electors had to be unmarried. To come to terms in some way with this contradictory circumstance, Korean monks were forced to reinterpret the status of *bhikṣu* and create a rationale that allowed them to live by and obey monastic rules in their own way. Even after the colonial government provided the definition of *bhikṣu*, monks' appropriation regarding *bhikṣu* did not change, as seen in the case of An Hyangdŏk.

Even if An Hyangdŏk was one of the married monks who were appointed as head monks soon after the revision of the temple laws and stood to benefit from it, his head monk appointment was not a watershed moment with regard to clerical marriage among head monks. Before the revision in the temple laws, some head monks married secretly or had biological children. For example, the colonial government had already discovered in 1923 that Kim Chŏnghae (金晶海, 1887–?), the head monk of Chŏndŭng Monastery from 1922 to 1928, covertly married in 1920.[81] In a sense, An Hyangdŏk's case was a sign of the times.

In addition, according to my analysis of the surviving household registers of sixty-seven monks who held head monk positions from 1926 to 1945 after the revision of the temple laws,[82] thirty-two head monks were unmarried, thirty-one were married,[83] three registered only their children in their household registers,[84] and one was divorced. Although monastic marriage was regarded as the norm after the revision of the temple laws, it can be assumed that it did not become an overwhelming phenomenon in the Korean Buddhist monastic community during these years. Further detailed analysis regarding clerical marriage among Korean monks in the late colonial period will be the subject of my future research.

Conclusion

With regard to the ordination tradition, one of the more interesting phenomena in the Korean Buddhist community during the early colonial period was the rise of the *bhikṣu* and bodhisattva ordination ceremonies among Korean monks and nuns. This can be explained in two ways. First, *bhikṣu* and bodhisattva ordinations were existing practices among Korean monks. As seen in the *Biographies of Korean Masters*, the two preceptors Ch'ŏŭi and Pŏmhae, who transmitted an ordination lineage from Taeŭn, strengthened the *bhikṣu* and bodhisattva ordination tradition. Moreover, the preceptor Manha began to bestow *bhikṣu* precepts around 1896 after he himself took them in China. This ordination trend continued in the colonial period. Second, in the temple laws, the Japanese colonial government required *bhikṣu* and bodhisattva ordinations as one of the qualifications for head monks, branch temple abbots, and Sŏn practitioners. The colonial government used these ordinations as criteria to divide elite monks from rank-and-file ones as a way of controlling the entire Buddhist community more effectively. The creation of ordination lineages in the nineteenth century can be seen as further evidence of Korean Buddhism's weak Vinaya tradition, allowing "married *bhikṣu*" to appear during the colonial period.

As Korean monks relied on temple laws for their education, clerical ranks, ordination, and even deportment, including clerical marriage, the temple laws soon replaced the Vinaya. The colonial government that had created these laws also enjoyed authority over whether major rules were being observed or not. To address this situation, Korean monks cleverly invented their own rationale: if they had fulfilled all of the requirements, including *bhikṣu* ordination, in their early years, they could be married with impunity later. In this context, so-called "married *bhikṣu*" appeared. Examining two head-monk elections, one in the T'ongdo Monastery parish and the other in the Magok Monastery parish, tells us that, in practice, "married *bhikṣu*" existed among Korean monks.

After the government revised the temple laws and removed these disadvantages for married monks while still requiring *bhikṣu* status for voters in elections, Korean monks were facing an ethical contradiction, because married monks were able to run for the elections, but voters had to be *bhikṣu*. They appropriated the monastic rules to give themselves the freedom to maintain their *bhikṣu* and married statuses at the same time. In this way, *bhikṣu* ordinations and clerical marriage among Korean monks coexisted during the colonial period.

Notes

1. A version of this chapter appeared in *Seoul Journal of Korean Studies* 30, no. 2 (2017): 131–63. The Kyujanggak Institute for Korean Studies granted permission to reuse the article.
2. Buswell, *The Zen Monastic Experience*, 25.
3. Sørensen, "Buddhism and Secular Powers in Twentieth-Century Korea," 133.
4. Park, "The Buddhist Purification Movement in Postcolonial South Korea," 135.
5. Ko, "Chogyejong ŭi kyejŏnghye samhak suhaeng chŏngch'aek: Yongsŏng, Yŏngho, Hanam, Chaun ŭl chungsim ŭro" (A Study on the Buddhist Research Trends of Japanese Students in the Korean Period Focused on Japanese Students in Japan during the Japanese Colonial Period), 184.
6. Kim, "Han Yongun kwa Paek Yongsŏng ŭi kŭndae Pulgyo kaehyŏngnon pigyo yŏn'gu" (Comparative Study in Modern Buddhist Reformation Ideas between Han Yongun and Paek Yongsŏng), 88.
7. Kim, "Yongsŏng ŭi kŏnbaeksŏ wa taech'ŏ sigyuk ŭi chaeinsik" (Yongsŏng's Petition and Re-examination of Clerical Marriage and Meat Eating), 233.
8. Prebish, "Varying the Vinaya: Creative Responses to Modernity," 62.
9. Prebish, "Varying the Vinaya: Creative Responses to Modernity," 57.
10. Blackburn, "Looking for the Vinaya: Monastic Discipline in the Practical Canons of the Theravāda," 285.
11. Kaplan, "Updating the Vinaya: Formulating Buddhist Monastic Laws and Pure Rules in Contemporary Korea," 254.
12. Ko, "Han'guk Pulgyo kangwŏn samigwa kyojae ŭi sŏjijŏk yŏn'gu" (A Bibliographic Research of the Study Materials of the Novice Course in Korean Buddhist Seminaries), 906.
13. Most head temples included "Awaken Your Mind and Practice," "Self-Admonitions," and "Admonitions for Beginning Students" as part of the novice monks' training course in their temple laws. Some head temples, such as Taehŭng Monastery and Wibong Monastery, also used the *Admonitions to the Gray-Robed Monks*. See Yi, *Chosŏn Pulgyo t'ongsa* (A Comprehensive History of Korean Buddhism), 285; Chōsen sōtokufu naimubu, "Honmatsu jihō ninka no ken" (Approval of Head-Branch Temple Laws), 42, 79.

14. The temple laws were not legally binding because the temple laws of a parish applied only to members of that parish, and the most serious punishment was expulsion from the sangha.

15. Chinese monks named Xinhai (K. Sinhae 信海) and Pujing (K. Pojŏng 普淨) came to Chosŏn Korea during the Imjin War.

16. Kim, *Chosŏn hugi Pulgyosa yŏn'gu* (A Study of the History of Late Chosŏn Buddhism), 125.

17. Yŏm, "Han'guk Pulgyo kyeyulgwan ŭi kŭnbon munje koch'al: Chungguk munhwa kwŏn ŭi t'ŭksusŏng ŭl chungsim ŭro" (An Examination of the Fundamental Problem for Vinaya Tradition of Korean Buddhism), 75.

18. Yi, *Han'guk Pulgyo kyeyul chŏnt'ong* (Vinaya and Precepts Tradition of Korean Buddhism), 150. When this visionary ordination of Taeŭn took place, Kŭmdam immediately asked Taeŭn to bestow ordination on him even though he was the teacher and Taeŭn, the pupil. In this way, Kŭmdam became capable of transmitting ordination lineage from Taeŭn.

19. However, in the *Tongsa yŏlchŏn*, Ch'oŭi's ordination was not recorded. According to "Biography of Venerable Sŏn Practitioner Ch'oŭi" (K. *Ch'oŭi sŏnbaek chŏn* 草衣禪伯傳), Ch'oŭi's original teacher was named Pŏkbong. He transmitted dharma lineage from a monk called Wanho and handed on Sŏn lineage from Kŭmdam. On the other hand, another record found on a stele does document Ch'oŭi's *bhikṣu* ordination. The inscription that commemorates Ch'oŭi says that he received *bhikṣu* precepts from Wanho. See Pŏmhae, *Tongsa yŏlchŏn* (The Biographies of Korean Masters), 10; Yi, *Han'guk kosŭng pimun ch'ongjip: Chosŏnjo kŭndaegi* (The Collection of Stele Inscriptions of Eminent Korean Buddhist Monks: Chosŏn and the Modern Periods), 696.

20. Yi, *Han'guk Pulgyo kyeyul chŏnt'ong*, 256–57.

21. Yi, *Han'guk Pulgyo kyeyul chŏnt'ong*, 146.

22. Chōsen sōtokufu gakumukyoku, "T'ongdosa jūji shūshoku ninka shinsei no ken" (On the Application for Approval of Head Monk Appointment for T'ongdosa), 325.

23. Pŏmhae wrote in "Biography of Venerable Sŏn Practitioner Taeŭn" (K. *Taeŭn sŏnbaek chŏn* 大隱禪伯傳): "Many people praised him [Taeŭn] as an incarnation of Daoxuan." See Pŏmhae, *Tongsa yŏlchŏn*, 1040.

24. Pŏmhae, *Tongsa yŏlchŏn*, 1032.

25. Pŏmhae, *Tongsa yŏlchŏn*, 1038, 1046.

26. Pŏmhae, *Tongsa yŏlchŏn*, 1033, 1055.

27. Ch'wiun was head monk at Taedun Monastery (which was called Taehŭng Monastery at the time) during the Japanese colonial period from 1912 to 1918 and 1923 to 1927.

28. For example, the *Four-Part Vinaya* prohibited manual labor, which was mandatory in Chan monasteries in China. Therefore, early Chinese Buddhists reclassified bodhisattva precepts in the *Brahmā Net Sūtra* as "supplements to

the Vinaya." See Ibuki, "Vinaya and the Chan School: Hīnayāna Precepts and Bodhisattva Precepts, Buddhism in the City and Buddhism in the Mountains, Religion and the State," 114; French and Nathan, "Introducing Buddhism and Law," in *Buddhism and Law: An Introduction*, 12.

29. Ch'oŭi, *Iljiam munjip* (Collected Works from Iljiam Hermitage), 865–66.
30. Ch'oŭi, *Iljiam munjip*, 264.
31. Pŏmhae, *Tongsa yŏlchŏn*, 1063–64.
32. Pŏmhae, *Tongsa yŏlchŏn*, 1052.
33. Pŏmhae, *Tongsa yŏlchŏn*, 1054.
34. Chōsen sōtokufu, "Seirei," *Ilche sidae Pulgyo chŏngch'aek kwa hyŏnhwang: Chosŏn ch'ongdokbu kwanbo Pulgyo kwallyŏn charyojip* (Buddhist Policy and Circumstance during the Japanese Colonial Period: Source Book of the Official Gazette of the Government General about Korean Buddhism) 7, no. 1 (June 3, 1911): 19.
35. It was Watanabe Akira (渡邊彰) who conducted a nationwide survey on Korean Buddhism between 1909 and 1910, and after annexation he worked in Buddhist Affairs in the Government-General Office. According to a statement he made in 1926, it can be surmised that Watanabe drafted the temple laws. For more information about Watanabe Akira, see Jeongeun Park, "Clerical Marriage and Buddhist Modernity in Early Twentieth-Century Korea," 89–91.
36. Yi, *Chosŏn Pulgyo t'ongsa*, 280.
37. Yi, *Chosŏn Pulgyo t'ongsa*, 276.
38. Yi, *Chosŏn Pulgyo t'ongsa*, 275.
39. Yi, *Chosŏn Pulgyo t'ongsa*, 286–87.
40. Yi, *Han'guk Pulgyo kyeyul chŏnt'ong*, 142.
41. "Chappo: Kyedan sŏngŭi" (Miscellaneous: Splendid Ordination Ceremony), 70.
42. "Chappo: Kyedan sŏngŭi."
43. Pŏmhae, *Tongsa yŏlchŏn*, 1075. Entries in the *Tongsa yŏljŏn* were chronicled. As Yi Hoegwang was the youngest monk whose biography was included, it was, therefore, the final entry. Yi Hoegwang was thirty-three years old when Pŏmhae completed the book in 1894.
44. "Chappo: Hŭngguk sŏlgye" (Miscellaneous: Sermon on the Precepts at Hŭngguk Monastery), 65.
45. His abbot position was approved by the Governor-General of Korea in December 1911, but he resigned in August 1912. See *Chōsen sōtokufu, Kanpō* No. 405 (January 6, 1912) and No. 27 (August 30, 1912).
46. "Sasŭng chosap'yo" (Survey of the Number of Buddhist Monks and Nuns).
47. "Chappo: Ilban ponmalsa sŭngni suhyo" (Miscellaneous: The Number of Monks and Nuns in the Head and Branch Temples), 94–96.
48. Chōsen sōtokufu naimubu, "Honmatsu jihō ninka no ken" (Approval of Head-Branch Temple Laws) (September 7, 1912), 42.
49. Jaffe, *Neither Monk nor Layman*, 54.

50. Borup, *Japanese Rinzai Zen Buddhism*, 22.

51. Chōsen sōtokufu gakumukyoku, "T'ongdosa jūji shūshoku ninka no ken" (On the Application for Approval of Head Monk Appointment for T'ongdosa) (August 9, 1926), 493.

52. Chōsen sōtokufu gakumukyoku, "T'ongdosa jūji sainin shūshoku ninka shinsei no ken" (On the Application for Approval of Head Monk Appointment for T'ongdosa) (March 4, 1924), 325.

53. Chōsen sōtokufu gakumukyoku, "T'ongdosa honmatsu jihō chū kaimei no ken" (Revision of Head-Branch Temple Laws of T'ongdosa) (December 21, 1926).

54. Chōsen sōtokufu gakumukyoku, "T'ongdosa jūji shūshoku ninka shinsei no ken" (August 9, 1926), 492–95.

55. Chōsen sōtokufu gakumukyoku, "T'ongdosa jūji shūshoku ninka shinsei no ken," 452–53.

56. Chōsen sōtokufu gakumukyoku, "T'ongdosa jūji shūshoku ninka shinsei no ken," 468–80.

57. Chōsen sōtokufu gakumukyoku, "T'ongdosa jūji shūshoku ninka shinsei no ken," 450.

58. Chōsen sōtokufu gakumukyoku, "T'ongdosa jūji shūshoku ninka shinsei no ken," 454–55.

59. Chōsen sōtokufu gakumukyoku, "Magoksa jūji shūnin ninka no ken" (Approval of Head Monk Appointment of Magoksa) (July 9, 1927), 651.

60. Chōsen sōtokufu gakumukyoku, "Kwijusa jūji shūshoku ninka no ken" (Approval of Head Monk Appointment of Kwijusa) (December 18, 1925), 334–36.

61. Park, "Clerical Marriage and Buddhist Modernity in Early Twentieth-Century Korea," 204–5.

62. Chōsen sōtokufu gakumukyoku, "Magoksa jūji shūnin ninka no ken" (July 9, 1927), 695.

63. Chōsen sōtokufu gakumukyoku, "Magoksa jūji shūnin ninka no ken," 716–17.

64. Chōsen sōtokufu gakumukyoku, "Magoksa jūji shūnin ninka no ken," 713–14.

65. Chōsen sōtokufu gakumukyoku, "Magoksa honmatsu jihō kaimei no ken" (August 27, 1926).

66. Chōsen sōtokufu naimubu, "Honmatsu jihō ninka no ken" (Approval of Head-Branch Temple Laws) (September 7, 1912), 33.

67. Chōsen sōtokufu gakumukyoku, "Kakuji honmatsu jihō chū shūsei o yōsubeki kajō no shūsei hyōjun o shimesu ken" (On the Guideline for the Standardized Revision of the Head-Branch Temples Laws of Each Buddhist Parish) (May 10, 1926), 1118.

68. After the revision, the Korean Buddhist communities were involved in a serious debate over the issue of clerical marriage and meat eating, and some Buddhists accused the colonial government of intending to promote clerical

marriage among Korean monks by breaking the authentic monastic rules of Korean Buddhism through this revision. In response to this criticism, the colonial government strongly defended itself by saying that the revision was not meant to promote the spread of clerical marriage but instead to appease demands from Korean monks to allow marriage.

69. Chōsen sōtokufu gakumukyoku, "Magoksa jūji shūnin ninka no ken" (July 9, 1927), 627–29.

70. Chōsen sōtokufu gakumukyoku, "Magoksa jūji shūnin ninka no ken," 805–7.

71. "Magoksa sinim chuji yussi pandae undong" (Magok Monastery's Movement against New Head Monk Yu), *Tong'a ilbo*, December 19, 1926; "Yu chuji pandae undong" (Movement against Head Monk Yu), December 21, 1926; and "Magoksa chuji huim chaengt'al chŏn" (Struggle for New Head Monk at Magoksa Monastery), February 6, 1927.

72. Chōsen sōtokufu gakumukyoku, "Magoksa jūji shūnin ninka no ken" (July 9, 1927), 724–25.

73. Chōsen sōtokufu gakumukyoku, "Magoksa jūji shūnin ninka no ken," 724–25. The original text is as follows: "有權者에 對하여서도 改正된 寺法의 解釋이 本山 及 郡道 當局으로부터 完全치 못함으로 帶妻者 非帶妻者를 不拘하고 全部를 比丘의 資格으로 有權者가 됨은 麻谷寺 本末寺法 第 二十一條의 違反된 不正選擧이 읍기에 玆에 陳情하오니."

74. "妻帶ノ比丘僧カ比丘僧ノ資格ヲ以テ住持選擧桝有無."

75. "妻帶ノ僧侶カ比丘戒ヲ受ク場合ニ於テハ比丘僧ト認ルヤ否ヤ."

76. "比丘戒ヲ受ク際ニ娶妻スル場合ニハ比丘戒ヲ消滅ナルヤ否ヤ," Chōsen sōtokufu gakumukyoku, "Magoksa jūji shūnin ninka no ken," 793–94.

77. Chōsen sōtokufu gakumukyoku, "Magoksa jūji shūnin ninka no ken," 788–89.

78. Chōsen sōtokufu gakumukyoku, "Magoksa jūji shūnin ninka no ken," 805–7.

79. Chōsen sōtokufu gakumukyoku, "Magoksa jūji shūnin ninka no ken," 623.

80. Chōsen sōtokufu gakumukyoku, "Magoksa jūji shūnin ninka no ken," 617–26.

81. Keijō Shōro keisatsusho, "Mimoto shōkai no ken" (Enquiry Request for Identification) (October 20, 1923), 540–42.

82. Park, "Clerical Marriage and Buddhist Modernity in Early Twentieth-Century Korea," 226–32.

83. A notable example is Na Chŏngho, who was head monk of the Pongŭn Monastery parish from 1912 to 1918 and from 1924 to 1934. The parish's temple laws were revised in September 1926. Na's household register indicates that he was married in 1930, but he had a son who was born in 1912. See Chōsen sōtokufu gakumukyoku, "Pongŭnsa jūji shūshoku ninka shinsei ni kansuru ken" (On the Application for Approval of Head Monk Appointment for Pongŭnsa) (May 12, 1934), 633.

84. For example, Kim Chŏngsŏp, the head monk of the Chŏndŭng Monastery parish from 1937 to 1945, listed seven illegitimate children (K. *sŏja* 庶子) in his household register but not their two mothers. See Chōsen sōtokufu gakumukyoku, "Chŏngdŭngsa jūji shūshoku ninka no ken" (Approval of Head Monk Appointment of Chŏngdŭngsa) (November 19, 1940), 56–57.

Chapter 6

Flesh in the Closet

The "Secret Wife" in Korean Buddhism

Su Jung Kim

> Wherever there is power, there is secrecy, except it is not only secrecy that lies at the core of power, but public secrecy.
>
> —Michael Taussig, *Defacement: Public Secrecy and the Labor of the Negative*

Introduction

In recent years, the Jogye Order, the biggest Buddhist sect in South Korea, has been mired in a slew of scandals.[1] In the spring of 2012, a number of senior Buddhist monks of the Order were forced to resign after a video surfaced showing them drinking, smoking, and playing a high-stakes poker game in a hotel room. After that incident, Chasŭng (慈乘, 1954–), the executive administrative director of the Jogye Order (K. *Chogyejong ch'ongmu wŏnjang* 曹溪宗總務院長), made a public apology and performed a 108-bow repentance. The scandal, however, sparked a series of other accusations against Jogye monks, including the claim that some of the senior leaders had secretly married women and fathered children. Three years later, another scandal erupted, an accusation that Sŏngwŏl (性月,

1954–), the newly elected abbot of Yongju Monastery (龍珠寺) in the city of Hwasŏng, had fathered twins. The temple's disillusioned followers have demanded his repentance and resignation ever since. Sŏngwŏl has not given in, and temple followers continue to protest.

The most recent high-profile scandal is the three corruption charges against Sŏlchŏng (雪靖, 1942–), the newly elected chief monk of the Jogye Order, that surfaced in May of 2018. The first alleged that he had forged his academic degree. He admitted to this, although he claimed that it should not disqualify him from being elected. He was also accused of financial corruption and of fathering a daughter with a Buddhist nun, charges that several citizen campaign groups had already leveled against him. But these did not resonate with the wider public. The allegations, however, gained widespread attention through coverage by *PD Notebook* (K. *PD Such'ŏp*), a weekly public television program known for tackling sensitive social issues produced by the Munhwa Broadcasting Corporation.[2] The episode "Can we ask questions, venerable monk? (K. *Kŭn sŭnimkke mutsŭmnida* 큰스님께 묻습니다)" was broadcast on May 1, 2018, and shed a critical light on the three charges. After the program's release, raging lay protestors were mobilized to demonstrate against Sŏlchŏng. Buddhist monastic members also demanded that he provide explanations about the charges, at the very least. The Order, however, remained silent. A couple of weeks later, it suddenly released a video clip in which the mother of Sŏlchŏng's alleged daughter testified that the monk had adopted her, denying that he was her biological father.[3] This testimony, however, still left the public full of questions. The testimony did not explain why the mother had brought a paternity suit against Sŏlchŏng several years earlier—a crucial point in the allegation. The chief monk promised to submit to a paternity test to settle the matter and insisted on his innocence. Yet he kept postponing taking the test. Without any explanation, Sŏlchŏng resigned in August 2018.

Regardless of whether the accusations are true, they have irreversibly damaged the public reputation of the Jogye Order. In South Korea, Buddhism had already been losing followers, according to a survey conducted by the Korean government in 2015.[4] The decline may in part reflect methodological flaws in the survey, as it included an online component that may have depressed response rates among seniors, the largest age group in the Korean Buddhist population. However, another recent survey conducted by Gallup Korea also indicates a significant decrease in religiosity among Buddhist followers. Cumulative data from 1984 to 2014 show that the number of Koreans who identify as Buddhist has held steady at approximately 20 percent, making Buddhism the most popular religion in Korea. However, the percentage of Buddhist followers who indicate that religion is "very important" in their lives has sharply declined. In 1984, it was 88 percent, and it declined to 59 percent by 2014. This figure may reflect an overall secularization of society, but the more modest reduction among Christians over the same period, from 97 percent to 90 percent, indicates otherwise. More significantly, the decline suggests that Buddhist institutions are gradually losing touch with their followers.[5] Also, the number of Buddhist monastics has fallen steadily in recent years. As a response to this, in 2017, the Order launched its first advertised recruitment campaign for novice monks and nuns with the slogan "Joining the clergy: the most brilliant choice of my life."[6]

For lay Buddhists, the accusations that high-ranking monks violated the monastic code of celibacy have been the most controversial; accusations of corruption and forgery generate far less outrage. For instance, Sŏlchŏng's forgery of his academic degree was easily pardoned by his followers, and he was allowed to continue as leader of his Order. However, some in the monastic community think differently. For example, Myŏngjin (明盡, 1950–), the former abbot of the Pongŭn Monastery (奉恩寺) in Seoul, one of the most influential temples in the country, has argued that Sŏlchŏng's forgery of his academic credentials is a more serious crime than having a secret relationship.[7] All of these responses suggest that there is a certain level of tolerance for secret wives in contemporary Korean Buddhism, and in fact their existence is in many cases an open secret.

Michael Taussig's notion of public secrecy provides a valuable analytical framework to untangle the phenomenon of secret wives in the monastic community. In his articulation of the social aspect of secrecy, Taussig defines public secrecy as a shared repression of information that "is generally known, but cannot be articulated."[8] In contrast to the Foucauldian notion of knowledge-power, Taussig argues that active not-knowing makes overt knowledge even more powerful.[9] Although I agree that attempting to unmask a secret does not necessarily reveal an undisclosed truth, this chapter is not designed to reveal the sexual transgressions of particular Buddhist monks. Keeping the complicated history of sex and Buddhism in mind, what I hope to advance is neither a condemnation nor a condonation of the practice. Rather, I seek to explain how the covert nature of the matter is deeply intertwined with the specific Korean Buddhist experience of modernity in the Japanese colonial period (1910–1945) and how the secret wife issue became an open secret in the postcolonial period of South Korean Buddhism. Furthermore, the secret wife issue illuminates various aspects of the development of modern Korean Buddhism, chiefly because monks' vows of celibacy played a tremendous role in both the identity formation of the Jogye Order and the establishment of its monastic authority. By highlighting the historical context in which accusations of having secret wives originated, developed, and entered public discourse, this chapter shows that the elusive presence of the secret wife is not just an issue within the history of the Jogye Order. Rather, it is closely related to several unresolved structural issues in the decolonization process in South Korean society.

What Is a Secret Wife?

The term *ŭnch'ŏsŭng* (隱妻僧) refers to a monk (K. *sŭng* 僧) who is in a secret relationship with a woman, whether the two are legally married or not. Throughout the chapter, I translate the term *ŭnch'ŏ* as "secret wife," although I recognize that the translation can be misleading because the word "wife" suggests a legal bonding in the relationship.[10] Although the corresponding term for the Korean word *ch'ŏ* is "wife," the term *ŭnch'ŏ* can mean a broad range of romantic but secretive relationships, such as a monk having a de facto wife, an unmarried spouse, or even a concubine or girlfriend. As the difficulty of translating the term already affirms, this is an intriguing phenomenon that has not been fully understood or explained. To complicate the term *ŭnch'ŏ* even further, a related term, *ŭnch'ŏja* (隱妻子), is worth mentioning here. This term encompasses any offspring who result from the secretive relationship and often require support over a long period of time. Although Buddhist nuns may well also violate their celibacy vows, this chapter focuses exclusively on male monastics because the prevailing gender inequality in Korean society and Korean Buddhism, I suggest, gives monks special power that may invite abuse.

Public secrecy about secret wives among Jogye Buddhist monks has been relatively common in Korea since the postcolonial period. One problem with this is that it is difficult to say whether this is particular to modern Korean Buddhism. Evidence suggests, for example, similar issues among priests and monks forbidden to marry in Christian sects[11] as well as in some traditions within Buddhism.[12] Media coverage in modern Taiwan indicates that, although the island was also a Japanese colony (1895–1945), Taiwanese Buddhists are not familiar with the concept of the secret wife, and Buddhist monastics are highly respected. Moreover, some neighboring Buddhist traditions, including Japanese Buddhism,[13] modern Mongolian Buddhism,[14] modern Newari Buddhism,[15] and some Tibetan Buddhist sects all recognize clerical marriage, and thus the concept becomes irrelevant. Most of the more than 200 contemporary Korean Buddhist sects, like the Jogye, Chŏnt'ae (天台), and Pomun (普門) Orders, accept only celibate clerics. However, a few sects, like the T'aego Order (太古宗), the second-largest sect, accept clerical marriage.

But are these clerical marriages a degenerated form of Buddhism, disobeying the original monastic regulations that originated in India? In theory, the Indian Buddhist monastic code bans any sexual activity, mostly for the protection of monastic members. According to *prātimokṣa* rules, which list regulations for monks and nuns hierarchically, the breaking of celibacy is the gravest infraction, even worse than murder.[16] In practice, however, since the early days of Buddhism, sexual transgression has been one of the most challenging issues for monasticism.[17] Borrowing Jan Nattier's words, "sex epitomizes the central problematic of Buddhism."[18] Although Nattier rightly points out the struggle between monasticism and celibacy throughout the history of Indian Buddhism, recent research on the Indian Vinaya literature, however, says that the picture was much more complicated. In his close reading of this literature, Shane Clarke suggests that the wholesale abandonment of familial ties among Buddhist monks is one side of an extreme and romanticized view that exists only in the scholarly imagination.[19] Clarke notes that Vinaya literature includes numerous stories in which monastic institutions treated monks' "visits" to their wives with leniency and points out that Indian Buddhism was neither antifamily nor antisocial. The author of the *Mahāvaṃsa* even states that "in the villages owned by the Sangha [in medieval Sri Lanka], the morality of the [Buddhist] monks consisted only in supporting their wives and children," suggesting that they were lax in every way except for feeding their families.[20] Clarke's findings do not undermine the gravity of sexual violation in the *sangha* or the Buddhist monastic order.[21] In fact, they provides us a more complex picture of a social tension between sexuality and celibacy among monastics in early Buddhism and the early Indian *sangha*'s practical approach to it.

The same complexity is found in the secret wife issue in modern Korean Buddhism. In the span of one hundred years, attitudes about monastic celibacy have oscillated. There was a time in the early twentieth century when clerical marriage was the norm; however, in twenty-first-century Korea, celibacy is expected for joining the Jogye Order, the country's largest and most influential Buddhist sect. Although there is a clear distinction between monks who marry in the sects that permit it and those who marry "secretly," the varied regulation of monastic celibacy reflects changing societal values and zeitgeists.

Historicizing the Secret Wife

The canonical source of the monastic celibacy that the Jogye Order upholds is the *Dharmaguptaka Vinaya* (K. *Sabun-yul* 四分律), one of the most influential monastic codes in East Asian Buddhism.[22] Such ancient codes, however, often play a symbolic rather than a concrete role in contemporary Korean Buddhist law, due in part to the challenge of adjusting these codes to the modern world. In the Jogye Order, there are supplementary rules that govern monastics' discipline and punishment, and celibacy is consistently mentioned in these regulations. For instance, by advocating for all of the precepts (K. *kujok-kye* 具足戒) of this *Dharmaguptaka Vinaya*, the Order's own constitution, called the "Jogye Order Constitution," disallows clerical marriage.[23] Another monastic law that regulates the Order's members' duties and rights, called the "Law of the Monastics" (K. *Sŭngnyŏ-pŏp* 僧侶法), also specifies that Jogye monks and nuns should remain celibate.[24] Whereas the T'aego Order embraces celibate clergy and married clergy (K. *kihonsŭng* 既婚僧/*taechŏsŭng* 帶妻僧) as equal members, the vow of celibacy is at the core of the Jogye Order's monastic identity and its authority; its members consider themselves the only legitimate successors to the Korean Buddhist tradition on the basis of this distinction.

This distinction also offers the Order leverage to project a more pure or holy public image than other sects, both on the religious and ideological levels. As celibate monastics, lay Buddhists may consider them more worthy of donations. Further, the Order connects its celibacy politics with timeless "tradition" and national pride.[25] The Order uses celibacy to legitimize itself through tactful association with Korean nationalism. The Order claims that it inherited the Buddhist tradition from the Silla (57 BCE–935 CE) and Koryŏ (918–1392) periods. However, this claim is not based on any historical evidence. We have no clear picture of these periods' monasticism, and recent scholarship has revealed that practices from the late Chosŏn period in fact dominate our understanding of "Korean

Buddhist tradition."²⁶ Although the Order militantly advocates celibacy as the core of its identity as well as the core of Korean Buddhist tradition, it is crucial to note that attitudes toward celibacy in past eras of Korean Buddhism were much more varied and ambiguous than is often assumed. Wŏnhyo (元曉, 617–686), for example, was neither a monk nor a layman, even though he is perceived as one of the most eminent "monks" in the history of Korean Buddhism.²⁷ Similarly, as Hwansoo Kim has illuminated, there have been lay Buddhist communities since the Chosŏn period (1392–1910) whose diversity displays a considerable range of Buddhist monastic identities.²⁸

The clerical marriage system was officially instituted in Korea during the Japanese colonial period, and this policy may have been the major reason that many Korean monks abandoned celibacy. The Korean monastic community suffered a loss of power and prestige over the course of the Chosŏn dynasty and was even barred from the capital until 1895. Moreover, the Korean monastic community also faced vigorous challenges from modernization and Christianization. For Korean Buddhist leaders, the advance of Japanese Buddhist missionaries was seen as both oppressive and an opportunity.²⁹ By the turn of the twentieth century, adherence to the Buddhist precepts had become increasingly lax among the Buddhist clergy, and married monks had become common in Korea.³⁰ Meanwhile, Japanese Buddhism had adopted a clerical marriage system in 1872, and its missionaries worked ardently to merge Korean Buddhism and Japanese Buddhism. With this historical association between the marriage practices of Korean and Japanese monastics, clerical marriage in Korea has been widely disparaged in the postcolonial public discourse as an effect of Japanese colonialism. But, as Micah Auerback points out, the truth may be more complicated. According to Auerback, it is still debatable whether or not the Japanese colonial government was primarily responsible for the abandonment of celibacy by Korean monks.³¹

Indeed, a wide range of opinions existed on the question of clerical marriage in the colonial space. A case in point is the prominent Buddhist monk, leader, social reformer, and poet Han Yongun (韓龍雲, 1879–1944).³² After his trip to Japan in 1908, Han sent two petitions to the Japanese cabinet and the monastery supervisory board, asking that they permit clerical marriage for monks and nuns. He later fully articulated this idea and others in the *Treatises on the Reformation of Korean Buddhism* (*Chosŏn Pulgyo Yusillon* 朝鮮佛教維新論), published in 1913.³³ Deeply influenced by the social Darwinism of the influential Chinese thinker Liang Qichiao

(梁啓超, 1873–1929),³⁴ he described clerical marriage as an opportunity to renew Korean Buddhism.³⁵ He enumerated the potential benefits for society and Buddhism itself of a change that he felt was common sense.³⁶ For Han, clerical marriage was ultimately connected to the greater issue of Buddhism's survival in Korea when the Christian population was growing rapidly. The crux of Han's argument was that, because many monks were privately ignoring the rule of celibacy, allowing them to marry and produce offspring who would become Buddhists would help Buddhism compete with other religions and widen its own sphere of influence in society, thereby ensuring its viability. Although Han's petitions may not have led to the institutionalization of clerical marriage by the colonial government more than a decade later, later Buddhist scholarship provides mixed evaluations of the influence of his petitions.³⁷

Paek Yongsŏng (白龍城, 1864–1940), a leading Buddhist intellectual of this period, was a prominent critic of clerical marriage.³⁸ Paek called for a revival of the traditional spirit among the clerics, emphasizing observance of the Vinaya generally and of celibacy in particular. In 1926, responding to the colonial government's institutionalization of clerical marriage and the candidacy of a married monk for abbot, Paek sent a petition to the government asking it to forbid monks' marriage and meat eating (K. *taechŏ sigyuk* 帶妻食肉).³⁹ As modern scholarship has pointed out, however, Paek and other Buddhist leaders may have objected more to married monks' leadership of the head temples than to all clerical marriage.⁴⁰

The official recognition of a married clergy system slowly but profoundly changed colonial Korean monastic life. By the late 1920s, more than half of all monks were married. Some 80 percent of the monasteries formally eliminated the restriction on having wives in residence by 1929. By the time colonization ended, fewer than 10 percent of Korean monks claimed to be celibate, or about 600 of 7,000.⁴¹ By contrast, the majority of the Japanese Buddhist clergy was unmarried in 1937. Although there had been no ban on clerical marriage since the beginning of the Meiji period (1868–1912), it was seen as an undesirable practice.⁴²

Clerical marriage became controversial again after the Korean War (1950–1953), when Korean society was caught in a vortex of postcolonial ideologies that advocated clearing away the remnants of Japanese colonialism. The monks who later became seminal members in the Jogye Order promoted a convincing narrative that clerical marriage, which they saw as the most conspicuous vestige of Japanese colonialism, had to be eliminated in the name of the "purification movement" (K. *chŏnghwa undong* 淨化

運動). On May 20, 1954, President Syngman Rhee (1875–1965) issued a presidential decree calling for the resignation of married monks and the appointment of celibate monks to leading posts. Although it was popularly believed that the government helped to restore the community of celibate monks, newer scholarship reveals that the president's interference had more to do with mending political fences than with Buddhist doctrine.[43] The government-supported purification movement became extremely powerful once its ideology was framed in the context of a dichotomy between anti-Japanese nationalist and pro-Japanese colonialist perspectives. This paradigm encouraged the uncritical assumption that celibate monks were anti-Japanese Buddhist leaders, that they were actively engaged in the liberation movement, and that married monks had been Japanese collaborators. In the highly politicized purification movement, married monks were considered remnants of Japanese occupation who therefore needed to be purged.

The Jogye Order was officially established with the support of the government in 1962, labeling itself "the order of pure celibate clergy" (K. *ch'ongjŏng pigu chongdan* 淸淨比丘宗團).[44] Largely based on their vow of celibacy, the Order also claimed to be "the representative order of traditional Korean Buddhism with roots that go all the way back 1,200 years to Unified Silla period National Master Toŭi (道義, d.u.), who brought Sŏn and the practice taught by the Sixth Patriarch, Huineng (慧能, 638–713)."[45] What the Jogye Order calls "the purification movement" legitimized the Order, and it was not until 1970 that the movement finally ended, when the T'aego Order was established as a separate Buddhist institution and absorbed the country's remaining married monks. Although the majority of Korean monks were married when the Jogye Order began the purification movement, by the 1970s, the Jogye Order was exclusively celibate and counted more monastic members than the T'aego Order.[46] The T'aego Order, however, is still in conflict with the Jogye Order on the issue of which of the two is the legitimate successor of the "1,700-year history of Korean Buddhism."[47]

Locating the Secret Wife

Meanwhile, the pure *sangha* image of the Jogye Order has been continuously damaged and its religious legitimacy undermined in the last several decades in South Korea. References to the secret wives of Jogye monks began to appear in newspapers in the late 1970s. Although such reports may have enraged some Buddhist followers, they also may have contributed to a certain level of public tolerance. This section explores how the issue became politicized by examining patterns in this media coverage.

On February 9, 1977, the *Kyunghyang Newspaper* (*Kyŏnghyang Sinmun*) reported that Park Kijong (朴淇宗, 1907–1987), the then chief administrative director of the Jogye Order, had set forth several new directives.[48] To establish stronger self-discipline among monastics, he instructed the Order to seek out any monastic who 1) had supported his family financially; 2) had a "so-called secret wife"; 3) had violated civil law and assumed the identity of a monk to escape prosecution; or 4) had manipulated their age for easy promotion in the monastic system. Clearly, Park considered secret wives a significant issue that needed to be confronted. During this period, the term "secret wife" was slowly introduced to the public.

The appearance of the term became more frequent in the 1980s because of the Jogye Order's internal conflicts during this time.[49] A news article titled "The Radical Attempt to Modernize Buddhism," published on August 19, 1982, reports the consequences of a tentative reformation plan that the Order had proposed a week prior. The controversial plan recommended permitting monks to marry and eat meat.[50] It further suggested two categories of monastics: those devoted to meditation practice (K. *sudosŭng* 修道僧) and those focused on propagation (K. *kyohwasŭng* 教化僧) of the religion. The idea was to allow married monks to be recognized as the *kyohwasŭng* group while limiting their opportunities for promotion and monastic roles in the Order.[51] What is intriguing here is that this proposed dual structure responded to a desire to incorporate married monks into the Order. The article also reported that there were more than 300 Jogye monks who had secret wives and that, in its attempt to resolve the long-standing issue, the Order came up with this plan despite the risk of public criticism.[52] The article further explains that, upon the release of this proposal, monastic opinions were very divided. The article continues to report that the Order's leadership had to scrap the plan because of "some senior monks' and Buddhist followers' objections" but does not provide further details.

This back-and-forth reveals a significant point for discussion. In the 1980s, there was a sizable number of married monks in the Jogye Order, a fact that the Order's leadership openly admitted. The chief of the Jogye Order at the time, Hwang Chin'gyŏng (黃軫經, 1936–), recounted that the Order came up with the plan to permit clerical marriage as a way to "save" married monks. He did not describe why the Order did not instead expel these monks as their traditions required. Why did the Order try to incorporate them instead of letting them join the T'aego Order? It seems likely that the Order wanted to retain secretly married monks because they stood to gain more than to lose by doing so. Perhaps by keeping these monks, the Order could claim more political influence or economic power. Interestingly, during this same period, the Jogye Order was reconciling various legal disputes over Buddhist temples and properties with the T'aego Order. The proposal was first publicized in 1982, the same year that the Jogye and T'aego Orders resumed these talks, which had been on hiatus since 1954.

In the 1990s, more frequent media coverage of the issue of secret wives further tarnished the public's perception of the Jogye Order's morality. A news article published on July 22, 1990, reported that Yi Pŏpchŏl (李法徹), the senior leader of the Order, had declared his sharp disdain for the prevalence of secret wives among its ranks.[53] The secret wife issue even triggered a schism in the Order and led to the establishment of a separate, second headquarters across the Han River from the Order's traditional headquarters in 1991. One headquarters stood on the north side of the river and was led by Sŏ Ŭihyŏn (徐義玄, b. 1936), and another, established by Chae Pyŏgam (蔡碧嚴, 1924–2005), stood on the south side of the river.[54] The split was only temporary, because the Sŏ Ŭihyŏn faction soon consolidated its power.

Another conflict arose between the two factions in January 1991 on the issue of voting procedures to elect the supreme patriarch (K. *chongjŏng* 宗正). Six months later, the confrontation escalated to personal attacks, and those who opposed Sŏ Ŭihyŏn, by then the chief monk, accused him of having a secret wife. After the Sŏ Ŭihyŏn scandal, his successor, Song Wŏlchu (宋月珠, b. 1935), openly acknowledged that some monks had secret wives and that this was a pressing issue in a 1996 report to the Order's supreme patriarch.[55] During Song's tenure, the Order made continuous attempts to realign the monastic registration system and to identify monastic members who had either a secret wife or a criminal history.[56]

With some exceptions, acknowledgement that some monks have secret wives tends to coincide with political conflict. Secret wife accusations have often taken the form of personal attacks against political rivals that surface during power struggles within the Order. As is confirmed by recent events in which other charges had little impact on the public's view of accused monks, the secret wife charge is the most effective. Yet it has always been common for monks to criticize one another for moral laxity, and this criticism is often viewed as a way to maintain standards. Genuine concerns about the degradation of the Order may motivate some calls to restore chastity among monks in the Order. Indeed, a sincere desire for reform is compatible with political conflict, and internal criticism has a history of sparking reform in Korea, such as when the Koryŏ monk Chinul (知訥, 1158–1210) denounced the moral failings of his fellow monks in medieval Korea and sparked a reform movement.[57]

At the same time, as long as the secret wife accusations do not lead to unfair political purges, these scandals may bring the monastic community one step closer to the democratic ideal of Buddhist monasticism. They have led to the creation of civic groups of lay Buddhist followers who are pushing for reform. In August 2017, more than twenty different Buddhist-aligned civic organizations launched a collaborative organization called "The People's Coalition for Purging the Jogye Order's Corruptions" (K. *Chogyejong chŏkp'ae chŏngsan simin yŏndae*). Through various channels, including social media, podcasts, and candlelight protests, members of the group have been involved in reform campaigns, drawing public and media attention. Monastic members interested in democracy and social justice have joined the movement as well. Although it is not necessarily related to the reform movements, there has been a renewed interest in Vinaya studies in monastic education. Some reform-minded leading monastics advocate installing a fortnightly confession ritual (K. *p'osal* 布薩, Skt. *poṣadha*), in which all monastic members recite their grave offenses to maintain high monastic ideals and live up to their public reputation.[58]

The secret wife issue is the most serious violation that a monk can commit in a traditional Buddhist sense, but the Jogye Order's current legal basis for the punishment of this sin is obscure. The *Law of the Monastics*, the current penal system of the Jogye Order (most recently revised in 2015), does not directly reference the secret wife or its legal consequences.[59] However, there is one justification in the *Law of the Monastics* for the Order to impose "permanent expulsion" (K. *myŏlbin* 滅擯), the most severe punishment codified in law: imprisonment of a monk for the violation of the four grave offenses, *pārājika*, which include sexual transgression.[60] But the requirement that a monk be imprisoned for the violation clouds the original spirit of the four *pārājika*, which were formulated to allow the harmonious coexistence of the monastic community and to maintain the community's reputation.[61] Adding the provision that a monk must be imprisoned to receive this punishment involves secular criminal law and effectively bars the Order from punishing monks who violate the four grave offenses (as well as seven other offenses for which expulsion can be a consequence) unless the offender has committed a crime before the state and is imprisoned for it.

According to Daniel Soloves, "the harm of disclosure is not so much the elimination of secrecy as it is the spreading of information beyond the expected boundaries."[62] Similarly, the mass media's repeated disclosure of the secret wife issue has harmed the reputation of the Order, but, more significantly, it has turned the issue into a political tool that encourages schisms in the monastic community. Although the series of disclosures in the mass media carries out the function of public shaming,[63] the results of most accusations have gone unreported, partly because of the difficulties in verifying them. Just as the secret wife issue is an open secret, secrecy and disclosure are both tolerated and coexist.

Making Sense of the Secret Wife

The recurring secret wife scandal in Korean Buddhism reflects several entwined issues that have not been fully resolved in Korean Buddhism's process of modernization and decolonization. In this final section, I examine this recurring problem from five different angles in an attempt to understand its underlying causes and make sense of how the transgression gained a certain level of tolerance in contemporary Korean society.

First, the prevailing Sŏn antinomianism in Korean Buddhist monasticism has contributed to the tolerance of secret wives in the Jogye Order. Since the birth of the Jogye Order in modern Korea, Sŏn Buddhism has been perceived as the dominant form of traditional Korean Buddhism, although scholars have pointed out that this may not be historically accurate.[64] In the context of this willfully constructed, Sŏn-centered Korean Buddhist identity, Sŏn antinomianism was actively reproduced and reinforced to create a modern lineage of "enlightened" monks. It came to be understood as a soteriological goal, and thus followers believe that a master's eccentric or transgressive behavior is merely the proper realization of Sŏn antinomianism. In reaction to the excesses of Indian legalism, some adherents of Mahāyāna Buddhism affirmed the amoral nature of awakening. Doctrinally speaking, Sŏn never considered sexual acts as a gateway to a higher truth.[65] However, because of the influence of

Chinese Chan, Korean Sŏn Buddhist followers often see what unenlightened ordinary people would call "transgression" as proof of awakening under the Mahāyāna Buddhist logic of nonduality.[66] This is evident in the case of the Sŏn "eccentric monks," whose tradition affirms the superiority of certain forms of transgression over strict observance of discipline.[67] Eccentric monks' transgressions are not considered true transgressions. Enlightened masters transgress intentionally, and this "intentional transgression" does not result in any moral sanction because, according to the antinomian logic, these enlightened Sŏn masters have transcended the mundane concept of morality.

The problem, however, lies in the uncritical idolization of eccentric monks and the related pursuit of mimicking symbolic figures' antinomianism. In modern Korean Buddhism, for instance, Kyŏnghŏ (鏡虛, 1849–1912) is revered as the enlightened master who revived the Korean Sŏn Buddhist tradition.[68] Contemporary Jogye Buddhist temples almost always include a portrait of Kyŏnghŏ mounted in the Patriarch's Hall, a token of his status as the patriarch of modern Korean Buddhism. Kyŏnghŏ was famous for both his enlightenment and unhindered behavior. Anecdotes describe him drinking, toying with a laywoman, and even having sex with a female leper—all actions that supposedly express his enlightenment.[69] These hagiographic stories mostly functioned as a didactic tool for monastic members of later generations. Stories of monks who break sexual taboos represent such transgressions as skillful means (K. pangp'yŏn 方便, Skt. upāya) for a monk to reveal higher truth. It needs to be clearly understood, however, that, although the uninhibited behavior of an enlightened master is glorified among the followers of Korean Sŏn, this Sŏn antinomianism has symbolic and soteriological functions.

Second, the secret wife issue speaks to ambivalent attitudes toward clerical marriage and sexual transgression more generally in the Korean Buddhist tradition, as demonstrated in the lionization of Wŏnhyo, for example. Based on the Mahāyāna logic of double negation, the enlightened master can readily reject the rules for the monastics. Therefore, Wŏnhyo's fathering of Sŏl Ch'ong (薛聰, ca, 660–720) with the widowed Silla princess Yosŏk (瑤石) becomes not an act of violation of Vinaya, but an expression of his internalization of nonduality, which is the ultimate expression of the Mahāyāna ideal because, in a way, Wŏnhyo "reconciled" the logics of transcendence and immanence. In this context, the Order has chosen to remember Wŏnhyo's family life as a fulfillment of his duty as a loyal subject of the emperor, a fulfillment of his filial duties as a human being, or even as a model of harmony between the Royal Way and the Buddhist Way.⁷⁰

Modern Korean Buddhist scholarship has also continued to idolize Wŏnhyo. Although Chinul, Hyujŏng (休靜, 1520–1604), Han Yongun, Kyŏnghŏ, and Sŏngch'ŏl (性徹, 1912–1993) receive some attention, Wŏnhyo is the most frequently researched Buddhist monk in modern scholarship.⁷¹ However, Wŏnhyo's veneration only goes back to the colonial period. Part of the "invented tradition," Wŏnhyo and the T'ong Pulgyo (通佛敎, Interpenetrated Buddhism) narrative around him were advanced by Korean intellectuals as a way to encourage Korean national pride. This began when the prominent historian Ch'oe Namsŏn (崔南善, 1890–1957) glorified Wŏnhyo as a nationalist response to the treatment of Korean Buddhism by Japanese historians like Takahashi Tōru (高橋亨, 1878–1967), who denounced Korean Buddhism as "a mere transplantation of Chinese Buddhism" in his influential 1929 work, *Richō Bukkyō* (李朝佛敎).⁷² According to Eun-su Cho, Rhi Kiyong (李箕永, 1922–1996), the well-respected Korean Buddhist scholar, founded what amounted to "a 'Wŏnhyo religion'" in the 1970s.⁷³ The sacralization of Wŏnhyo uncritically continues today in Korean Buddhist scholarship. Wŏnhyo is an indisputable cultural icon, the archetypal representation and embodiment of today's national pride in Korean Buddhism. Tolerance of Wŏnhyo's violation of the chastity vow may not relate directly to the tolerance of secret wives, but it certainly reflects the Korean Buddhist tradition's rather ambiguous position on sexual transgression.

Third, although the Japanese colonial influence has been blamed for the Korean Buddhist practice of taking a wife, this broad-brush accusation has obscured the roots of the issue. Anticolonialism and anticommunism are the two ideological mainstays of postwar South Korea. As a result, the political frameworks of nationalism versus colonialism have dominated public and scholarly discussions of the Korean Buddhist experience. Furthermore, similar to the Meiji government's intervention in Japanese Buddhism's celibacy debate, South Korea's secular government has interfered in monastic questions since the time of Syngman Rhee's regime. With its close ties to secular power during different periods of the postcolonial era, the Jogye Order took advantage of the discourse of nationalism. Postcolonial Korean Buddhism has imagined only two categories of monks: married monks who collaborated with Japanese-style Buddhism (K. *woesaek Pulgyo* 倭色佛敎), and celibate monks, upholders of the true

Korean Buddhist spirit. In this way, monastic celibacy is undergirded by discourses that favor a complete expulsion of Japanese-style Buddhism, and the secret wife issue is perceived as an extension of Japanese-style Buddhism. These sentiments of anti-Japanese colonialism and puritan rhetoric have long reinforced each other. This puritanical anticolonialism is so ingrained that, instead of making an effort to understand the deeper nature of the problem, the secret wife issue is quickly dismissed as a result of Japanese colonialism or simply the moral laxity of individual monks.[74]

Challenges to the nationalist paradigm have come about slowly as newer scholarship has debunked the myth that married monks were collaborators and unmarried monks were necessarily nationalist.[75] Research has illuminated more complicated pictures of modern Korean Buddhism and reevaluated the roles of clerical marriage and meat eating in modern Korean Buddhism.[76] Evidence suggests that married as well as celibate monks were among the leaders of both the Korean anti-Japanese Buddhist movement and the resistance to the colonial power.[77] These actors operated on the basis of a far more complicated agency. They also constantly negotiated their positions in the rapidly changing political context of the colonial period.[78]

Fourth, the secret wife issue indicates a lack of open discussion on the question of celibacy in modern Korean Buddhism. As Carl Olson points out, celibacy may appear to be an antisocial choice, but embracing celibacy enables a person to construct a new social order, identity, and status.[79] Celibacy is essentially a personal choice, but also one that is social in nature because it encourages camaraderie among monastics who engage in it, thus fostering group identity and an elevated religious status. The Jogye Order's embrace of celibacy reflects its concern for maintaining purity and social authority. And yet the Order has not made much effort to prevent the recurrence of secret wife scandals, which continue to threaten its moral authority. Moreover, while the accused and the accusers have been quick to deny or attack, neither side of any of the scandals in the past fifty years has shown an interest in discussing the complexity of celibacy or the social role of the Jogye Order in Korea's highly secularized, hypercapitalist society.

Fifth, the secret wife issue reveals asymmetrical gender relations that pervade and persist in the Jogye Order as well as in Korean secular society at large. Whether they willingly become secret wives or not, women and their children have had neither voice nor agency in the issue. Even the term "secret wife" itself points to a gendered structure and the patriarchal nature of Buddhist culture. There is, for example, no equivalent term to "secret wife" for the spouses of Jogye Buddhist nuns, who comprise almost half of the monastic population. Buddhist nuns are expected to keep the Vinaya more strictly than monks, and there is no tolerance for nuns if they fail to be celibate in androcentric Korean Buddhist culture. Accusations revolve around monks because they are the ones with the power.

Conclusion

In a sense, the act of becoming a monk in itself constitutes a social transgression. But having a secret wife constitutes a double transgression of another level for a Buddhist monk: a violation of monastic regulations and a deception before fellow monastics and lay followers. While the secret wife issue is an extremely personal matter, I have shown that it is a social, religious, and political one as well. Although this highly controversial practice is intimately tied to Korean Buddhism's experience of modernization and colonization, it has become highly politicized since the postcolonial period. It has also, in the relatively short history of the Jogye Order, constantly undermined the legitimacy of the Order's very foundational principle. Yet the transgression remains an open secret even after decades of scandal. As Taussig suggests, unmasking the transgressions of particular monks does not necessarily reveal undisclosed truths, but rather produces new masks. As monks continue to shroud the secret wife issue, the issue slips further into obscurity as its invisible presence increases. Perhaps the truly transgressive aspect of secretive clerical marriage is not the violation of celibacy, but the secrecy itself.

Notes

1. According to the Jogye Order's official records, it has more than 3,000 branch temples and Buddhist centers with 12,000 ordained monastics. Of the 870 traditional temples, more than 90 percent belong to the Order. See Jogye Order, "Jogye Principles and Organization." The Order's annual budget is 33 billion Korean wŏn ($30 million), and it holds millions more in property. See "Monkey Business: Buddhism in Korea."

2. The episode focused on allegations against Sŏlchŏng, but it also discussed allegations of sexual harassment against another high-profile monk. PD Notebook aired a follow-up on May 29. For the entire series, see "MBC PD Notebook—Kŭn sŭnimkke mutsŭmnida I"; "MBC PD Notebook—Kŭn sŭnimkke mutsŭmnida II."

3. Paek, "Sŏlchŏng Sŭnim ŭi sumŭn ttal" (The Chief Monk's Accusation Is Untrue. He Adopted Her)."

4. The South Korean government's Office of Statistics releases results from the religious census of the country every ten years. According to 2015 statistics, almost half of the population described themselves as having no religion. According to the survey by the government's Office of Statistics, Buddhism is the second most common faith in the country, and according to the survey by Gallup Korea, it is the most common faith. Still, the numbers of South Korean Buddhists are continuously decreasing. Buddhists were 23.2 percent of the population in 1995, 22.8 percent in 2005, and 15.5 percent in 2015. See Statistics Korea, "2015 Demographic Data."

5. Gallup Korea, "Gallup Report on Korean Religions."

6. Kim, "Chogyejong ch'ulgaja chikjŏb ch'aja nasŏnda" (The Jogye Order Recruits Members); Jackson, "Karma Back! Buddhist Ad Campaign Tries to Reverse Falling Numbers."

7. Kim, "Sŏlchŏng sŭnim, ŭnch'ŏja ŭihok poda hakryŏk wijo tŏ nappa" (Ven. Sŏlchŏng's Academic Fraud Is Worse Than His Charge of a Secret Wife)."

8. Taussig, *Defacement*, 5.

9. Taussig, *Defacement*, 7.

10. I am very grateful to Gregory Evon for pointing out the complexity of the translation and for giving me several helpful suggestions.

11. For a detailed case study of priests' wives and children and their lived experience in medieval England, see Janelle Werner, "'Just as the Priests Have Their Wives': Priests and Their Concubines in England, 1375–1549," PhD diss.

12. For examples of the numerous sexual scandals of Thai Buddhist monks, see Ekachai, *Keeping the Faith: Thai Buddhism at the Crossroads*. For sex scandals in North American Buddhist centers, see Coleman, *The New Buddhism: The Western Transformation of an Ancient Tradition*.

13. For a detailed account, see Jaffe, *Neither Monk nor Layman*. Japanese Buddhism required its monks to be celibate for centuries. The marriage of Shinran (親鸞, 1173–1263), the founder of the Jōdo Shinshū sect (浄土真宗), is an exception. For more on Shinran's open marriage, see James Dobbins, *Jōdo Shinshū: Shin Buddhism in Medieval Japan*. Also, for more general questions of celibacy in East Asia and the case of Japanese practice, see Kieschnick, "Celibacy in East Asian Buddhism," 225–40.

14. Sagaster, "The History of Buddhism among the Mongols," 426.

15. Tuladhar-Douglas, *Remaking Buddhism for Medieval Nepal: The Fifteenth-Century Reformation of Newar Buddhism*, 9.

16. Clarke, *Family Matters*, 30.

17. On the issue of Buddhism and sexuality, see Cabezón, *Buddhism, Sexuality, and Gender*; Faure, *The Red Thread: Buddhist Approaches to Sexuality*; Faure, *The Power of Denial: Buddhism, Purity, and Gender*.

18. Nattier, "Sex," 274.
19. Clarke, *Family Matters in Indian Buddhist Monasticisms*.
20. Mahāvaṃsa no. 77: 3–4. Cited from Boucher, *Bodhisattvas of the Forest and the Formation of the Mahayana*, 65.
21. Citing Hirakawa Akira, Clarke points out that "the term sangha carries with it no inherent, implicit, or any other sense of 'celibacy.'" Clarke, *Family Matters*, 214, n. 257.
22. The tradition holds that the Silla monk Chajang (慈藏, 590–658) studied with the Chinese Vinaya master Daoxuan (道宣, 596–667) and introduced Vinaya studies upon his return in 643. For an overview of the Vinaya tradition from the Silla period to the Koryŏ period, see Sem Vermeersch, "Views on Buddhist Precepts and Morality in Late Koryŏ," 38–44. In China, Taiwan, and Korea, Buddhist monastic rules are based on the *Dharmaguptaka Vinaya*, although Japanese Buddhism requires only the bodhisattva precepts. While different Vinaya texts had arrived in China, the *Dharmaguptaka Vinaya* was imposed on all of China in the eighth century. For more about the history of Vinaya in India and China, see Heirman, "Vinaya: From India to China," 167–202.
23. The constitution was first established in 1961 and revised twenty-one times by 2015.
24. See the thirty-fourth article of the "Jogye Order Constitution."
25. For more about the term "tradition," see Hobsbawm and Ranger, *The Invention of Tradition*.
26. Yi, "Pong'amsa kyŏlsa wa kŭ Pulgyosa chŏk ŭmi" (Pong'amsa Association and Its Historical Significances), 112–13.
27. Whereas Wŏnhyo referred to himself as a śramaṇa (K. samun 沙門) in his scholarly writings, he also called himself "Humble Householder" (K. sosŏng kŏsa 小性居士) after his affair with the Princess Yosŏk, according to the *Samguk sagi* and *Samguk yusa*. For more on this, see McBride, "Wŏnhyo," 913–17. I thank an anonymous reviewer for helpful comments on this issue.
28. Kim, "'The Mystery of the Century': Lay Buddhist Monk Villages (Chaegasŭngch'on) near Korea's northernmost Border, 1600s–1960s," 269–305.
29. Sanō Zenrei (佐野前励, 1859–1912), a Japanese Nichiren (日蓮) monk, filed a petition to appeal for Buddhist monks' passage to the capital of Korea in 1895. For more on this, see Robert Buswell, *The Zen Monastic Experience*, 24. For how colonial-period monastics responded to the trauma of Chosŏn's anti-Buddhist paradigm, see Kim, "Buddhism during the Chosŏn Period (1392–1910): A Collective Trauma?" 101–42.
30. Buswell, *The Zen Monastic Experience*, 25.
31. On the criticism of Korean scholarship's tendency to ascribe the married clergy in Korean Buddhism to Japanese rule, see Auerback, "Ch'in-il Pulgyo yŏksahak ŭi chaego: Chosŏn Pulgyodan kwa 1920 nyŏndae Chosŏn esŏ ŭi sŭnggryŏ kyŏlhon e kwanhan nonjaeng" (Rethinking the Historiography of "Ch'in-Il"

Buddhism: The Chōsen Bukkyōdan and the Debate over Clerical Marriage in 1920s Korea), 15–53.

32. For more about Han Yongun, Park, see "A Korean Buddhist Response to Modernity: Manhae Han Yongun's Doctrinal Reinterpretation for His Reformist Thought," 41–60; Kim, "A Study of Han Yong-un's 'On the Reform of Korean Buddhism,'" 64–86.

33. For the English translation, see Vladimir and Owen, trans., *Selected Writings of Han Yong'un*.

34. Auerback, "Japanese Buddhism in an Age of Empire: Mission and Reform in Colonial Korea, 1877–1931," 214–16.

35. In the section titled "The Future of Buddhism Depends on Whether Monks and Nuns Marry," Han writes, "if somebody were to ask me how to revive Buddhism in the future, I would always reply that one of the most important and urgent measures is to abolish the prohibition on marriage among monks and nuns." Advocating for married clergy as "the Mahayana truth of the unobstructed interpenetration," Han invoked the necessity to reform and to secularize Buddhism in the modern climate. He presented four reasons to abolish monastic celibacy: "1. Celibates are not filial; 2. Clerical marriage will help to expand the population rapidly and also allow rapid economic and social progress; 3. It will help proselytization; 4. It follows the law of nature." Tikhonov and Miller, *Selected Writings of Han Yongun*, 106–9.

36. Buswell, *The Zen Monastic Experience*, 27.

37. Postwar scholarship often portrays Han as a national hero of modern Korean Buddhism. He was among the thirty-three representatives of the Korean people who signed the document that declared Korea's independence from Japanese colonial rule in 1919. Studies of him constitute almost 30 percent of the studies of modern Korean monks. In particular, after 2000, the research on Han drastically increased because of its active promotion by several organizations. See Yi, "Il-je ha inmul ŭi saeng'ae wa sasang" (The Life and Thought of Buddhist Figures during the Colonial Period). Unpublished paper presented at the conference "Han'guk kŭnhyŏndae pulgyo sa yŏn'gu ŭi tonghyang kwa kwaje," 43–72.

38. For the details of Paek Yongsŏng's argument, see Kim, "1926 nŏn Pulgyogye ŭi taechŏ sikukron kwa Paek Yongsŏng ŭi kŏnbaeksŏ" (The Dispute over the Buddhist Priests' Marriage and Meat-Eating in 1926 and Paek Yongsŏng's Proposal), 195–221.

39. The whole petition is translated into English. See Auerback, "Japanese Buddhism in an Age of Empire," 298–99.

40. Kim, "The Mystery of Century," 293.

41. Kim, *Hanguk kŭndae Pulgyo ŭi hyŏnsil insik, Hanguk hyŏndae Pulgyosa yŏn'gu* (The Study on Korean Contemporary Buddhist History), 293.

42. Jaffe, *Neither Monk nor Layman*, 243. In the Edo period, outside the Ture Pure Land and the Tōzan (当山派) branch of Shugendō (修験道), the shogunate

banned all sexual relationships for monks and imposed the death penalty for monks who took wives. On this, see Ruppert, "Buddhism and Law in Japan," 286.

43. Kim, "1950 nŏndae Yi Sungman Taet'ong'ryŏng ui Pulgyo chŏnghwa yushi wa Pulgyogye ui chŏngch'i kaeyib" (The "Buddhist Purification" Instructions of the President Yi Sungman and the Political Intervention of the Buddhists in the 1950s), 306-7.

44. For a detailed description of the process of establishing the Jogye Order, see Buswell, *The Zen Monastic Experience*, 30-33. Also, for more details on the contemporary history of Korean Buddhism, see Kim, *Hanguk hyŏndae Pulgyosa yŏn'gu*.

45. See Jogye Order, "Jogye Principles & Organization." The Order also claims that the Chan transmission has remained only in Korea and that Chinje, the current supreme patriarch, is the 79th patriarch in the lineage of Shakyamuni Buddha ("Patriarch of Jogye Order"). While the Order traces its historical roots to Toŭi, Chinul, and T'aego Pou (太古 普愚, 1301-1382), recent scholarship has shown that this lineage is an invented one. Kim Yongt'ae, "Chosŏn hugi kŭndae ŭi chongmyŏng gwa chongjo inshik ŭi yŏksajŏk goch'al: Chogyejong gwa T'aego pŏpt'ong ŭi kyŏlyŏn" (The Name and the Patriarch of the Buddhist Order in the Late Chosŏn and Modern Periods: The Complicated History between the Jogye Order and the T'aego Order), 43-81; Kim, "Chogyejong chongt'ong ŭi yŏksajŏk ihae: Kŭn·hyŏndae chongmyŏng, chongjo, chongji nonŭi rŭl chungshim ŭro" (The History of the Jogye Order: Its Focus on the Discussions of the Name, Patriarch, and Identity), 144-68.

46. In his memoir, Sungsan (崇山, 1927-2004), one of the prominent members of the movement, criticizes the Jogye Order by stating that, in their attempt to forcefully increase the number, the pikusŭng hastily mobilized disqualified monks (K. kŭbjŏsŭng 急造僧) in the early periods of the purification movement and that these groups of incapable monks caused moral corruption in the later periods. Cited from Kim Kwangsik, "Chŏng Kŭm-o ui Pulgyo chŏnghwa ŭndong" (The Buddhist Purification Movement Led by Chŏng Kŭmo), 165.

47. The narratives of modern/contemporary Korean Buddhist history are mostly from the Jogye Order's side. In 2006, the T'aego Order published its own history, in which it claims to be the orthodox Buddhist order in Korea. Upon the Jogye Order's protest, the book was recalled immediately after its publication. See Kim, *T'aegojongsa: Han'guk Pulgyo chŏngt'ong chongdan ŭi yŏksa* (The History of the T'aego Order: The History of the Legitimate Buddhist Order in Korea).

48. "Chogyejong sach'al chongmu kamsa dŭng kanghwa" (The Jogye Order Reinforces Its Inspection of the Administration).

49. Cho, "Chogyejong ch'ongmu haengjŏng chedo koch'al" (Studies on the Administrative System of the Jogye Order).

50. Park, "Ppuri hŭndŭnŭn Pulgyo hyŏndaehwa param" (A Radical Modernization Movement in Buddhism).

51. The plan limits the kyohwasŭng's rights greatly. According to the plan, kyohwasŭng cannot serve any important administrative positions, including as abbots, and they are not allowed to perform major Buddhist ceremonies at a temple.

52. In the Jogye Order, Buddhist chaplains can get married.

53. "Chogyejong chŏnghwa moksori nop'a" (Increasing Demand for the Reformation of the Jogye Order).

54. Chŏng, "Chogyejong ittan sokari Ch'op'ail maji tŭisungsung" (Continuous Scandals of the Jogye Order Cause Internal Chaos before the Buddha's Birthday). During his tenure as chief monk from 1986 to 1994, several lawsuits were filed against Sŏ Ŭi-hyŏn. Sŏ purportedly hired a gang of thugs to attack monks and laypeople who protested his bid for a third term as head monk in 1994, and he was permanently expelled from the Order, only to be reinstated in 2015, sparking public outrage. For more examples of monastic scandals in the 1990s, see Uri Kaplan, "Updating the Vinaya: Formulating Buddhist Monastic Laws and Pure Rules in Contemporary Korea," 252–53.

55. Sŏ, "Tobak ŭnchŏsŭng chingye chŏt kŏron" (The First Attempt to Take a Disciplinary Action against Those Monks Who Have Wives or Gamble).

56. Cho, "Chogyejong kaehyŏk kadak chapnŭnda" (Jogye Order Works on Reformation).

57. Vermeersch, "Views on Buddhist Precepts and Morality in Late Koryŏ," 44.

58. Kaplan, "Updating the Vinaya," 256–62.

59. Kaplan notes that the "Law of the Monastics" focuses on material and financial vices, ignoring sexual and dietary issues. Kaplan, "Updating the Vinaya," 258. Also, on the problems and suggestions for the Jogye Order's Law, see Ch'a Ch'asŏk, "Chogyejong jongbŏp e nat'anan chingye chedo wa yuljang ŭi pigyo goch'al" (Comparing the Disciplinary System between Jogyejong's Law and the Vinaya), 201–6.

60. Jogye Order, "Sŭngryŏ-pŏp." The other three grave offenses are stealing, killing, and lying about one's spiritual attainment.

61. Jogye Order, "Sŭngryŏ-pŏp." The emphasis is mine.

62. Soloves, *Understanding Privacy*, 145.

63. For the idea of public shaming, see Petley, *Media and Public Shaming: Drawing the Boundaries of Disclosure*.

64. According to Yi Nŭnghwa's *Chosŏn Pulgyo t'ongsa* (1918), in the early twentieth century, few monks practiced Sŏn. Yi states that, among the fifty leading monks of his time, only three to four practiced Sŏn, and 80 percent to 90 percent were engaged in doctrinal studies. Song, "Chogyejong chŏnt'ong ŭi ch'angjo wa honjongjŏk kŭndaesŏng: Sŏgu kŭndae Pulgyo waŭi pigyo rŭl chungshim ŭro" (The Invention of the Jogye Order and Hybrid Modernity: In Comparison with the Modern Buddhism in the West), 30. Sim Chaeryong, Kil Hŭisŏng, and Kim Yongt'ae note the historical fallacy of the Order's identification of Sŏn as the traditional form of Korean Buddhism. Shim, "Hanguk Pulgyo nun hoet'ong Pulgyo inga?" (Is Korean

Buddhism Hoet'ong Pulgyo?), 190; Kil, "Hanguk Pulgyo chŏngch'aesŏng ŭi t'amgu: Chogyejong ŭi yŏksa wa sasang ŭl chungshim ŭro" (The Identity of Korean Buddhism: Its Focus on the Jogye Order's History and Thought), 67–92; Kim, "Ton'gashia kŭndae Pulgyo yŏn'gu ŭi t'uksŏng gwa orientalism ŭi t'uyŏng" (The Characteristics of the Study of the Modern Buddhism in East Asia and Its Orientalism), 249–51.

65. For the Vajrayāna's view on sexual desire and its techniques for transmuting, see Powers, "Celibacy in Indian and Tibetan Buddhism," 201–24.

66. For the various transgressions of Bodhidharma, the first Chinese Chan patriarch, in the Edo period Japan, see Faure, "From Bodhidharma to Daruma: The Hidden Life of a Zen Patriarch," 45–71.

67. Faure, *The Read Thread*, 98.

68. On Kyŏnghŏ, see Sørensen, "Mirror of Emptiness: The Life and Times of the Sŏn Master Kyŏnghŏ Sŏngu," 131–56.

69. For details of Kyŏnghŏ's story with the leper woman, see Yun, *Kyŏnghŏ Kŭn Sŭnim: ch'akhan il mani hage kŭdae ka puchŏ ilse* (Great Master Kyŏnghŏ: Do Many Good Deeds, You Are the Buddha), 225–36.

70. Interestingly, all of the paradigmatic elements of Wŏnhyo's life story are found in the life of the Buddha. It is said that Wŏnhyo's mother gave birth to him under a tree. The tree is called "Sara," and this birth takes place in a village called the Buddha's Land (K. *pulji* 佛地). The name of Wŏnhyo's wife, Princess Yosŏk, also invokes Śākyamuni's royal wife, Yasodharā. Wŏnhyo also repeats Śākyamuni's long abandonment of his son. In fact, these narrative elements are not unique to Wŏnhyo, but are commonly found in the biographical narratives in Chinese Buddhist literature such as Yongming Yanshou's (永明延壽, 904–75) Zongjing lu (宗鏡錄, 961), Zanning's (贊寧, 919–1001), Song gaoseng zhuan (宋高僧傳, 988), and Juefan Huihong's (覺範慧洪, 1071–1128) Linjian lu (林間錄, 1107). On this see, Richard D. McBride II, "Pŏmhae's Hagiography of Wŏnhyo from the Late Chosŏn Period," *International Journal of Buddhist Thought & Culture* 20 (February 2013): 59–73. In Korea, Wŏnhyo's story experienced a second life in the modern period when it appeared in Yi Kwangsu's novel, *Wŏnhyo Taesa* [The Great Master Wŏnhyo], first published in a daily newspaper in 1942.

71. For example, with the goal of "globalizing Wŏnhyo's thought," two volumes of the *Complete Works of Wŏnhyo* (five volumes in total) were translated into English and published in 2007 and 2011.

72. Taka hashi, *Richō Bukkyō* (Buddhism in the Chosŏn Dynasty), 12.

73. Cho, "The Uses and Abuses of Wŏnhyo and the 'T'ong Pulgyo' Narrative," 48.

74. For instance, Ch'oi Pyŏnghŏn, one of the leading scholars of Korean Buddhist history, argues that the Jogye Order was considered a pro-Japanese organization that collaborated with the colonial government when it was established in 1941. See Ch'oi, *Hanguk Pulgyosa yŏn'gu immun* (Introduction to Korean Buddhist History), 277–313.

75. Auerback criticizes the old paradigm as a problem of the "presentist" tendency in historiography. Auerback, "Ch'inil Pulgyo," 5. Pori Park also problematizes previous scholarly evaluations that posit a sharp division between nationalists and collaborators and tradition versus modernity. Pori Park, *Trial and Error in Modernist Reforms: Korean Buddhism under Colonial Rule* (Berkeley, CA: Institute of East Asian Studies, 2009). Korean scholarship presents a similar critique. Cho, *Pulgyo wa Pulgyohak* (Buddhism and Buddhist Studies), 229–66; O Kyŏnghu, "Ilche sikminji chŏngch'aek gwa Chosŏn Pulgyo ŭi ilbonhwa e taehan chaegŏmťo (Reexamination of Japanese Colonial Policies and Japanization of Korean Buddhism), 37–57.

76. For a critical review of Korean scholarship's approach to the issue of meat-eating and marriage among Buddhist monks, see Sim, "Kundae Pulgyo ui han jingyong: Gogi mokgi wa Manura kkwechagi" (An Exotic Scene of Modern Buddhism: Eating Meats and Taking Wives), 58–74; Park, "Kŭndae Pulgyo ŭi taech'o shikuk munje e kwanhan yunlijŏk koch'al" (Ethical Dimensions on the Issue of Taking a Wife and Eating Meat in Modern Buddhism), 47–70.

77. Kang, "Haebang hu Pulgyo wa kukka, 1945–1960: Pigu taechŏ kaldŭng ŭl chungshim ŭro'" (Buddhism and the State after the Liberation, 1945–1960: The Struggle between the Celibate Monk and the Married Monk), 88.

78. Auerback, "Ch'inil Pulgyo," 15–53.

79. Olson, "Celibacy and Human Body: An Introduction," 5.

Chapter 7

Monastic Regulations in Contemporary Korea

Uri Kaplan

Introduction

A series of scandals rattled the Korean Buddhist community during the 1990s.[1] News reports of monastic leaders laundering money through the construction of Buddhist statues in 1991[2] and using donated cash to fund a presidential candidate in the 1992 general elections[3] provoked great social outcry. The administrative head of the Jogye Order at the time, Sŏ Ŭihyŏn (徐義玄, 1936–), was eventually banished from the organization in 1994, but he did not leave without a fight. In April of that year, he allegedly hired thugs to violently beat monks and laymen who protested against him in central Seoul's Jogye Temple (曹溪寺), the head temple of the Order. Four years later, in 1998, Jogye Temple resembled a war zone yet again as factional fights erupted surrounding the Order's elections, and videos of barricaded monks combating the riot police were broadcasted across the world. Smaller-scale monastic scandals have continued to surface every once in a while in recent years. In 2012, several monks from Paegyang Monastery (白羊寺) were caught on candid camera spending an evening in a hotel room, drinking, smoking, and playing cards, allegedly gambling with money that was donated to their temple. The incident instigated a flood of videos and media images of corrupt monks, sometimes caricatured as praying to the "flush" and "full-house" bodhisattvas. Another controversial video found its way online in 2013, showing a novice by the name of Chŏkkwang forcefully dragged out of Jogye Temple by other monks after making severe accusations against the current leaders of the Order. In 2014, a couple of monastic embezzlement cases made the news; in October 2015, a large lay demonstration was held in front of Jogye Temple demanding the expulsion of an abbot accused of being secretly married.

Rumors of religious corruption, whether real or imagined, seem to be a common pastime of people throughout the world. Just as tales of Catholic priest-pedophiles ignite the imaginations of Europeans, East Asian folktales, drama, fiction, and official histories often depict Buddhist monks as greedy, decadent, devious, and lascivious.[4] Nonetheless, I believe that, rather than indicating a general degeneration of the monastic community, Buddhist scandals demonstrate that a higher moral purity is still expected from the sangha. In other words, reports of individual monks fighting, playing cards, or having relationships with women would not have provoked public commotion unless Korean monastics were still held and mostly conformed to a higher ascetic ethical ideal.[5] More important, the public condemnation invoked by such incidents sometimes functions as a catalyst for the formation of new Vinaya literature. In Korea, the scandals of the 1990s stimulated an overarching reconstruction of the laws and proceedings regulating the Order, and the 2012 Paegyang Monastery incident motivated the creation of the modern common Jogye Order Pure Rules in the spirit of Baizhang (百丈, 720–814). This contemporary Vinaya manufacturing stands at the center of this chapter.

To be sure, this is certainly not the first time that Buddhist Vinaya regulations were written as a direct response to social criticism. The Indian Vinayas make it clear that the regulations were not given all at once, instead accumulating gradually whenever a stipulation was called for by particular social circumstances. This process is exemplified in the Vinaya rule against handling money that we are told was enacted by the Buddha after the monk Upananda was criticized by bystanders for shopping in the market[6] as well as in the provision forbidding the ordination of famous thieves that was enacted after people were shocked to discover the notorious bandit Aṅgulimāla standing at their doorstep wearing robes and asking for alms.[7] Additionally, at times, exemptions to rules were added to the Vinaya in situations where social culpability did not pose a threat any longer. The Buddha allowed his disciple Kātyāyana, for example, to wear leather shoes while propagating in Avanti, a stony place where such commodities were common enough and were unlikely to provoke reproach.⁸

Other Vinaya regulations were written as precautions against potential future criticism and clashes with society. It has been argued, for instance, that the specific Vinaya rules against sangha consumption of horse and elephant meat were meant to avoid complications with politicians and military men who used them as vehicles, and the stipulation forbidding snake intake was intended to dodge conflict with local *nāga* groups who believed snakes to be sacred.⁹ The Vinaya prohibitions on ordinations of people with scars and other physical deformities as well as the stricter rules established to ensure the sexual purity of nuns could be similarly understood as attempts to establish a favorable image and avoid social suspicion. Pure Rules written in Song and Yuan China reiterated a similar concern, stipulating, for example, that an abbot going into retirement should carry few possessions because "if he has too much luggage, he is likely to be ridiculed or criticized."¹⁰ Paul Numrich further reported that contemporary monastic Theravāda communities in the United States were also inclined to conform their Vinaya rules to the attitudes of their affiliated laity: monastics serving liberal lay communities tended to be more flexible with the Vinaya, and those dependent on more conservative communities tended to strictly adhere to the historical guidelines.¹¹

Hence, Lambert Schmithausen's claim that the Vinaya is primarily concerned with internal harmony and external reputation rather than with morality proper certainly seems to be on target.¹² Yi Charang recently showed that the Vinaya, in fact, makes these goals fairly explicit. The various Indian Vinayas explain their own raison d'être by enlisting the "ten benefits of keeping the precepts" (C. *zhijie shili* 制戒十利), which may be grouped into three general objectives: increasing the joy and comfort of the sangha, contributing to individual practice toward enlightenment, and supporting the sangha's relationship with secular society.¹³ By keeping the precepts, the sangha maintains the trust of the people, which is necessary for both the economic continuity of monasteries and the general spiritual authority of the religion. After all, monastics are the *face* of Buddhism, and the future of Buddhist faith and practice rests to a large extent on the public image of the sangha. Social criticism of monks in contemporary Korea has triggered the re-creation of various laws, organizational structures, and monastic codes, aiming first and foremost to improve the image and reputation of the sangha and ensure the continuity of the Buddhist tradition on the peninsula.

My main aim in this chapter is to illustrate the fascinating ways in which contemporary Buddhist monastics of the Korean Jogye Order negotiate with their accumulated historical disciplinary codes, supplementing, updating, and reformulating them to match the realities of the modern day. It begins with a short discussion of the actual use of the historical Vinayas in Korea, demonstrating that "Admonitions" collections[14] have been the most widely studied Vinaya literature in recent centuries and that, although the *Dharmaguptaka Vinaya* has been partially recited during ordinations and increasingly studied in specialized institutions, it is researched today primarily as an inspiration for the creation of new codes. This research then turns to the current penal system of the Order, which for all practical purposes precedes all other Vinayas in Korea, and examines its recent reconstruction into a more democratic, objectified, transparent, punishment-based mechanism, in imitation of the secular national government administration. Finally, attention is given to the new Pure Rules that have been produced by the Jogye Order in the past several years. Just as early Chinese Pure Rules embodied the Sinification and Confucianization of the Vinaya,[15] these new Korean codes illustrate attempts to Koreanize and modernize the Pure Rules via the codification of contemporary consumerism, technology, and environmental issues as well as local Korean-specific practices. As we shall see, spiritual attainments are hardly taken into consideration in the making of these modern codes. Instead, their primary aim is to improve the social reputation of the sangha.

Practical Vinayas

With approximately 12,000 monks and nuns, two degree-granting universities, several newspapers and TV channels, and close to 3,000 monasteries, including nearly all of the historical mountain complexes, the Jogye Order is by far the most dominant Buddhist organization in Korea. It was established in 1962 by celibate monastics wishing to separate themselves from married Buddhist clerics, whose number increased significantly in the early twentieth century.[16] Its newly founded constitution prescribes a mix of several Vinayas: both the prātimokṣa and the Bodhisattva Precepts are to be taken and upheld by all affiliated monastics, and the "admonitions of the patriarchs and Baizhang's Pure Rules" (C. *Baizhang qinggui* 百丈清規) guide monastic bureaucracies and ritual procedures.[17] In addition to these four bodies of rules, one must take into consideration the Order's constitution and laws as well as the regulations of individual temples, the result being a broad and inclusive Vinayic amalgam that is certainly not without ambivalence and inconsistency. Perhaps most noticeable is its disagreement on meat consumption: the *Dharmaguptaka Vinaya* allows meat in several circumstances, but the Bodhisattva Precepts and the Pure Rules forbid all meat eating,[18] and the Jogye Order's penal laws ignore the subject altogether, thus tacitly allowing meat ingestion to go unpunished. In fact, it has been convincingly argued that taking the Indian precepts during ordinations is simply a symbolic formality in Korea and that what really matters are the Order's newly enacted laws and regulations.[19]

Scholars have long noted that the formal historical canons were often unsatisfactory for understanding the actual practices of Buddhists on the ground; as such, scholars have offered to talk of "ritual canons,"[20] "practical canons,"[21] and "curricular canons"[22] instead as the actual literature that was studied, ritualized, and has regulated monastic lives. The *Dharmaguptaka Vinaya*, which has been used in Chinese ordinations since the third century,[23] has been known in Korea at least since the seventh century, yet the scarcity of references to and commentaries on it between the eighth and twentieth centuries proves that it has not been widely studied on the peninsula.[24] Neither this Vinaya, nor the *Brahmā Net Sūtra*, nor the historical Pure Rules have been included in the traditional monastic curriculum in Korea, which was first used at major monasteries in the seventeenth century and has become the mandatory common program for monastics in the twentieth century.[25] Instead, different texts have been responsible for the actual ethical standards of Korean monastics going back at least four centuries: the historical Vinaya genre of "Admonitions" that has been mostly neglected in scholarship.

Perhaps the most elementary practical Vinaya of contemporary Korean Buddhism is a compilation of three short texts written by Wŏnhyo (617–686), Chinul (知訥, 1158–1210), and Yaun (fifteenth century) titled the *Admonitions to Beginners* (*Ch'obalsim chagyŏngmun* 初發心自警文).[26] The three essays were first put together in 1567 and published as a set at least thirteen times before the twentieth century.[27] In modern times, this collection has become the sole Vinaya text to be memorized by all prospective monastic postulants.[28] The second Admonitions text that has taken the place of the *Dharmaguptaka Vinaya* and the Pure Rules in regulating the actual lives of Korean monastics is another compilation that was first assembled in 1313 by Zhixian Yongzhong in Yuan China, titled the *Admonitions to the Gray-Robed Monks* (C. *Zimen jingxun* 緇門警訓).

This collection was republished in Korea numerous times, had a detailed commentary written to it on the peninsula in the seventeenth century, and became the focus of the first stage of learning in Korean monastic seminaries in the beginning of the twentieth century at least.[29] In fact, until very recent reforms, this was the only Vinaya-related literature studied in modern Korean monastic seminaries.[30] More than half of the essays in the collection deal with monastic conduct and rituals, some of which exhibit direct influence by the Pure Rules.[31] As could be expected, the ethical ideals reflected in these Admonitions compilations correspond more closely to East Asian Confucian models of morality than to the Indian Vinayas, and the focus shifts from the authority of Shakyamuni to the warnings and advice of the Chinese patriarchs. If the formal Vinayas emphasize issues of material possessions, sexuality, and dietary restrictions, these practical Vinayas are more concerned with speaking and behaving in a solemn and dignified manner, studying hard, and maintaining harmonious relationships with others.

Recent years, however, have brought new attitudes. The focus of western Buddhist scholarship on the so-called "early" and "original" Buddhist Tripitaka has been imitated by Japanese, Chinese, and Korean modern Buddhists, who began to doubt their own traditions and to search for authenticity in the Pali and the Sanskrit.[32] Consequently, the first full translation of the Pali Canon into Korean was published in recent years, monastic curriculums were supplemented by classes on Indian Buddhism, and the study of the *Dharmaguptaka Vinaya* has been promoted on a larger scale than ever before. A few small monastic Vinaya Schools (K. *yurwŏn* 律院) specializing in the research of the *Dharmaguptaka Vinaya* operated sporadically throughout the twentieth century, but seven others have been founded in the new millennium (including three run by nuns), and the number of Jogye monastics actually studying the Indian Vinaya increased by ten times during the last ten years (see table 7.1). In 2010, a unified curriculum of two to five years was fixed for these schools, in which readings of the *Dharmaguptaka Vinaya* have been supplemented by the study of the *Brahmā Net Sūtra*, Pure Rules, and the Order's laws as well as research on other Vinaya-related texts (see table 7.2). Still, these institutes only cater to a minute percentage of the sangha. Accordingly, their objective does not lie in encouraging all monastics to abide by these ancient Indian rules, but rather in fostering specialists in the various historical codes who would be able to reconstruct and formulate new laws, regulations, and proceedings in the spirit of the old Vinayas for the development of the Order today. Graduates of these schools often

Table 7.1. Number of students in Korean Vinaya Schools, multiple sources[1]

	1998	2003	2013–4
1. Tʻongdosa Vinaya School (reinstated in 2005)			21
2. Haeinsa Vinaya School (since 1968)	6	9	11
3. Songwangsa Vinaya School (since 1988)		10	3
4. Paegyangsa Vinaya School (since 2006)			4
5. Chŏngamsa Vinaya School (since 2008)			20
6. Pongnyŏngsa Vinaya School (since 1999)		5	16
7. Unmunsa Vinaya School (since 2008)			10
8. Pŏmŏsa Vinaya School (since 2013)			8
9. Tonghwasa Vinaya School (since 2011)			20
10. Pagyesa Vinaya School (since 1997)	5	4	Closed
Sum	11	28	113

[1]Statistics assembled by the author from official documents and Vinaya School personnel.

Table 7.2. The Curriculum of the Vinaya Schools, multiple sources[1]

Course	First Semester	Second Semester
Year 1	—*Dharmaguptaka Vinaya* —General Ethics *Developing novice ordination ceremonies	—*Dharmaguptaka Vinaya* —Mahāyāna Precepts *Developing ordination ceremonies and culinary regulations
Year 2	—*Brahmā Net Sūtra* —Buddhist Ethics *Developing Bodhisattva precept ceremonies and uposathas	—Baizhang's Pure Rules and the new Chogye Order Pure Rules —The Chogye Order Constitution and Laws —Thesis writing
Research 1st year	Research of the various Vinayas of the early Indian sects	Research of the various Vinayas of the early Indian sects
Research 2nd year	Research of Chinese Vinaya-related Buddhist texts	Research of Korean Vinaya-related Buddhist texts, as well as modern ethics.
Research 3rd year	Individual specialized research	Thesis writing

[1]This curriculum can be found on the Chogye Order's website: http://www.buddhism.or.kr/bbs/board.php?bo_table=DN_Content_edu&wr_id=21&DNUX=edu_03_03 (accessed December 15, 2015).

take part in the legislative and judicial activities of the Order, which are discussed next.

Legislating Buddhism

Unlike in Southeast Asia and in China, where the secular government continues to enforce the Vinaya and reportedly arrests monastics who violate its prohibitions,[33] the national authorities in Japan and Korea have ceased their historical supervision of monastic affairs. Thus, the Jogye Order had to formulate its own autonomous governing administration and proceedings from its very beginning. Enacted in 1962, its first laws provided the Supreme Patriarch of the Order (K. *chongjŏng* 宗正) with almost absolute authority over abbot appointments and financial issues, but multiple revisions in subsequent years gradually stripped this position of its powers.[34] It was the scandals of the early 1990s that triggered the entire reconstruction of the Order's headquarters and the development of semi-independent legislative, administrative, judicial, and censorial bodies, reflecting the transformation into democracy that took place in the national government just a few years earlier. Thirty-four of the current fifty comprehensive laws of the Order were written in 1994 or afterward, ensuring legal objectification of monastic bureaucratic appointments, transparency in finance, and rationalized equality in ranks and positions to avoid the reoccurrence of leadership corruption that damaged both the internal harmony and the external reputation of the sangha. Not only does this new body of laws precede all earlier Vinayas in regulating the actual lives of Jogye monastics today, but it also symbolizes a significant shift from local lineage-focused communities into a standardized national Buddhist Order.

This transformation of the Jogye Order into a modern democratic organization can be illustrated by examining its new penal system. As is well known, the *Dharmaguptaka prātimokṣa* is composed of 250 rules for monks and 348 for nuns, categorized according to eight types of expiation procedures.[35] In comparison, the Jogye Order's Law of the Monastics (K. *Sŭngnyŏbŏp* 僧侶法) lists a total of seventy-two offenses divided into seven categories of punishments, ranging from permanent expulsion from the Order to suspensions, demotions, and official reproaches (for details, see table 7.3).[36] Unlike the Indian Vinayas, this new code does not distinguish between monks and nuns and mostly ignores sexual and dietary issues.

Table 7.3. The penal system of the Chogye Order in comparison to the *Dharmaguptaka Vinaya*

Chogye Order Punishment	Chogye Order	Dharmaguptaka Vinaya
Permanent Expulsion	1. Disrespectful action toward patriarchs 2. Forming factions 3. Breaking the four pārājika rules 4. Not abiding by Chogye procedures 5. Violence toward outsiders 6. Prior suspension without repentance 7. Simultaneous registry in another order 8. Runaway	Only the four pārājika defeats of sex, theft, killing, and false claims of spiritual attainment require expulsion.
Suspension for More Than Five Years	Twenty-seven offenses listed: — Eleven of which are related to handling money (using temple money for personal shopping or travel without approval, losing or damaging temple money or valuables, gambling temple money, habitually begging for alms, receiving money from monastic students, etc.) — Four are related to disobedience to authority (violent language to elders, arrogance to teachers, rejecting the authority of abbots and central Chogye organs) — Two involve secular law (imprisoned by secular authorities or registered in an illegal group) — Two involve prior offenses (did not reform after prior punishment, three-time offender)	There is no such punishment in the Indian Vinayas, but perhaps the closest category is the thirteen Sanghadisesa rules, which necessitate separate habitation for the length of time the offense has been concealed, followed by possible return to the sangha after repentance in front of twenty monastics. Only a few of the Chogye rules here could be viewed as related to Sanghadisesa stipulations, especially those regarding rejection of authority. Most of the other Chogye stipulations here either do not have a counterpart in the Vinaya or correspond to far less grave Vinaya categories. (Note that five of the thirteen Sanghadisesa are sex related, a matter that is ignored in the Chogye law.)

continued on next page

Table 7.3. Continued.

Chogye Order Punishment	Chogye Order	Dharmaguptaka Vinaya
	— The rest are miscellaneous offenses such as going to public entertainment places, drunkenness, establishing a private temple, and forging monastic documents	
Suspension for Three to Five Years	Fourteen offenses listed: — Nine are related to money and property (cheating laity for money, owning a private hermitage, buying and wearing secular clothes, etc.) — The rest are miscellaneous offenses such as abandoning one's temple position, intentionally obstructing religious affairs, second-time offenders, etc.	Same as above.
Suspension for One to Three Years	Eight miscellaneous offenses such as not shaving one's head, staying too long in secular habitation, spreading rumors about other monastics, damaging the harmony of the sangha, receiving punishment for the third time, etc.	Same as above.
Demotion in Rank	Four offenses (immoral behavior, receiving precepts without proper qualifications, accepting apprentices without proper qualifications, neglecting teacher responsibilities).	No corresponding punishment in the Vinaya.

Dismissal from Position	Seven offenses (illegal use of funding and temple property, damaging cultural assets (even accidently), not conforming to the Order's instructions, using personal connection to receive position, refusal to disperse medicine, etc.).	Same as above.
Official Reproach	Four offenses (tardiness in following the Order's instructions, unreasonably misunderstanding instructions, unintentionally breaking the Order's laws, inadequate documentation).	Same as above.

†Table partially adapted from Ch'a Ch'a-sŏk, "Chogyejong chongbŏp e nat'anan chinggye chedo wa yulchang ŭi pigyo koch'al" [Comparison of the Chogye Order's penal law system and the Vinaya], *Sŏnmunhwa yŏngu* 13 (2012): 201–26.

It focuses on material and financial vice, again in response to the public criticisms voiced in the second half of the twentieth century. More significantly, in imitation of the contemporary secular legal system, these new monastic rules stipulate the distribution of objectified punishments rather than attempt to rehabilitate offenders via atonement and repentance, which stand at the core of the Indian Vinayas.[37] Several Korean lay professors and monastic Vinaya School teachers recently suggested replacing this punishment-centered system with specialized Repentance Halls (K. *ch'amhoewŏn* 懺悔院) in head parish temples where offenders would be able to atone during suspensions, but no such developments have occurred to date.[38] If we recall that only the four *pārājika* defeats of killing, theft, sex, and false claims of spiritual attainment demand expulsion in the Indian Vinayas (and still, this is only eviction from the local community and is often impermanent),[39] the severity of the Jogye system seems ever more apparent. Seven additional offenses on top of the *pārājikas* entail the grave punishment of permanent expulsion (K. *myŏlbin* 滅擯) from the Order according to the law; forty-nine regulations—some as simple as neglecting to shave one's head—necessitate suspension from the sangha; and even unintentional damage to temple property requires punishment of abbots and other position holders.

To evaluate offenders and distribute punishments in an impartial and rational way, the Jogye Order recently established its very own central monastic court of law called the Precepts-Court (K. *Hogyewŏn* 護戒院). The court began its activity gradually in the 1980s, and its first major ruling took place following the Jogye Temple havoc of 1994. As many as 143 monastics received punishments at the time, and the chief administrative director of the Order was expelled along with twenty other leading monks.[40] I have been told by the court personnel that more than 1,000 cases have been brought to justice since, most of these apparently regarding minor bureaucratic matters. Stepping away from the Indian Vinayic system of repentance in front of members of the local community, the Precept-Court Law has been revised no fewer than twenty-three times to ensure that the proceedings and rulings tallied with the disinterested judicial attitudes of the modern world. Trials take place in front of seven central monastic judges, who are elected by the legislative organ (K. *Chungang chonghoe* 中央宗會) for four-year terms. At least twenty-five years in the sangha and previous study in Vinaya Schools or participation in the general assembly are required of all prospective judges.[41] Defenders are entitled to lawyers and may appeal after the first ruling for a retrial in front of nine judges. Once a year, during Buddha's birthday celebrations, amnesty is sometimes given to those who have shown remorse.⁴²

Current Jogye Vinaya manufacturing involves ambivalent attempts to both modernize and democratize the system while at the same time resuscitating old Indian traditions. Buddhist scholarship often mentions, for instance, the Indian Vinaya stipulation for a twice-monthly *uposatha* (K. *p'osal* 布薩) ritual, in which the precepts are chanted and memorized to ensure the ethical "quality control" of the community.⁴³ It is unclear, however, whether such rituals ever played a significant role in East Asian monasticism. Zongze's (宗賾, died c. 1107) twelfth-century Pure Rules document, for one, makes no mention of such a ceremony, and it was rarely if ever performed in twentieth-century Korea.⁴⁴ Nonetheless, with the increased study of the Indian Vinayas (as well as the increase of English language scholarship on Buddhism), leading Jogye monastics recently began to advocate for a re-creation of this ritual. In 2007, the first official Korean vernacular liturgy for the rite was published by the Order, and by 2008 the ceremony was legislated as an obligatory service to be performed in all twenty-five head parish temples several times a year and attended at least twice a year by every affiliated monastic.⁴⁵ Only elders who have spent at least forty years in the Order and monastics studying or teaching abroad are excused. The law is unclear regarding the actual precepts to be chanted in these rites, mentioning the *prātimokṣa*, the Bodhisattva precepts, the novice precepts, and the Pure Rules as possible candidates. It seems, however, that in most cases it is the short list of the ten major Bodhisattva precepts that is chosen.

Modern Pure Rules

The 2012 Paegyang Monastery scandal caused great shame and concern for the monastic community. In subsequent Jogye Order assemblies and seminars, speakers often noted the need to remedy such monastic ethical laxity either by more extensive study of the ancient Vinayas or through their creative adaptation for contemporary times. The abbot of a famous temple in the south of the peninsula, for example, argued in a recent Jogyesa colloquium that the Order must create modern Vinayas because "the world changes and if Buddhism will not change with it—it will demise."⁴⁶ His respondent, the head of a major Vinaya School by the name of Tŏngmun, reminded the audience that the Buddha explicitly instructed Ananda in the *Mahaparinibbana Sutta* that only minor rules may be abolished and the Order must be cautious not to overly deviate from the ancient codes. Debates regarding which rules were the "minor" ones and to what extent it would be legitimate to alter the Vinaya have occupied monastics from the time of the early Buddhist councils to the modern day. Charles Prebish reported that a parallel debate took place in the 1987 Conference on World Buddhism in North America, where two prominent South Asian monks expressed opposing opinions regarding the legitimacy of revising the canonical Vinaya.[47] Numrich quoted the Dalai Lama's argument that, although exceptions can be made, the basic Vinaya rules must not be changed.[48]

Shizuka Sasaki offered a way out of this conundrum. He explained that the Vinaya incorporates both precepts (Skt. *sila*, K. *kye* 戒) and monastic procedures (Skt. *vinaya*, K. *yul* 律), and whereas ritual proceedings are linked to society and may be altered according to circumstances, the precepts regulate individual spiritual practice, so changing societies should not have any effect on them.[49] They should thus remain intact. To be sure, this sort of division is not always clear-cut, and it is possible to argue that, at least to some extent, precepts serve to regulate harmonious societies and rituals to foster individual attainments. Nevertheless, it seems that the Pure Rules literature of Song and Yuan China may serve as an example for formulating new Vinaya proceedings without making major changes to the *prātimokṣa*. These Chinese codes do not contain long discussions of the precepts per se and focus mainly on monastic schedules, rituals, and bureaucratic positions. Scholars agree that the Pure Rules were probably meant to be supplements rather than substitutions for the Indian Vinaya, yet they admit that the later Chan tradition understood them as replacements for the earlier rules.[50] In fact, Korean monastics today often view the historical formation of the Chinese Pure Rules as proof of the legitimacy of deviation from the Indian Vinayas and as sanction for the creation of their own new sets of regulations.[51]

Evidence suggests that individual monastic communities in Korea have been creating localized codes, often explicitly calling them Pure Rules, at least since the eleventh century.[52] In modern times, a 1928 survey discovered that eighteen of the seventy-three Sŏn Halls (K. *sŏnppang* 선방 or *sŏnwŏn* 선원) operating at the time legislated their own short Pure Rules, focusing on monastic positions, schedules, and ritual proceedings, but also containing stipulations of precept-related prohibitions and punishments. In some locations, for example, fighting or missing the morning rituals required expulsion from the community; in others, bathing on the wrong day or asking questions during lectures was punishable by long prostration sessions.[53] These penalties are certainly stricter than the ones found in the *Dharmaguptaka Vinaya*. In the twenty-first century, approximately twenty of the larger Sŏn Halls and monastic seminaries impose their own Pure Rules. Most are composed of provisions regarding schedules and positions, new objective criteria for admissions and remunerations, and short lists of behavioral rules and punishments. Sŏn Halls today frequently require expulsion of those drinking or smoking, watching TV, or walking beyond the main gate of the temple during retreats.[54] Seminary Pure Rules tend to reflect the contents of the various Admonitions collections and prohibit behaviors such as running, walking hand in hand, shouting, laughing, singing, putting hands in pockets, and lateness. Their penalties range from expulsions to suspensions, prostrations, and even small monetary fines.[55]

As part of the recent inclination to standardize and centralize the Order's system of laws, punishments, ranks, curriculums, rituals, and so forth, a national Sŏn Hall Elders Committee (K. *Sŏnwŏn sujwahoe* 禪院首座會) was assembled in the early 2000s and began to work toward the first Korean unified Sŏn Halls Pure Rules (K. *Sŏnwŏn chŏnggyu* 禪院清規). A rather long 200-page document was finally published by the Jogye Order on this topic in 2010.[56] It begins by explaining that, just as the Chinese Pure Rules "replaced" the Indian texts to adapt to Chinese cultural circumstances, another millennium has passed, and it is time for a new update to the Vinaya. The following ten chapters of the work (see details in table 7.4) exhibit both the modernization and the Koreanization of the Pure Rules. Codification of current monastic tourist programs,[57] technology use, Sŏn psychology sessions, and ecological behavior accompanies explicit endorsement of the Korean Kanhwa Sŏn (看話禪) retreat system as the only legitimized method of meditation. It also provides Korean vernacular renditions for part of the liturgy, which until then had remained in Chinese.

Still, this new code contains numerous allusions to and quotations from the ancient Pure Rules. A substantial part of the work deals with the monastic bureaucracy, listing no fewer than forty-four different administrative positions. Most are taken directly out of the Chinese codes, but some, such as the Monastic Publicist (K. *sahoe* 社會) in charge of representing the temple in its communications with the outside world, are completely original. It also reiterates the Chinese Pure Rules in detailing the procedures of eight kinds of formal tea ceremonies and in encouraging a return to large-scale monastic farming. However, the text diverges from actual practice in contemporary Korean Sŏn Halls to such an extent that at times it is read more as a history or a mythology than a code that is actually expected to be applied in full. Formal communal tea ceremonies, for one thing, are not very common in Korean temples today, and many of the monastics in fact prefer to drink coffee;[58] further, as the absolute majority of Sŏn meditation halls are rather small and house fewer than ten meditators, forty-four administrative positions are certainly superfluous. For this reason as well as for its sheer length, these Pure Rules have not been able to make much impact on contemporary Sŏn meditation halls to date. Their contents, however, are noteworthy for demonstrating the constant negotiations between reform and revival, modernization and traditionalism that seem to surround much of the Jogye Order's contemporary undertakings (see table 7.4).

In 2012, two years after the publication of the unified Sŏn meditation hall Pure Rules and only a few months after the Paegyang Monastery scandal, the Jogye administration came to the conclusion that the most

Table 7.4. The new 2010 Chogye Order Chan Hall Pure Rules, multiple sources

Chapter 1: General Summary (the uniqueness of Korean Buddhism, the objectives for this work)	Chapter 6: Retreats and Practice (schedules, etiquette, and rituals during meditation retreats)
Chapter 2: The Chogye Order (short history of Korean Buddhism)	Chapter 7: Communal Work (farming, social welfare, and propagation responsibilities)
Chapter 3: The Vinayas of the Chogye Order (the various Vinayas in Korean history)	Chapter 8: Yearly Events and Tea Ceremonies (Buddhist and national holiday proceedings and tea ceremonies)
Chapter 4: The Chogye Order's Sangha Ranks and Education System (explaining the new Chogye education system)	Chapter 9: Economy and Welfare (clothing, food, housing, property, money, and general behavioral rules)
Chapter 5: Chan Hall Structures (different types of Chan Halls and administrative positions)	Chapter 10: Death Rites (funeral and memorial proceedings)

elementary problem was that the average monastic simply did not know the Vinayas well enough. The Indian codes, the Chinese Pure Rules, the Order's laws, and the new Pure Rules were all long, complicated, and often irrelevant to current conditions. Short, succinct, standardized new guidelines that could be widely disseminated and easily studied were needed instead. A committee of ten respected elders led by Sŏru, a long-time meditator and contributor to seminary textbooks, was formed to formulate new Pure Rules for the entire sangha of the Order (rather than only for the Sŏn meditation halls). The first draft was ready in 2013 and subsequently revised in several Jogye colloquiums. The final version of the Pure Rules for the Sangha (K. sŭngga chŏnggyu 僧伽清規) was completed in 2015, printed in several thousand nicely designed booklets, and disseminated to all Jogye-affiliated temples and hermitages.[59] Its introduction reveals that this document was written as a response to contemporary monastic disgraces in an attempt to regain the trust of society. It reads:

> The sangha is a community that embodies wisdom and compassion. Since the time of the Buddha, the sangha practiced the Dharma and the Vinaya, maintained a religious community, and prospered. But as the will to uphold the Vinaya has weakened recently, Korean Buddhism today is facing various difficulties. The firm conviction and motivation to practice is lost day by day, and the virtuous tradition of lowering desire and being content (K. *soyok chijok* 小慾知足) is becoming vaguer. Moral laxity brought by secularism and lack of concern for social justice causes the loss of respect and trust from our neighbors and society. . . . For that reason, we must succeed to the spirit of the Buddha, bodhisattvas, and patriarchs, create Pure Rules that satisfy the social values and common sense of today, and serve as models for fostering the faith of the laity and raising the trust of society [in Buddhism].

This new code is divided into two short sections. The first is further subdivided into forty stipulations encouraging general attitudes of sincere Buddhist practice, social justice, peace, material sharing, and propagation. The second part is composed of seventy-seven specific regulations regarding food, habitation, clothing, possessions, rituals, and monastic etiquette. Instead of the list of monastery positions commonly included in Pure Rules texts, this new centralized code expounds on the bureaucracy of the

Order as a whole. Regulations take the form of both recommendations and prohibitions but do not specify punishments—an issue that provoked some degree of internal controversy. While some monastics believe that the Pure Rules should maintain their authority by consensus rather than legalization, others think they must be made into law and perhaps even enforced by the secular government.[60] Overall, this new Pure Rules manuscript does not attempt a comprehensive structuring and disciplining of the sangha; rather, it develops a concentrated treatment of the burning Vinaya issues of the day. It is mainly concerned with regulating monastic consumerism and technology and fostering simplicity, communal spirit, and modern, environmental-friendly consciousness among the sangha. In the following, I present some of its central agendas.

Cars, Cell Phones, Recycling, and the Stock Market

Driving has become a contested issue in modern Buddhist monastic communities worldwide. The Indian Vinaya rule against monks riding in carts was supplemented by an exception allowing the old, weakening Pilinda to ride in a wagon.[61] This episode could be interpreted in a narrow way, meaning that riding in vehicles is not allowed unless one is a respected elder or has illnesses that forbid one from walking, or in a more flexible manner, allowing vehicle transportation unless it appears lazy or extravagant. Most sanghas today seem to adhere to the more flexible interpretation, at times arguing that driving is necessary to propagate the religion.[62] Thus, the issue has mainly shifted from the action of driving itself to the kind of vehicles ridden. There have been reports of public criticism of monks driving overly luxurious cars in Japan and in Sri Lanka,[63] and I have personally witnessed laypeople surveying the parking lot at a major Chinese monastery and shaking their heads in disapproval.

In Korea, although most individual seminaries and Sŏn meditation hall regulations strictly prohibit student novices and meditators from using personal cars, it is common to see other monastic bureaucrats driving. In 2010, the unified Sŏn meditation hall Pure Rules attempted to standardize monastic auto usage by determining that novices were not allowed to own cars and clarifying that vehicles should be registered to the temple rather than to individuals and used for religious purposes only. More important, no foreign or luxurious brands were allowed in order to avoid social reproach. The earlier draft of the Pure Rules for the Sangha took it perhaps a step too far in stipulating car use according to rank: novices were not allowed to drive, fifth-rank monastics could only drive communal temple cars, those of the fourth rank could drive cars with an engine smaller than 1500cc, the third monastic rank could operate vehicles with an engine up to 2000cc, and the second and first ranks were authorized to use cars with up to 3000cc engines.[64] This hierarchy, however, has been disputed, and the final 2015 version of the Pure Rules has left us with a more modest and somewhat abstract exhortation for the use of frugal, simple cars according to the social standards of the day.

Similar general encouragement to live more prudent and simple lives seems to be the core message of these new, unified Pure Rules. The text cautions against wearing expensive hiking boots, owning too many undergarments, eating at lavish restaurants, drinking expensive teas, participating in leisure sports, traveling abroad for nonreligious purposes, and holding extravagant personal celebrations of birthdays, funerals, and memorials. Rules are normally made according to transgressions, and it is likely that this specific list was meant to remedy particular issues that have provoked reproach of the monastic community. Modern technological apparatuses such as TVs and cell phones are usually prohibited in seminaries and during Sŏn retreats, but, as they are ubiquitous among all strata of society and therefore are unlikely to provoke rebuke, they are mostly ignored by the new Pure Rules. In fact, cell phone apps are increasingly being applied by monastics for Buddhist propagation in Korea. Nevertheless, the new text does demand that all video/audio equipment at temples be communally owned and admonishes against aimless internet gaming. In addition, registry in, association with, and support or critique of any secular political party is forbidden, yet backing the peace movement between the two Koreas is encouraged, and so is engagement in nonviolent struggles against all forms of social injustice. The unified Sŏn Pure Rules also encourages monastics to participate in anti-abortion and anti–capital punishment movements.

Possibly the most original contribution to the Vinaya made by the new Pure Rules is the codification of contemporary ecological behaviors. Both of the new unified texts emphasize the importance of recycling in monasteries. The Sŏn Halls' Pure Rules further prohibit the application of chemical fertilizers in farming, the use of sprays, and the burning of plastic. They also admonish monastics to dispose of organic garbage by compost, to plant trees, to moderate refrigerator thermostats and lower air conditioner usage in summers, and, when possible, to apply a direct-exchange market of farming goods between temples. Finally, both new texts encourage monastics to donate blood and sign up as postmortem organ donors. Without diminishing these admirable endeavors of the contemporary sangha, it must be noted that these rules demonstrate attempts to regain moral authority through participating in the secular ethical agendas of today rather than by appealing to traditional Buddhist ascetic practices.

Finally, a substantial portion of the new Pure Rules codifies contemporary monetary and property-related matters. Gregory Schopen has shown that the *prātimokṣa* rule against handling gold and silver was supplemented by numerous exceptions, suggesting that ancient Indian monastics not only retained personal wealth for purchasing medicine and paying taxes, but also made loans and charged interest, inherited money, and made donations.[65] Unlike some contemporary Southeast Asian and Taiwanese communities that make use of lay attendants as intermediators substituting monastics in monetary dealings,[66] Korean monks and nuns continue to use their personal bank accounts after ordination. The new Pure Rules acknowledge that the sangha is increasingly involved with welfare and propagation initiatives outside the monasteries proper, and so it must make use of money. However, it attempts to make sure that this monastic cash is used in a moderate, non-ostentatious manner.

First, the codes specify that bank accounts should all be registered under the Buddhist names of monastics, probably to monitor possible corruption and to ensure the smooth transition of all assets to the Order after death. Furthermore, personal monetary transactions with visiting laity are forbidden, as well as personal investment for gain in the stock market or in real estate. In fact, the new Pure Rules caution against all private ownership of houses and apartments, and monastics are encouraged to stay overnight as little as possible outside the communal temples of the Order to avoid provoking suspicion. The document also exhorts monastics to donate their personal money to the Order or to welfare agendas every month. Instead of specifying all legitimate and illegitimate uses of money, the document offers three considerations that a monastic should keep in mind before a purchase is made: whether it is needed for religious practice and propagation rather than for individual comfort, whether it could be used communally rather than individually, and whether it will appear ethical to society at large. Even if the historical Vinayas allow it, the text clarifies that monastics should refrain from any possession that contemporary society would be likely to criticize.

Monastic Regulations in Contemporary Korea | 201

The Reputation of the Sangha

A little over a decade ago, a Jogye Order monk courageously published an uncomfortable personal story in a Korean journal. He recounted a time when he was traveling south from Seoul to visit his teacher in a remote mountain monastery. He made a lunch stop at a highway rest area, and, as there was not much of a culinary selection at the place, he ordered a dish that contained some fish. When he sat down to eat, he noticed a ten-year-old boy staring at him. With wide eyes, the boy asked his mother why the monk was eating meat. The monk remembered feeling so utterly ashamed that he quickly left and resolved to repent by eating only raw herbs for the next two years, yet the gaze of the little boy continued to haunt him. Even young children in Korea expect Buddhist monastics to behave in certain ways, he exclaimed, and thus the sangha must strive to live up to this social ideal.[67]

Maintaining a favorable social reputation has played a major role in the creation of monastic regulations throughout history, and it has certainly been a central objective in the recent Vinaya debates of the Jogye Order. Increased study in Vinaya Schools in Korea inspired the revival of ancient rites such as the uposatha repentance. It also informed the creation of new Vinaya literature. The contemporary Jogye constitution and laws reformulate the Indian prātimokṣa into a modern, objectified, judicial monastic penal system in line with the democratic structures of today, and the new unified Pure Rules update the ancient regulations with modern consumerist, technological, and environmental agendas. Although the *Dharmaguptaka* precepts are still formally taken during ordinations, the Admonitions of the patriarchs are learned by all novice monastics, and it is the Jogye laws that guide monastic procedures and retributions. In addition, the Order is currently attempting to popularize the 2015 Pure Rules for the Sangha as the new universal ethical standard, though it may still be too early to determine its success. Overall, I hope I was able to illustrate the manner in which Korean monastics today formulate their ethical codes in continuous conversation with both their historical traditions and the contemporary secular world, imitating and reacting to its values and criticisms.

One final story must be told before this chapter is concluded. As was mentioned at the beginning of this chapter, Sŏ Ŭihyŏn, the former chief administrative director of the Jogye Order, was banished after the mayhem of 1994. In 2015, a full twenty-one years later, he was allowed to return to the sangha. He reportedly appeared in front of the Precepts-Court and repented profusely with tears in his eyes. The judges considered how he had continued to live as a monk outside the organization for the duration of his exile and that he was now more than eighty years old. They decided to let him end his life as a Jogye monk.[68] Needless to say, this decision provoked some controversy, but I think it demonstrates that, regardless of the increasing legalization and objectification of the Order, simple repentance and compassion still play a role in the modern system. Korean monastics generally do not regard any of their multiple Vinayas as ultimate truths to be followed indiscriminately, but rather as skillful means to be reconsidered and updated according to changing conditions. Thus, the current Jogye disciplinary system continually balances itself between modern, centralized, objectified standardization and more flexible considerations of subjective intentions and personal compunction.

Notes

1. This chapter is an adapted version of Uri Kaplan, "Updating the Vinaya: Formulating Buddhist Monastic Laws and Pure Rules in Contemporary Korea," *Contemporary Buddhism* 17, no. 2 (2016): 252–74. Reproduced with permission.

2. Kim Sunsŏk, "1994 nyŏn Taehan Pulgyo Chogyejong kaehyŏk chongdan ŭi sŏngnip kwa ŭiŭi" (The Formation and Significance of the 1994 Reformed Jogye Order), 327–59.

3. Sorensen, "Buddhism and Secular Power in Twentieth-Century Korea."

4. Han, *Korean Folk & Fairy Tales*, 158–60; Kieschnick, *The Eminent Monk: Buddhist Ideals in Medieval Chinese Hagiography*, 19–21; Vermeersch, "Views on Buddhist Precepts and Morality in Late Koryŏ," 35–65.

5. By comparison, in Japan, Buddhist priests drinking and playing games is common enough not to instigate any public outrage.

6. Chiu, "Rethinking the Precept of Not Taking Money in Contemporary Taiwanese and Mainland Chinese Buddhist Nunneries," 9–56.

7. Yi, "Yulchang ŭl t'ongae pon sŭngdan kwa hyŏndae sahoe ŭi chohwa" (The Monastic Order Seen through the Vinaya and Its Agreement with Contemporary Society).

8. Chahyŏn, "Yul ŭi kaep'yŏn kanŭngsŏng kwa sŭnggabŏp ŭi tangwisŏng kŏmt'o" (Examination of the Possibility of Reforming the Vinaya and of the Properness of the Sangha Law), 375–415. This *Dharmaguptaka Vinaya* episode is found in T1428.22.0845b28-c02.

9. Chahyŏn, "Yul ŭi kaep'yŏn kanŭngsŏng kwa sŭnggabŏp ŭi tangwisŏng kŏmt'o."

10. Yifa, *The Origins of Buddhist Monastic Codes in China*, 219.

11. Numrich, "Old Wisdom in the New World: Americanization in Two Immigrant Theravada Buddhist Temples," 53–54.

12. Prebish, "Varying the Vinaya: Creative Responses to Modernity," 60.

13. Yi, "Yulchang ŭi kŭnbon inyŏm e ipkakhan Chogyejong chŏnggyu chejŏng ŭi pangyang: Chegyesimni nŭl chungsimŭro" (The Creation of Jogye Order Pure Rules Based on the Fundamental Principles of the Vinaya with Focus on the "Ten Benefits of Keeping the Precepts"), 9–42. The list of ten benefits is found in *Sifen lu* (Dharamguptaka Vinaya), T22.1428 570c3-7, and is as follows: 1. Cohesion for the sangha (*she qu yu seng* 攝取於僧); 2. Joy for the sangha (*ling seng huan xi* 令僧歡喜); 3. Comfort for the sangha (*ling seng an le* 令僧安樂); 4. Fostering faith among those who do not have it (*wei xin ling xin* 未信令信); 5. Raising faith among those who have it (*yixin ling zeng zhang* 已信令增長); 6. Re-tuning those who are out of tune with the community (*nan diao zhe diao shun* 難調者調順); 7. Returning to peace through repentance (*can kui zhe an le* 慚愧者安樂); 8. Cutting off present defilements (*duan xian zai you lou* 斷現在有漏); 9. Cutting off future defilements (*duan wei lai you lou* 斷未來有漏), 10. Ensuring the future continuity of the correct dharma (*zheng fa de jiu zhu* 正法得久住). Yi uses commentaries to argue that numbers four and five deal specifically with fostering a harmonious relationship between the sangha and secular society.

14. I am referring here to texts usually titled "Admonitions" using the characters *kyŏng* 警, *kyŏnghun* 警訓, *kyŏngmun* 警文, or *kyŏngch'aek* 警策. For a more detailed analysis of this little-discussed genre, see Kaplan, *Monastic Education in Korea: Teaching Monks about Buddhism in the Modern Age*.

15. Yifa, *The Origins of Buddhist Monastic Codes*, 74–87.

16. Mun, *Purification Buddhist Movement 1954–1970*.

17. Taehan Pulgyo Chogyejong (The Korean Jogye Order), Chonghŏn (Order Constitution), 1962. Note that Baizhang's Pure Rules is not extant, and it is unclear whether it ever existed at all. When Koreans refer to Baizhang's Pure Rules, they are likely to be talking about another text, the Chixiu Baizhang qinggui, which was written in the fourteenth century, 500 years after the death of Baizhang.

18. Yifa, *The Origins of Buddhist Monastic Codes*, 115, 168.

19. Ch'a, "Chogyejong chongbŏp e nat'anan chinggye chedo wa yulchang ŭi pigyo koch'al" (Comparison of the Jogye Order's Penal Law System and the Vinaya), 201–26; Wŏnyŏng, "Yulchang kwa Chogyejongbŏp ŭi ihae" (Understanding the Vinaya and the Jogye Order Laws), 227–67. Note that Georges Dreyfus similarly argued that monasticism in Tibet is mostly organized according to monastic constitutions rather than the formal Vinaya: Dreyfus, *The Sound of Two Hands Clapping: The Education of a Tibetan Buddhist Monk*, 114. Interestingly, Richard Jaffe argued that in Japan, where even the prohibitions on marriage and alcohol consumption are not commonly observed by Buddhist clerics, the Indian Vinaya still holds great significance as an ideal to be reflected on and contemplated. See

Jaffe, *Neither Monk nor Layman: Clerical Marriage in Modern Japanese Buddhism*, 240–41.

20. Collins, "On the Very Idea of the Pali Canon," 89–126.

21. Blackburn, "Looking for the Vinaya: Monastic Discipline in the Practical Canons of the Theravada," 281–311.

22. McDaniel, "Gathering Leaves and Lifting Words: Histories of Buddhist Monastic Education in Laos and Thailand."

23. Heirman, "Can We Trace the Early Dharmaguptakas?" 396–429; "Indian Disciplinary Rules and Their Early Chinese Adepts: A Buddhist Reality," 257–72.

24. Jonathan Best recently debunked the legend of an earlier sixth-century Korean monk by the name of Kyŏmik, who has been claimed in modern Korean historiography to have gone to India, brought the Vinaya to Korea, and translated it: Best, "Tales of Three Paekche Monks Who Traveled Afar in Search of the Law," 139–97. Richard McBride explains that, although Chajang (590–658) wrote essays on the *Dharmaguptaka Vinaya* in the seventh century, there is no proof that he actually brought the text from China to Korea, and only after the fourteenth century did he become known as a Vinaya Master: McBride, "The Complex Origins of the Vinaya in Korean Buddhism," 151–78. Sem Vermeersch collected interesting data from the Koryŏ period that show that some basic knowledge of the Indian Vinaya rules was prevalent at the time: Vermeersch, "Views on Buddhist Precepts and Morality in Late Koryŏ," 35–65.

25. Kaplan, "Monastic Education in Korea: Teaching Monks about Buddhism in the Modern Age."

26. Wŏnhyo's *Arouse the Mind and Practice* was translated by Buswell, "Arouse Your Mind and Practice!," 154–57; and by Charles Muller, "Awaken Your Mind and Practice" (*Balsim suhaeng jang* 發心修行章). Chinul's "Admonitions to Neophytes" was translated by Robert Buswell, "Admonitions to Neophytes" (*Kye chosim hagin mun* 誡初心學人文), 195–205. Yaun's "Self-Admonitions" was translated by Richard McBride, "Watch Yourself!" (*Jagyeongmun* 自警文).

27. Ko, "Han'guk Pulgyo kangwŏn samigwa kyoje ŭi sŏjijŏk yŏn'gu" (A Bibliographic Research of the Study Materials of the Novice Course in Korean Buddhist Seminaries), 883–932.

28. Since the 1990s, a few additional short Chinese apocryphal Vinaya texts have been added to the Buddhist novice curriculum in Korea. For details, see Kaplan, *Monastic Education in Korea*.

29. Sin, "Ch'imun kyŏnghunju ŭi kyoyukchŏk kach'i e kwanhan yŏn'gu" (Research on the Educational Value of the Commentary to the *Admonitions to the Gray-Robed Monks*); Wang, "Yŏngnamdae tosŏgwan tongbin mun'go sojang p'yohun sap'an Ch'imun kyŏnghun ŭi Sŏji mit Kugyŏl" (A Study of the Bibliography and Kugyŏl of Ch'imun Kyŏnghun at Yŏngnam University's Central Library), 147–67.

30. Kaplan, *Monastic Education in Korea*.

31. Sin, "Ch'imun kyŏnghunju ŭi kyoyukchŏk kach'i e kwanhan yŏn'gu"; Hyewŏn, "Hyŏndae Han'guk Sŏnwŏn ch'ŏnggyu ŭi mosŭp kwa naagal pangyang" (The Shape of Modern Korean Sŏn Monastic Pure Rules and Future Objectives), 259–75.

32. For Japan, see Jaffe, "Seeking Sakyamuni: Travel and the Reconstruction of Japanese Buddhism," 65–96. For China, see Tarocco, *The Cultural Practices of Modern Chinese Buddhism: Attuning the Dharma*, 66–71. For Korea, see Joo, "Countercurrents from the West: 'Blue-Eyed' Zen Masters, Vipassana Meditation, and Buddhist Psychotherapy in Contemporary Korea," 614–38.

33. Dicks, "Buddhism and Law in China: Qing Dynasty to the Present"; Schonthal, "Guest Editor's Introduction: Buddhist Legal Pluralism? Looking Again at Monastic Governance in Modern South and Southeast Asia," vii–xxx.

34. Taehan Pulgyo Chogyejong (The Korean Jogye Order), *Chonggyejongbŏp ŭi ihae* (Understanding the Jogye Order Laws), 87–88.

35. For example, see Prebish, "Varying the Vinaya."

36. Taehan Pulgyo Chogyejong (The Korean Jogye Order), "Sŭngnyŏbŏp" (Law of the Monastics).

37. Yi, "Yulchang e kŭn'gŏhan Chogyejongdan chinggye chedo ŭi kaesŏn pangyang: Sŭngnyŏbŏp, Hogyewŏnbŏp ŭl chungsimŭro" (Reforming the Penal System of the Jogye Order Based on the Vinaya: Focusing on the Law of the Monastics and the Precepts-Court Law), 223–53.

38. Ch'oe, "Pŏmgyu haengwi wa chejae" (Legislation and Discipline); Tŏngmun, "Yulchang ŭi chinggye kalma wa hogyewŏnbŏp" (The Penal Proceedings in the Vinaya and the Precepts-Court Law), 43–77.

39. Clarke, "Monks Who Have Sex: Parajika Penance in Indian Buddhist Monasticisms," 1–43; "Where and When Is a Monk No Longer a Monk? On Communion and Communities in Indian Buddhist Monastic Law Codes," 115–41.

40. Kwŏn, "Ŭihyŏn chŏn ch'ongmuwŏnjang 21yŏn mane 'myŏlbin kulle' pŏdŏ" (Previous Administrative Head Ŭihyŏn Takes Off the Shackles of Expulsion after 21 Years).

41. Taehan Pulgyo Chogyejong (The Korean Jogye Order), *Hogyewŏnbŏp* (The Precepts-Court Law).

42. Yŏ, "Hobŏp pun'gwawi 't'ŭkpyŏl samyŏn' taesangja 52myŏng kŏmt'o" (The Precepts Department Examines Special Amnesties for 52 Monastics).

43. Wijayaratna quoted in Prebish, "Varying the Vinaya," 60.

44. For Zongze's Pure Rules, see Yifa, *The Origins of Buddhist Monastic Codes*. There may be some exceptions. According to the *Samguk Yusa*, for example, Chajang organized what seem to be *uposatha* rites in seventh-century Silla. Interestingly, Ester Bianchi reports of similar attempts to "revive" the *uposatha* tradition in modern China as well: Bianchi, "Yi jie wei shi 以戒為師: Theory and Practice of Monastic Discipline in Modern and Contemporary Chinese Buddhism," 111–41.

45. Taehan Pulgyo Chogyejong (The Korean Jogye Order), Kyŏlgye mit p'osal e kwanhan pŏp (Law Regarding Habitation and Uposatha Rites); Pŏmmanggyŏng posalgye p'osalbon (The Bodhisattva Precepts of the *Brahmā Net Sūtra* for Uposatha Ceremonies).

46. Kŭmgang, "Hyŏndae sahoe sŭngga chŏnggyu nŭn ŏttŏn naeyong ŭro chejŏng toeaya hanŭn'ga" (How Should We Formulate the Monastic Pure Rules of Modern Society?) (Paper presented at Hyŏndae sahoe sŭngga chŏnggyu, Chogyesa, 2015).

47. Prebish, "Varying the Vinaya."

48. Numrich, *Old Wisdom in the New World*, 52.

49. Sasaki, "Bukkyō ni okeru kai to ritsu no imi" (The Meaning of Precepts and Discipline in Buddhism), 73–97.

50. Poceski, "Xuefeng's Code and the Chan School's Participation in the Development of Monastic Regulations," 33–56; Jia, "The Creation and Codification of Monastic Regulations at Mount Baizhang," 39–59.

51. Chasŭng (Introduction), in *Sŭngga chŏnggyu* (The Pure Rules for the Sangha), ed. Taehan Pulgyo Chogyejong; Hyewŏn, "Hyŏndae Han'guk Sŏnwŏn chŏnggyu ŭi mosŭp kwa naagal pangyang."

52. Vermeersch, "Views on Buddhist Precepts and Morality in Late Koryŏ."

53. Taehan Pulgyo Chogyejong (The Korean Jogye Order), *Sŏnwŏn ch'ongnam* (A Comprehensive Survey of Sŏn Halls), 1478–81.

54. Chŏngmyŏl, "Kŭnhyŏndae Han'guk Sŏnjong kyodan esŏ chejŏngdoen chŏnggyu e kwanhan koch'al" (Inquiry into the Formulation of Pure Rules in Modern and Contemporary Korean Chan), 193–240.

55. See, for example, the portrayal of Unmunsa's regulations in Unsan, "Unmun sŭngga taehak ŭi chŏnt'ong kwa hyŏnjaesŏng" (The Traditional and Present Character of Unmunsa's Sangha University), 11–52. On Pongnyŏngsa's rules, see Yogyŏng, "Piguni kyoyuk toryang Pongnyŏngsa sŭngga taehak e taehan koch'al" (Inquiry into the Nun Education at Pongnyŏngsa's Sangha University), 83–136.

56. Taehan Pulgyo Chogyejong (The Korean Jogye Order), *Sŏnwŏn chŏnggyu* (Pure Rules for the Sŏn Halls).

57. With this document, the touristic Temple Stay program turned into an integral part of Korean Buddhist law. For details on this program and on tourism in Korean Buddhist temples, see Kaplan, "Images of Monasticism: The Temple Stay Program and the Re-branding of Korean Buddhist Temples," 127–46.

58. Kaplan, "From the Tea to the Coffee Ceremony: Modernizing Buddhist Material Culture in Contemporary Korea," 1–22.

59. Taehan Pulgyo Chogyejong (The Korean Jogye Order), *Sŭngga chŏnggyu* (Pure Rules for the Sangha).

60. Chahyŏn, "Kŭmgang sŭnim palche e taehan tappyŏn" (Response to Ven. Kŭmgang's Presentation); Chugyŏng, "Saeroun sŭngga chŏnggyu ŏttŏk'e chongdan e chŏngch'ak sik'il kŏdin'ga?" (How Can We Make the New Pure Rules for the Sangha Strike Root in the Order?).

61. *Sifen lu* (Dharamguptaka Vinaya), T1428.22.0848c01–3: "時長老畢 陵伽婆蹉 老羸不堪步涉白佛 佛言 聽 作步挽車若輿若乘." In free translation, this reads: "It was told to the Buddha that the elder Pilinda-Vatsa was old and weak and could not walk, so the Buddha ordered that a cart/palanquin be made to carry him."

62. See, for example, the discussion in Prebish, "Varying the Vinaya."

63. For Japan, see Stephen Covell, "Money and the Temple: Law, Taxes and the Image of Buddhism." For Sri Lanka, see Kinnard, "Proper Possessions: Buddhist Attitudes toward Material Property."

64. The rank system of the Jogye Order has been recently standardized through a system of seniority, education, retreats, and examinations. For details, see Kaplan, *Monastic Education in Korea*.

65. Schopen, "Doing Business for the Lord: Lending on Interest and Written Loan Contracts in the Mulasarvastivada-Vinaya," 527–54; "Monastic Law Meets the Real World: A Monk's Continuing Right to Inherit Family Property in Classical India," 101–23; "The Good Monk and His Money in Buddhist Monasticism of 'The Mahayana Period,'" 85–105.

66. Chiu, "Rethinking the Precept of Not Taking Money in Contemporary Taiwanese and Mainland Chinese Buddhist Nunneries."

67. Mun'gwang, "Milleniŏm sidae ŭi sŭngga wa suhaeng: Kyeyul kwa ch'ŏnggyu chŏngsin ŭi pokkich'o rŭl parwŏn hamyŏ" (The Sangha and Buddhist Practice in the Millennial Age: Praying for a Revival of the Spirit of the Vinaya and the Pure Rules), 110–25.

68. Kwŏn, "Ŭihyŏn chŏn ch'ongmuwŏnjang 21nyŏn mane 'myŏlbin kullae' pŏsŏ."

PART 4

SECULARITY, SOCIETY, AND POLITICS

Chapter 8

Han Yongun, Fukuzawa Yukichi, and Questions of Nationalism and Colonialism

GREGORY N. EVON

Introduction

The amount of research on Han Yongun (韓龍雲, 1879–1944) is so great that one could be kept busy by focusing on distinct aspects of his career—Han as Buddhist reformer, Han as an independence activist, and of course, Han as a Korean vernacular poet—with little need to peer over the walls of one's own academic enclosure.[1] However, the general dangers of academic specialization are particularly acute in the case of Han Yongun. This is not simply a result of the array of his activities or the connections between those activities, but also of the overlapping historical contexts in which he lived and worked. The Japanese colonial period (1910–1945) is especially thorny in that respect for three distinct reasons. First, there is a marked tendency in the scholarship to emphasize the effects of Japanese colonialism in Korea at the expense of inquiry into the background of Japanese colonialism in both Japan and Korea. Such oversight is problematic in relation to Korean Buddhism in general and Han Yongun in particular. Second, there is a tacit assumption that "modernity" (broadly construed) is the necessary point of comparison in relation to Japanese colonialism. Hence notions of individual freedom, national autonomy, and social progress become central points of reference.

The problem is that such ideas were initially inspired by the Japanese among a minority of the late Chosŏn elite. The third problem may be called "language ideology" or "linguistic nationalism" and the range of postcolonial assumptions-cum-assertions related to the situation of the Korean language during the Japanese colonial period.

As a consequence, scholars are inclined to overlook certain questions. Two of these interest me here. First, notwithstanding censorship in the Japanese colonial context, there developed a robust commercial publication industry in which Buddhists—clerics and the laity, male and female—participated, and these publications sat within a larger commercial publication industry. Nothing like this had existed prior to the Japanese colonial period, and reflexive appeals to Japanese censorship blind us to this critical fact. Second, increasing rates of vernacular literacy drove—and were driven by—commercial publication. To be sure, there are great difficulties in attempting to determine overall literacy rates, but the mere fact of commercial publication demonstrates the existence of a readership sufficient for selling books and journals. Han Yongun's work is illustrative of these broad cultural changes in terms of what was written, for whom it was written, and how it was written. This chapter is driven by these two questions and in turn their relationship to Han's *A Miserable Fate* (K. *Pangmyŏng* 薄命), a novel serialized late in the Japanese colonial period from 1938 and 1939. However, the wider significance of Han's novel cannot be seen without reference to the broader intellectual context in which it was written. That broader intellectual context is the focus of this chapter. In what follows, I trace key ideas that influenced Han and to which he responded, placing these in comparative frameworks to bypass some of the pitfalls potentially generated by focusing on a single country, person, or topic. I conclude with a short analysis of *A Miserable Fate* that highlights the importance of Walter D. Mignolo's "exteriorities," to which I now turn.

Reframing Mignolo's "Darker Side of Modernity"

In *The Darker Side of Western Modernity*, Mignolo raises the question of how colonialism continues to influence the ways in which the views of people from colonized parts of the world contrast with the views of those from former colonial powers. Discussing the self-critiques offered by "two Third World intellectuals," Mignolo emphasizes that they were "looking at the global conditions, being where they think, dwelling in the *exteriorities* [italics in original] of the modern colonial world. These views have not been accounted for in the analysis of globalization and modernity."²

In the case of East Asia, it is true that there has been less attention given to the thinking of those "dwelling in the exteriorities" than is warranted, although there are notable exceptions.³ One problem is that the general issues involved are not explicitly marked but rather commonplace in the majority of studies dealing with East Asia from the late nineteenth to the early twentieth centuries. An additional factor is perhaps signaled in Mignolo's subtle shift in emphasis, from "Coloniality: The Darker Side of Modernity" to *The Darker Side of Western Modernity*.⁴ Put briefly, the explicit connection between modernity and coloniality was a consequence of Western activities, but modernity—or, at least, incipient modernities— did exist in East Asia, as Alexander Woodside has argued.⁵ What changed quickly and dramatically in East Asia in the late nineteenth century was how to define culture and civilization. This question was assessed insistently in Japan by Fukuzawa Yukichi (福澤諭吉, 1835–1901).

A significant example of how the world came to be interpreted differently can be seen through a meeting over the question of Korea held in 1875 between the Japanese Mori Arinori (森 有礼, 1847–1889) and his Chinese counterpart, Li Hongzhang (李鴻章, 1823–1901). When Mori argued that international laws and treaties were useless for anything other than trade, Li was so shocked that he pronounced Mori's views "heresy."⁶ But Mori was heretical in other respects as well, including his attitudes toward women. One significant marker of "Asian backwardness," he argued, "was the near contempt he thought Asian peoples had for female intelligence and ability," and his point of comparison was the "Western respect for women."⁷ By that point, he had studied in England and traveled throughout the United States. Li, however, was yet again shocked by Mori's views, and guessed—incorrectly, as Mori explained—that Mori was a Christian. Mori was instead an atheist whose marriage the following month "took the form of an equal contract for both parties," witnessed by his close friend and colleague, Fukuzawa Yukichi.⁸

Read from the vantage of Japan's victory in the Sino-Japanese War (1894–1895), its increasing militarization, and the memories of cruelty toward women that remain contentious throughout East Asia, it is easy to dismiss Mori as insincere. Fukuzawa's increasing belligerence over the following two decades poses yet another problem. But on balance, the problem seems to stem from our assumptions that do not easily fit with their assumptions. To be sure, Fukuzawa saw the world in terms of struggle, and that way of interpreting the world became commonplace throughout East Asia through the end of the nineteenth century, with Fukuzawa's writings playing a pivotal role in their dissemination. What is instead of greater interest is Fukuzawa's attitude toward the weak and dispossessed and his more general attitude toward the consequences of Western imperialism and colonialism. The well-known shift in his thinking in the middle of the 1870s was largely a matter of emphasis, from a slightly more positive view of international relations to one marked by the same deep skepticism that was displayed by Mori and deemed heretical by Li. But it would be difficult to argue that Fukuzawa was ever confused about the costs of Western power. Depending on one's point of view, his attitude toward the history of Western conquest was either immoral or, at best, amoral. But even when he wrote *An Outline of a Theory of Civilization* (J. *Bunmei-ron no gairyaku* 文明論之概略, 1875), he was in no way blinkered. On the contrary, he prefigured Schumpeter's appropriation of the notion of creative destruction without any discernible sense of unease. I return to this issue below in relation to Han.

Framed in terms of Mignolo's thesis, Fukuzawa did not see colonialism as the dark side of modernity; rather, he saw modernity as the bright side of colonialism. As terrible as this idea seems—or perhaps, precisely because it is so terrible—it points to Fukuzawa's assessment of the world and the reasons why he insisted that Japan had to modernize. Yet it is impossible to think that he saw modernization as simply a burdensome but necessary imposition from without. He recognized the threats posed by the West to Japan as well as the consequences of Western imperialism and colonial dispossession throughout the world; even so, he genuinely found much in the West that was admirable. By contrast, he was highly critical of the East, and his main point of reference was the disparity between the possible effects of individual initiative in the West and the East.[9] He was particularly sharp on this point in relation to Japanese history and its effects on the well-being of the people in general.[10] Although not clearly stated, we can glimpse another idea that is deeply embedded in the work, which becomes all but explicit in his discussion of national independence: that internal divisions within Japan itself had mimicked the worst aspects of the international conflict, but on a single-country scale and without any of the benefits, resulting in Japan's then current weakness.[11] For Fukuzawa, the West posed danger, but it was not the source of the problem.

The Flow of Ideas

Whether or not Han Yongun had directly read Fukuzawa's work, Fukuzawa's influence is palpable throughout Han's *Treatise on the Restoration of Korean Buddhism* (K. *Chosŏn Pulgyo yusillon* 朝鮮佛教維新論, 1913). This is not surprising. The Chinese modernizer Liang Qichao (梁啟超, 1873–1929) was Han's favored source in *Restoration* and cited liberally throughout, and Fukuzawa's "writings directly influenced" Liang.[12] In this respect, the flow of ideas had reversed, with Fukuzawa, a Japanese thinker, becoming the source of inspiration and guidance to thinkers in China and Korea. But Japanese influence in *Restoration* was evident in many other respects. Among these, the best-known—and still notorious—was Han's arguments on behalf of the Buddhist clergy's right to marry. In this and many other ways, his writings reflected an understanding of the effects of modernization within Japanese Buddhism. As made clear through Richard M. Jaffe's magnificent study of clerical marriage in Japanese Buddhism, Han's arguments on behalf of modernizing Korean Buddhism cannot be adequately understood without reference to Japan.[13]

However, Japanese influence also showed up in a much subtler way in *Restoration*, underscoring thorny questions surrounding the interrelationships of identity (both personal and national), the influence of ideas, and the various meanings of ideas in different contexts. The instance in question is found in the first section of *Restoration*, where Han explains the excellence of Buddhism as a philosophical and religious system. In support of his argument, Han notes in passing the similarities between the Chinese Neo-Confucian tradition associated with Lu Xiangshan (陸象山, 1139–1192) and Wang Yangming (王陽明, 1472–1529) and the teachings of Zen Buddhism.[14]

Seen in terms of the tradition of Korean scholarship during the Chosŏn dynasty and how the Chosŏn Korean elite identified themselves, this claim is shocking precisely because it is true. No one would have argued against the claim that Lu and Wang had been influenced by Zen Buddhism. But they saw in such influence the very reasons why the teachings of Lu and Wang were so dangerous. The Chosŏn Korean elite could conclude that their suspicions about Wang and his followers in particular had been confirmed by the fall of China's Ming dynasty (1368–1644). By contrast, Wang's school of thought had enjoyed great popularity in Japan, remained popular even after the Meiji restoration, and eventually influenced Liang Qichao. As Joshua A. Fogel describes the situation, "historiographical currents, and ideological currents as well, followed a two-way course between China and Japan."[15] As Han's *Restoration* shows, Korea too was involved in this interchange of ideas, but because the line between what was deemed right and wrong had been drawn so sharply in the Korean context, Han's offhanded reference to Lu and Wang was shocking in a way that would have made no sense in Japan.

Read in terms of the larger historical-intellectual context, Han's reference to Lu and Wang conveyed a Japanese intellectual sensibility that had, perhaps, been mediated by China, but nonetheless marked a break with his own national tradition. On the other hand, the very idea of a national intellectual tradition raises a pointy problem. Should Han, a Buddhist, have sided with a point of view that denigrated his own religion? At what point does tradition become an impediment? And above all else, at what point does an individual assume the right to make judgments about his or her place in the world?

These are questions with which Fukuzawa and then Han as well as many others throughout East Asia grappled. It is therefore useful to think through the implications of Taiaiake Alfred and Jeff Corntassel's examination of "indigenousness" in relation to Fukuzawa and the larger East Asian context. Of particular importance is their discussion of "indigenous pathways of action and freedom," which emphasizes that "authentic action and freedom" proceed on an "individual basis—a strength that soon reverberates outward from the self to the family, clan, community, and into all of the broader relationships that form an indigenous existence."[16] This prescription would look very familiar to anyone acquainted with Korean cultural nationalism during the Japanese colonial era, and once one makes the shift from one historically specific example to another—and is thus able to see them in the abstract—it becomes easy to see definite parallels in Fukuzawa's thinking too.

There is, however, a profound difference. Like Alfred and Corntassel as well as Han, Fukuzawa was, in Mignolo's terms, "dwelling in the *exteriorities*." But unlike them, Fukuzawa was working from a position of near-coloniality, and coloniality was precisely what he sought to avoid. This helps to explain another distinguishing feature in Fukuzawa: individual freedom—and the change that was to derive from it—was to be directed at a radical transformation of tradition rather than functioning as a means to recapture the past. Indeed, the prescription in Alfred and Corntassel that one's freedom is to be directed at "comprehend[ing] the teachings and values of the ancestors" is an inversion of what Fukuzawa prescribed.[17] In many ways, Han sat between these two positions. Like Fukuzawa, he saw that tradition was not necessarily good because it was one's own tradition. On the other hand, he saw that tradition could contribute to the present, if properly reconstituted. As he described the matter, the "destruction" (K. p'agoe 破壞) of Korean Buddhism was the necessary precondition for its "restoration/reformation" (K. yusin 維新).[18]

The biggest difference between Han and Fukuzawa, however, rested in their discrepant views of the role of religion, ethics, and morality in individual development. For Fukuzawa, such questions were themselves a problem because, in a traditional Confucian fashion, they conflated quantifiable knowledge and ability with virtue. Or put simply, a kind and personally virtuous surgeon is not necessarily a skilled surgeon any more than a surgeon who is a rascal is necessarily unskilled. Han clearly understood that idea; for him, however, Buddhism was to play a crucial role in guiding the individual, and, like that of Alfred and Corntassel, his vision of authentic action and freedom commenced with the individual, whose influence would reverberate outward. As seen below, that vision was central to his novel *A Miserable Fate*.

The Stuff of Self-Understandings and Knowledges, Buddhist and Otherwise

As Jaffe has shown in considerable detail, the increasingly globalized and interconnected world of the late nineteenth century led to exchanges of ideas and information that had significant consequences in shaping Buddhism throughout the world: "What emerged as modern Buddhism in Japan and elsewhere in Asia was a result of this complex, tangled set of exchanges that resulted in the production of a discourse that wove together traditional Buddhist self-understandings with knowledges received in a wide variety of contact zones."[19] Jaffe's analysis can be read as an example of what Thomas A. Tweed has termed "translocative," and it particularly fits with Tweed's emphasis on the need for scholars of Buddhism to "follow the flows," because "[r]eligions are spatial processes . . . [and] even things that seem static . . . are always changing."[20] More recently, Alicia Turner, Laurence Cox, and Brian Bocking have argued that "[s]ingle country approaches to the study of Buddhism miss the crucial significance of international networks in the making of modern Buddhism."[21] That is all certainly true, but it does not go nearly far enough for my purposes here. The history and spread of Buddhism were a result of diffusion across networks of trade that crossed what would now (albeit anachronistically) be called "national boundaries," and Buddhism's spread out of India secured its survival. As a result, the push in the late nineteenth century was to dispatch "clerics to India to help restore Buddhist sites and counter the actions of Christian missionaries."[22] The flow of ideas of which Buddhism had historically been a part intensified in the mid- to late nineteenth century and grew more complex because the world was growing more complex. In Korea, the link between "Buddhist self-understandings" and "knowledges" was reflected in the production of Buddhist journals, as seen below. But that link pointed to broader changes in what was available for self-understanding and what was seen to constitute knowledge.

A seemingly innocuous entry contained in virtually any chronology of Han Yongun's life provides a remarkable example of the historical changes that occurred in Korea as the Chosŏn (1392–1910) dynasty was replaced by the Japanese colonial regime (1910–1945). Despite some differences in wording, such chronologies typically note that, by the age of nine—or eight, by Western reckoning—he was regarded as an unusually bright youngster because of the Chinese works he had read. Such a setup was nearly a cliché in premodern biographies, in which adult accomplishment was prefigured by a precocious mastery of literary Chinese, poetic composition, and Confucian texts. In Han's case, much of this commonplace format was preserved, albeit with one significant difference. One of the texts that he is said to have read was *The Story of the Western Wing* (C. *Xixiang ji* 西廂記), a Chinese dramatic love story that dated to the Yuan dynasty (1271–1368).

If true, Han's precociousness extended far beyond matters of literacy. Although by modern standards little about *The Story of the Western Wing* seems scandalous, it was regarded as morally noxious at least by some in both China and Korea because it contravened a central tenet of the Confucian patriarchal regulations that were fundamental to sociopolitical order: in the story, the protagonists put their love for each other before the demands of their parents. Roughly a century before Han is said to have read *The Story of the Western Wing*, it was a source of moral panic among the Chosŏn elite. The specific concern was the quality of elite male education and the overall sociopolitical vitality of the Chosŏn dynasty that such education was meant to preserve. *The Story of the Western Wing* therefore represented not merely an unacceptable view of interpersonal relations and disregard for parental authority—and thus disregard for the moral order as defined by the state—but also a dangerous distraction to one's studies. To be sure, the worries over the work around the turn of the nineteenth century meant that it was being read, but such worries expressed elite assumptions about social regulation and the proper role of literacy in reinforcing social regulation. By the early decades of the twentieth century, however, the work was commercially published with vernacular Korean glosses so as to make it more accessible to a wider readership.[23]

What is of specific importance here is not whether Han actually read *The Western Wing* in 1878, but rather the massive sociopolitical and cultural changes that are reflected in the claim itself. If he did, in fact, read the work at the age of eight, then his family appears to have been as unusual as his reading skills were great. But notwithstanding difficulties in reconstructing some of the events of his early life, it is clear that he was the source of the claim. Writing in 1933 to give his "account of first going to the capital" (K. *ch'o sanggyŏnggi* 初上京記), that is, Seoul, he claimed that, in a moment of stress thirty years earlier, he had recalled the "*The Story of the Western Wing*, which I had read at the age of nine."[24] His stress was caused by his recognition that, beyond his provincial hometown, his basic education in literary Chinese (*Hanhak* 漢學) was insufficient to his goal of accomplishing something great. The world had changed, and he was ill-equipped to deal with such changes. Lurking in the background of this account is Japan's increasing control in the lead-up to making Korea a protectorate (1905) before finally establishing Korea as a colony. Upon recognizing his educational inadequacy and remembering the heartbreak in *The Story of the Western Wing*, he despaired in a conventionally Buddhist manner: struck by the "emptiness" (K. *kong* 空) of human aspirations for fame and wealth, he decided to become a monk.

Han's presentation of how he became who he was reflected the vast changes that Korea experienced over his lifetime. In this account, his classical education was stripped of its value by external circumstances, and it is easy to see this as a criticism of the Chosŏn elite's failure to modernize and make the necessary reforms that might have secured Korean sovereignty against Japanese aggression. In the Korean case, modernity and colonialism were interlocked. But Han was no archaist, nor some advocate of traditional values, and many of the causes that he publicly championed—popular education, women's rights, relative freedom and individual autonomy from the state, and the right to choose one's spouse, to name the most obvious—reflected the breakdown of the Chosŏn dynasty. What is easy to overlook is how the past remained in the present and how the present provided new ways of interpreting the past. A commitment to Korean independence did not entail an automatic rejection of many of the elements of colonial modernity, nor did it render the past in any way good simply because it was Korea's past.

The case of Japanese colonialism in Korea was influenced by another factor that did not exist in the case of British imperialism in China and India—two examples that animated Japanese fears and sparked Japanese colonial ambitions, as seen below—and that further influenced the ways in which one could look at the past. This factor was a similarity between Japan and Korea that was founded on a common repertoire of ideas and texts as well as the historical use of literary Chinese as an elite language of intellectual accomplishment. Educated Koreans and Japanese had at least some shared understanding of Confucianism and Buddhism, and if they could not speak to each other face to face, they certainly could at least communicate through writing in literary Chinese in what is typically referred to as "brush dialogues" (K. *p'iltam* 筆談). But over the final quarter of the nineteenth century, that situation began to change. A full accounting of these not altogether straightforward changes is beyond the scope of this discussion, but it is sufficient to emphasize that the recognition of a changing world order necessitated widespread popular education and that this, in turn, necessitated widespread vernacular literacy. When Han recalled how he suddenly recognized in 1903 the limitations of his education in literary Chinese, he was referring to that historical shift. By 1903, that shift was well underway in Japan and in an incipient phase in Korea.

The historical implications of that shift soon appeared in *Restoration*. Bearing a preface dated 1910 but published in 1913, this work seems to have been Han's first attempt at employing an easier (albeit far from perfectly vernacular) literary style for a larger Buddhist audience. Of interest here is the starting passage in Han's attempt to impress upon his readers the need for Buddhist clerics to engage in the propagation of Buddhist teachings with the same degree of vigor as shown by Christian missionaries. He begins by noting that "[there is a] saying in the West . . . that 'one thousand words of law are not as good as a single cannon'" (K. *Sŏjiŏn-e wal kongbŏp ch'onŏn-i puryŏ taep'o-ilmun irahani* 西之言에曰公法千言이不如大砲一門이라ᄒ·니).[25]

That quote was derived from Fukuzawa Yukichi when he concluded that he had been previously wrong to take the rhetoric of Western democracies at face value. Their appeals to international law and order were instead a subterfuge masking their national self-interest. The change in

Fukuzawa's thinking was subtle. In 1875, he praised the effects of international law and the restraint it imposed on overt acts of aggression in his *An Outline of a Theory of Civilization*; in drawing a sharp distinction between knowledge and practical knowhow on the one hand and the influence of religion and philosophy on moral conduct on the other, he also unfavorably compared Japanese religiosity with Western Christians and their eagerness to propagate their religion throughout the world.[26] Even then, however, he was under no illusions about the historical consequences of European expansion, taking note of the decimation of Indigenous populations throughout the Americas, among many other things. The question of national strength was thus of paramount importance, and as Fukuzawa astutely observed of some of his contemporaries, it was a mistake to think that military strength could be measured by the number of warships and cannons. What mattered instead were the conditions that led to the creation of such *matériel*: "[Their] idea seems to be that, if England has one thousand warships, and we too have one thousand warships, then we can stand against them. Now, this is the thinking of men who are ignorant of the proportion of things . . . If there are [in England] one thousand warships, there have to be at least ten thousand merchant ships, which in turn require at least one hundred thousand navigators; and to create navigators there must be naval science."[27]

In 1878, however, he published a lengthy tract under the title *On Popular National Sovereignty* (J. *Tsūzoku kokken ron* 通俗國「論). Here he attacked international law, noting that "A few cannons are worth more than a hundred volumes of international law." Following this source for Han's quote above, Fukuzawa pressed on, leaving no doubt over how his thought had evolved: "A case of ammunition is of more use than innumerable treaties of friendship. Cannons and bullets are not means of asserting a reason already existing. They are instruments for making a reason of their own."[28] Intimations of this viewpoint were evident three years earlier in his *An Outline of a Theory of Civilization*, but at that time he had counseled restraint: Japan had neither the financial nor the human resources to compete with the West.[29] Hard work and patience were therefore critical if Japan was to avoid being taken over by the West. By 1878, however, his earlier sense of caution had undergone modification. Shortly after laying out the relationship between international law and military power, he offered a variation on his previous estimation of the English military that emphasized not its strength, but rather the weakness of those it faced: "The English excel at choosing their opponents well"

(J. *Ei wa yoku teki o erabu no jutsu ni chōji* 英はよく敵を撰ぶの術に長じ).[30] One critical event had occurred in the intervening three years, and it demonstrated an underlying truth in Fukuzawa's calculation. In 1876, the Japanese "opened" Korea, securing a treaty after they had provoked a naval skirmish the previous year.

Born three years after Japan opened Korea and dying the year before Korea's liberation, the entirety of Han Yongun's life overlapped with Korea's increasing weakness vis-à-vis Japan. But in the early stages, that outcome did not look inevitable. Writing in the decade before Japan's initial show of force in Korea in 1875, a Vietnamese Catholic priest favorably compared Japan and Korea with each other and appealed to their efforts to modernize as a model for Vietnam to follow.[31] The magnitude of the shift that occurred over the final quarter of the nineteenth century was astonishing and had no shortage of historical resonance. The Japanese had been keen to conceive of themselves and their political order as equal to China by the early seventh century.[32] Cultural flows, however, continued to move from China and Korea to Japan for well over the following millennium, and long before—and long after—the devastation caused by the Japanese invasions of Korea in the late sixteenth century, the Japanese were not seen as culturally or intellectually accomplished. After the fall of the "Chinese" Ming dynasty (1368–1644) and the founding of the "barbarian" Qing (1644–1911), a crucial element in the Korean elite's self-understanding was that they were civilized, whereas China had succumbed to Manchu barbarism and Japan remained largely unaffected by the civilizing influences of orthodox Confucian culture. When this began to change in the late nineteenth century, so too did the basic assumptions, and Fukuzawa was a key figure in defining the change. The long-standing cultural/civilizational frameworks of analysis could no longer be taken for granted. Whereas the Japanese elite of the seventh century wished to see themselves as counterparts to the Chinese, what was wanted in the late nineteenth century was to be unlike the Chinese.

The question of identity is crucial in this regard. At the end of the nineteenth century, the problem was not simply identifying oneself or one's cultural-intellectual milieu in relation to something else, as the Koreans and Japanese had done in various ways and to various degrees in relation to China for well over 1,000 years. Instead, the pressing question was how one was defined and seen by others. From a Chinese historical perspective, this was a novel question because the Chinese assumed that they were to judge civilization on Chinese terms. As the rulers of

China, the Manchus arrogated the same right as well. It was this point of view that was evident in the Qianlong (r. 1735–1796) emperor's famous letter to England's King George III. As Kate Teltscher puts it, "Qianlong believed that he had no reason to pay any attention to the demands of a tiny island state, situated so far from the center of the world."[33] Qianlong's letter reflected a Chinese-Confucian worldview of which Qianlong, as an ethnic Manchu—that is, foreign—emperor, had every reason to be suspicious. But as he contemplated his counterpart far off to the West—on "the lonely remoteness of your island, cut off from the world by intervening wastes of sea"—he instead stressed the classic Chinese Confucian conception of a civilized Chinese center surrounded by barbarism, noting that the "distinction between Chinese and barbarian is most strict" and thus forgetting—or ignoring—that he, too, was a barbarian by Chinese standards.[34] At that moment, however, such confidence was not misplaced. As Charles Holcombe neatly summarizes the on-the-ground reality, the tiny Manchu minority ruled "a vast, multiethnic conquest empire that, by the eighteenth century, may have ruled over as much as 40 percent of the world's total population."[35]

Fukuzawa grasped, however, that that way of looking at the world was dangerous, and he came to view Japan differently by looking at the West and attempting to understand as much of the world as he could. Although examining a different set of issues, Jane Caplan's formulation regarding personal identity can be applied equally well in this context: "Identity is something that depends on other people as much as ourselves; it depends on difference as much as on sameness, and on groups or categories as much as on individuation."[36] It is no surprise that this definition can be applied to Korea and Japan, but it must be emphasized that it can also be applied to China, not only in terms of the geographic-civilizational distinction between a civilized center (China) surrounded by barbarians (non-Chinese), but also because those who, like the Koreans, wished to be part of the Chinese world order regularly dispatched diplomatic missions to China, which, in turn, convinced China's ruling elites that they were at the center of the world.

During the late eighteenth and early nineteenth centuries, some of the assumptions in this construction of identity came to be questioned on the Korean side, but such questioning was marginalized. Too much was at stake not only in terms of Chosŏn-Qing relations, but also in terms of how the Chosŏn elite identified themselves: they could not consider themselves properly cultured and civilized—the true heirs to the Chinese

Confucian tradition—without the existence of Manchu rule in China. But by the second half of the nineteenth century, that question was becoming irrelevant, and a new, more complicated question would take its place. How could one respond to the increasing aggressions of Japan, a neighbor that had long been regarded as culturally inferior? Among the many great paradoxes of this cultural and political shift, one is of specific concern here: how the increasing weakness of the Chosŏn dynasty coincided with an increasingly robust culture of commercial publication in which Buddhists actively participated.

Interactions of the Past and Present

To read through the collected writings of colonial-era Buddhist figures such as Han Yongun, Kwŏn Sangno (權相老, 1879–1965), or Paek Yongsŏng (白龍城, 1864–1940) is not the same as reading their works as initially published. At issue here are not simply questions of orthography, typesetting, or even translation to varying degrees. The problem instead is that their individual careers become the overarching context. Another element is the materiality of those journals, and apart from the often rambunctious use of designs and illustrations, their standout feature was the nature of the advertisements. The advertisements marked these journals as modern products of the twentieth century: commercial enterprises functioning symbiotically with businesses that traded in everything from clerical robes to Western-style clothes, to sports equipment, to paint, to typesetting and publication. If the reader had a question about any of the products or services on offer, all they had to do was pick up a telephone and dial the number! But apart from the telephone numbers, what occurred during the colonial period was a truncated developmental process of something that had existed for a long time in Japan and much longer in China but had been forestalled in Chosŏn Korea for hundreds of years by the governing elite.[37]

An equally important question is what else was being published at the time. This too showed signs of commercialization, and for good reason: you publish what people want to buy and read, and if people want to buy and read what you publish, then you attract advertisers. In saying this, I emphasize that I am not dismissing commercialized literary and intellectual activity. Money is crucial, but it is only one factor. Public intellectuals are only public intellectuals insofar as people care about what they have to say and write. And the general quality of what was published during the colonial period is astonishing, not simply because of the topics and expansive vision of some of the leading contributors such as Yang Kŏnsik (梁建植,1889–1944; aka Paekhwa [白華], among many other pen names), but also because it forces us to recognize how the past interacted with the present.

Ko Chaesŏk makes this point in a study that includes a detailed analysis of Yang, a Buddhist layman who was a modern intellectual with an eye firmly trained on the past. Apart from his own stories, poems, and essays, he also translated *A Doll's House* by Ibsen (1828–1906) and wrote criticism of the work as well as what appears to have been his own adaptation of it. Two years after the publication of *Siddhartha* (1922) by Herman Hesse (1877–1962), Yang brought out his own translation, which ran in the journal *Buddhism* (K. *Pulgyo* 佛敎) from April to November 1926. And in 1930, he brought out *The True Story of Ah Q* (C. *Ā Q zhengzhuan* 阿Q正傳) by Lu Xun (魯迅, 1881–1936). This is merely a brief sketch to provide a general indication of his modern literary interests; a fuller inventory of his output would take up nine dense pages.[38] But Yang's "modern" interests sat alongside equally extensive interests in premodern works ranging from Yuan dynasty drama to the great novels of Ming and Qing China; he also did work on premodern Korean literature, although to a lesser extent.

When we examine Yang's works in relation to other things published around the same time, we can glean a crucial piece of contextual information that is ignored in studies on Han Yongun. A major element of Han's reputation rests on his 1926 collection of Korean vernacular poems published under the title *Silence of Love* (K. *Nim-ŭi ch'immuk* 님의 沈默). This collection is typically read, at least to some degree, as a patriotic statement of commitment to Korean independence couched in the form of love poetry; inasmuch as Han was a Buddhist cleric and had spent time in prison for his involvement in the March First Independence Movement of 1919, the collection itself has attained an exalted status and is seen to be invested with vast patriotic and Buddhist religious profundity. I do not question that. However, it was also quite simply a product of its time. In the mid-1920s, the idea of "love" (K. *yŏnae* 戀愛) was commonplace in the Korean publishing industry.

This question of "love" in the context of publishing and public intellectual life—both within and beyond Buddhism—is extremely important for reasons that are not apparent if one focuses solely on the Japanese colonial period. The reason is that this interest in "love" sat within a much deeper and broader context. The intellectual-literary work of Yang Kŏnsik makes this clear, particularly his work on Ming and Qing novels. What was happening in Korea during the 1920s can best be characterized as a "catch-up" driven by translation and mass publication. In one respect, Korea was not unique: similar interests were evident in China. There was, however, a difference. In the Chinese context, the interest in "love" as an idea had a long pedigree, stretching back to the late Ming intellectuals' interest in love and emotion, something now typically referred to as the "cult of *qing* [feeling]."[39]

In the Korean context, the Ming "cult of feeling" was known—and it was vigorously attacked around the turn of the nineteenth century, which is to say, roughly one hundred years before the publishing boom of love-related titles during the Japanese colonial period. An additional crucial factor—and one that remains easy to overlook if one focuses on the Japanese colonial period as a discrete topic—is that premodern Korean literary works were also published in massive quantities during the colonial period. A sharp division between the premodern and modern is therefore untenable, and once one takes into consideration the translation and adaptation of foreign works—both premodern and contemporary, East Asian and Western—into the Korean vernacular, the situation becomes even more complex and much more interesting. As a result, we see that the late Ming "cult of feeling," which had been held in check during the Chosŏn dynasty, came to the foreground in the mid-1920s. Korean readers were able to read in their own language works that had driven the elite to distraction not so long before.[40]

When we examine these changes in relation to the debates over the establishment of bookstores in the fifteenth through sixteenth centuries, it becomes clear that the Chosŏn elite grasped the power inherent in an ability to control the written word.[41] Their control was never complete, but it was extensive, and at the outset it was targeted at subduing Buddhism. To examine the situation of books and publishing during the colonial period yields a necessary—albeit heretical—insight: Korean Buddhist intellectuals, eager to extend their influence and engage with the world, were far better off in the early twentieth century than at any point during the Chosŏn dynasty. Han Yongun was a principal beneficiary of that change, and, for him, the printed and published word was a critical means for the propagation of Buddhism (K. *p'ogyo* 布教).[42] That very fact entailed his involvement in the political and economic world in which he lived, which in turn entailed his dealings with the Japanese.

Much of the Korean scholarship on Han therefore has kept the rich texture and multifaceted problems of the colonial period to a minimum for a very understandable reason: to do otherwise would make it impossible to present a neat, seamless picture of a steadfast nationalist and opponent of Japanese colonialism. More recent critical work suggests that this situation has changed somewhat.[43] At the same time, the need to "revisit" nationalism demonstrates that *nationalism* is still the main concern. Park's edited volume on modern Korean Buddhism contains more than enough material to show why an overwhelming emphasis on nationalism might, at least at times, be misplaced. In that respect, the key contribution is to be found in Woosung Huh's examination of the aforementioned cantankerous Korean Buddhist monk, Paek Yongsŏng.[44]

Paek was fascinating for many reasons, but what is of principal interest here is the sharp contrast we can draw between him and others such as Han Yongun and Yang Kŏnsik. Paek lived in a world that was self-consciously modernizing, but he was never of that world in any comfortable way, as far as I can see. He was an anachronism, but an anachronism who made use of at least certain elements of modernity. This is well illustrated in an advertisement for his twelve-volume Korean vernacular translation of the *Avataṃsaka Sūtra* (K. *Hwaŏm-gyŏng*華嚴經), which boldly began by explaining: "In world literature, the most expansive thing is Buddhism; within expansive Buddhism, the most profound thing is the *Avataṃsaka Sūtra*."[45] This was a commercial advertisement, and access to such expansiveness and profundity was neither free nor amenable to an honor system. Although one could have the books delivered to one's home, the advertisement reminds the reader that the "delivery fee" (K. *songnyo* 送料) and the cost of the books "must be paid in advance" (K. *yo sŏn'gŭm* 要先金).[46]

Han and Yang no doubt agreed with Paek on the superiority of Buddhism, but they also knew that claims of superiority demanded an explanation for Korean Buddhism's relative weakness and that this, in turn, required an understanding of the larger world. The result is that Paek Yongsŏng appears to be a Korean Buddhist example of Robert N. Bellah's characterization of Japan as adopting the "axial traditions" of Buddhism, Confucianism, Christianity, and Western civilization, only to use these traditions to maintain its own archaic past.[47] In a fundamental sense, Paek did much the same, adopting the trappings and techniques of modernity to preserve his own vision of what constituted Buddhism.

By contrast, Han was at home in the modern world. It is necessary to grasp that personality and disposition are of the utmost importance because such characteristics fundamentally affect how one is oriented toward—and reacts to—the world. The colonial period was fraught with tensions that many people would have preferred simply to forget. And forget they did, as Nayoung Aimee Kwon now reminds us in her recent examination of collaboration in *Intimate Empire*.[48] But even in the forced intimacy of empire, truly religious questions could come under scrutiny. Han's 1939 novel, *A Miserable Fate*, did just that.

The Buddhist Question in *A Miserable Fate*

The general lack of sustained interest in Han's novels is curious given the reasonably good-sized corpus of his collected works. Put cynically, I suspect the reason for this is quite simple: it becomes difficult to focus largely on nationalist issues if one does so. *A Miserable Fate* puts this issue in a pointed form because it is clearly—and self-consciously—a work conceived to make a Buddhist point.[49] The question is, what is that point?

The story recounts the life of its female protagonist, Sunyŏng, who at the age of fourteen is under the care of her stepmother after the death of her mother and then her father, who had remarried. For all intents and purposes, she is an orphan, and what she lacks—and this is crucial, for reasons made clear above—is love and affection. Han was in no way squeamish about human desires and feelings, and his real—if unacknowledged, again for reasons made clear above—Buddhist pedigree should be traced as much to Japan's True Pure Land Sect (J. *Jōdo shinshū* 浄土真宗) as anything that can be counted as Korean Buddhism, however construed.[50] What drives the novel is Sunyŏng's search for a sense of belonging and caring among other people.

In the first instance, this desire for friendship leads to her being tricked into going to Seoul. And that initial moment of trickery leads to many others. By the end of the story, she discovers that the people who seemed to care for her had instead sought to use her for their own gain. This includes not only the women, one old and one young, who conspire to bring her to Seoul, but also the man whom she marries and deeply loves. The grimness of the novel is consistent, involving lies, slander, sex work, and heavy drug abuse. Han deftly portrays the nasty, self-serving psychology of the majority of his characters. The one character who does not make sense is the protagonist, simply because she seems too good, too caring, and too forgiving, a point made inescapable after her husband causes the death of their daughter. And in the end, Sunyŏng, after all of her suffering and demonstrations of compassion, decides to become a Buddhist nun.

The references to Buddhism that recur through the novel are too numerous to be treated here in detail. However, two points must be emphasized. First, Han was using Sunyŏng to illustrate—in a modern format and setting—the values of compassion associated with Guanyin (K. Kwanŭm) or Avalokiteśvara, the exemplar of compassion in Buddhism. Second, Han plays with the idea of causality in both its commonsense and Buddhist meanings. When Sunyŏng's husband ends up dying because of his drug use, his death is not surprising. But that is not the sense of causality that operates in relation to Sunyŏng. Instead, she suffers because she is compassionate.

The austerity of this vision is startling. Yet it is in no way difficult to reconcile it with anything that Han ever wrote. It reads like a culmination-cum-clarification of the vision for Buddhism that had animated his career from the very beginning. Indeed, the novel makes that very point in its closing section, when a Buddhist monk praises Sunyŏng's compassion and sacrifice, explaining at some length that relationships between individuals form the basis for society and the nation.[51] Written nearly thirty years into the Japanese colonial period, it is striking to encounter this none-too-subtle reference to how to be a nationalist and respond to Japanese colonialism. But while this emphasis on the individual as an agent of change is nearly identical to the propositions made by Alfred and Corntassel on how to respond to colonialism, it also resembles Fukuzawa's propositions, albeit with one significant difference, made clear at the end of the novel. As a Buddhist reformer intent on modernizing Buddhism and making it relevant for the twentieth century, Han could take a view of tradition that was every bit as critical as anything found in Fukuzawa's writings, but he could not envision modernity without reference to the Buddhist ethical principle exemplified by Sunyŏng.

Conclusion

Han could not countenance Fukuzawa's acceptance that colonialism was simply the price to be paid for the benefits of modernity. That refusal on Han's part was perhaps nowhere more evident than in his shock over Fukuzawa's assessment that law meant nothing in a contest with raw power. At the same time, Han's response to that assessment underscores how Mignolo's emphasis on "exteriorities" must itself be relativized in an East Asian context, where highly developed notions of a Chinese-inspired cultural core had been commonplace for centuries. To be sure, there were vast differences in how that cultural core was conceptualized and used, but such differences did not make it any less significant. Much of the modern Korean Buddhist scholarship typically blocks this from view because it reflects coloniality; also, in its concern with some singular Korean Buddhist identity, it necessarily bypasses the question of multiple identities and the differences in how people could—and did—see themselves.

Most important of all is to recognize that multiple possibilities for self-understanding were enabled by a flow of ideas across the top of a deep reservoir of cultural resources that were shared throughout East Asia. What was translocal in the late nineteenth and early twentieth centuries extended far beyond Buddhism. Indeed, in explaining civilization in 1875, Fukuzawa could simply take it for granted that his audience knew about the central events and people of China's classical past. Precisely the same was true thirty-five years later in Han's *Restoration*. Yet the commonality of cultural resources did not dictate their use; more than anything else, this underscores the dangers inherent in attempting to fix some settled identity. When Han wrote of how he had gone to the capital and recognized the insufficiency of his classical education, he referred to the romantic *Story of the Western Wing* rather than a proper Confucian classic. That sliver of personal biography pointed at astonishing changes within Korea that began in the nineteenth century and gathered speed over the following decades.

Notes

1. This work was supported by the Academy of Korean Studies (KSPS) Grant funded by the Korean Government (MOE) (AKS-2011-AAA-2103). The author gratefully acknowledges the Academy for its support and would also like to thank Lee Dong-Eun at the Dongguk University Central Library for providing invaluable assistance during a research trip in November 2015.

2. Mignolo, *The Darker Side of Western Modernity*, 104.

3. See, for example, Larsen, *Tradition, Treaties, and Trade* and Tang, *Global Space and the Nationalist Discourse of Modernity*.

4. For this earlier version, see Mignolo, "Coloniality: The Darker Side of Modernity."

5. Woodside, "Territorial Order and Collective-Identity Tensions in Confucian Asia: China, Vietnam, Korea," 191–220; Woodside, *Lost Modernities: China, Vietnam, Korea, and the Hazards of World History*.
6. Larsen, *Tradition, Treaties, and Trade*, 283.
7. Jansen, *China in the Tokugawa World*, 118.
8. Jansen, *China in the Tokugawa World*, 118.
9. Fukuzawa, *An Outline of a Theory of Civilization*, 94.
10. Fukuzawa, *An Outline of a Theory of Civilization*, 206–23.
11. Fukuzawa, *An Outline of a Theory of Civilization*, 250.
12. Tang, *Global Space and the Nationalist Discourse of Modernity*, 62.
13. Jaffe, *Neither Monk nor Layman*.
14. Han, *Chosŏn Pulgyo yusillon*, ed. and trans. Yi Wŏnsŏp, with photo-reprint of original 1913 text 27, 30n15 and original text 11, line 10.
15. Fogel, *The Cultural Dimension of Sino-Japanese Relations*, 18.
16. Alfred and Corntassel, "Being Indigenous: Resurgences against Contemporary Colonialism," 612.
17. Alfred and Corntassel, "Being Indigenous," 613.
18. Han, *Chosŏn Pulgyo yusillon*, 37–39.
19. Jaffe, "Seeking Śākyamuni," 68.
20. Tweed, "Theory and Method in the Study of Buddhism," 24.
21. Turner, Cox, and Bocking, "A Buddhist Crossroads: Pioneer European Buddhists and Globalizing Asian Networks 1860–1960," 1.
22. Jaffe, "Seeking Śākyamuni," 95.
23. Wang, *(Sŏn-Han Ssangmun) Sŏsang-gi*; Wang, *(Hyŏnt'o chuhae) Sŏsang-gi*.
24. An, ed., *Han Yongun*, 243.
25. Han, *Chosŏn Pulgyo yusillon*, 31, line 12.
26. Fukuzawa, *An Outline*, 123–26, 160, 235.
27. Fukuzawa, *An Outline*, 253.
28. Translation from Blacker, *The Japanese Enlightenment: A Study of the Writings of Fukuzawa Yukichi*, 129; for the original, see Fukuzawa, *Tsūzoku kokken ron*, reprinted in *Fukuzawa zenshū*, 4: 51 [line 14]–52 [line 2].
29. Fukuzawa, *An Outline*, 253.
30. Fukuzawa, *Tsūzoku kokken ron*, 53 [line 14].
31. Kathirithamby-Wells, "The Age of Transition: The Mid-Eighteenth to the Early Nineteenth Centuries," 248.
32. Duthie, "Poetry and Kingship in Ancient Japan," 127.
33. Teltscher, *The High Road to China*, 250.
34. "Ch'ien Lung, (Qianlong) Letter to George III (1792)"; "Chinese Cultural Studies: Emperor Qian Long [sic]: Letter to George III, 1793 [sic]."
35. Holcombe, *A History of East Asia: From the Origins of Civilization to the Twenty-First Century*, 171.
36. Caplan, "Identity and Identification," lecture delivered at Gresham College, June 9, 2014, 3–4.

37. Evon, "The Conceptualization of Qing-Era (1644–1911) Chinese Literature in Nineteenth Century Chosŏn (1392–1910) Korea," 396–421.

38. Ko, *Han'guk k'ŭndae munhak chisŏng-sa*, 66; for Yang's output, see 393–401.

39. On the "cult of *qing* [feeling]," see Haiyan Lee, *Revolution of the Heart: A Genealogy of Love in China, 1900–1950*, 25–59; Wang, "The Cult of Qing: Romanticism in the Late Ming Period and in the Novel *Jiao Hong Ji*."

40. See especially the comments on the "four great works" of Chinese fiction in relation to Yang Kŏnsik in Ko, *Han'guk k'ŭndae munhak chisŏngsa*, 126.

41. Evon, "The Conceptualization of Qing-Era (1644–1911) Chinese Literature."

42. For an excellent study of propagation, see Nathan, "Buddhist Propagation and Modernization: The Significance of P'ogyo in Twentieth-Century Korean Buddhism."

43. Lee, "A Doubtful National Hero: Han Yong'un's Buddhist Nationalism Revisited," 35–52.

44. Huh, "Individual Salvation and Compassionate Action: The Life and Thoughts of Paek Yongsŏng," 19–40.

45. K. *segye munhak chung-e kajang wangyanghan kŏs-ŭn Pulgyo-yo wangyanghan Pulgyo chung-e kajang ch'ungsimhan kŏs-ŭn Hwaŏm-gyŏng imnida* (世界文學中에 가장汪洋한것은佛敎요. 汪洋한佛敎中에 가장沖深한것은華嚴經임니다).

46. Advertisement for Paek, *Chosŏn'gŭl Hwaŏmgyŏng*, back cover of *Pulgyo*, 49 (1928).

47. Bellah, *Religion in Human Evolution*, 654–55n155.

48. Kwon, *Intimate Empire*.

49. Han, *Pangmyŏng*, 286–90.

50. For a useful survey on the importance of the True Pure Land Sect in Japan, see Amstutz, "Missing Hongan-ji in Japanese Studies," 155–78.

51. Han, *Pangmyŏng*, 288–90.

Chapter 9

Kim Kugyŏng's Liminal Life
Between Nationalism and Scholarship

KIM CHEONHAK

Introduction

Most Korean-language research on modern and contemporary Korean Buddhism still tends to adopt the dichotomous pro- and anti-Japanese framework used by the nationalist perspective. It also has a general tendency to stigmatize people who lived their lives as scholars and carried out research at the borderline between nationalism and scholarship as pro-Japanese collaborators. However, it is problematic to unilaterally condemn these scholars on the grounds of ideological and political standards. Their achievements should also be evaluated objectively from an academic point of view. This chapter examines Kim Kugyŏng (金九經, 1899–1950?) as an example of these "liminal figures" in the Japanese empire and considers his life and research, which have not received sufficient attention. Kim lived during the tumultuous colonial and immediate postliberation periods, facing numerous national misfortunes, and he nevertheless made a significant contribution to the field of philology.

Some encyclopedias sketch Kim's life and scholarly achievements,[1] and several Buddhism-related books and research articles mention him briefly.[2] One recent article introduces his life in somewhat more detail,[3] but no substantial research has been conducted on the liminal nature of his life and academic work. Building on previous scholarship, I explore Kim's dynamic life, which can be divided into four major turning points: his study in Japan, his stay in Beijing, his work in Manchuria, and his return to Korea. Through this, I hope to bring to light the wide network of relationships that he built around his scholarly work for the Japanese empire and to evaluate the accomplishments he made in his research on Buddhism and beyond.

Turning Points in Kim Kugyŏng's Life

Study in Japan

Kim Kugyŏng was born in the city of Kyŏngju in Kyŏngsang Province in 1899. He took "Kyerim," an old name for the city of Kyŏngju, the capital of Silla, as his moniker. He studied at Kyŏngsŏng High School (K. *Kodŭng Pot'ong Hakkyo* 高等普通學校) in colonial Seoul from 1917 to 1920[4] and then began a career teaching at an elementary school; less than a year later, however, he went to Japan to pursue a degree.[5] He was accepted at Ōtani University, which was affiliated with the Ōtani branch of the Jōdo Shinshū, and he studied Chinese literature under Kuraishi Takeshirō (倉石武四郎, 1897–1975) and Buddhism under Suzuki Daisetsu (鈴木大拙, 1870–1966). Kim finished his degree after six years and returned to Korea in 1927.[6]

The reason Kim left his teaching job to study in Japan is unknown. An article from a daily newspaper offers a clue to this mystery, however. In "To Those Who Would Like to Come to Japan for Studying," Kim reminisces on his decision and mentions "great hope," which suggests that he intended to gain a higher degree in Japan to achieve his scholarly dreams.[7] He was not alone in this: a great many ambitious young Koreans wanted to study abroad to gain a modern education and knowledge, and their first choice of destination was Japan. Not only was Japan an empire that ruled Korea as a colony; it was also a land where they could advance their education and their chances of success not only in Korea but in the Japanese empire at large. As such, the number of Korean students studying in Japan increased drastically, exceeding 1,000 after the March First Movement of 1919.[8]

Stay in Beijing

After returning to Korea, Kim did not wait long before landing a job as acting director of the Keijō Imperial University Library.[9] However, he soon returned to a teaching position. He worked at Songdo High School at Kaesŏng for a while, but he was forced to resign when his students boycotted him. According to an article in the *Tonga* daily newspaper on June 14, 1928, all of the high school's senior students submitted a petition to the school on June 11 demanding that more teachers be hired and three be fired: vice principal Im Tuhwa (林斗華, 1886–1948), teacher Kō no Hyōma (河野兵馬), and Kim Kugyŏng. A June 15 article from the same paper repeated the story. It is not known why Kim was boycotted, though it is certain that he and a Japanese teacher had created discontent in the student community. Kim revealed the reason for this later after he moved to Beijing. According to Li Jiye (李霽野, 1904–1997), when Kim met with the famous Chinese writer Lu Xun (魯迅, 1881–1936) in China, Kim divulged that he had been deeply dissatisfied with the measures the Japanese took to handle the school affairs, so he decided to leave the school run by the Japanese and came to Beijing.[10] This means that the school must have caved to the students' demands and let him go.

In Beijing, Kim found a place to stay with the help of a Chinese linguist on the Peking University faculty, Wei Jiangong (魏建功, 1901–1980), with whom he had developed a friendship. According to Hong Sŏkp'yo, when Wei was a visiting scholar at the Department of Chinese Literature at Keijo Imperial University in Seoul in 1926, he was beholden to Kim, who worked in the university library at the time.[11] When Kim moved to Beijing in late 1928, Wei Jiangong asked his friend, the prominent poet Tai Jingnong (臺靜農, 1902–1990), to prepare a temporary residence for Kim in Weiming Temple to repay his kindness.

As late as May 1929, Kim was lecturing at Peking University.[12] Around this time, he befriended Lu Xun and his younger brother Zhou Zuoren (周作人, 1885–1967), a writer and a professor at Peking University. Kim's name appears frequently in Zhou's diary from the time.[13] Zhou recorded sending a Chan Buddhist text to Kim on December 15, 1930, and Kim subsequently visited Zhou but failed to meet him. Kim also sent a copy of *Record of the Masters and Disciples of the Laṅkāvatāra School* (C. *Lengjia shizi ji* 楞伽師資記) to Zhou sometime in 1932. From these records, although the details of their interactions are not known, we can assume that when

Kim met with Lu Xun and Zhou Zuoren, they discussed Buddhism in one way or another. In addition, Kim's research on Buddhism must have become more prominent when he relocated to Beijing.

Research in Manchuria

After the Manchurian Incident in 1931, Kim relocated to Fengtian in Manchuria.[14] What led him to this move was a coincidental encounter with descendants of the Three Scholars (K. *Samhaksa* 三學士): Hong Ikhan (洪翼漢, 1586–1637), Yun Chip (尹集, 1606–1637), and O Talche (吳達濟, 1609–1637). During the Manchurian invasion of Korea in 1636, these three had vehemently objected to the Chosŏn court making peace with Qing and, as a result, were arrested and taken to China for execution. Kim later stated that he had developed a rapport with descendants of these scholars who served in the military. These included a Military Department advisor, Lieutenant Colonel Hong (洪); the captain of the Fourth Division of the Kwantung Army, Yun (尹); and the vice consul of the Fengtian Consulate, O (吳).[15] Thanks to these descendants, Kim was able to locate the memorial stones for the Three Scholars in 1933,[16] and this discovery resulted in the publication of biographies of all three.[17]

After the Manchukuo State was established in 1932, the Fengtian National Library was constructed to promote cultural activities in the area, and Kim was hired as a part-time employee on June 7 of the same year.[18] On September 10, he was reassigned as a book organizer and secretary for the deputy director of the library.[19] On April 1, 1933, he was promoted to a full-time librarian with more responsibilities.[20] When the library began collecting rare ancient texts, he was in charge of organizing and preserving materials, including many rubbed copies. By this time, Kim had gained recognition from the Manchukuo government as a valuable employee. This recognition and his rather speedy promotion were attributed in part to the fact that the three descendants he had befriended worked for the Kwangtung army and were influential in the Manchu government.

While serving at the Fengtian National Library, Kim also worked as a journalist for the Fengtian branch of the *Tonga* newspaper[21] and was involved in the local Korean community. In 1933, he participated in an event organized by the Hangul Study Group (K. *Han'gŭl yŏn'guhoe* 한글 연구회) to commemorate the creation of the Korean vernacular *hangul* scripts.[22] Later, he was instrumental in founding a secondary school for

Korean children living in Fengtian.²³ Amid all of these activities, he continued to work at the library until 1954.²⁴

However, his career took another turn in 1936 when he landed a teaching position as an assistant professor at Fengtian Agricultural College.²⁵ This was when he adopted a Japanese name. According to the *Three Thousand Li* (*Samchŏlli* 三千里) in 1940, "Among those who changed their names recently, the Fengtian National Agricultural College professor Kim Kugyŏng submitted his new name, 'Shinba Susumu' (新馬晉), to several places with a long footnote for the name."²⁶ Although the details of this footnote are not known, one can at least guess that Kim changed his name at some point in 1940.

The colonial government initiated its name-change policy in February 1940 and ordered Koreans to submit their new names by August. Only about 7.6 percent of the population had done so by May, but the number jumped to almost 80 percent following government coercion through legal stipulations and encouragement by celebrities.²⁷ As someone who held a public office, it was inevitable that Kim would follow government policy.

In his 1940 book *The History of the Development of Manchuria* (*Manshū hattatsu shi*), historian Inaba Iwakichi (1876–1940) discusses Kim's name change²⁸ because Kim played a role in having Inaba's book translated into Chinese.²⁹ In the preface, Inaba introduces Kim by saying, "Professor Shinba's family name is Kim and his first name Kugyŏng. He is a remarkable scholar in recent history, and he was trained under the auspices of the historian and Sinologist Naitō Konan (内藤湖南 or Naitō Torajirō 内藤虎次郎, 1866–1934). This spring, he [Kim] changed his last name to Shinba and his first name to Susumu. Tainyo (退如) is his penname."³⁰ Korean scholar Yi Kŭnbok speculates that Inaba made this statement because he was glad that Japan's name-change policy had been successful. Given that Kim had changed his name a month after the policy was promulgated, Inaba might have been happy that a prominent Korean scholar such as Kim faithfully followed the imperialization movement (J. *kōminka undō* 皇民化運動).³¹ Based on the extant sources, it is at least safe to say that Kim might have considered himself a citizen of the Japanese empire, regardless of whether this was forced or voluntary. At any rate, Kim continued to publish academic articles and other writings under his new name.³²

In Fengtian, Kim devoted himself to research on Buddhism, the Korean alphabet, and the Manchurian language. The prominent Korean scholar Kim T'aejun (金台俊, 1905–1949) wrote in a 1935 journal article "Impressions of Fengtian" (K. *Pongch'ŏn insang ki* 奉天印象記):

> Kim Kugyŏng had profound knowledge of the Manchurian and Mongolian languages. In Fengtian, he published texts such as Yu Hŭi's [柳僖, 1773–1837] *Monograph on Korean Language* [Ŏnmunji 諺文誌] and Yu Tŭkkong's [柳得恭, 1748–1807] *Record of Luanyang* [K. *Nanyangnok* 灤陽錄] and included them in the *Ginger Garden Collection* [K. *Kangwŏn ch'ongsŏ* 薑園叢書]. Recently, he also published the *Lives of Three Scholars* [K. *Samhaksachŏn* 三學士傳] and expressed his plan to publish Sin Kyŏngjun's [申景濬, 1712–1781] *Phonological Explanation of the Korean Alphabet* [K. *Hunmin chŏngŭm unhae* 訓民正音韻解].[33]

As we can see, Kim's scholarly works and compilations were included in the *Ginger Garden Collection*, and Kim expanded his research into linguistics, most likely because he came to Manchuria through his relationship with the descendants of the Three Scholars. He maintained his interest in these scholars, but it is not known whether he actually published Sin Kyŏngjun's *Hunmin chŏngŭm unhae*.

At this time, Kim Kugyŏng's scholarly work became a catalyst for East Asian scholars' academic networks. For example, he collated and published the Dunhuang version of the *Record of the Masters and Disciples of the Laṅkāvatāra School* that Hu Shi (胡適, 1891–1962) had obtained from France. On the basis of Kim's publication, his former teacher Suzuki Daisetsu published a book in English called *Studies in the Laṅkāvatāra Sūtra* in 1930.[34] Kim tirelessly worked as a translator for Japanese scholars in their research and academic exchanges. He also served as a translator for Chinese scholars when they visited Seoul or interacted with their Japanese counterparts. This was possible because Kim was a seasoned researcher who was fluent in Chinese and Japanese and well connected.[35]

RETURN TO KOREA

Kim returned to Korea shortly after Japan was defeated by the Allied Forces and Korea gained independence in 1945. With his rich experience in teaching and research, he easily landed a teaching job and lectured at Seoul National University. He also instituted the Bibliography of Korean Society (K. *Chosŏn sŏji hakhoe* 朝鮮書誌學會) in 1947 in collaboration with the prominent librarian Pak Pongsŏk (朴奉石, 1905–?), then deputy-director of the National Library of Korea.[36] However, because of the sociopolitical unrest, his scholarly output diminished to just a single article on Hu Shi, who had discovered the *Record of the Masters and Disciples of the Laṅkāvatāra School*. Kim was also mired in the ideological confrontation between the left and the right in postcolonial Korea and went missing during the Korean War of 1950, a fate that befell Pak Pongsŏk as well. Kim disappeared from history at the age of fifty-one.

Academic Accomplishments

Drawing on his multilingual capabilities, Kim published articles on the Korean alphabet and compiled Korean exegeses of Chinese writings.[37] Based on his knowledge of the Manchurian language,[38] in 1935 he published the *Second Edited Canonical Rites of Manchurian Offerings to the Spirits and Heaven* (K. *Chungjŏng Manju chesin chechŏn chŏllye* 重訂滿州祭神祭天典禮), a compilation of the Manchurian rituals for heaven. This book contains a preface from Chinese historian Jin Yufu (金毓黻, 1887–1962), who worked with him in the Fengtian library.

On Buddhism, Kim was the first person to collate and publish the *Record of the Masters and Disciples of the Laṅkāvatāra School*. This great achievement was relatively well recognized in comparison with his other research activities.[39] The prominent Zen scholar Yanagida Seizan (柳田聖山, 1922–2006) later said that Kim Kugyŏng had been asked to combine Stein 2054 and Pelliot 3436, both of which Hu Shi had discovered in 1926, into a single text. Kim undertook the project and published the results under the title *The Corrected Edition of the Copy of the Tang Dynasty's Record of the Masters and Disciples of the Laṅkāvatāra School* (C. *Jiaokan Tangxieben Lengjia shizi ji* 校刊唐寫本楞伽師資記) in 1931, with a preface by Chinese scholar and reformer monk Taixu (太虛, 1890–1947). The lost writings in the *Taisho New Edition of the Buddhist Canon* (J. *Taishō Shinshū Daizōkyō* 大正新修大藏經) include Kim's edition collated with Stein 2054 as the primary source text.[40] In the meantime, Kim Kugyŏng included another revision he made from 1933 to 1934 in the *Ginger Garden Collection* and published it in Shenyang, Manchuria.

The *Ginger Garden Collection* includes the following texts: (1) *The Corrected Edition of the Copy of the Tang Dynasty's Record of the Masters and Disciples of the Laṅkāvatāra School* (校刊唐寫本楞伽師資記), (2) *The*

Corrected Edition on the Record of the Dharma-Jewel through the Generations (C. *Xiaokan lidai fabao ji* 校刊歷代法寶記), (3) *The Corrected Edition of the Treatise on the True School of Awakening the Mind and Returning to One's Original Nature through Sudden Enlightenment of Mahayana* (C. *Xiaokan dasheng kaixin xianxing dunwu zhenzong lun* 校刊大乘開心顯性頓悟眞宗論), (4) *The Corrected Edition of the Anshin-ji version of Bodhidharma's Treatise on Observing the Mind* (C. *Xiaokan anxinsiben Damo dashi guanxin lun* 校刊安心寺本達摩大師觀心論), and (5) *The Corrected Edition of Mr. Yu's Treatise on Han'gŭl* (C. *Xiaokan liushi yanwen zhi* 校刊柳氏諺文志). The first four are all Buddhist texts. According to Yanagida, the Taishō version of (2) is basically a combined version without corrections, whereas Kim's edition in the *Ginger Garden Collection* is straightforward to read and contains the proper corrections.[41] Kim published (3) after collating P 2162 with the Taishō version. He added (4) by combining the Anshin-ji and *Ginger Garden Collection* versions.[42] As such, Kim used a comparative method that was new at the time and was instrumental in creating a more accurate text through meticulous collation.

Kim also published his own research findings based on analyses of these texts. For example, in "The Place Name of Tōwan and Śarīra Stūpa" (J. *Tōwan no chimei to sharitō* 塔湾の地名と舎利塔), he investigated the *stūpas* in Fengtian[43] with a special focus on the reliquary *stūpa* in Tōwan (塔湾), a region that had been largely forgotten. The name "Tōwan" probably came from the reliquary *stūpa*, a thirteen-story octagonal brick structure built during the reign of Emperor Xingzong (興宗, r. 1016–1055) of the Liao (遼) dynasty. This *stūpa* is called "Immaculately Pure Light Śarīra Stūpa" (*Wugou jingguang sheli fota* 無垢淨光舍利佛塔). From the sections on ancient traces in the *Unified Gazetteer of the Great Qing* (C. *Da Qing yitongzhi* 大淸一統志) and the *Unified Gazetteer of Shengjing* (C. *Shengjing tongzhi* 盛京通志), Kim discovered that, behind the *stūpa*, there had been a temple called Sheli-si (舍利寺) or Huilong-si (回龍寺). In his discussion, Kim cited Japanese geographer Tanaka Hidesaku's (田中秀作, 1885–1963) assessment in the *Studies on the Geography of Manchuria* (J. *Manshū chishi kenkyū* 滿洲地誌研究) that this *stūpa* followed a typical Liao style. Tanaka argued that, as a rule, buildings in this style contained *śarīra*. Kim did not fully concur, and by cross-referencing the Classical Chinese, Mongolian, and Manchurian renditions of the *Inscription on the Stele on the Restoration* (C. *Chongxiu beiwen* 重修碑文), he countered that there had been no *śarīra* inside the *stūpa*. He translated the whole Manchurian rendition of the epitaph and determined that it differed in sentence structure from the Chinese version but had the same content. He also identified some misleading records in the Chinese rendition by comparing it with the Manchurian one.

The scholar Okamura Keiji (岡村敬二, 1947–), who first introduced Kim's article, said that Kim had developed his argument from his fieldwork and a thorough reading of the materials.[44] Okamura also confirmed that Kim had taken part in the investigation of the Liaoyang region in 1933 to take rubbings of memorial steles from the Liao and Jin (金) periods after he became a librarian at Fengtian. Kim subsequently investigated the ancient Parhae (渤海, 698–926) region in collaboration with a Japanese research group in 1933 and 1934.[45] His studies of the reliquary *stūpa* resulted from his field-trip research experience.

In Korea, the first article on the *stūpa* that Kim worked on was not published until 2005, and it failed to mention his extensive research on the subject,[46] meaning that Kim's research is not fully recognized in his motherland even now. However, the 2005 study revealed that Kim's claim that the *stūpa* contained no ornaments was incorrect: during repair work, *śarīra* adornments were discovered inside. On the *stūpa*'s style, another study argued, "Considering the importance of Koryŏ in Liao's diplomacy, not to mention the resuming of the close and stable diplomatic relationship between Liao and Koryŏ, it is highly likely that a new way of decorating *śarīra*, which started during the reign of Liao Emperor Xingzong (興宗, r. 1031–1055), was a Buddhist ritual element that was transmitted from Koryŏ."[47] This is a significant point and offers a new view that enhances the academic research on this reliquary *stūpa*.

Although Kim paid attention to Liao culture with a keen interest, he overlooked the crucial connection between Koryŏ and Liao. In his translation of the chapter "Khitan Culture in Manchuria and Mongolia" (C. *Manmeng zhi Qidan wenhua* 滿蒙之契丹文化) from the Records on the Collection of the Stone Carving in Liaoling (C. *Liaoling shikeji lu* 遼陵石刻集錄), which the famous Chinese epigrapher Luo Zhenyu (羅振玉, 1866–1940) compiled in 1934,[48] Kim simply compared the *stūpa* with its Japanese counterparts and failed to even consider comparing Koryŏ and Liao, although they had a close relationship at the time the *stūpa* was erected.

One of his articles on Buddhism from this time was "On *Nanming's Ode to the Song about Realizing the Truth* in the Koryŏ Dynasty's Tripitaka-Woodblock of Mr. Kamio's Shinjuzō Collection" (J. *Kamioshi shinjuzo Koraiban nameisen shodoka nitsuite* 神尾氏眞珠莊藏高麗板南明

泉頌證道歌について).⁴⁹ "Kamio" refers to Kamio Kazuharu, a researcher on the cultural history of Liao (Khitan), and the term "shinjuzō" (眞珠莊) was the name of Kamio Kazuharu's (神尾弌春, 1893–?) personal study room. Kamio owned many rare books in Korean editions and provided Zen-related texts to several experts. From Kamio, Kim also borrowed the *Great Master Bodhidharma's Treatise on Contemplation* (C. *Damo dashi guanxin lun* 達磨大師觀心論) and included it in the *Kangwŏn ch'ongsŏ*. When Kamio made public all of the books he owned in 1942 for the first time, Kim had a chance to read the Koryŏ edition of *Nanming's Ode to the Song about Realizing the Truth* (C. *Nanmingquan song zhengdaoge* 南明泉頌證道歌, 1239) and the *Work on the Song about Realizing the Truth* (C. *Zhengdaoge shishi* 證道歌事實, 1248). In his article, Kim evaluated these two texts as valuable references that would generate a lot of scholarly questions and provided his reasons for this judgment. Through a close reading of the *Nanmingquan song zhengdaoge*, he found the thirty-two missing words from the "Song of the Dharma Spring" (Faquan song 法泉頌) in the *Xu zang jing* (Supplemental Buddhist Canon). He also argued that the text appeared to come from wooden printing type but in fact came from woodblocks. In addition, he drew attention to the five words on the title page: "重彫鑄字本" (C. *zhong diao zhu zi ben* or "Revised Steel Type Edition"). At the time, it was generally agreed in scholarly circles that Korean printing type had spread only during the Chosŏn period. Kim corrected this view by demonstrating advanced printing technology from Korea. He expressed amazement at this, saying, "The fact that the metal type was re-created [in Chosŏn Korea] 200 years prior to the Yongle [永樂, the reign of Yongle Emperor of the Ming dynasty in the fifteenth century] is marvelous." As evidence for this chronology, Kim noted that the phrase "steel type" (*zhu zi* 鑄字) was a Korean-style Chinese term that had never been used in China. As for the *Work on the Song about Realizing the Truth*, Kim pointed out that the text was significant because it was a commentary on the *Song about Realizing the Truth* (C. *Zhengdao ge* 證道歌) and its author was a Koryŏ monk.

Kim's arguments and bibliographical acumen in this case have not received scholarly attention. However, it is necessary to reflect on the meaning of the five words *zhong diao zhu zi ben* that Kim noticed. It recently made headlines that new metal-typed text had been found in Korea that was about 130 years older than the *Essentials of Pointing Directly to the Essence of Mind* (K. *Chikchi simch'e yojŏl* 直指心體要節, 1377), previously the oldest-known such text. The new document was the aforementioned

Nanming's Ode to the Song about Realizing the Truth (*Nanmingquan song zhengdao ge*). However, because there was no mention of the Kamio edition in a recent research article, further inquiry is needed into what happened to the Kamio edition.[50] Kim understood the five words to mean "The metal type was re-created." But he left it an open question whether the Kamio version had been created in Koryŏ or imported from Song China. In Kim's time, the existence of the *Essentials of Pointing Directly to the Essence of Mind* was not yet known, so there is no possibility that he recognized *Nanming's Ode to the Song about Realizing the Truth* as a text produced with full metal type. Rather, he found a phrase that could overturn the dismissive Japanese scholarly view and give historical significance to the printing culture of the Chosŏn period. His challenge to Japanese scholarship on Korean printing technology is a testament to the fact that he did not merely cater to the needs of colonial scholarship, but instead asserted the significance of Korean culture and identity in East Asian civilization.

COLLATING OF THE GINGER GARDEN COLLECTION

The most significant achievement in Kim Kugyŏng's Buddhist scholarship may be found in his attempt to compile an accurate text of the *Ginger Garden Collection* through his collating work. Two texts show in detail how meticulously he collated the *Ginger Garden Collection*: (1) *The Corrected Edition of the Treatise on the True School of Awakening the Mind and Returning to One's Original Nature through Sudden Enlightenment of Mahayana* (校刊大乘開心顯性頓悟眞宗論) and (2) *The Corrected Edition of the Anshin-ji Version of Bodhidharma's Treatise on Observing the Mind* (C. *Xiaokan Anxinsiben Damo dashi guanxin lun* 刊安心寺本達摩大師觀心論). The records of his collating work for these two texts are still extant.

On the other hand, the texts (1) The Corrected Edition of the Copy of the Tang Dynasty's Record of the Masters and Disciples of the Laṅkāvatāra School (校刊唐寫本楞伽師資記) and (2) The Corrected Edition on the Record of the Dharma-Jewel through the Generations (校刊歷代法寶記) were also published after being collated, but we do not have the records of their collation. The passages regarded as most accurate were selected after the collating work and then published. However, according to the collation records, (3) *Xiaokan dasheng kaixin xianxing dunwu zhenzong lun* and (4) *Xiaokan anxinsiben Damo dashi guanxin lun* retain distinct features of each text, although they are not unitary. As mentioned above,

Yanagada reported that Kim did not use the collation method employed in the Taishō canon. This was the case with (1) and (2) but not (3) and (4). Here, I discuss Kim's collation method with (3) and (4).

I first describe Kim's collation method in the Treatise on Contemplating Mind (K. *Kwansim non* 觀心論). The *Kwansim non* is included in volume 85 of the Taishō canon. Kim compared this text with the Anshin-ji (安心寺) version (1570) owned by Kamio Kazuharu. Kim's collated text is divided into two parts. The first part consists of the preface by Pak Isŏng (朴移成, fifteenth century) and "Errata in the Treatise on Contemplating Mind" (K. *Kwansim non* kano p'yo 觀心論刊誤表), which is a single page of corrections of errors in the main text of the Taishō version of the *Kwansim non*. During his collation, Kim did not correct the main text of the Taishō version; he pointed out errors only by presenting the list of corrections. According to Kim's preface to the *Kyogan kwansim non* (The Corrected Edition of the Treatise on Contemplating Mind), he had no base text other than the Anshin-ji version with which he could proofread. It appears that, because the corresponding part of the Taishō version was missing, Kim had to collate Pak Isŏng's preface and the first chapter up to where the Dunhuang manuscript begins entirely on the basis of his own judgment. Kim corrected three errors in Pak's preface, however, and later discoveries from other versions have shown that Kim's corrections were right. In the main text before the Dunhuang manuscript begins, Kim also made three corrections. The sentences containing the errors run as follows:

問曰云何觀心稱心爲了

雖假緣和合本不相生淨人恒樂善因染心常思惡業

Kim changed the underlined words 心 (C. *xin*), 本 (C. *ben*), and 人 (C. *ren*) to 之 (C. *Zhi*), 無 (C. *wu*), and 心, respectively. According to the oldest extant version of Wŏn'gaksa (1538), which is available at the Archives of Buddhist Culture at Dongguk University, the word 本 should be 互, not 無. This is also the case with the version compiled in 1580, which is kept in the National Library of Korea. In these versions, the phrase reads "cannot mutually generate each other." Kim probably read it as "There is no case in which they do not produce each other."

Kim also fixed the errors in the part that appears in the Dunhuang version on the basis of his own judgment. For instance, one appears in the sentence:

答曰. 欲修六度當淨六根欲淨六根先降六賊

The underlined word, 當 (C. *dang*), is 常 (C. *chang*) in the Anshin-ji version, but Kim corrected it to 當. Given that 常 appears in both the 1538 and 1580 versions, the versions popular in Korea also contain 常. However, Kim seems to have read the phrase as "[One] should purify six faculties" rather than "[One] always purifies six faculties." This was the way Kim corrected the errors for his version.

Second, at the end of the *Kwansim non*, there is a record of collation with the Taishō version. This collation amounts to seventeen and a half pages. Notably, Kim did not make any comments about errors in the Dunhuang part of the text. Therefore, the collation records prove that Kim adopted the Taishō canon's collation method. But the list of corrections demonstrates that his system was distinctive and analogous to the critical approach to text collation.

Next, (3) *Xiaokan dasheng kaixin xianxing dunwu zhenzong lun* has a collation record that amounts to about three pages but no list of corrections. In this text, Kim collated the Taishō version of P. 2162 directly with the Dunhuang manuscript. For instance, he read "☐☐☐" in the Taishō version as "作夢大" (C. *zuo meng da*), but he kept the "☐☐☐" in the original text of the *Ginger Garden Collection*. Kim also changed "名之心" (C. *ming zhi xin*) in the Taishō version to "明之爲心" (C. *ming zhi wei xin*) in the *Ginger Garden Collection* and "境智無二" (C. *jing zhi wu er*) to "境智不二" (C. *jing zhi bu er*). Thus, Kim's collation methods can be seen as demonstrating his scholastic abilities and acute judgment. Kim Kugyŏng emphasized the importance of philology and archaeology in his study of Buddhism. As a polyglot who could handle both Manchurian and Mongolian, Kim was able to deal confidently enough with Chinese texts to make careful revisions for the *Taishō shinshū daizōkyō*.

Unlike his contributions to textual and archeological analyses, it is not easy to find sources that illuminate Kim's insights into Buddhist teachings and practice. In his scholarship, he seemed less concerned with Buddhist thought than with categorizing and organizing texts. As Son Chihye shows by way of Hu Shi's letter, however, Kim seems to have had insufficient knowledge of the history of the Chan school, at least, as Hu Shi criticized Kim for not grasping the history of Chan after the Lengjia school.[51] This is probably because he was familiar only with the old history of Chan and did not properly understand the value of the Dunhuang texts.

Conclusion

We have explored Kim Kugyŏng's life, addressed some important turning points, and assessed his academic achievements. Kim was a nomad who wandered Korea, Japan, China, and Manchuria, a liminal person who was a product of a tumultuous time in Korea.

Kim's nomadic lifestyle might have been driven by multiple factors. The fact that he was expelled from a teaching position because of a student boycott after returning to Korea and finished his studies in Japan raises a question about his national identity. It appears that he opened his eyes to national consciousness in Beijing, where he befriended several renowned scholars. The fact that he was also involved in promoting the Korean vernacular hangul demonstrates that he was conscious of his Korean identity. At the same time, he probably considered himself a citizen of the Japanese empire, as he moved to Fengtian in Manchuguo to work for the National Library there after the Manchurian Incident. That he defended changing his name to a Japanese one and published under his new name is further evidence of this. After the collapse of Imperial Japan, Kim tried to assume an academic and social role among the intellectual elite of postcolonial Korea, lecturing at Seoul National University and founding the Bibliography Society, but he met an unfortunate fate, disappearing from public view during the Korean War.

One of Kim's remarkable research accomplishments was his publication of collated and corrected editions. The new method of collation he employed was published in the *Ginger Garden Collection*. This did not include the Yuan Dynasty block-printed edition *Song about Realizing the Truth* (C. *Yuan keben Zhengdao ge* 元刻本 證道歌, 1942) that Kim had corrected and published in Fengtian. Nonetheless, the publication of the corrected edition of *Record of the Masters and Disciples of the Laṅkāvatāra School* triggered meaningful debates among renowned scholars in China and Japan. In his research on the reliquary *stūpa* in Tōwan, Kim thoroughly investigated a *stūpa* that had received little attention and even drew a sectional diagram of it for close analysis. His ability to read Manchurian was also fully demonstrated in this research. Another study of his on the Yuan dynasty block-printed edition *Song about Realizing the Truth* was an examination of the meaning of the text through the Kamio edition.

Kim was neither a nationalist nor a socialist who sacrificed his life for the pain and suffering of his time. Still less was he either anti-Japanese or a pro-Japanese collaborator with no sense of Korean nationalist identity. Rather, he was a transnational scholar who sought to expand his own horizons and adapt himself to the currents of his time. His life might have been interrupted by the invisible obstacles that lay between nationalism, colonialism, and scholarship. However, it is also undeniable that he was able to crisscross national, ethnic, linguistic, and cultural boundaries and engage with scholars from China, Japan, and Manchuria, which was facilitated and augmented by opportunities made available in the Japanese empire. He was not an exception in this; many intellectuals and scholars faced similar situations. Unfortunately, many of their dynamic life stories and the contributions they made to their professions have been forgotten in postcolonial Korean nationalist historiography. It is rather a relief that recent research has begun to reveal Kim's accomplishments. I expect that his scholarship and his scholarly role as a bridge between China, Korea, and Japan in modern times will come to be better recognized and appreciated.

Notes

1. Internet dictionaries such as *Encyclopedia of Korean Culture* and *Doosan Encyclopedia* define him as a Zen historian and mention the correction and publication of some Dunhuang texts as his accomplishments.

2. Kim, *Sŏn munhŏn yŏn'gu-Yukcho tangyŏng ŭi segye* (A Study on the Text of Sŏn-Platform Sutra of Sixth Patriarchs); Ilchi, *Ttŏdonŭn Tonhwang* (A Floating Dunwhang).

3. Son, "Wasurerareta kindai no chishikijin Kim Kyūkei ni kansuru chōsa" (A Study on a Forgotten Modern Intellectual, Kim Kugyŏng), 91–119. Here, Kim's life was divided into the following periods, introducing his research attainments: (1) his study in Japan; (2) correcting and publishing Dunhuang Texts; (3) his stay in Beijing, interacting with writers and scholars; (4) his stay in Manchuria, investigating and researching ancient remains and history; (5) after returning to Korea.

4. Previous researchers have called this school "Kyŏngsŏng cheil kodŭng pot'ong hakkyo"; it was renamed in 1921. Because Kim graduated before that, I use the former name.

5. He contributed an article titled "Tongmo ŭi chŏng" (Friend's Affection) in October 1919 to the journal's publisher, *Chungjŏn posŏngsa*, which accorded with his occupation as an elementary school teacher.

6. Son, "Wasurerareta kindai no chishikijin Kim Kyūkei," 93. Because Kuraishi worked for Tokyo University and Kyoto University during this time, he probably lectured at Ōtani University.

7. Kim, "Kohak ŭl mokchŏk ŭro Ilbon ŭro osiryŏ hasinun yŏrŏ hyŏngnim-kke" (Dear Brothers Who Would Like to Come to Japan for Studying).

8. Ko, "Taehan sidae Ilbon yuhaksaeng tŭrŭi Pulgyo yŏn'gu tonghyang" (A Study on the Buddhist Research Trends of Japanese Students in the Korean Period—Focused on Japanese Students in Japan during the Japanese Colonial Period), 145–67.

9. Cho, "Seoul Taehakkyo Chungang Tosŏgwan ŭi palchok" (Establishment of the Central Library of Seoul National University). In a letter to Naitō Konan (1866–1933) in April 1927, Kim reported that he would work for the university starting April 9. This probably refers to the fact that he worked for Kyŏngsŏng Imperial University Library (Son, "Wasurerareta kindai no chishikijin Kim Kyūkei," 97).

10. Kim, "Nosin i mannan Han'gugin" (The Korean Whom Lu Xun Met), 149.

11. Hong, "Nosin i kwa kŭ chejadŭl, kŭrigo Chosŏn insik" (Lu Xun and His Disciples and Korea Recognition), 265.

12. Kim, "Nosin i mannan Han'gugin," 153.

13. Kim, "Nosin i mannan Han'gugin," 150–52.

14. In "Wasurerareta kindai," Son Chihye mentions the possibility that Kim participated in the Korean independence movement between 1933 and 1934. However, this seems unlikely because he was in Manchuria at that time. Son Chihye probably confused him with the female activist Kim Kugyŏng, who joined the Korean Young Women's Union, the organization that Kim Kyŏngae (1889–1976), wife of the Korean politician Kim Kyusik (1881–1950), formed in Shanghai in August 1930. The fact that Kim Kugyŏng went to Fengtian right after the Manchurian Incident is recorded in "Hojŏk ssi ŭi haksul tongnip simnyŏn kyehoegan" (Mr. Hu Shi's [1891–1962] Ten-Year Plan for Scholarly Liberation), 9–12.

15. Kim, "Shinyō to Chōsen no sangakushi" (Shenyang and the Three Scholars of Korea), 44–46.

16. "Injo tangnyŏn ŭi samhaksa Pongchŏn esŏ pisŏk palgyŏn" (The Discovery of the Memorial Stone for Three Scholars during the Years of King Injo (r. 1623–1649).

17. Kim, "Shinyō to Chōsen," 46.

18. Okamura, "Ryōneishō toshokan hōmonki" (A Record on the Visit to the Liaoning Library), 189.

19. Okamura, "Ryōneishō toshokan hōmonki," 190–91.

20. Okamura, "Ryōneishō toshokan hōmonki," 190–91.

21. "Kŭn'go" (Announcement); Suzuki, "Toshokan fugō (Toshokan chizu kigō) to to kuni kamae ni to" (Library Symbols [Library Map symbols and ㅏ]), 1–7.

22. "Han'gŭl kinyŏmsik Pongchŏn esŏ kŏhaeng" (The Founding of Hangul Celebrated at Fengtian).

23. "Toman palsimnyŏn ŭi kyŏlchŏng!" (The Fruit of the Eighty Years of Korean Immigration to Manchuria).

24. Suzuki, "Toshokan fugō," 1–7.

25. Kim, "Tōwan no chimei to sharitō" (The Place Name of Tawan and the Shari Stūpa).
26. Gaodeng Nongye Xuexiao in Manchuria was renamed to Guoli Gaodeng Nongye Daxue in 1938 (Okamura, "Ryōneishō toshokan hōmonki," 191).
27. Yi, "Ch'angssi kaemyŏng chŏngch'aek kwa chosŏnin ŭi taeŭng" (The Name-Changing Program and the Reaction of Koreans Under Japan's Compulsory Occupation Period), 180.
28. Qinpu Li, *Tuo jie, lama, Jin Jiujing* (Nirvana, Lama, Kim Kugyŏng), 193.
29. Mori, "Manshū shi to Tōhoku shi no aida—Inaba Iwakichi to Jin Yufu no kōryū yori," Kansai daigaku tozai gakushutsu kenkyu kiyo (Between the History of Manchuria and Dongbei: The Relationship between Inaba Iwakichi and Jin Yufu as Observed in Jingwushi—Riji), 343–63.
30. Mori, "Manshū shi to Tōhoku shi no aida," 343–63.
31. Q. Li, *Tuo jie, lama, Jin Jiujing*, 194. In providing Kim's profile, Yi Kŭnbok interestingly presents Kim as a Buddhist priest of the Ōtani branch of the Jōdōshinshū without giving any further details.
32. Shinma, "Aru hi no kenryūtei" (One Day, Emperor Qianlon); Shinma, "Kamioshi shinjuzō Koraiban nameisen shōdōka ni tsuite" (On *Nanmingquan song zheng dao ge* in the Koryŏ Dynasty's Tripitaka-Woodblock of Mr. Kamio shinjuzō's Collection), 13–21. For more details, see Mori's "Manshū shi to tōhoku shi no aida," footnote 25.
33. *Samch'ŏlli* 7/9 (October 1, 1935), 58. It was quoted again by Son Chihye (2015).
34. Suzuki, *Studies in the Lankavatara Sutra*.
35. Son, "Wasurerareta kindai no chishikijin Kim Kyūkei," 343–63; Sū Sōsō, "Sanjū nendai no Pekin ni okeru Sen Tōson-zō no—Nihonjin ryūgakusei no me wo tōshite" (The Image of Qian Daosun in Beijing in 1930s: Through the Eyes of Japanese Overseas Students), 89–101; Sakayori Masashi, "Bokkaishi kenkyū to kindai nihon" (Research on Bohai History and Modern Japan), 1–12.
36. Lee Ch'ŏlgyo, "Pak Pong-sŏk ŭi saengae wa chŏjak e taehaesŏ" (On the Life and Work of Park Bongsŏk), 101–18.
37. Kim, *Kyogan yussi ŏnmunji* (The Printing and Proofreading of *yussi ŏnmunji*).
38. Kim, "Manshūgo to kango o konyū sitaru kitsu hōkai" (A Type of Chipangxie That Uses Both Manchu and Chinese), 222–42; Kim, *Manshū jibo*.
39. For details, see Ilchi, *Ttŏdonŭn Tonhwang* and Son, *Wasurerareta kindai no chishikijin Kim Kyūkei ni kansuru chōsa*.
40. Yanagida, *Shoki no zenshi I* (Early Zen History I), 40.
41. Yanagida, *Shoki no zenshi II* (Early Zen History II), 32.
42. Tanaka, "Tonkō Zenshū siryō bunrui mokuroku shoko" (A Draft of the Classified Catalogue of the Zen Buddhist Texts from Tunhuang), 1–18.

43. Kim, "Tōwan no chimei to sharitō," 1–14.

44. Okamura, *Nichi-Man Bunka Kyōkai no rekishi: Sōsōki o chūshin ni* (History of the Nichiman Cultural Association), 191.

45. *Tōa Kogo gakkai, Tokyojo* (Tokyo Castle), *Tōa Kogo gakkai* (1939).

46. Chu, "Yo Hŭngjong nyŏngan (1031–1055) ŭi Pulsari changŏm yŏn'gu" (A Study on the Buddhist Reliquaries during the Reign of Xingzong [1031–1055] of the Liao Dynasty), 197–221.

47. Chu, "Yo Hŭngjong nyŏngan," 217.

48. Lua, *Liaoling shikejilu vol. 6* (Records on the Collection of the Stone Carving in Liaoling, vol. 6), 1–2.

49. Shinma, "Kamioshi shinjuzō Koraiban nameisen shōdōka ni tsuite."

50. Nam, "Chŭngdogaja ŭi palgyŏn kwa Nammyŏng Chŏnhwa song Chŭngdoga ŭi yŏn'gu" (The Discovery of the Chŭngdoga's Movable Metal Type and the Study of *The Song of Enlightenment*), 5–84.

51. Son, "Wasurerareta kindai no chishikijin Kim Kyūkei," 100–3.

Chapter 10

Praying in Kangnam and Longing for the Mountains

The Dilemma of Centrality in Contemporary Korean Buddhism

Florence Galmiche

Introduction

Buddhism in contemporary South Korea evokes contrasting ideas that verge sometimes on contradiction.[1] Temples in beautiful landscapes never fail to captivate hikers and tourists; beyond their picturesque quality, however, they often house monastic communities.[2] Some temples seem rustic and simple, while others may impress visitors with their brand-new facilities, projecting wealth and consumption. The most universally promoted images of Buddhism emphasize serene and remote monasteries, but everyday life in many temples revolves primarily around lively meetings of followers and the eclectic prayers and offerings of a busy audience. Such differences and contrasts within the "Buddhist world" are not superficial, nor are they simple indications of false appearances or a lack of authenticity. Instead, they echo lasting tensions that have marked Korean Buddhism for more than a century. They speak of the challenges met by Buddhism when it was called upon to prove its relevance to modern society and also questioned regarding its fundamental principles and purposes.

One of the major dilemmas faced by contemporary mainstream Buddhism, as represented notably by the Jogye Order, revolves around its place and status in society. Since at least the end of the nineteenth century, Korean Buddhists have striven to give their faith and institutions greater social prominence, but this aspiration has also been a major source of contention. On the basis of ethnographic fieldwork conducted in Buddhist temples and associations mostly from 2006 to 2015, this chapter analyzes how the desire to rebuild the status of Buddhism in society has been manifested in temples affiliated with the Jogye Order. It also addresses the questions and consequences, sometimes unexpected, that these renovation initiatives have provoked.

This chapter shows that several reforms and modernization projects have been achieved by Buddhists, bringing profound changes in the life of temples. At the dawn of the twenty-first century, Buddhism is backed by powerful religious institutions that can count on officially affiliated followers who are organized in various associations and share at least the basis of a common orthodoxy. As a crucial consequence of these reforms, the center of gravity of the Buddhist world has partly moved from the monks to the laypeople. Attention to the needs and demands of a large audience and adaptation to contemporary society have become imperatives for temples and are seen as evidence of their social utility. However, reform projects, together with historical circumstances, have also contributed to strengthening monastic status and revalorizing asceticism, helping to restore weight and prestige to the monastic ideal. This double movement—massification of the audience and valorization of the monastic ideal—has given Buddhism a stronger place in society and a renewed influence, even beyond the country.

However, it has also laid the foundation for a difficult equation. Currently, Buddhism is experiencing tension between very different sources of legitimacy: its active role in society and its status as a religion with a universal vocation on the one hand and the value of ascetic renunciation on the other, which implies maintaining a distance from the objectives and values of society.

Aspiration for the Center

Most urban temples in today's South Korea actively undertake outreach initiatives and other activities to respond to the diverse demands of the public. For a few, such as Pongŭn Monastery (奉恩寺)[3] in the wealthy neighborhood of Kangnam, for example, such initiatives have led to gigantic development projects in line with the dominant conception of what a "successful religious institution" is in contemporary South Korea. In a stately complex of freshly renovated buildings and green spaces, Pongŭn Temple hosts a wide range of rituals and ceremonies as well as many types of classes, cultural programs, and social activities. It also offers many amenities for members, visitors, and tourists. Supporters of such initiatives value them as a means for Buddhism to engage with urban life and rebuild its relevance and centrality in Korea and beyond. They also assign them values according to the precepts of Mahāyāna Buddhism, especially the responsibility to spiritually educate the population. In some cases, this perspective is accompanied by a critical view of some monasteries' distance from society and a denunciation of ascetic remoteness. This ambition to better integrate Buddhism into society and to increase its visibility is far from a recent phenomenon. Instead, it echoes a recurrent concern throughout the history of Buddhism: to demonstrate its relevance and usefulness for society and the nation. This priority has taken on new importance in the modern context of increased concern about the prosperity and even the survival of Buddhism, especially as other religions have competed for prominence.[4]

After five centuries of relegation to a secondary position during the Chosŏn period (1392–1897),[5] Buddhism's status achieved a significant revival at the end of the nineteenth century.[6] However, this new opportunity for Buddhist communities to increase their influence in society occurred in a context of conflict and growing Japanese and Western influence.[7] When the law that prohibited Buddhist monks from entering the capital was suspended in 1895, missionaries from various Japanese Buddhist schools as well as Protestant and Catholic missionaries were already actively proselytizing in Korea. Buddhist monks expected to revive Buddhism, but they also faced a need to redefine their identities in the face of ongoing modernization efforts as well as several other competing religions. Worried that Buddhism would be further marginalized or even disappear and looking for a way to give the Dharma a greater importance in the "new society," some intellectuals called for a reform of Korean Buddhism and particularly criticized the chasm between the monastic community and society.

In spite of significant differences, Korean Buddhist reformists in modern times were particularly active in denouncing the isolation of

Buddhism and the distance between the monastic community and the social concerns of the laity. Emphasizing both the survival of Buddhism and its duty to work toward a better society, they advocated for a process of secularization (in the sense of engagement with the world), and some supported the authorization of clerical marriage. In this intellectual context, critics particularly targeted the remote locations of monasteries and their tendency to overvalue renunciation. One of the influential figures of the time, the monk Han Yongun (韓龍雲, also known as Manhae 萬海, 1879–1944), was particularly vehement in criticizing monastic withdrawal. He ironically described monasteries as "a special world outside of the normal world . . . concerned only with their own cleanliness" and wondered with regret "how many of the accomplished and famous have entered these formal 'separate universes'—from the point of view of the spirit, these devil-inhabited black mountains—to decay there in silence, together with the grass and the trees, without sending a single message to the outside world?"[8] In his treatise "On the Reformation of Korean Buddhism," he points out that this distance from the rest of the world was a major cause of what he describes as the social and spiritual decay of Korean Buddhism.

To compete with other religions and counteract monastic withdrawal from the world, modernist reformers of Buddhism have emphasized propagation as their most crucial priority. As extensively analyzed by Mark Nathan, the concept of "Buddhist propagation" (K. *p'ogyo* 布教) was "a ubiquitous feature in nearly all the writings on Korean Buddhist reform in the first two decades of colonial rule."[9] Closely associated with a concern for developing religious education for both monastics and the laity, this new emphasis on propagation was accompanied by a movement of Buddhist activities from the mountains to the cities.[10] Several schools were created with the aim of giving monks an education in line with modernity, integrating, for example, geography, natural sciences, and history.[11] In addition, Buddhist monks attempted to create "propagation centers" aimed at the laity in villages and cities. In 1910, several monasteries collaborated to open the "Central Propagation Center of Korean Buddhism" (*Chosŏn Pulgyo chungang p'ogyodang* 朝鮮佛教中央布教堂) in Seoul, which was followed in 1912 by the "Central Propagation Center of the Korean Sŏn Order" (*Chosŏn Sŏnjong chungang p'ogyodang* 朝鮮禪宗中央布教堂). In 1913, there were eighteen propagation centers in Korea. This number increased to 117 by 1930.[12] The success of these new institutions remained limited, and many closed their doors after a few years. However, they contributed to the development of Buddhism in urban areas as well as the emergence of Buddhist temples primarily directed to the laity.

Recent historiography has brought necessary nuances to the excessively negative characterization that was generally made of Chosŏn Buddhism. Nonetheless, at the dawn of the twentieth century, the main priority for many monastics was to rebuild and revitalize Korean Buddhism and its status in society. Many Korean and foreign observers of that time noticed the generally degraded status of monastics, sometimes with surprise or concern. Maurice Courant, for example, a pioneer of Korean studies in France, noted that when he was in Korea (1890–1892), monastics were reduced to the lowest social rank "together with witches, butchers and prostitutes."[13] Although traditional Buddhism in the early twentieth century was still struggling with discrimination and negative portrayals that had not completely disappeared, new schools of Buddhism and other religions such as Christianity were benefiting from a growing audience and a reputation for modernity and social engagement. This situation as a whole contributed to sow the seeds in Buddhist circles of an acute concern, if not obsession, with revitalization and improved social status. Moreover, the strength and influence of Silla and Koryŏ Buddhism and the power attributed to Christianity in the West became lasting models and goals for reformers. As Hwansoo Kim stated, "reinsert[ing] itself into the center of society" has since then become a crucial priority for the Buddhist institution; as a result, "to return to the center of society figuratively, Korean Buddhists sought to return to the center literally."[14] More than a century later, this ambition of returning "to the center of society" still resounds with the aspirations of mainstream temples, especially those striving to strengthen their position in affluent areas. This chapter describes a few specific cases of such temples.

Buddhacizing Laity and Promoting Buddhism in the Public Sphere

To increase Buddhism's influence in society and give it the status of a proper religion in the eyes of the public, Buddhist institutions faced a challenge that remained crucial throughout the twentieth century: the integration of laity. Even today, the definition and the role of lay Buddhists remain critical questions; in spite of repeated attempts to reduce the distance between monastics and laity, this issue is a recurrent concern in

Buddhist circles. In the second half of the twentieth century, lay Buddhist intellectuals expressed sharp criticism of the monastic community, accusing it of neglecting "common believers" and failing to spread Buddhist teachings. These criticisms were notably voiced by the movement of Minjung Buddhism (民衆佛敎) and by socially engaged lay groups.[15] More broadly, they reproached dominant Buddhist institutions for their lack of social investment and politically conservative positions. Alternative Buddhist schools have further challenged the Jogye Order by strongly emphasizing the importance of lay practice and adaptation to modern society.[16] Many lay Buddhists have come together in relatively independent associations in which they organize classes, lectures, and reflections on the reform of Buddhist institutions.

In contrast with this generally intellectual and sometimes militant form of lay Buddhism, the majority of temple attendees did not self-identify as "Buddhist" until recently. Yoon Yee-Heum analyzed religion surveys conducted in Korea in the 1980s and noted, "[In contrast to] Christians [who] can accurately be counted by a questionnaire, Buddhism shows a very high difference between self-identified members and those who can be classified as 'practical.' . . . 'Practical' Buddhists outnumber self-identified Buddhists by a ratio of more than two to one."[17]

This discrepancy between the number of people who took part in Buddhist prayers and ceremonies and those who self-identified as "Buddhist" has also been documented in detail by anthropologists who conducted fieldwork in South Korea in the 1970s and the early 1980s. Alexandre Guillemoz[18] and Laurel Kendall,[19] for example, shed light on the prevailing "continuum" of the religious life of villagers and the proximity between prayers to Shamanist and Buddhist shrines. In reaction to this context, gaining, maintaining, and making membership visible became a guiding principle for Buddhism, reinforced by competition with Christian (especially Protestant) churches that promote strong and visible affiliation among their members.

Since the early twentieth century, Buddhist reformers have worked to counter such religious continuums and strengthen believers' loose affiliations with Buddhism. They have particularly targeted prayers for practical or worldly benefits,[20] denouncing them as a symbol of incorrect and superstitious (K. *misinjŏk* 迷信的) practice. Today, mothers' prayers and bows in temples for the academic success of their children are frequently criticized as examples of the so-called shamanistic and mundane excesses of popular Buddhism. Even if Buddhism in the Korean peninsula has always given a prominent place to practical religiosity, since the end of the nineteenth century, prayers for good fortune have tended to be regarded in religious circles as resulting from the "polluting" influence of popular beliefs and Shamanism.[21] This view is generally based on the idea that prayers for success, luck, or any other kind of practical benefit do not comply with Buddhist teachings and values. In temples today, one hears often that Buddhism does not mean praying for benefits or luck but instead finding one's true self through cultivation practices like meditation. Criticism of practical religiosity is sometimes sharp and stigmatizes prayers for success in harsh terms: "Today, you can see a lot of people praying for success in the University Entrance Examination. . . . You are not beggars who beg the Buddha or the Bodhisattvas to receive something. Ah, Buddha, give me this, give me that! While rubbing one's hands [in prayer]. . . . This is not Buddhism! You should not do that!"[22] Such teachings and admonitions are common among the Buddhist clerics and laypeople who are engaged in temple life and management.

These warnings do not mean, however, that propitiatory rites are altogether forbidden in temples. Most temples continue to organize ceremonies for practical benefits, even as they also offer sutra or meditation training classes. Propitiatory rites frequently coexist with warnings against prayers for good fortune. One of the most salient aspects of these contemporary teachings is the clear distinction between "prayers for good fortune" (K. *kibok* 祈福) and "correct prayers" (K. *parŭn kido* 바른 기도). But importantly enough, all prayers for worldly benefits are not regarded as "prayers for good fortune." What seems to be problematic here is less a matter of wanting practical benefits than the forms that the prayers take and the ways practitioners understand and describe the outcomes of their devotion. Key issues in these public teachings include understanding whether a given practice is a Buddhist one and praying and practicing in a *properly Buddhist way*, even when prayers aim at solving practical problems. This is clearly illustrated in a teaching given at Pongŭn Temple on August 1, 2007, by the monk Hyegŏ (慧炬). His talk was published the day after in an online Buddhist journal with the title "If you want to pray correctly for the students who are taking university entrance exam."[23] In this talk attended by about 500 people, Hyegŏ expressed his understanding and empathy with the anguish of parents whose children were preparing for the difficult test. His teaching condemned direct solicitations to the Buddhas and Bodhisattvas but praised the opportunity for parents to wholeheartedly experience authentic prayer and faith (K. *illyŏm* 一念) by sincerely trying to understand Buddhist doctrines and values, even while praying for the success of their children.

The current movements to reform popular Buddhism are less aimed at suppressing practical religiosity than at regulating and rephrasing it in accord with contemporary orthodoxy. As noted by Richard D. McBride, the contemporary success of handbooks and manuals where Buddhist monks explain to the general public how to choose and use *dhāraṇi* (K. *tarani* 陀羅尼) and mantras (K. *chinŏn* 眞言) when praying for worldly benefits shows that practical religiosity is far from being simply condemned in the Buddhist world.[24] Religious institutions, however, are concerned about integrating it into Buddhist orthodoxy, especially when the related prayers and rites are done within temples.

In this context, temples give central importance to educational programs that aim to regulate practices. The increase and systematization of progressive courses for laity have been conceptualized by Buddhist institutions and intellectuals[25] as crucial tools to transform "the common people who come to the temple with the vague thought that they may be Buddhist into real Buddhists."[26] In their teachings, monastics emphasize the need for believers to learn about the central principles of Buddhism so that they can avoid superstitious practices (K. *mishinjŏgin shinang* 迷信的인 信仰) and follow a proper Buddhist path. The underlying idea is that correct prayer requires education. Monastics and laypeople in charge of temples put considerable effort into encouraging the public to participate in diverse training programs. During these courses, monastics initiate newcomers into the basics of Buddhist history, culture, and doctrine. In addition, these courses also encourage new believers to establish deeper connections to the Buddhist community. Such programs frequently aim to establish a community of educated followers who can correctly engage in the daily and ritual activities of the temple. They are often regarded as a first step in a longer curriculum. This process resonates with the way propagation is conceptualized in Buddhist circles. Despite almost unanimous criticism, the favorable reception of propitiatory prayers such as prayers for academic success is commonly justified by monastics as a way to encourage propagation and public participation. It is also regarded as a form of "expedient means" (K. *pangp'yŏn* 方便, Skt. *upāya*).

The emphasis on the religious education of the laity and on the abundance of educational programs is an important characteristic of how Buddhism is developing in South Korean cities. This movement toward a systematized religious education of the public is also closely related to the effort to cultivate stronger formal ties to Buddhist institutions among followers. The emphasis on the doctrinal education of believers is related not only to a quest for orthodoxy, but also to the development of a collective identity and the promotion of Buddhism as a form of social affiliation. When newcomers participate in the educational curriculums offered by temples, they are often encouraged to join the temple's followers' association (K. *sindohoe* 信徒會) and participate in the association's various activities. Education is designed by Buddhist institutions as a means to transform individual temple attendance into a collective commitment. This phenomenon is particularly evident in the case of Pongŭn Temple, where involvement in the followers' association and participation in the educational program are almost inseparable. In this temple, the structure of the association itself is partly based on the various courses of the education curriculum.[27] When a person wants to participate in the temple's activities, they are strongly encouraged to enroll in a class for beginners (K. *kich'o haktang* 基礎學堂), which leads to membership in the temple association. During my fieldwork in this temple (2006–2010), the diploma ceremony that closed the beginner class coincided with both the students' integration into the followers' association and a ceremony of lay precepts (K. *sugyesik* 受戒式) in which most students received a Buddhist name.[28]

Although individual attendance at Buddhist monasteries remains important, a new form of religious participation has developed over the last two or three decades. Buddhist institutions promote formal affiliation for attendees so that those who participate individually in religious activities also become members of an organization. This tendency is demonstrated through the promotion of membership cards for believers. These membership cards have been widely encouraged and tend to formalize both membership in the central organization of the Jogye Order and affiliation with a specific monastery. In 2009, a movement was even launched to promote Buddhist cards for children and teenagers.

Education and Propagation: Making "Highest-Quality Buddhists"

When we examine the ambition of Buddhist institutions to regulate lay practice, a specific demographic stands out: women, and in particular the so-called housewives who comprise the overwhelming majority of the attendees of mainstream Buddhist temples. In spite of their importance in the history and present of Buddhism, women practitioners frequently face a perceived lack of legitimacy that is perceptible in both twentieth-century texts and contemporary discourses.[29] For religious reasons (such as disqualification of practical religiosity) and political ones (attendees of mainstream temples tend to be more conservative than attendees of socially engaged Buddhist temples), this demographic is commonly regarded by new movements as a drag on the cultivation of authentic lay Buddhism. Regardless of this suspicion, in most active temples, many apparently traditional Buddhist women assert their search for authentic Buddhism and for modern and educated forms of practice. The ambition to develop religious education among the laity is clearly an institutional objective, but it is also nourished by a strong demand from the laypeople themselves. As observation in temples has shown, laywomen are frequently involved in the creation of Buddhist classes. During my field research, the enthusiasm of these active lay Buddhists to promote their discovery of more about Buddhism was almost a constant. In contrast to common pejorative descriptions of Buddhist women as prone to superstition, a very general statement I heard and observed from them during my fieldwork was that being "a real Buddhist" (K. *ch'am pulcha* 참불자) requires training, knowledge, and skills.

The women followers I interviewed also frequently expressed their concern for renovating Buddhism. Many were critical of the doctrinal ignorance of "previous generations of grandmothers" and were clearly affirming their responsibility to transform common Buddhism into educated practice. A laywoman of Pongŭn Temple summed up this goal in clear terms: "We Buddhist lay followers should *upgrade* ourselves."[30] This statement resonates with one of the slogans chosen by the temple shortly afterward, in 2010: "Through the highest-quality education, we will foster the highest-quality Buddhists" (K. *myŏngp'um kyoyug ŭro myŏngp'um pulcha yangsŏng hal kŏt* 명품 교육으로 명품 불자 양성할 것). This ubiquitous idea was explained by a monk in charge of lay education in an interview published by the temple's journal in February 2010:

> The role of education is to *produce Buddhists who correctly practice and understand Buddhism* through a comprehensive range of educational programs, such as doctrinal education, retreats, and pilgrimages. The Buddhists who are formed through such educational programs will be able to *actively participate in social activities* and the management of the temple, *helping their*

neighbors and the whole society. Hence, this kind of practice will become the religious practice of the sincere Buddhists, *of the highest-quality Buddhists* [K. *myŏngp'um pulcha* 명품불자].³¹

This quotation also illustrates that the prioritization in Buddhist temples of the education and involvement of believers has multiple dimensions. The development of collective activities and relationships among practitioners is encouraged in religious terms as a means to nourish their motivation and deepen their devotion, but also as a way to improve the image of Buddhism and its social status. Together with other goals, education and community building among laypeople aim to contribute to a collective Buddhist identity that is expected to reinforce the place of Buddhism in society.

This "formation of the highest-quality Buddhists" is meant to produce followers who are socialized in accordance with Buddhist institutions, but also to broaden this Buddhist identity (and, in this case, the identity of "a Pongŭn Temple member") beyond the temple in society at large. This aim is not restricted to Pongŭn Temple; rather, similar discourses can be found in many other temples, especially in metropolitan areas. At Jogye Temple (曹溪寺), the abbot clearly noted the importance of knowledgeable lay followers to the outreach and social influence of Buddhism. During a forum on "followers management,"³² he exhorted followers to take on this responsibility and play an active role in the development of South Korean Buddhism.

At the turn of the twenty-first century, Buddhism narrowly appeared in the national census as the religion with the highest number of followers in South Korea.³³ However, both practitioners and observers felt that it had a secondary, if not marginal, position in society.³⁴ The feeling of being in a fairly fragile position *as Buddhists* has been particularly present among upper-middle-class Buddhists in Seoul, where Protestants are the majority and frequently enjoy more symbolic power. In the context of religious competition, many monastic and lay Buddhists have regarded the temples of affluent districts as strategic terrain for spreading Buddhism among those considered to be "leading members of society." Although this strategic view is obviously not the first reason for Buddhists to develop collective activities, it is nonetheless an explicit and very present concern in the temples of the affluent district of Kangnam. Monastics, laypeople, and the journals published by these temples tend to emphasize how the development of religious education and socialization among believers is crucial for improving the image of Buddhism in society and increasing its influence as a social force. Temples' emphasis on the "highest-quality education" is directly correlated with the idea that the "highest-quality Buddhists" should proudly represent Buddhism in society and contribute to its new visibility. In competition with neighboring, active, and visible Protestant megachurches, urban temples have been particularly committed to expressing a sense of confidence and extroverted belonging among their believers.

On several points, Buddhist temples have reacted to the success of Protestant churches, even if this relationship is ambiguous. The "megachurch model" is an ambivalent reference in Buddhist circles that elicits both fascination and repugnance. Even so, Christian techniques of believer management have had a significant influence on the new Buddhist emphasis on community building among believers and the praise of a more conscious and vocal Buddhist identity.

Adapting their propagation strategies to a modern and urban society has been a key concern for Buddhist institutions throughout the twentieth and twenty-first centuries. In this context, various comparative studies have been undertaken in Buddhist circles. Several temples in Seoul have even organized official "equipment study tours" (K. *sisŏl kyŏnhak* 施設見學) and "benchmarking for adherent management" (K. *sindo kwalli pench'imak'ing* 신도관리 벤치마킹) in successful churches to determine what Buddhist institutions can learn from them.[35]

Transformations and Dilemmas

Urban temples are trying to respond to demand and multiply services in a way that is comparable to what Danièle Hervieu-Léger observed in contemporary Catholic churches in Western Europe. She noted that among these churches, the multiplication of responses to the diverse demands of the public were in general loosely coordinated and had contributed to a growing "illegibility" (F. *illisibilité*)[36] of the institution. In Korean temples as well, ongoing transformations and the priority given to propagation and social influence have brought deep changes in the everyday life and the social organization of Buddhism, leading to an acute questioning of the roles and identities of monastics.

Urban temples have become increasingly concerned about their adaptation to the needs of an urban population and have endeavored to broaden their activities to new sectors such as health, social work, and education. The active role of followers in temple management and everyday activities has also been emphasized as crucial for both local development and the social integration of Buddhism in general. This has led to a continuous quest to increase the number of affiliated followers and develop wide and influential networks of believers. Accordingly, the activities of the small communities of monastics who live in urban temples have been largely designed to engage themselves with lay audiences. This phenomenon has led to significant changes in the relationship between "renouncers" (K. *ch'ulga* 出家) and "householders" (K. *chaega* 在家) and in the definition of their roles. In mainstream temples, new forms of relationships between monastic communities and laity have been established through the development of lay follower associations and the transition from occasional and individual (or familial) attendance to a more collectively organized and regular participation.

In addition, the importance and centrality of lay followers, communalized and organized, has increased in temples. In a process similar to what Max Weber described when he created the sociological ideal type of "communal religiosity" (G. *Gemeindereligiosität*), the centrality of followers' communalization in the relationship between temples and laity has increasingly driven monastics and religious institutions to heed and adapt to the public's demands.[37] In follower associations, lay members generally operate under the respected authority of monastics, but the role of monastics is increasingly moving toward a function of service to the laity.

Urban temples and, to a lesser extent, remote temples both show a reorientation toward laity. This change does not, however, imply a reversal in hierarchy or a decrease in monastic authority. In fact, it implies the opposite. Even so, the increasing opening of the monastic community to lay demands is accompanied by a profound redefinition of the monastic identity, role, and source of authority, especially in cities. In remote temples, there is generally a significant distance between monastics and the laity; outside of specific ceremonies, most monastics have little contact with the public, and a large part of their activities takes place among themselves. Apart from weekends and festivals, monasteries are primarily devoted to monastic life. The situation is different in urban temples, where clerics are fewer and their role is mostly considered, by both themselves and the laity, as oriented toward the diffusion of Buddhism and, hence, teaching and public relations. The role of monastics has been redefined in relation to the laity, with an emphasis on their educational mission. Their identity as ritual specialists remains present (in funerals, for instance), but this function is also frequently associated with their pedagogical role, because participants increasingly expect advice on practice from monastics. When lay Buddhists speak during interviews about monks' and nuns' commitment to meditation, they frequently stress the need for monastics to know how to transmit this practice and criticize their "traditional" remoteness and lack of engagement toward sentient beings. Almost unanimously, ideal monks and nuns have been described as specialized Buddhists who possess a high degree of doctrinal understanding and knowledge and are also able to transmit "Buddha's teaching" to the general public to help common people pray correctly and achieve a correct/Buddhist understanding of the world.

In this context, and with the growing scale and role of follower associations, lay Buddhists have tended to express their expectations toward monastics in a more direct if not exigent way. In particular, practitioners are now inclined to strongly demand that teachings be accessible and directly compatible with a modern lay lifestyle. Now that a wide range of Buddhist classes are available in urban areas, many potential students attempt to find the lectures that are the most "interesting," "deep," "entertaining," "easy to understand," and relevant to the participant's life. This is also a common topic of discussion among friends or members of Buddhist associations. During an interview, a lay Buddhist described how she moved from one temple to another looking for teachings that would suit her:

> I used to attend Sach'al[38] [temple], since it's close to our house in Chongno. But studying in Sŏnwŏn[39] [temple] is so much better. . . . The monk teaches in a way that directly enters our minds. At first, when I heard about Buddhism at Sach'al . . . [She expresses annoyance.] But now it has changed at Sach'al as well! But at first, what eminent monks [K. *k'ŭn sŭnim* 큰스님] were teaching was so difficult and boring. Their lectures also . . . I could not really understand their meaning. . . . [At Sŏnwŏn], this monk is extremely interesting! And he's so entertaining. And as people get enthusiastic, it increases even more the popularity [of the temple]. This monk is really smart. He knows exactly how to do it.[40]

This demand for easily graspable and entertaining teachings sometimes creates tensions with monastics. In the "Buddhist classes for beginners" that I observed in a large Seoul temple, for example, on several occasions,

I saw lay followers talking about their frustration with the instruction, lamenting that the concepts used by the monk were "too abstract" and the Chinese characters "too numerous." After a time, someone with responsibilities in the followers' association informed the monk about this and asked him to make his lectures more accessible. The monk answered that he would take this remark into consideration but also showed annoyance, stressing that Buddhist doctrine "is complex, and monastics also have to make an effort in order to learn and understand it."[41]

Expecting monastics to be attentive to the needs and demands of the public is obviously neither new nor strange. When Buddhists talk about the monastic duty of dedication to others, this role is not regarded as a result of the new place of temples in society. Instead, it is valued from a religious perspective as a traditional and foundational dimension of monastic spiritual practice. Nonetheless, tensions can arise between the importance given to this duty of service and other monastic duties. Monks and nuns who have commitments with laity commonly speak about how they must juggle different roles and how this sometimes challenges the foundations of their religious practice. During an interview, a monk who was living in a large temple in Seoul explained that cultivation in a remote monastery is essential to become a renouncer before adding that this training should lead to "sharing the fate of all beings" after a time. He then described engagement with society and laity as the result of a deep understanding of the world's true nature and of the relationship between every being. In a city temple, he noted, this usually means actively taking part in diverse and numerous activities with followers, which comes with new attributions and a redefinition of the monastic role.

> [Staying in a remote temple for practice] is not about personal interest and selfish desire. If one speaks precisely and with a broad perspective, "purifying and improving oneself" is something exactly directed toward others. . . . In cities, we have to constantly share the suffering of other beings and, somehow, we have to live together. Now, in my case, I am staying like that [calmly sitting], but if the phone rings I have to go out and do all kind of things . . . and then, for example, immediately, or tomorrow, or the day after, students or members from the youth association are going to visit me so that I can give them advice on spiritual practice, and I will talk with them. If one speaks about my role, that's exactly what it is in an urban temple.[42]

With the urban development of Buddhism and the transformations in the organization of temples and lay attendance, the role of urban monastics has moved toward "ministerialization" with central and everyday responsibilities toward the laity.

Reform of Monasticism and Revival of Asceticism

How should the current roles of monastics be understood? They are expected (and frequently aspire) to be guidance counselors, teachers, and temple managers, attuned to the needs of modern society, but their identity also remains based on a foundation of rupture with society. The tension between engagement and withdrawal is of course a classical matter and almost a cliché, but it has been shaped by new developments, combining issues of secularization and modernization as well as the contemporary history of Korea. The place and meaning of the monastic tradition today is particularly ambivalent. It has been regularly questioned and criticized in the name of opening Buddhism to the needs and constraints of society. In the meantime, ascetic meditation monks and the traditional lifestyle of the monastic sangha enjoy increasing prestige among lay and monastic Buddhists and even outside Buddhist circles. Ascetic traditions have also been regarded as a crucial basis for the refoundation and revival of Korean Buddhism. This importance given to the monastic aspects of Buddhism in the midst of calls for a greater secularization is neither an anecdotic phenomenon nor a mere issue of distinction but rather has roots in the complex history of contemporary Buddhism. Reforming and rejuvenating monasticism has been a crucial concern for more than a century. This emphasis on monastic tradition is less directly visible than secularization projects, but the current situation of Korean Buddhism cannot be understood without taking this side of its recent history into consideration.

Significantly, in November 2007, the Jogye Order organized a large and official ceremony to commemorate the sixtieth anniversary of the Pongam Monastery Compact Community (K. *Pongamsa kyŏlsa* 鳳巖寺結社). The Pongam Monastery Compact Community was interrupted by the Korean War after three years, but, in spite of its brevity, it produced significant parts of the doctrinal foundation of the current Jogye Order and directly influenced its leaders.[43] This initiative began in 1947, two years after the end of Japanese colonization, when a few monastics founded a new community at Pongam Monastery with the aim of reestablishing the tradition of Korean monasticism. About twenty monks gathered and committed to live "in accordance with the Buddha's law." With references to Koryŏ Buddhism, they set up a compact community based on a shared commitment and ideal to both renew Buddhism and reestablish it in its original form and genuine meaning.[44] The main slogan of the community was to live as much as possible according to the original teachings of the Buddha. As in the processes of monastic foundation analyzed by sociologist Jean Séguy, the vision of Buddhism and monasticism claimed by this group was based on "the requirement to go back to the primitive monastic ideal" and on a "protest against the previous form of monastic institution," while also maintaining a strong "innovative" dimension where "an ancient myth . . . becomes an utopia by a forward projection."[45] As a matter of fact, this movement had concerns similar to modern reformist movements, such as the goal of dismissing the practices and divinities regarded as external to Buddhism. However, its main aspirations and goals were radically different from the modern calls for the massification, mundanization, and social engagement of Buddhism advocated by, for example, Han Yongun in the early twentieth century.

The priority in this renovation of Buddhism was to refound the monastic community with an emphasis on its detachment from the world, on the strengthening of monastic precepts, and on the redefinition of the monastic ethos. The role of monastics was defined by intensive practice and study, and their relationship with society was conceived at least partially in terms of separation. For this purpose, this group established a new set of rules, the Community Regulation (K. *kongju kyuyak* 共住規約), as the basis for a renewed monastic life.[46] This convention aimed at reinforcing traditional rules and precepts in monasteries, but it was not widely adopted. However, this primacy of asceticism and monastic independence from society has had a deep and lasting impact on the understanding of monastics' roles and relationships with laity. In addition, the principles established by the Pongam Monastery Compact Community have contributed to the rebuilding of the social and symbolic status of monks after its weakening during the Chosŏn period. Sŏngch'ŏl (性徹, 1912–1993), one of this initiative's leading monks, recounted how this community was particularly critical in the name of original Buddhism of propitiatory offerings and the role of monastics as intermediaries in popular prayers.[47] By suppressing offerings, they were attempting to give monastics greater autonomy from laity, and they accompanied this new principle with recommendations to generalize work (in agriculture, woodcutting, etc.) as a way for monastic communities to support their needs. An explicit ambition to strengthen monastic authority and status came into play in the redefinition of monks' identity; the radicality of their commitment to the "Buddha's teaching" was supposed to free them from worldly demands and requests and give them a higher status than common people. To this effect, the Pongam Monastery Compact Community has also called for a general use of the respectful title "venerable" (K. *sŭnim* 스님) when talking to a monastic and has given new importance to visible signs of monastic status, such as the robe and a characteristic stick and hat.[48] When talking about this goal to achieve higher status, Sŏngch'ŏl described the lack of consideration, if not the contempt, toward monastics that he commonly witnessed during his first years as a monk.[49] To counter this low position of the monastics, he made a point of asserting the primacy of the monastic community over laity. These views and reforms deeply influenced the organization of the Jogye Order when it was established several years later, in 1962. They became a significant part of the organization's self-definition and culture and are still noticeable today.

Through the influence of the Pongam Monastery Compact Community movement, a dominant part of contemporary Buddhism's ideological basis has been built around a monastic project that distances itself from the world. Moreover, mistrust toward secularization has been reinforced by a severe conflict on the issue of "clerical marriage," which profoundly divided Buddhist circles from the 1950s to at least the 1970s.[50] The so-called "purification movement" (K. *chŏnghwa undong* 淨化運動) triggered violent conflicts over legitimacy and temple property and led to the creation of two separate orders, the Jogye Order of Korean Buddhism (*Taehan Pulgyo Chogyejong* 大韓佛教曹溪宗) in 1962 and the Taego Order of Korean Buddhism (*Han'guk Pulgyo T'aegojong* 韓國佛教太古宗) in 1970. These power struggles continued after the official resolution of the conflict and have reinforced the emphasis on monastic and ascetic identity by the largest part of the Jogye Order.

Today, the image of "mountain monastics" and ascetic meditators has a great deal of prestige among Buddhist laity and clerics alike. In addition, withdrawal, renunciation, and remote monasteries are central parts of the image cultivated by contemporary Korean Buddhism. However, this ideal is today a confluence of very different—sometimes antagonistic—perspectives; it brings together historical emphasis on monastic tradition, the importance given to asceticism and renunciation, urban aspirations for a different and more authentic lifestyle, and also explicit strategies of communication and branding.

The success of "Temple Stay" programs illustrates this phenomenon. The Ministry of Culture and Tourism launched this project in anticipation of the FIFA World Cup in 2002 to provide accommodation for some of the many foreign visitors expected to visit Korea. As noted by Uri Kaplan, the Jogye Order at first opposed this idea, but a compromise was finally reached on the basis of a "package of both accommodation and a cultural/spiritual experience."[51] First aimed at foreigners, this program has had important success among Koreans as well. It is now widely spread across South Korean monasteries. The program is not exclusively for Buddhist practitioners; instead, it is open to the general public and consists of a mixture of spiritual, cultural, and touristic activities. Temple Stay retreats are generally, but not exclusively, organized in traditional monasteries located in the mountains, and the Buddhism that is emphasized through this program is mostly monastic with a focus on the monastic lifestyle and "emblematic" activities such as the art of tea (K. *tado* 茶道) and the formal monastic meal (K. *paru kongyang* 鉢盂供養). These retreats are not oriented toward a specific soteriological goal, but rather claim (quoting their advertisements) to offer participants a "transformative experience" and an "occasion to connect with Korean tradition, nature, and one's peace of mind."

Outside of this touristic program, the ideal of a temple among Buddhists remains mostly based on images of mountains and monasticism. Nonetheless, this phenomenon is not only a matter of "image." Even if the representations of Korean Buddhism promoted by the Jogye Order and programs like Temple Stay are not completely congruent with its actual practices and reality, they cannot be reduced to mere promotion strategies. Redefining Korean Buddhism is a concern shared not only among monks and nuns, but also by a large part of the general lay audience. Above all, this issue reflects a significant tension in the current reorganization of Buddhist temples in urban areas. Most temples affirm an ambition to prove their relevance to the "new" South Korean society. While urban monasteries tend to differentiate themselves more and more from a monastic lifestyle, mountain temples are celebrated and sometimes idealized. The increasing success, especially among young adults, of programs offering a temporary experience of monastic lifestyle illustrates this tendency. Likewise, the recent development of urban temples is praised by Buddhist individuals and institutions even as they might also, on some occasions, distance themselves from Buddhist "mega-temples." As observed during my ethnographic fieldwork, it is common for Buddhists to express reservations toward a transformation of temples that would make them look like churches. Urban monasteries are widely valued, as they bring Buddhism to the world and participate in its development and visibility. However, equally omnipresent is the idea that the "real monasteries" that constitute the "essential foundation" of Buddhism are located in the mountains. Hence, believers who actively engage in the lay association of a large urban temple near their home may both emphasize its conveniences and social role and criticize its "mundanity" and "noisiness" while expressing a stronger attachment to a more remote mountain temple.

In spite of rapidly growing dynamism and success, and even if they benefit in practice from a larger degree of autonomy and generally larger incomes, urban monasteries are nevertheless relatively dependent, symbolically and in terms of human resources, on the more traditional ones located in mountains. An illustration of this can be found in the new variety of pilgrimages offered by city temples, sometimes several times a month. The rotation of monks and nuns between mountain and urban areas constitutes another circulation; most of them are not steadily located in a remote monastery or a busy one, but rather move between them. However, these two locations have different meanings, as remote monasteries are frequently described by monastics as places where they can restore their physical and spiritual forces to contribute to the propagation of Buddhism in cities.

Conclusion

Contemporary mainstream Buddhism has inherited a complex heritage regarding modernization and adaptation to urban society. Even if the Jogye Order may seem more traditional than new schools of Buddhism, this "mainstream" Buddhism has been deeply engaged in issues of reform and modernization. The commonness of propitiatory practices and the primacy of monastic culture frequently appear as symbols of its attachment to the past, but this chapter stresses that these aspects have also been deeply influenced and reshaped by contemporary priorities and concerns.

Another salient point has emerged: the ubiquity and importance in Buddhist circles of issues related to the social recognition of Buddhism. In very different contexts, from urban projects aiming at developing gigantic temples to monastics trying to reestablish an ascetic lifestyle, one can find the aspiration for Buddhism to regain the vitality and prestige that used to characterize its social position. This recurrent matter, however, has diverse implications with regard to the favored sources for legitimacy and recognition. The way mainstream Buddhism has drawn from very different registers of value (social usefulness, ascetic radicality, etc.) has benefited its vitality and sparked a profusion of initiatives that have contributed to its adaptability and outreach. However, this use of very different registers of value is not without tension and has sometimes brought illegibility to Buddhist institutions.

Buddhism's aspirations to universality have encouraged its institutions and actors to embrace and maintain diverse and sometimes antagonistic currents. In the twentieth century, this view (together with other causes) contributed to the development of the Jogye Order as a dominant organization that claims the role of a representative umbrella for Korean Buddhism in general. This is, however, a double-edged success; some of the difficulties faced by Korean Buddhism today echo those faced by other dominant and institutionally powerful religions in the world. This is especially true of the contemporary disaffection of members[52] or potential members, who may favor smaller religious or spiritual groups with more flexible structures and, often, more radicality in the implementation of principles; they may also choose to keep their distance from major religious institutions. After important efforts to gain recognition as a "fully modern religion," Korean Buddhism now seems to be experiencing the same difficulties as other "fully modern religions" that it has regarded as models.

Notes

1. The starting point of this chapter was a previous article: "A Space of Mountain within a Forest of Buildings? Urban Buddhist Monasteries in Contemporary Korea," 227–39. It has been largely rewritten to fit the collective project of this book, and new sections have been added with unpublished materials.

2. The Korean term *sach'al* (寺刹) can be translated as either a Buddhist monastery or a Buddhist temple. The ambiguity appearing in this translation reflects the issue presented in this chapter. Here, both terms are used in an almost interchangeable way.

3. I anonymized names of individuals and monasteries (or temples) when they are associated with privately expressed ideas. However, I kept real names when it comes to publicly expressed policies, teachings, or opinions.

4. Regarding the issue in modern Korean Buddhism, see Park, ed., *Makers of Modern Korean Buddhism*.

5. For a more nuanced view on the repression of Buddhism in Korea, see Bruneton, "Comment la répression du religieux a-t-elle accompagné la réforme du régime monarchique de T'aejong? Les mesures antibouddhiques au début du XVe Siècle en Corée" (How Did the Repression of Religion Go Along with the Reform of the T'aejong Monarchy? Anti-Buddhist Measures at the Beginning of the Fifteenth Century in Korea), 73–147.

6. The history of Chosŏn Buddhism has recently attracted new attention. Historians have nuanced the excessively negative depictions of its weaknesses as well as the overemphasis on the consequences of the Korean port opening of 1876. See Cho, "Re-thinking Late 19th Century Chosŏn Buddhist Society," and Walraven, "A Re-examination of the Social Basis of Buddhism in Late Chosŏn Korea."

7. The Yi dynasty was overthrown in 1910, and Korea was officially annexed by Japan the same year.

8. Han, "On the Reformation of Korean Buddhism," 78, 84.

9. Nathan, "Buddhist Propagation and Modernization: The Significance of P'ogyo in Twentieth-Century Korean Buddhism," 41–42.

10. On the "Mountain Buddhism trope," see Nathan, *From the Mountains to the Cities: A History of Buddhist Propagation in Modern Korea*.

11. Taehan Pulgyo Chogyejong Kyoyugwŏn, ed., *Chogyejong-sa kŭnhyondaep'yŏn* (History of the Jogye Order), 104–8.

12. Park, "Korean Buddhist Reforms and Problems in the Adoption of Modernity during the Colonial Period," 101.

13. Courant, *Sommaire et Historique Des Cultes Coréens—Conférence Faite Au Musée Guimet Le 17 Décembre 1899* (Summary and History of Korean Religions—Lecture at the Guimet Museum, December 17, 1899), 29.

14. Kim, *Empire of the Dharma: Korean and Japanese Buddhism, 1877–1912*, 49.

15. Chung, "The Buddhist Lay Movement in Korean Society," 91.

16. For example, see Kim Hyun Mee's research on the Jungto Society (Chŏngt'ohoe 淨土會): "Many young people also regard Buddhism as traditional and conservative. Young urbanites who are attracted to Buddhist spirituality and mediation thus represent a counter-trend. Their quest for spirituality represents a novel and highly distinctive form of social reproduction in contemporary South Korea." Kim, "Becoming a City Buddhist among the Young Generation in Seoul," 451.

17. Yoon, "The Contemporary Religious Situation in Korea," 11–12.

18. Guillemoz, *Les algues, les anciens, les dieux. La vie et la religion d'un village de pêcheurs-agriculteurs coréens* (Seaweed, Ancestors, and Gods: Daily Life and Religion in a Village of Korean Fishermen-Farmers).

19. "The women of Enduring Pine Village themselves consider seasonal offerings at the mansin's shrine and seasonal offerings at the Buddhist temple analogous practices. . . . The Christians stand outside the folk religious system, but shamanism and Buddhism blur. From the perspective of women worshipers,

shrine and temple do not represent discrete religions, but rather the different traditions of separate households." Kendall, *Shamans, Housewives, and Other Restless Spirits. Women in Korean Ritual Life*, 83–84.

20. On this concept, see Reader and Tanabe, *Practically Religious: Worldly Benefits and the Common Religion of Japan*.

21. The concept that authentic Buddhism has been degraded by popular religions was particularly developed and supported during the twentieth century. In academic circles, this idea has been recently contextualized and criticized: cf. Walraven, "A Re-examination of the Social Basis of Buddhism in Late Chosŏn Korea."

22. Notes taken during a Buddhist teaching (K. *pŏmmun* 법문) given to a lay audience at Chikehi Monastery (直指寺) in October 2007 (my translation).

23. A transcription of this lecture was published online on August 2, 2007, on HMBC (Hyŏndae Pulgyo Media Center) under the title "If You Want to Pray Correctly for the Students Who Are Taking the University Entrance Examination."

24. McBride, "Dhāraṇī and Mantra in Contemporary Korean Buddhism: A Textual Ethnography of Spell Materials for Popular Consumption."

25. Riw Ho Sun wrote: "Nowadays, what is called 'movement for the renovation of faith and practice' [K. *sin sinhaeng undong* 新信行運動] is gaining momentum. The 'movement for the renovation of faith and practice' is a central mission in Jogye Order propagation centers: its goal is to overcome invocation practices directed toward good fortune and to reform them in concordance with the system of correct faith and practice. The people in charge of propagation in the Jogye Order administration try to bring some order to the religious life of the Buddhists. This process is as follows: 'Introduction → basic education → practice of self-cultivation [*suhaeng*] → application on a social level.'" Riw, "Han'guk Pulgyo ŭi sinhaeng kaenyŏm e kwanhan yŏn'gu," 708 (my translation).

26. From an extract of *P'anjŏn* 板殿 (February 2010), the monthly journal published by Pongŭn Temple (my translation).

27. Some subgroups in the association gather alumni of the temple's teaching program and are named in accordance with the year of their class: "primary class 1," "primary class 2" (K. *kich'o* 1, 2), etc.

28. Galmiche, "La construction d'une identité religieuse bouddhiste en Corée du Sud" (The Making of a Buddhist Religious Identity in South Korea), 135–46.

29. Nowadays, this negative view may also echo the criticism directed more generally toward "education mothers" accused of being too ambition driven and centered on private and familial interests. See Park, "Mother's Anxious Management of the Private After-School Education Market," 194–95.

30. Interview conducted in November 2008 with a member of the followers' association of Pongŭn Temple (my translation).

31. "Int'ŏbyu Pongŭnsa kyoyuk kukchang Kwangmyŏng sŭnim" (Interview with the Monk Kwangmyŏng, in Charge of the Laity Education in Pongŭn Temple), 10–11 (my translation and emphasis).

32. *Chogyesa sindo kwalli hwalsŏnghwa t'oronhoe* (Jogye Temple's Forum for the Invigoration of Followers Management), December 8, 2010.

33. According to a census by Gallup, in 2004, 47 percent of the South Korean population declared no religion, while Buddhists were estimated at 24 percent, Protestants at 21 percent, Catholics at 7 percent, and other religions at 1 percent.

34. Frank Tedesco, for example, has shed light on this seemingly paradoxical situation: "In general, Korean Buddhists do not view themselves as an influential or prestigious force in Korean society and they have little political clout compared to well-organized, wealthy Protestant and Catholic factions. . . . Buddhism has low status in contemporary Korea and engaged Buddhists who work in public often feel self-conscious and sometimes react with defiance or timidity when ostracized." Tedesco, "Social Engagement in South Korean Buddhism," 158.

35. This concern for growth and the use of management and communication methods in Buddhist temples has been further developed in a previous article, Galmiche, "'Upgrading' Buddhism?"

36. Hervieu-Léger, *Catholicisme, la fin d'un monde* (Catholicism, the End of a World), 326–29.

37. Weber, *Wirtschaft und Gesellschaft* (Economy and Society), 278.

38. The choice of this pseudonym is inspired by the one chosen by Sharon Suh in her inspirational research on a large Buddhist temple in Los Angeles, Suh, *Being Buddhist in a Christian World. Gender and Community in a Korean American Temple.*

39. "Sŏnwŏn" (禪院) is used as a pseudonym for an urban temple in Seoul. On my use of pseudonyms, see note 3.

40. Interview conducted in September 2008 with a laywoman regularly attending Sŏnwŏn [temple].

41. Observations conducted in a temple located in Seoul in November 2009.

42. Interview conducted in December 2008 (Seoul).

43. Sŏngch'ŏl (性徹, 1912–1993) (one of the founding members of the Community) was the Supreme Patriarch of the Jogye Order from 1981 to 1993. Chigwan (止觀, 1932–2012), who was the disciple of Chaun (慈雲, 1911–1992), another founding member of the Community, was the executive director of administration (K. *ch'ongmu wŏnjang* 總務院長) of the Jogye Order from 2005 to 2009.

44. See Sŏ, "Pongamsa kyŏlsa ŭi chŏngsin kwa T'oeong Sŏngch'ŏl ŭi yŏkhal" (The Spirit of Pongam Monastery Compact Community and the Role of T'oeong Sŏngch'ŏl).

45. Séguy, "Une sociologie des sociétés imaginées: monachisme et utopie" (A Sociology of Imagined Societies: Monasticism and Utopia), 338.

46. Sŏngch'ŏl presented these rules publicly in the spring of 1948. See Kim, *Han'guk hyŏndae pulgyosa yŏn'gu* (Research on the History of Contemporary Korean Buddhism), 56–57.

47. Taehan Pulgyo Chogyejong kyoyuk-wŏn Purhak yŏn'guso, ed., *Pongamsa kyŏlsa wa hyŏndae Han'guk Pulgyo* (The Pongam Monastery Community and Contemporary Korean Buddhism), 272.

48. Sections 6, 7, and 8 of the Community Regulations (K. *kongju kyuyak* 共住規約) address this topic. Kim Kwang-sik presented accounts made by Sŏngch'ŏl on this matter, *Han'guk hyŏndae pulgyosa yŏn'gu* (Study on Modern Korean Buddhism), 61.

49. Taehan Pulgyo Chogyejong kyoyuk-wŏn pulhak yŏn'guso, *Pongamsa kyŏlsa wa hyŏndae Han'guk Pulgyo* (Pongam Monastery Compact Community Movement and Modern Korean Buddhism), 274–75.

50. In 1954, the South Korean President Syngman Rhee ordered married clerics, the majority among clerics since the Japanese colonization, to leave the Buddhist community and to hand monasteries over to celibate monks.

51. Kaplan, "Images of Monasticism: The Temple Stay Program and the Re-branding of Korean Buddhist Temples," 132–33.

52. The national census of 2015 reported 15.5 percent Buddhists in 2015. This proportion was 22.8 percent in 2005 and 23.5 percent in 1995. We can also note that the proportion of the population who declared themselves "to have a religion" decreased from 52.9 percent in 2005 to 43.9 percent in 2015. See the South Korean website, Statistics Korea: http://kostat.go.kr/.

Bibliography

Alfred, Taiaiake, and Jeff Corntassel. "Being Indigenous: Resurgences against Contemporary Colonialism." *Government and Opposition* 40, no. 4 (2005): 597–614.
Amstutz, Galen. "Missing Hongan-ji in Japanese Studies." *Japanese Journal of Religious Studies* 23, no. 1/2 (1996): 155–78.
An Munok. "Suok sunim" (Nun Suok). *Pŏbpo sinmun*. March 22, 2004. https://www.beopbo.com/news/articleView.html?idxno=30682.
An P'yŏngjik, ed. *Han Yongun*. Seoul: Han'gilsa, 1988.
Asahi shinbun 朝日新聞 (1879–present). Tokyo: Asahi shinbunsha.
Auerback, Micah. "Ch'inil Pulgyo yŏksahak ŭi chaego" '친일불교' 역사학의 재고 (Rethinking the Historiography of Pro-Japanese Buddhism). *Asea yŏn'gu* 51, no. 3 (2008): 15–53.
Auerback, Micah. "Japanese Buddhism in an Age of Empire: Mission and Reform in Colonial Korea, 1877–1931." PhD diss., Princeton University, 2007.
Batchelor, Martine. *Women in Korean Zen: Lives and Practices*. Syracuse: Syracuse University Press, 2006.
Bellah, Robert N. *Religion in Human Evolution: From the Paleolithic to the Axial Age*. Cambridge: Harvard University Press, 2011.
Best, Jonathan. "Tales of Three Paekche Monks Who Traveled Afar in Search of the Law." *Harvard Journal of Asiatic Studies* 51, no. 1 (1991): 139–97.
Bianchi, Ester. "Yi jie wei shi 以戒為師: Theory and Practice of Monastic Discipline in Modern and Contemporary Chinese Buddhism." *Studies in Chinese Religions* 3, no. 2 (2017): 111–41.
Blackburn, Anne M. "Looking for the Vinaya: Monastic Discipline in the Practical Canons of the Theravāda." *Journal of the International Association of Buddhist Studies* 22, no. 2 (1999): 281–309.
Blackburn, Anne M. *Locations of Buddhism: Colonialism and Modernity in Sri Lanka*. Chicago: University of Chicago Press, 2010.
Blacker, Carmen. *The Japanese Enlightenment: A Study of the Writings of Fukuzawa Yukichi*. Cambridge: Cambridge University Press, 1964.

Borup, Jørn. *Japanese Rinzai Zen Buddhism: Myōshinji, a Living Religion*. Leiden: Brill, 2008.

Boucher, Daniel. *Bodhisattvas of the Forest and the Formation of the Mahayana: A Study and Translation of the Rastrapalapariprccha-sutra*. Honolulu: University of Hawai'i Press, 2008.

Bruneton, Yannick. "Comment la répression du religieux a-t-elle accompagné la réforme du régime monarchique de T'aejong? Les mesures antibouddhiques au début du XVe siècle en Corée" (How Does the Suppression of Religion Accompany the Reform of Monarch of T'aejong?: Anti-Buddhist Measurements at the Beginning of the 15th Century in Korea). In *État, religion et répression en Asie. Chine, Corée, Japon, Vietnam (XIIIe-XXIe siècles)* (State, Religion, and Suppression in Asia: China, Korea, Japan, Vietnam (XIIIth-XXIst century), edited by Arnaud Brotons, Yannick Bruneton, and Nathalie Kouamé, 73-147. Paris: Karthala, 2011.

Burton Watson, trans. *The Lotus Sutra*. New York: Columbia University, 1993.

Buswell, Robert E. Jr., trans. "Secrets on Cultivating the Mind." In *Tracing Back the Radiance: Chinul's Korean Way of Zen*, by Robert E. Buswell Jr., 98-117. Honolulu: University of Hawai'i Press, 1991.

Buswell, Robert E., Jr. "Admonitions to Neophytes (Kye ch'osim hag'in mun 誡初心學人文)." In *The Collected Works of Korean Buddhism Vol. 2*, edited by Robert Buswell, 195-205. Seoul: The Jogye Order of Korean Buddhism, 2012.

Buswell, Robert E., Jr. "Arouse Your Mind and Practice!" In *Sourcebook of Korean Civilization, Volume 1: From Early Times to the Sixteenth Century*, edited by Peter H. Lee, 154-57. New York: Columbia University Press, 1993.

Buswell, Robert E., Jr. "Buddhist Reform Movements in Korea during the Japanese Colonial Period: Precepts and the Challenge of Modernity." In *Buddhist Behavioral Codes and the Modern World: An International Symposium*, edited by Charles Wei-hsun Fu and Sandra A. Wawrytko, 141-60. Westport, CT: Greenwood Press, 1994.

Buswell, Robert E., Jr., trans. *Chinul: Selected Works*. Collected Works of Korean Buddhism. Vol. 2. Paju, Korea: Chun-il Munhwasa, 2012.

Buswell, Robert E., Jr. *The Zen Monastic Experience*. Princeton, NJ: Princeton University Press, 1992.

Cabezón, José I., ed. *Buddhism, Sexuality, and Gender*. Albany: State University of New York Press, 1991.

Caplan, Jane. "Identity and Identification." Lecture delivered at Gresham College, June 9, 2014. http://www.gresham.ac.uk/lectures-and-events/identity-and-identification.

Ch'a Ch'asŏk 차차석. "Chogyejong chongbŏp e nat'anan chinggye chedo wa yulchang ŭi pigyo koch'al" 조계종 종법에 나타난 징계 제도와 율장의 비교 고찰 (Comparison of the Jogye Order's Penal Law System and the Vinaya). *Sŏnmunhwa yŏn'gu* 13 (2012): 201-26.

"Ch'anggyŏnggung yang chŏngha" 昌慶宮兩陛下 (Two Highnesses of Ch'anggyŏng Place). *Maeil sinbo*, March 24, 1921.

Ch'ien Lung. "Ch'ien Lung (Qianlong) Letter to George III (1792)." http://www.history.ucsb.edu/faculty/marcuse/classes/2c/texts/1792QianlongLetterGeorgeIII.htm.

Ch'oe Chŏnghŭi 최정희. *Puch'ŏnim Pŏpdaero Sarara—Kwangwu Sŭnim kwaŭi taedam* 부처님 법대로 살아라—광우스님과의 대담 (Live by the Buddha's Dharma—The Interviews with Venerable Kwangwu). Seoul: Choggyejong Ch'ulp'ansa, 2008.

Ch'oe Pyŏnghŏn 최병헌. *Han'guk Pulgyosa yŏn'gu immun* 한국 불교사 연구 입문 (Introduction to Korean Buddhist History). Vol. 2. Seoul: Chisik Sanŏpsa, 2013.

Ch'oe Yongch'un 최용춘. "Pŏmgyu haengwi wa chejae" 범규행위와 제재 (Legislation and Discipline). In *Chongdan chinggye chedo kaesŏn ŭl wihan kongch'ŏngoe*, edited by Taehan Pulgyo Chogyejong. Seoul: Chogyejong Ch'ulpansa, 2008.

"Ch'ojo uryŏ ro palgŭn oilya ŭi Ch'anggyŏnggung" 焦燥憂慮로밝은五日夜의昌德宮 (Fifth Night of Ch'anggyŏng Palace Dawning with Restlessness and Worry). *Maeil sinbo*, May 8, 1926.

Chŏn Ilchŏng. "*Sanggung Chŏn Ilchŏng t'anwŏnsŏ*" 상궁천일청탄원서 (Court Lady Chŏn Ilchŏng's Petition), 1934. http://yoksa.aks.ac.kr/jsp/aa/ImageView.jsp?aa10up=kh2_je_a_vsu_81908_000&aa10no=kh2_je_a_vsu_81908_001.

"Chŏnsanggung sogigo sammanwŏn kich'ŭihan Chang'il Kŏmsaguk haeng" 千尙宮속히고 三萬圓欺取한 張一 사긔한 장일 검사국행 (Chang'il Arrested in Charge of Deceptively Extorting 30,000 Wŏn from Court Lady Chŏn). *Maeil sinbo*, August 17, 1927.

"Chŏnsanggung ŭi karyŏnhan p'alja" 千尙宮의 可憐한八字 (Court Lady Chŏn's Pitiful Fate). *Tonga ilbo*, March 31, 1925.

"Ch'unsaek tŭngjin kokung e yŏgwan tot'aesŏl taedu" 春色등진古宮에 女官淘汰說擡頭 (Rumors about the Disestablishment of the Court Lady System Comes to the Fore to the Old Palace Against Spring). *Tonga ilbo*, April 22, 1930.

Chahyŏn 자현. "Kŭmgang sŭnim palche e taehan tappyŏn" 금강스님 발제에 대한 답변 (Response to Ven. Kŭmgang's Presentation). Paper presented at Hyŏndae sahoe sŭngga chŏnggyu. Chogyesa, 2015.

Chahyŏn 자현. "Yul ŭi kaep'yŏn kanŭngsŏng kwa sŭnggabŏp ŭi tangwisŏng kŏmt'o" 율의 개편 가능성과 승가법의 다위성 검토 (Examination of the Possibility of Reforming the Vinaya and of the Properness of the Sangha Law). *Pulgyo hakpo* 61 (2012): 375–415.

"Chang Il susongguk" 張一遂送局 (Chang'il Finally Sent to the Prosecutor's Office). *Chungwae ilbo*, August 19, 1927.

"Chappo: Chŏnssi kwŏnhak" 雜報: 千氏勸學 (Miscellaneous: Chŏn's Recommendation of Education). *Chosŏn Pulgyo wŏlbo* 5 (June 1912): 73.

"Chappo: Hŭngguk sŏlgye" 雜報: 興國說戒 (Miscellaneous: Sermon on the Precepts at Hŭngguk Monastery). *Chosŏn Pulgyo wŏlbo* 3 (April 1912): 65.

"Chappo: Ilban ponmalsa sŭngni suhyo" 雜報: 一般本末寺僧尼數爻 (Miscellaneous: The Number of Monks and Nuns in the Head and Branch Temples). *Haedong pulbo* 4 (February 1914): 94–96.

"Chappo: Kakhwangsa pulsang pongansik" 雜報: 覺皇寺 佛像奉安式 (Miscellaneous: the Enshrinement Ceremony of the Buddha Statue). *Maeil sinbo*, October 27, 1910.

"Chappo: Kyedan sŏngŭi" 雜報: 戒壇盛儀 (Miscellaneous: Splendid Ordination Ceremony). *Chosŏn Pulgyo wŏlbo* 1 (February 1912): 70.

"Chappo: P'aril sŏnghwang" 雜報: 八日盛況 (Miscellaneous: A Great Success of [April] Eight), *Chosŏn Pulgyo wŏlbo* 5 (June 1912): 67–69.

Chasŭng. "Introduction." In *Sŭngga chŏnggyu* 승가청규 (The Pure Rules for the Sangha), edited by Taehan Pulgyo Chogyejong. Seoul: Chogyejong Ch'ulp'ansa, 2015.

"Che ilhoe kaech'oe toen Chosŏn puinhoe" 제1회 개최된 朝鮮婦人會 (The First Meeting of the Association of Chosŏn Women). *Maeil sinbo*, March 6, 1920.

"Chinese Cultural Studies: Emperor Qian Long [sic]: Letter to George III, 1793." http://acc6.its.brooklyn.cuny.edu/~phalsall/texts/qianlong.html.

Chinul 知訥. *Kanhwa Kyŏrŭi Ron* 看話決疑論 (Resolving Doubts about Observing the Hwadu). *Han'guk Pulgyo Chŏnsŏ* 韓國佛教全書 (Collected Works of Korean Buddhism). Vol. 4, 732c–737c. Seoul: Tongguk Taehakkyo Ch'ulp'anbu, 1982.

Chinul 知訥. *Hwaŏmnon Chŏryo Sŏ* 華嚴論節要序 (Preface to the Excerpts from the Flower Garland Sutra). *Han'guk Pulgyo Chŏnsŏ* 韓國佛教全書 *(Collected Works of Korean Buddhism).* Vol. 4, 767c–768b. Seoul: Tongguk Taehakkyo Ch'ulp'anbu, 1982.

Chinul 知訥. *Susim kyŏl* 修心訣 (Secrets on Cultivating the Mind). In *Han'guk Pulgyo Chŏnsŏ* 韓國佛教全書 (Collected Works of Korean Buddhism). Vol. 4, 708b–714c. Seoul: Tongguk Taehakkyo Ch'ulp'anbu, 1982.

Chiu, Tzu-Lung. "Rethinking the Precept of Not Taking Money in Contemporary Taiwanese and Mainland Chinese Buddhist Nunneries." *Journal of Buddhist Ethics* 21 (2014): 9–56.

Cho Chaesun 조재순. *Seoul Taehakkyo Chungang Tosŏgwan ŭi palchok* 서울대학교 중앙도서관 발족 (Establishment of the Central Library of Seoul National University). Newsletter of Libraries (2003). http://www.nl.go.kr/pds/research_data/text/newsletter/200311/200311history.htm.

Cho Kiryong 조기룡. "Chogyejong ŭi chongdan kaehyŏk kwa Hyeam Sŏnggwan ŭi hwaldong" 조계종의 종단 개혁과 혜암성관의 활동 (The Reformation of the Jogye Order and the Activities of Hyeam Sŏnggwan). *Han'guk kyosu pulcha yŏnhap hakhoeji* 26, no. 1 (2020): 65–88.

Cho Kiryong 조기룡. "Chogyejong ch'ongmu haengjŏng chedo koch'al" 조계종 총무행정 제도 고찰 (Studies on the Administrative System of the Jogye Order).

Pulgyo pyŏngnon 7 (2001). http://www.budreview.com/news/articleView. html?idxno=607.

Cho Sŏngha 조성하. "Chogyejong kaehyŏk kadak chapnŭnda" 조계종 개혁 가닥 잡는다 (Jogye Order Works on Reformation). *Tonga ilbo*, June 14, 1994. http://newslibrary.naver.com/viewer/index.nhn?articleId=199406 1400209114001&editNo=45&printCount=1&publishDate=1994-06-14&office Id=00020&pageNo=14&printNo=22541&publishType=00010.

Cho Sŭngmi 조승미. "Paek Yongsŏng ŭi ch'amsŏn taejunghwa undong kwa puinsŏnwŏn" 백용성의 참선 대중화 운동과 부인선원 (Paek Yongsŏng's Movement of the Popularization of Sŏn and the Women Meditation Center). *Taegak sasang* 27 (July 2017): 191–223.

Cho Sungtaek 조성택. *Pulgyo wa Pulgyohak* 불교와 불교학 (Buddhism and Buddhist Studies). Seoul: Tolbegae, 2012.

Cho, Eun-su. "Re-thinking Late 19th Century Chosŏn Buddhist Society." *Acta Koreana* 6, no. 2 (2003): 87–109.

Cho, Eun-su. "The Religious Life of Buddhist Women in Chosŏn Korea." In *Buddhist Feminism(s) and Femininities*, edited by Karma Lekshe Tsomo, 67–83. Albany: State University of New York Press, 2019.

Cho, Eun-su. "The Uses and Abuses of Wŏnhyo and the 'T'ong Pulgyo' Narrative." *Journal of Korean Studies* 9, no. 1 (2004): 33–59.

Cho, Eun-su. *Korean Buddhist Nuns and Laywomen: Hidden Histories, Enduring Vitality*. Albany: State University of New York Press, 2011.

Cho, Francesca, and Richard King Squier. "Religion as a Complex and Dynamic System." *Journal of the American Academy of Religion* 81, no. 2 (June 2013): 357–98.

"Chogyejong chŏnghwa moksori nop'a" 조계종 정화 목소리 높아 (Increasing Demand for the Reformation of the Jogye Order). *Hangyŏre sinmun*, July 22, 1990. http://newslibrary.naver.com/viewer/index.nhn?articleId=199007 2200289109006&editNo=4&printCount=1&publishDate=1990-07-22&office Id=00028&pageNo=9&printNo=677&publishType=00010.

"Chogyejong sach'al ch'ongmu kamsa dŭng kanghwa" 조계종 사찰총무 감사 등 강화 (The Jogye Order Reinforces Its Inspection on the Administration). *Kyŏnghyang sinmun*, February 9, 1977. http://newslibrary.naver.com/viewer/index.nhn? articleId=1977020900329205006&editNo=2&printCount=1&publishDate= 1977-02-09&officeId=00032&pageNo=5&printNo=9652&publishType=00020.

Choi, Hyaeweol. *Gender and Mission Encounters in Korea: New Women, Old Ways*. Berkeley: University of California Press, 2009.

Chŏng Ch'anju 정찬주. *Kayasan Chŏngjin Pul* 가야산 정진불 (The Buddha in Practice in Kaya Mountain). 2 vols. Seoul: Random House Korea, 2010.

Chŏng Ch'anju 정찬주. *Kongbu hada chugŏra* 공부하다 죽어라 (Practice until Die). Seoul: Yŏlimwŏn, 2013.

Chŏng Insik 정인식. "Chogyejong ittan sogari Ch'op'ail maji tŭisungsung" 조계종 잇단 속앓이 초파일 맞이 뒤숭숭 (Continuous Scandals of the Jogye Order

Cause Internal Chaos before the Buddha's Birthday). *Hangyŏre sinmun*, May 9, 1993. http://newslibrary.naver.com/viewer/index.nhn?articleId=1993050900289109001&editNo=5&printCount=1&publishDate=1993-05-09&officeId=00028&pageNo=9&printNo=1554&publishType=00010.

Chŏng Suok. "Naeji Pulgyo kyŏnhakki (ha)" 內地佛教見學記 (下) (Observations from a Tour of Japanese Buddhism: Part 2). *Pulgyo sibo* 49 (August 1939): 6.

Chŏng Suok. "Naeji Pulgyo kyŏnhakki (sang)" 內地佛教見學記 (上) (Observations from a Tour of Japanese Buddhism: Part 1). *Pulgyo sibo* 48 (July 1939): 6–7.

"Chonggyo paengnyŏn (wan): Ch'inilsŭng Yi Hoegwang" 宗教百年 (完): 親日僧 李晦光 (The Recent Hundred Years of Religion [final]: Pro-Japanese Monk Yi Hoegwang). *Kyŏnghyang sinmun*, June 4, 1974.

"Chonggyo paengnyŏn 14: Ch'inilsŭng Yi Hoegwang" 宗教百年14: 親日僧 李晦光 (The Recent Hundred Years of Religion [14]: Pro-Japanese Monk Yi Hoegwang). *Kyŏnghyang sinmun*, May 18, 1970.

Chonghyŏn 종현. "Sobang chŏngt'o rŭl hyanghayŏ-Namu amit'abul kwa pŏmsŏ" 서방정토를 향하여—나무아미타불과 범서 (Toward the Western Pure Land—Paying Homage to the Amida Buddha and Sanskrit Writing). *Haein* 392 (October 2014). http://haein.or.kr/contents/?pgv=v&wno=408&cno=7384.

Chongmuk 종묵. "Ch'ongnim ŭi chindan, naagal panghyang: Haein ch'ongnim chungsim ŭro" 총림의 진단, 나아갈 방향: 해인총림 중심으로 (Diagnosis of the Chan Community and Objectives for Its Development: Focusing on the Haeinsa Community). In *Chogyejong ch'ongnim ŭi yŏksa wa munhwa*, edited by Taehan Pulgyo Chogyejong Kyoyugwŏn, 170–246. Seoul: Chogyejong Ch'ulp'ansa, 2009.

Chongmuk 종묵. "Kŭnhyŏndae Han'guk Sŏnjong kyodan esŏ chejŏngdoen chŏnggyu e kwanhan koch'al" 근현대 한국 선종 교단에서 제정된 청규에 관한 고찰 (Inquiry into the Formulation of Pure Rules in Modern and Contemporary Korean Chan). *Taegak sasang* 10 (2007): 193–240.

"Chongmuwŏn kŭp Pulygodang" 宗務院及佛教堂 (The Administrative Office and Buddhist Hall). *Hwangsŏng sinmun*, February 8, 1910.

"Chorŏpsaeng illan" 卒業生一覽 (List of Graduates). *Taehan hŭnghakbo* 5 (July 1909). http://db.history.go.kr/id/ma_011_0050_0010.

Chōsen Sōtokufu Gakumukyoku 朝鮮總督府 學務局. "Chŏngdŭngsa jūji shūshoku ninka no ken" 傳燈寺住持就職認可ノ件 (Approval of Head Monk Appointment of Chŏngdŭng Monastery). November 19, 1940. https://theme.archives.go.kr/next/government/viewGovernmentArchivesEvent.do?id=0001565561&docid=0027157644.

Chōsen Sōtokufu Gakumukyoku 朝鮮總督府 學務局. "Kakuji honmatsu jihō chū shūsei o yōsubeki kajō no shūsei hyōjūn o shimesu ken" 各寺本末寺法中修正ヲ要スヘキ箇條ノ修正標準ヲ示ス件 (On the Guideline for the Standardized Revision of the Head-Branch Temples Laws of Each Buddhist Parish). May

10, 1926. https://theme.archives.go.kr/next/government/viewGovernment ArchivesEvent.do?id=0001565460&docid=0027159455.

Chōsen Sōtokufu Gakumukyoku 朝鮮總督府 學務局. "Kwijusa jūji shūshoku ninka no ken" 歸州寺住持就職認可ノ件 (Approval of Head Monk Appointment of Kwiju Monastery). December 18, 1925. https://theme.archives.go.kr/next/government/viewGovernmentArchivesEvent.do?id=0001565460&docid=0027159423.

Chōsen Sōtokufu Gakumukyoku 朝鮮總督府 學務局. "Magoksa honmatsu jihō kaimei no ken" 麻谷寺本末寺法改正ノ件 (Revision of Head-Branch Temple Laws of Magok Monastery). August 27, 1926. https://theme.archives.go.kr/next/government/viewGovernmentArchivesEvent.do?id=0001565460&docid=0027159445.

Chōsen Sōtokufu Gakumukyoku 朝鮮總督府 學務局. "Magoksa jūji shūnin ninka no ken" 麻谷寺住持就任認可ノ件 (Approval of Head Monk Appointment of Magok Monastery). July 9, 1927. https://theme.archives.go.kr/next/government/viewGovernmentArchivesEvent.do?id=0001565465&docid=0027157331.

Chōsen Sōtokufu Gakumukyoku 朝鮮總督府 學務局. "Makokuji jūji shūshoku ninka shinsei no ken" 麻谷寺住持就職認可申請ノ件 (On the Application of Magok Monastery for the Approval of Head Monk Appointment). July 2, 1930. https://theme.archives.go.kr/next/government/viewGovernmentArchivesEvent.do?id=0001565479&docid=0027157450.

Chōsen Sōtokufu Gakumukyoku 朝鮮總督府 學務局. "Pongŭnsa jūji shūshoku ninka shinsei ni kansuru ken" 奉恩寺住持就職認可申請ニ關スル件 (On the Application for the Approval of Head Monk Appointment for Pongŭn Monastery). May 12, 1934. https://theme.archives.go.kr/next/government/viewGovernmentArchivesEvent.do?id=0001565499&docid=0027157550.

Chōsen Sōtokufu Gakumukyoku 朝鮮總督府 學務局. "T'ongdosa honmatsu jihō chū kaimei no ken" 通度寺本末寺法中改正ノ件 (Revision of Head-Branch Temple Laws of T'ongdo Monastery). December 21, 1926. https://theme.archives.go.kr/next/government/viewGovernmentArchivesEvent.do?id=0001565460&docid=0027159454.

Chōsen Sōtokufu Gakumukyoku 朝鮮總督府 學務局. "T'ongdosa jūji shūshoku ninka no ken" 通度寺住持就職認可申請ノ件 (On the Application for the Approval of Head Monk Appointment for T'ongdo Monastery). August 9, 1926. https://theme.archives.go.kr/next/government/viewGovernmentArchivesEvent.do?id=0001565460&docid=0027159428.

Chōsen Sōtokufu Gakumukyoku 朝鮮總督府 學務局. "T'ongdosa jūji shūshoku ninka shinsei no ken" 通度寺住持就職認可申請ノ件 (On the Application for the Approval of Head Monk Appointment for T'ongdo Monastery). March 4, 1924. https://theme.archives.go.kr/next/government/viewGovernmentArchivesEvent.do?id=0001565456&docid=0027157305.

Chōsen Sōtokufu Naimubu 朝鮮總督府 內務部. "Honmatsu jihō ninka no ken 本末寺法認可ノ件" (Approval of Head-Branch Temple Laws). September 7, 1912. https://theme.archives.go.kr/next/government/viewGovernmentArchivesEvent.do?id=0001565442&docid=0027157166.

Chōsen Sōtokufu Naimubu 朝鮮總督府 內務部. "Honmatsu jihō ninka shinsei no ken" 本末寺法認可申請ノ件 (Approval of Head-Branch Temple Laws). December 20, 1912. https://theme.archives.go.kr/next/government/viewGovernmentArchivesEvent.do?id=0001565442&docid=0027157167.

Chōsen Sōtokufu 朝鮮總督府. *Kanpō* 官報 (Official Gazette) (1910–1945). https://theme.archives.go.kr//next/gazette/listDateSearch.do?TP=000006&sort=2.

Chosŏn chungang ilbo 朝鮮中央日報 (1933–1937). Seoul: Chosŏn chungang ilbosa.

Chosŏn ilbo 朝鮮日報 (1920–present). Seoul: Chosŏn ilbosa.

Chosŏn Pulgyo wŏlbo 朝鮮佛敎月報 (1912–1913). Keijō: Pulgyo Chinhŭnghoe Ponbu.

Chu Kyŏngmi 周炅美. "Yo Hŭngjong nyŏn'gan (1031–1055) ŭi Pulsari changŏm yŏn'gu" 遼 興宗年間 (1031–1055) 의 佛舍利莊嚴 硏究 (A Study on the Buddhist Reliquaries during the Reign of Xingzong [興宗, 1031–1055] of the Liao Dynasty). *Chungguksa yŏn'gu* 35 (2005): 197–221.

Chūgai nippō 中外日報 (1897–present). Kyoto: Kōrakudō.

Chugyŏng 주경. "Saeroun sŭngga chŏnggyu ŏttŏk'e chongdan e chŏngch'ak sik'il kŏshin'ga?" 새로운 승가 규정 어떻게 종단에 정착시킬 것인가? (How Can We Make the New Pure Rules for the Sangha Strike Roots in the Order?). Paper presented at the conference "Hyŏndae sahoe sŭngga chŏnggyu" (The Pure Rules of the Sangha in Modern Society). Chogyesa, 2015.

Chung Byungjo 정병조. "The Buddhist Lay Movement in Korean Society." In *Religion and Society in Contemporary Korea*, edited by Lewis R. Lancaster and Richard K. Payne, 87–100. Berkeley: Institute of East Asian Studies, University of California, 1997.

Chungwae ilbo 中外日報 (1926–31). Kyŏngsŏng-pu: Chungwae ilbosa.

Clarke, Shayne. "Monks Who Have Sex: Parajika Penance in Indian Buddhist Monasticisms." *Journal of Indian Philosophy* 37 (2009a): 1–43.

Clarke, Shayne. "Where and When Is a Monk No Longer a Monk? On Communion and Communities in Indian Buddhist Monastic Law Codes." *Indo-Iranian Journal* 52 (2009b): 115–41.

Clarke, Shayne. *Family Matters in Indian Buddhist Monasticisms*. Honolulu: University of Hawai'i Press, 2014.

Coleman, James W. *The New Buddhism: The Western Transformation of an Ancient Tradition*. New York: Oxford University Press, 2001.

Collins, Steven. "On the Very Idea of the Pali Canon." *Journal of the Pali Text Society* 15 (1990): 89–126.

Courant, Maurice. *Sommaire et historique des cultes coréens—Conférence faite au musée Guimet le 17 décembre 1899* (Summary and History of Korean Cults,

Conference at the Guimet Museum, December 17, 1899). Vol. IV. T'oung-Pao, Série II. Leiden: E.J. Brill, 1900.
Covell, Stephen Grover. "Money and the Temple: Law, Taxes and the Image of Buddhism." In *Handbook of Contemporary Japanese Religions*, edited by Inken Prohl and John Nelson, 159–76. Leiden: Brill, 2012.
Covell, Stephen Grover. *Japanese Temple Buddhism: Worldliness in a Religion of Renunciation*. Honolulu: University of Hawai'i Press, 2005.
Daoyuan道原. *Jǐngdé chuándēng lù* 景德傳燈錄. T 2076.51.196–467.
Derrida, Jacques. "Faith and Epoché." In *Derrida and Religion: Other Testaments*, edited by Yvonne Sherwood & Kevin Hart, 27–50. New York: Routledge, 2005.
Dicks, Anthony. "Buddhism and Law in China: Qing Dynasty to the Present." In *Buddhism and Law: An Introduction*, edited by Rebecca French and Mark Nathan, 234–54. New York: Cambridge University Press, 2014.
Dobbins, James C. *Jōdo Shinshū: Shin Buddhism in Medieval Japan*. Honolulu: University of Hawai'i Press, 1989.
Dreyfus, Georges. *The Sound of Two Hands Clapping: The Education of a Tibetan Buddhist Monk*. Berkeley: University of California Press, 2003.
Duthie, Torquil Michael Stephen. "Poetry and Kingship in Ancient Japan." PhD diss., Columbia University, 2005.
Ekachai, Sanitsuda. *Keeping the Faith: Thai Buddhism at the Crossroads*. Bangkok: Bangkok Post, 2002.
Evon, Gregory N. "The Conceptualization of Qing-Era (1644–1911) Chinese Literature in Nineteenth Century Chosŏn (1392–1910) Korea." *Frontiers of Literary Studies in China* 7, no. 3 (2013): 396–421.
Faure, Bernard. "From Bodhidharma to Daruma: The Hidden Life of a Zen Patriarch." *Japan Review* 23 (2011): 45–71.
Faure, Bernard. *The Power of Denial: Buddhism, Purity, and Gender*. Princeton, NJ: Princeton University Press, 2003.
Faure, Bernard. *The Read Thread: Buddhist Approaches to Sexuality*. Princeton, NJ: Princeton University Press, 1998.
Fogel, Joshua A. *The Cultural Dimension of Sino-Japanese Relations: Essays on the Nineteenth and Twentieth Centuries*. Armonk, NY: M.E. Sharpe, Inc., 1995.
French, Rebecca Redwood, and Mark A. Nathan. "Introducing Buddhism and Law." In *Buddhism and Law: An Introduction*, edited by Rebecca Redwood French and Mark A. Nathan, 1–30. New York: Cambridge University Press, 2014.
Fukuzawa Yukichi. *An Outline of a Theory of Civilization* (Bunmeiron no gairyaku, 文明論之概略, 1875). Translated by David A. Dilworth and G. Cameron Hurst III. New York: Columbia University Press, 2008.
Fukuzawa Yukichi. *Tsūzoku kokken ron* 通俗國ｒ論 (On Popular National Sovereignty, 1878). Reprinted in *Fukuzawa zenshū* 福ｒ全集 (Collected Works of Fukuzawa). Vol. 4. Tokyo: Jiji Shinpō-sha, 1898. Accessed January 20, 2016,

through the National Diet Library (of Japan). http://dl.ndl.go.jp/info:ndljp/pid/898730.

Gallup Korea. "Gallup Report on Korean Religions." http://www.gallup.co.kr/gallupdb/reportContent.asp?seqNo=625.

Galmiche, Florence. " 'Upgrading' Buddhism? Methods from the Business World in South Korean Buddhism." *Review of Korean Studies* 18, no. 2 (2015): 35–61.

Galmiche, Florence. "A Retreat in a South Korean Buddhist Monastery. Becoming a Lay Devotee Through Monastic Life." *European Journal of East Asian Studies* 9, no. 1 (2010): 47–66.

Galmiche, Florence. "A Space of Mountain within a Forest of Buildings? Urban Buddhist Monasteries in Contemporary Korea." In *Sociology and Monasticism*, edited by Isabelle Jonveaux, Enzo Pace, and Stefania Palmisano, 227–39. Leiden: Brill, 2014.

Galmiche, Florence. "La construction d'une identité religieuse bouddhiste en Corée du Sud." (A Making of Buddhist Religious Identity in South Korea). PhD diss. École des hautes études en sciences sociales (EHESS), Paris, 2011.

Gondō Shirōsuke 權藤四郞介. *Ri Ōkyū hishi* 李王宮秘史 (A Secret History of the Yi Royal Palace). Keijō: Chōsen Shinbunsha, 1926.

Guillemoz, Alexandre. *Les algues, les anciens, les dieux. La vie et la religion d'un village de pêcheurs-agriculteurs coréens.* Paris: Le léopard d'or, 1983.

Ha Ch'unsaeng 하춘생. *Kkaedarŭm ŭi kkot* 깨달음의 꽃 (The Flower of Enlightenment). Seoul: Tosŏ Ch'ulp'an Yŏrae, 2001.

Haedong pulkyo 해동불교 (1914). Seoul: Haedong pulbosa.

Hall, David. *Lived Religion in America: Toward a History of Practice.* Princeton, NJ: Princeton University Press, 1997.

Han Chunggwang 한중광. *Kyŏnghŏ: Kil wŭiŭi k'ŭn sŭnim* 경허: 길위의 큰 스님 (Kyŏnghŏ: The Great Master on the Road). Seoul: Han'gilsa, 1999.

Han Heesook. "Women's Life during the Chosŏn Dynasty." *International Journal of Korean History* 6 (December 2004): 113–62.

Han Hŭisuk 한희숙. "KuHanmal Sunhŏn hwanggwibi Ŏmbi ŭi saengae wa hwaltong" 구한말 순헌황귀비 엄비의 생애와 활동 (Empress Um's Life and Activities at the End of the Chosŏn Dynasty). *Asia yŏsŏng yŏn'gu* 45/2 (2006): 195–239.

Han Pogwang 한보광. "Taegaksa ch'anggŏn sijŏm e kwanhan chemunje" 대각사 창건 시점에 관한 제문제 (Problems Regarding the Timing of Taegaksa's Founding). *Taegak sasang* 10 (2007): 245–83.

Han Pogwang 한보광. "Yongsŏng sŭnim ŭi chŏnban'gi ŭi saengae" 龍城스님의 前半期의 生涯 (The Early Part of Venerable Yongsŏng's Life). *Taegak sasang* 1 (1998): 27–50.

Han Pogwang 한보광. "Yongsŏng sŭnim ŭi chungban'gi ŭi saengae" 龍城스님의 중반기의 생애 (The Middle Part of Venerable Yongsŏng's Life). *Taegak sasang* 2 (1999): 13–46.

Han Pogwang 한보광. "Yongsŏng sŭnim ŭi huban'gi ŭi saengae (I)" 龍城스님 의 후반기의 생애 (The Last Part of Venerable Yongsŏng's Life (I)). *Taegak sasang* 3 (2001): 9–64.

Han Pogwang 한보광. "Yongsŏng sŭnim ŭi huban'gi ŭi saengae (II)" 龍城스님 의 후반기의 생애 (The Last Part of Venerable Yongsŏng's Life (II)). *Taegak sasang* 4 (2002): 9–74.

Han Pogwang 한보광. *Yongsŏng sŏnsa yŏn'gu* 龍城禪師研究 (A Study of the Sŏn Master Yongsŏng). Seoul: Kamnodang, 1981.

Han Sanggil 한상길. "Kyŏnghŏ Sŏngu ŭi Pulgyosa chŏk wisang" 경허성우의 불교사적 위상 (Seon Master Kyŏnghŏ Sŏngu's Thought and His Status in Buddhist History). *Pulgyo p'yŏngnon* 57 (March 2014).

Han T'aesik 한태식. "Paek Yongsŏng ŭi Haeinsa mit Koam Sŭnim kwa ŭi inyŏn 백용성스님의 해인사 및 고암스님과의 인연 (Paek Yongsŏng and Haeinsa and His Affinity with Koam Sŭnim). *Taegak sasang* 20 (December 2013): 26–27.

Han Yongun 한용운. "*Pangmyŏng*" 薄命 (A Miserable Fate). In *Han Yongun chŏnjip* 韓龍雲全集 (The Collected Works of Han Yongun), edited by Cho Myŏnggi, Sŏ Kyŏngbo, Paek Chŏl, Chŏng Pyŏnguk, Chŏn Kwanu, Sin Tongmun, and Kim Yŏngho, 286–90. Seoul: Sin'gu Munhwasa, 1980.

Han Yongun 한용운. *Chosŏn Pulgyo yusillon* 朝鮮佛教維新論 (Treatise on the Restoration of Korean Buddhism. Edited and translated by Yi Wŏnsŏp, with photo-reprint of original text. Seoul: Unjusa, 1992.

Han Yongun. "On the Reformation of Korean Buddhism (1913)." In *Selected Writings of Han Yongun. From Social Darwinism to "Socialism with a Buddhist Face,"* edited by Vladimir Tikhonov and Owen Miller, 41–152. Folkestone: Global Oriental, 2008.

Han, Suzanne Crowder. *Korean Folk & Fairy Tales*. New Jersey: Hollym, 1991.

Hanam Chungwŏn 漢巖重遠. "Sŏnsa Kyŏnghŏ Hwasang haengjang" 先師鏡虛和尚行狀 (A Record of the Deceased Teacher Master Kyŏnghŏ). In *Kyŏnghŏ chip* 鏡虛集 (Collected Works by Kyŏnghŏ), edited by Kŭngnak sŏnwŏn, 399–421. Seoul: Moa, 1990.

"Han'gŭl kinyŏmsik Pongch'ŏn esŏ kŏhaeng" 한글記念式봉천에서거행 (The Founding of Hangul Celebrated at Fengtian). *Tonga ilbo*, October 29, 1933.

Heine, Steven. *Existential and Ontological Dimensions of Time in Dōgen and Heidegger*. Albany: State University of New York Press, 1985.

Heirman, Ann. "Can We Trace the Early Dharmaguptakas?" *T'oung Pao* 88 (2002): 396–429.

Heirman, Ann. "Indian Disciplinary Rules and Their Early Chinese Adepts: A Buddhist Reality." *Journal of the American Oriental Society* 128, no. 2 (2008): 257–72.

Heirman, Ann. "Vinaya: From India to China." In *The Spread of Buddhism*, edited by Ann Heirman and Stephan Peter Bumbacher, 167–202. Leiden: Brill, 2007.

Hervieu-Léger, Danièle. *Catholicisme, la fin d'un monde*. Paris: Bayard, 2003.

Hobsbawm, Eric, and Terence Ranger. *The Invention of Tradition*. Cambridge: Cambridge University Press, 1983.

Hŏjŏng 허정. "Kyŏnghŏ tamnon ŭi chaengjŏm kwa hyŏnjae chŏk ŭimi" 경허 담론의 쟁점과 현재적 의미" (Focus and Contemporary Implication of Discourse on Kyŏnghŏ). *Pulgyo p'yŏngnon* 57 (Spring 2014).

Holcombe, Charles. *A History of East Asia: From the Origins of Civilization to the Twenty-First Century*. New York: Cambridge University Press, 2011.

Hong Sŏkp'yo 홍석표. "Luswin kwa kŭ chejadŭl, kŭrigo Chosŏn insik" 루쉰과 그 제자들, 그리고 '조선'인식 (Lu Xun and His Disciples, and the Recognition of Korea). *Chungguk munhakchi* 47 (2014): 245–75.

Hong Sunmin 홍순민. "Chosŏn sidae ŭi kungnyŏ ŭi wisang" 조선시대 궁녀의 위상 (The Status of the Court Ladies during the Chosŏn Dynasty). *Yŏksa pip'yŏng* (August 2004): 241–67.

Hong Tayŏng 홍다영. "Hanam sunim kasa" 한암스님 가사 (Master Hanam's Robes). *Pulgyo sinmun*, April 28, 2015. http://www.ibulgyo.com/news/articleView.html?idxno=140756.

Huh, Woosung. "A Monk of Mukti and Karma: The Life and Thought of Baek Yongseong." *Korea Journal* 45, no. 1 (Spring 2005): 29–63.

Huh, Woosung. "Individual Salvation and Compassionate Action: The Life and Thoughts of Paek Yongsŏng." In *Makers of Modern Korean Buddhism*, edited by Jin Y. Park, 19–40. Albany: State University of New York Press, 2010.

Hwang Ingyu 황인규. "Kŭnhyŏndae piguni wa Pulgyo chŏnghwa undong" 근현대 비구니와 불교정화운동 (Modern Bhiksunis and the Buddhist Purification Movement). *In Pulgyo Chŏnghwa Undong ŭi Chaejomyŏng* (Shedding New Light on the Buddhist Purification Movement in Korea). Edited by Taehan Pulgyo Chogyejong Pulhak Yŏn'guso, 267–308. Seoul: Chogyejong Ch'ulp'ansa, 2008.

Hwangsŏng sinmun 皇城新聞 (1898–1910). Seoul: Hwangsŏng Sinmunsa.

Hyeam Mundohoe, ed. 혜암문도회. *Hyeam Taejongsa Pŏpŏjip* 혜암대종사 법어집 (Collection of the Dharma Talks by Great Master Hyeam). 2 vols. Seoul: Gimmyoungsa, 2007.

Hyeam Sŏnsa Munhwa Chinhŭng hoe, ed. 혜암선사문화진흥회. *Hyeam Sŏnsa ŭi sam kwa sasang* 혜암선사의 삶과 사상 (Life and Thoughts of Sŏn Master Hyeam). Seoul: Sihwaŭm, 2019.

Hyeam Sŏnsa Munhwa Chinhŭng hoe, ed. 혜암선사문화진흥회. *Sŭsŭng Hyeam* 스승혜암 (Teacher Hyeam). Seoul: Gimmyoungsa, 2019.

Hyeam Sŏnsa Munhwa Chinhŭnghoe, ed. 혜암선사문화진흥회. *Haksul taehoe* 학술대회 (Conference Proceedings). 2014.

Hyeam Sŏnsa Munhwa Chinhŭnghoe, ed. 혜암선사문화진흥회. *Hyeam Sŏnsa ŭi Sŏn sasang kwa segyehwa* 혜암선사의 선사상과 세계화 (Sŏn Master Hyeam's Sŏn Thought and Globalization). Seoul: Sihwaŭm, 2020.

Hyeam Taejongsa Mundohoe 혜암대종사문도회. "Hyeam Taejongsa Haengjang" 慧菴大宗師行狀 (Short Biography of Great Master Hyeam). In *Sŭsŭng Hyeam* 스승혜암 (Teacher Hyeam), edited by Hyeam Taejongsa Munhwa Chinhŭnghoe, 12–19. Seoul: Gimmyoungsa, 2019.

Hyewŏn 혜원. "Hyŏndae Han'guk Sŏnwŏn chŏnggyu ŭi mosŭp kwa naagal pangyang" 현대 한국 선원 청규의 모습과 나아갈 방향 (The Shape of Modern Korean Chan Monastic Pure Rules and Future Objectives). In *Sŭngga kyoyuk 5*, edited by Taehan Pulgyo Chogyejong Kyoyugwŏn, 259–75. Seoul: Chogyejong Ch'ulp'ansa, 2004.

Hyewŏn 혜원. "Kyeyul kwa chŏnggyu ŭi kwan'gye esŏ pon hyŏndae Han'guk ŭi Sŏnwŏn Chŏnggyu" 계율과 청규의 관계에서 본 현대 한국의 선원청규 (The Modern Korean Chan Hall Pure Rules Seen through the Relationship between the Vinaya and the Pure Rules). Paper presented at "Kyeyul ŭi hyŏndaejŏk chomyŏng." Dongguk University, 2006.

Hyŏndae Pulgyo 현대불교 (1994–present). Seoul: Hyŏndae pulgyo sinmunsa.

Hyŏndam 현담. *Kyŏnghŏ Sŏnsa iltaegi* 경허 선사 일대기 (Life of Zen Master Kyŏnghŏ). Seoul: Sŏn, 2010.

"Hyujit'ong" 휴지통 (Wastebasket). *Tonga ilbo*, January 20, 1925.

Ibuki, Atsushi. "Vinaya and the Chan School: Hīnayāna Precepts and Bodhisattva Precepts, Buddhism in the City and Buddhism in the Mountains, Religion and the State." *Studies in Chinese Religions* 1, no. 2 (2015): 105–30.

Ilchi 일지. *Ttŏdonŭn Tonhwang* 떠도는 돈황 (Floating Dunhuang). Taegu: Haein Ch'ulp'ansa, 1993.

Im Hyebong 임혜봉. *Ch'inil sŭngnyŏ 108-in: kkŭnnaji anŭn yŏksa ŭi murŭm* 친일승려108인: 끝나지 않은 역사의 물음 (108 Pro-Japanese Korean monks: Unfinished Questions of History). P'aju, South Korea: Chŏngnyŏnsa, 2005.

Im Sŏkchin 임석진. *Kisan munjip* 綺山文集 (Collection of the Writings). Seoul: Pulgyo T'ongsinwŏn, 1998.

"Injo tangnyŏn ŭi samhaksa Pongch'ŏn esŏ pisŏk palgyŏn" 仁祖當年의 三學士奉天에서 碑石發見 (The Discovery of the Memorial Stone for Three Scholars during the Years of King Injo (r. 1623–1649). *Tonga ilbo*, May 13, 1933.

"Insa sosik" 人事消息 (Personnel News). *Chosŏn chungang ilbo*, May 17, 1936.

"Int'ŏbyu Pongŭnsa kyoyuk kukchang Kwangmyŏng sŭnim" 인터뷰 봉은사 교육국장 광명스님 (Interview with the Monk Kwangmyŏng, in Charge of Laity Education in Pongŭn Temple). *P'anjŏn* (February 10, 2010): 10–11.

Iryŏn 一然. "Wŏnhyo pulgi" 元曉不羈 (Wŏnhyo the Unbridled). In *Samguk yusa* 三國遺事. *Han'guk Pulgyo Chŏnsŏ* 韓國佛教全書 (Collected Works of Korean Buddhism). Seoul: Tongguk Taehakkyo Ch'ulp'anbu, 1984, vol. 6, 347b–348b.

Jackson, Ben. "Karma Back! Buddhist Ad Campaign Tries to Reverse Falling Numbers." *Korea Exposé*, January 30, 2018. https://www.koreaexpose.com/buddhist-south-korea-declining-jogye/.

Jaffe, Richard M. "Seeking Śākyamuni: Travel and the Reconstruction of Japanese Buddhism." *Journal of Japanese Studies* 30, no. 1 (2004): 65–96.

Jaffe, Richard M. *Neither Monk Nor Layman: Clerical Marriage in Modern Japanese Buddhism*. Princeton, NJ: Princeton University Press, 2001.

Jansen, Maurius B. *China in the Tokugawa World*. Cambridge: Harvard University Press, 1992.

Jia, Jinhua. "The Creation and Codification of Monastic Regulations at Mount Baizhang." *Journal of Chinese Religion* 33, no. 1 (2005): 39–59.

Jogye Order 조계종. "Jogye Order Constitution." http://law.buddhism.or.kr/asp/_view/linkView.asp?lawid=1478.

Jogye Order. "Jogye Principles and Organization." http://www.koreanbuddhism.net/bbs/content.php?co_id=230.

Jogye Order. "Patriarch of Jogye Order." http://www.koreanbuddhism.net/bbs/board.php?bo_table=2030.

Joo, Ryan Bongseok. "Countercurrents from the West: "Blue-Eyed" Zen Masters, Vipassana Meditation, and Buddhist Psychotherapy in Contemporary Korea." *Journal of the American Academy of Religion* 79, no. 3 (2011): 614–38.

Jorgensen, John. "Marginalized and Silenced: Buddhist Nuns of the Choson Period." In *Korean Buddhist Nuns and Laywomen: Hidden Histories, Enduring Vitality*, edited by Eun-su Cho, 119–46. Albany: State University of New York Press, 2011.

Jorgensen, John. "Minjung Buddhism: A Buddhist Critique of the Status Quo—Its History, Philosophy and Critique." In *Makers of Modern Korean Buddhism*, edited by Jin Y. Park, 275–314. Albany: State University of New York Press, 2010.

Jung Ji-Young. "Buddhist Nuns and Alternative Space in Confucian Chosŏn Society." In *Korean Buddhist Nuns and Laywomen: Hidden Histories, Enduring Vitality*, edited by Eun-Su Cho, 147–64. Albany: State University of New York Press, 2011.

Kaebyŏk 開闢 (1920–26). Seoul: Ch'ŏndogyo Ch'ŏngnyŏnhoe.

Kagan. *Tongsa yŏlchŏn* 東師列傳 (Biographies of Korean Masters). Seoul: Tongguk Taehakkyo Ch'ulp'anbu, 2015.

Kakhun 覺訓. Haedong kosŭng chŏn 海東高僧傳 (Lives of Eminent Korean Monks), T 2065.50.1015a–1023a.

Kang Inch'ŏl 강인철. "Haebang hu Pulgyo wa kukka: 1945–1960: Pigu taechŏ kaldŭng ŭl chungsim ŭro'" 해방 후 불교와 국가: 1945–1960: 비구-대처 갈등을 중심으로 (Buddhism and the State after the Liberation: 1945–1960: The Struggle between the Celibate Monk and the Married Monk). *Sahwoe wa yŏksa* 57 (2000): 79–114.

Kang Sŏkchu 강석주, and Pak Kyŏnghun 박경훈. *Pulgyo kŭnse paengnyŏn* 불교근세백년 (Recent Hundred Years of Buddhism). Seoul: Minjoksa, 2002.

"Kankoku no jokan seikatsu" 韓國の女官生活 (Life of Korean Court Ladies). *Yomiuri shinbun*, February 18, 1909.
"Kankoku Shaonshi to jokan" 韓國謝恩使と女官 (Korea's Gratitude Delegates and the Court Ladies). *Yomiuri shinbun*, February 14, 1909.
Kaplan, Uri. "From the Tea to the Coffee Ceremony: Modernizing Buddhist Material Culture in Contemporary Korea." *Material Religion* 13, no. 1 (2017): 1–22.
Kaplan, Uri. "Images of Monasticism: The Temple Stay Program and the Re-branding of Korean Buddhist Temples." *Korean Studies* 34 (2010): 127–46.
Kaplan, Uri. *Monastic Education in Korea: Teaching Monks about Buddhism in the Modern Age*. Honolulu: University of Hawai'i Press, 2020.
Kaplan, Uri. "Updating the Vinaya: Formulating Buddhist Monastic Laws and Pure Rules in Contemporary Korea." *Contemporary Buddhism* 17, no. 2 (2016): 252–74.
"Karye ch'amgaja ch'uga" 嘉禮參列者追加 (Additional Participants in the Royal Wedding). *Tonga ilbo*, April 23, 1920.
Kathirithamby-Wells, J. "The Age of Transition: The Mid-Eighteenth to the Early Nineteenth Centuries." In *The Cambridge History of Southeast Asia: Volume Two, From c. 1500 to c. 1800*, edited by Nicholas Tarling, 228–75. Cambridge: Cambridge University Press, 1999.
Kawakami Zenbē 川上善兵衛. *Takeda hanshi den* 武田範之伝 (A Biography of Takeda Hanshi). Tōkyō: Nihon Keizai Hyōronsha, 1987.
Keijō Chongno keisatsusho 京城 鍾路 警察署. "Mimoto shōkai no ken" 身元照會ノ件 (Enquiry Request for Identification). October 20, 1923. https://theme.archives.go.kr/next/government/viewGovernmentArchivesEvent.do?id=0001565471&docid=0027157437.
Kendall, Laurel. *Shamans, Housewives, and Other Restless Spirits. Women in Korean Ritual Life*. Studies of the East Asian Institute. Honolulu: University of Hawai'i Press, 1985.
Kieschnick, John. "Celibacy in East Asian Buddhism." In *Celibacy and Religious Tradition*, edited by Carl Olson, 225–40. New York: Oxford University Press, 2008.
Kieschnick, John. *The Eminent Monk: Buddhist Ideals in Medieval Chinese Hagiography*. Honolulu: University of Hawai'i Press, 1997.
Kil Hŭisŏng 길희성. "Hanguk Pulgyo chŏngch'esŏng ŭi t'amgu: Chogyejong ŭi yŏksa wa sasang ŭl chungsim ŭro" 한국불교 정체성의 탐구: 조계종의 역사와 사상을 중심으로 (The Identity of Korean Buddhism: Its Focus on the Jogye Order's History and Thought). *Han'guk chongyo yŏn'gu* 2 (2000): 67–92.
Kim Ch'anggyŏm, ed. 김창겸. *Han'guk yugyŏng saŏp ŭi ŏmŏni Ch'oe Songsŏltang* (한국 육영사업의 어머니 최송설당 (The Mother of Korea's Educational Work). Seoul: Kyŏngin Munhwasa, 2008.

Kim Chigyŏn 김지견. *Sŏn munhŏn yŏn'gu-Yukcho tangyŏng ŭi segye* 선문헌 연 구-六祖壇經의 세계 (A Study on the Text of Sŏn-Platform Sutra of Sixth Patriarchs). Seoul: Minjoksa, 1989.

Kim Chinhŭm 김진흠. "1950 nyŏndae Yi Sŭngman Taet'ong'ryŏng ŭi Pulgyo chŏnghwa yushi wa Pulgyogye ŭi chŏngch'i kaeyib" 1950년대 이승만 대 통령의 불교 정화 유시와 불교계의 정치개입 (The "Buddhist Purification" Instructions of the President Syngman Rhee and the Political Intervention of the Buddhist in the 1950s). *Sarim* 53 (2015): 305–40.

Kim Chŏnghyŏn 김정현. "Sŏlchŏng sŭnim, ŭnch'ŏja ŭihok poda hangnyŏk wijo tŏ nappa" 설정스님, 은처자 의혹보다 학력위조 더 나빠 (Ven. Sŏljŏng's Academic Fraud Is Worse Than His Charge of a Secret Wife). *Bulgyo Focus*, May 22, 2018. http://m.bulgyofocus.net/news/articleView.html?idxno=79504.

Kim Chŏngja (Unsŏng) 김정자 (운성). "Pŏpkye Myŏngsŏng ŭi Pulgyogwan kwa piguni sŭngga kyoyukkwan yŏn'gu" 법계 명성의 불교관과 비구니 승가교육 관 연구 (A Study on Pŏpkye Myŏngsŏng's Buddhist Thought and Her Perspectives on Bhiksuni Sangha Education). PhD diss. Yŏngnam University, Kyŏngsan, Korea, 2012.

Kim Ho Sung 김호성. "Kyŏnghŏ ŭi 'Chŏnghye Kyesa' e nat'anan suhaeng inyŏm chaego" 경허(鏡虛)의 정혜계사 (定慧稧社)에 나타난 수행 이념 재고 (Reexamination of the Idea of "Practice" in Kyŏnghŏ's Society of Samādhi and Prajñā). *Pulgyo hak yŏn'gu* 33 (2012): 347–95.

Kim Hŭisŏn 김희선. "Chogyejong ch'ulgaja chikjŏb ch'aja nasŏnda" 조계종 출가자 직접 찾아 나선다 (The Jogye Order Recruits Its Members). *Yŏnhap News*, November 29, 2017. http://www.yonhapnews.co.kr/bulletin/2017/11/29/02 00000000AKR20171129161600005.HTML.

Kim Iryŏp 金一葉. *Haengbok kwa pulhaeng ŭi kalp'i esŏ* 幸福과 不幸의 갈피에서 (In Between Happiness and Misfortune). Seoul: Whimun Ch'ulp'ansa, 1964.

Kim Iryŏp. *Ŏnŭ sudoin ŭi hoesang* 어느 수도인의 회상 (Reflections of a Zen Buddhist Nun). Ch'ungnam, South Korea: Sudŏksa, 1960.

Kim Jongmyung 김종명. "Ijong Sŏn, Samjong Sŏn nonjaeng" 이종선, 삼종선 논 쟁 (Debate on the Types of Sŏn Buddhism). In *Nonjaeng ŭro ponŭn Pulgyo ch'ŏrhak* 논쟁으로 보는 불교 철학 (Buddhist Philosophy Seen through Debates), coedited by Yi Hyogŏl, 224–61. Seoul: Yemun sŏwŏn, 1998.

Kim Kijong 김기종. "Kim T'aehŭp—Pulgyo taejunghwa e saengae rŭl hŏnsin hada" 김태흡: 불교대중화에 생애를 헌신하다 (Kim T'aehŭp: Devoting His Life to the Popularization of Buddhism). *Pulgyo P'yŏngnon* 49 (2011): 385–90.

Kim Kugyŏng 김구경. "Sutch'a ro ponun Pulgyo wa Chogyejong" 숫자로 보는 불 교와 조계종 2017 (Buddhism and Jogye Order Seen through Numbers). *Pulgyo p'ocŏsŭ*, January 18, 2019. http://www.bulgyofocus.net/news/articleView.html?idxno=76958.

Kim Kugyŏng 金九經. "Manshūgo to kango wo konyū sitaru kahon 'kitsu hōkai'" 滿洲語と漢語を混用したる歌本吃螃蟹 (A Type of Chipangxie That Uses Both Manchu and Chinese). *ManMō* 16, no. 9 (1935): 222–42.

Kim Kugyŏng 金九經. "Shinyō to Chōsen no sangakushi" 瀋陽と朝鮮の三學士 (Shenyang and Three Scholars of Korea). *Kōa kyōkai* 6 (1939).

Kim Kugyŏng 金九經. "Tōwan no chimei to sharitō" 塔湾の地名と舎利塔 (The Place Name of Tawan and the Shari Stupa). *Kōnō* 3 (1936): 1–14.

Kim Kugyŏng 金九經. "Kohak ŭl mokchŏk ŭro Ilbon ŭro osiryŏ hasinŭn yŏrŏ hyŏngnim-kke" 苦學을 目的하고 日本으로 오시려하시는 여러兄님께 (To Those Who Would Like to Come to Japan for Studying). *Tonga ilbo*, July 29, 1923.

Kim Kugyŏng 金九經. *Kyogan yussi ŏnmunji* 校刊柳氏諺文志 (The Printing and Proofreading of *Yussi ŏnmunji*). Simyang, China, 1934.

Kim Kugyŏng 金九經. *Manshū jibo* 滿洲字母 (The Manchu Alphabet). Beiping: Daishutang, 1900.

Kim Kwangsik 김광식. "1926 nyŏn Pulgyogye ŭi taechŏ sikyugnon kwa Paek Yongsŏng ŭi kŏnbaeksŏ" 1926년 불교계의 대처 식육론과 백용성의 건백서 (The Dispute over the Buddhist Priests' Marriage and Meat-eating in 1926 and Paek Yongsŏng's Proposal). *Han'guk tonib undongsa yŏn'gu* 11 (1997): 195–221.

Kim Kwangsik 김광식. "A Study of Han Yong-un's 'On the Reform of Korean Buddhism.'" *Korea Journal* 45, no. 1 (2005): 64–86.

Kim Kwangsik 김광식. "Chŏng Kŭm-o ŭi Pulgyo chŏnghwa ŭndong" 정금오의 불교 정화운동 (The Buddhist Purification Movement led by Chŏng Kŭm-o). *Pulgyo hakpo* 57 (2011): 145–79.

Kim Kwangsik 김광식. "Hwagwawŏn ŭi yŏksa wa sŏngkyŏk" 화과원의 역사와 성격 (History and Characteristics of Hwagwawŏn). *Taegak sasang* 28 (2017): 9–48.

Kim Kwangsik 김광식. "Paek Yongsŏng yŏn'gu ŭi hoego wa chŏnmang" 백용성 연구의 회고와 전망 (A Retrospective and Prospective Look at Research on Paek Yongsŏng). *Taegak sasang* 14 (2011): 31–57.

Kim Kwangsik 김광식. "Pulgyo Chŏnghwa Undong kwa Hwadong Wiwŏnhoe" 불교정화운동과 화동위원회 (Movement for the Purification of Buddhism and the Hwadong Committee). In *Pulgyo Chŏnghwa Undong ŭi chaejomyŏng* 불교정화운동의 재조명 (Re-examination of the Buddhist Purification Movement), 223–66. Seoul: Chogyejong Ch'ulp'ansa, 2008.

Kim Kwangsik 김광식. "Yongsŏng ŭi kŏnbaeksŏ wa taechŏ sigyuk ŭi chaeinsik" 용성의 건백서와 대처식육의 재인식 (Yongsŏng's Petition and Re-examination of Clerical Marriage and Meat-eating). *Sŏnmunhwa yŏn'gu* 4 (2008): 213–51.

Kim Kwangsik 김광식. *Han'guk hyŏndae Pulgyosa yŏn'gu* 한국현대불교사 연구 (Research on the History of Contemporary Korean Buddhism). Seoul: Pulgyo Sidaesa, 2006.

Kim Kwangsik 김광식. *Han'guk kŭndae Pulgyosa yŏn'gu* 한국 근대불교사 연구 (Study of Modern Korean Buddhism). Seoul: Minjoksa, 1996, 2006.

Kim Kwangsik 김광식. *Pulgyo kŭndaehwa ŭi isang kwa hyŏnsil* 불교 근대화의 이상과 현실 (The Ideal and Reality of Buddhist Modernization). Seoul: Sŏnin, 2014.

Kim Kyŏngjip 김경집. *Han'guk kŭndae Pulgyo sa* 한국근대불교사 (History of Modern Korean Buddhism). Seoul: Kyŏngsŏwŏn, 1998.

Kim Min'gu 김민구. "Chosŏn-jo majimak Sangung Ttŏnada" 조선조 마지막 상궁 떠나다 (The Last Court Lady of Choson Korea Passes Away). *Chosŏn ilbo*, May 8, 2001. https://www.chosun.com/site/data/html_dir/2001/05/07/2001050770018.html.

Kim Pyŏg'ong 金璧翁. "Chosŏn Pulgyo ki'uron" 朝鮮佛敎杞憂論 (Debates in Rethinking the Issues of Chosŏn Buddhism). *Pulgyo* 32 (1927): 22–26.

Kim Sangyŏng 김상영. "Chŏn kŭndae Chogyejong yŏksa ŭi chŏn'gye yangsang kwa kŭ t'ŭksŏng" 전 근대 조계종 역사의 전개양상과 그 특성 (Evolution and Characteristics of the History of the Jogye Order in the Premodern Period). *Han'guk sŏnhak* 36 (December 2013): 454–92.

Kim Sijun 김시준. "Nosin i mannan Han'gugin 魯迅이 만난 韓國人" (The Korean Whom Lu Xun Met). *Chungguk hyŏndae munhak* 13 (1997): 127–63.

Kim Sunsŏk 김순석. "1994-nyŏn Taehan Pulgyo Chogyejong kaehyŏk chongdan ŭi sŏngnip kwa ŭiŭi" 1994년 대한 불교 조계종 개혁 종단의 성립과 의의 (The Formation and Significance of the 1994 Reformed Chogye Order). *Taegak sasang* 20 (2013): 327–59.

Kim Sunsŏk 김순석. "Han Yongun kwa Paek Yongsŏng ŭi kŭndae pulgyo kaehyŏngnon pigyo yŏn'gu" 한용운과 백용성의 근대 불교개혁론 비교 연구 (Comparative Study in Modern Buddhist Reformation Ideas between Han Yongun and Paek Yongsŏng). *Han'guk kŭnhyŏndaesa yŏn'gu* 35 (2005): 68–91.

Kim Sunsŏk 김순석. *Ilchesidae Chosŏn ch'ongdokpu ŭi Pulgyo chŏngch'aek kwa Pulgyogye ŭi taeŭng* 일제시대 조선 총독부의 불교 정책과 불교계의 대응 (The Colonial Government's Policies on Buddhism and the Response of the Buddhist Community during the Japanese Colonial Period). Seoul: Kyŏngin Munhwasa, 2003.

Kim Yongsuk 金用淑. *Chōsenchō kyūchū fūzoku no kenkyū* 朝鮮朝宮中風俗の研究 (A Study on the Court Customs of the Chosŏn Dynasty). Tokyo: Hōsei Daigaku Shūppansha, 2008.

Kim, Yongsuk 金用淑. "KuHanmal ŭi kungjung p'ungsok" 구한말의 궁중풍속 (The Court Custom in the Last Chosŏn Period). *Munhwajae* 16 (1983): 178–201.

Kim Yŏngt'ae 김영태. *T'aegojongsa: Han'guk Pulgyo chŏngt'ong chongdan ŭi yŏksa* 태고종사: 한국불교 정통종단의 역사 (The History of the T'aego Order: The History of the Legitimate Order of Korea Buddhism). Seoul: Han'guk Pulgyo Ch'ulp'anbu, 2006.

Kim Yongt'ae 김용태. "Chogyejong chongt'ong ŭi yŏksajŏk ihae: Kŭn·hyŏndae chongmyŏng, chongjo, chongji nonŭi rŭl chungshim ŭro" 조계종 종통의 역사적 이해: 근·현대 종명, 종조, 종지 논의를 중심으로 (The History of the Jogye Order: Its Focus on the Discussions of the Name, Patriarch, and Identity). *Han'guk sŏnhak* 35 (2013): 144–68.

Kim Yongt'ae 김용태. "Chosŏn hugi kŭndae ŭi chongmyŏng gwa chongjo inshik ŭi yŏksajŏk goch'al: Chogyejong kwa T'aego pŏpt'ong ŭi kyŏryŏn" 조선 후기·근대의 종명과 종조 인식의 역사적 고찰: 조계종과 태고 법통의 결연 (The

Name and the Patriarch of the Buddhist Order in the Late Chosŏn and Modern Periods: The Complicated History between the Jogye Order and the T'aego Order). *Sŏn munhwa yŏn'gu* 8 (2010): 43–81.

Kim Yongt'ae 김용태. "Han'guk kŭndae Pulgyo ŭi taejunghwa mosaek kwa chŏngch'ijŏk sesokhwa" 한국 근대불교의 대중화 모색과 정치적 세속화 (Study of the Popularization of Modern Korean Buddhism and Political Secularization). *Pulgyo yŏn'gu* 35 (2011): 109–38.

Kim Yongt'ae 김용태. "Tong'asia kŭndae Pulgyo yŏn'gu ŭi t'ŭksŏng kwa orientalism ŭi t'uyŏng" 동아시아 근대 불교 연구의 특성과 오리엔탈리즘 의 투영 (The Characteristics of the Study of the Modern Buddhism in East Asia and Its Orientalism). *Yŏksa hakpo* 210 (2011): 229–58.

Kim Yongt'ae 김용태. *Chosŏn hugi pulgyosa yŏn'gu* 조선 후기 불교사 연구 (A Study of the History of Late Chosŏn Buddhism). Seoul: Sin'gu Munhwasa, 2010.

Kim, Hwansoo Ilmee. " 'The Mystery of the Century': Lay Buddhist Monk Villages (Chaegasŭngch'on) Near Korea's Northernmost Border, 1600s–1960s." *Seoul Journal of Korean Studies* 26, no. 2 (2013): 269–305.

Kim, Hwansoo Ilmee. "Buddhism during the Chosŏn Period (1392–1910): A Collective Trauma?" *Journal of Korean Studies* 22, no. 1 (2017): 101–42.

Kim, Hwansoo Ilmee. "Seeking the Colonizer's Favors for a Buddhist Vision: The Korean Buddhist Nationalist Paek Yongsŏng's (1864–1940) Imje Sŏn Movement and His Relationship with the Japanese Colonizer Abe Mitsuie (1862–1936)." *Sungkyun Journal of East Asian Studies* 14, no. 2 (2014): 171–93.

Kim, Hwansoo Ilmee. *Empire of the Dharma: Korean and Japanese Buddhism, 1877–1912*. Cambridge: Harvard University Asia Center, Harvard University Press, 2012.

Kim, Hyun Mee. "Becoming a City Buddhist among the Young Generation in Seoul." *International Sociology* 31, no. 4 (2016): 450–66.

Kim, Seong Uk. "The Re-invention of Koran Sŏn Buddhism in the Late Chosŏn." *Journal of Korean Religions* 8, no. 1 (2017): 161–83.

Kinnard, Jacob. "Proper Possessions: Buddhist Attitudes toward Material Property." In *Buddhism and Law: An Introduction*, edited by Rebecca French and Mark A. Nathan, 78–90. New York: Cambridge University Press, 2014.

Kirk, Dan. "Monk Factions Vie to Control Korea's Biggest Sect: Buddhist Temple Tug-of-War." *New York Times*, December 5, 1998. https://www.nytimes.com/1998/12/05/news/monk-factions-vie-to-control-koreas-biggest-sect-buddhist-temple.html.

Ko Chaesŏk. *Han'guk kŭndae munhak chisŏngsa* 韓國近代文學知性史 (Korean Modern Literary and Intellectual History). Seoul: Kip'ŭnsaem, 1991.

Ko Hŭisuk 고희숙. "Han'guk Pulgyo kangwŏn samikwa kyoje ŭi sŏjijŏk yŏn'gu" 한국불교 강원 사미과 교제의 서지적 연구 (A Bibliographic Research of the Study Materials of the Novice Course in Korean Buddhist Seminaries). *Sŏjihak yŏn'gu* 10 (1994): 883–932.

Ko Taesŏk 고대석. *Han'guk k'ŭndae munhak chisŏngsa* 한국 근대 문학 지성사 (The Intellectual History of Modern Korean Literature). Seoul: Kip'unsaem, 1991.

Ko Yŏngsŏp 고영섭. "Chogyejong ŭi kyejŏnghye samhak suhaeng chŏngch'aek: Yongsŏng, Yŏngho, Hanam, Chaun ŭl chungsim ŭro" 조계종의 계정혜 삼학 수행 정책: 용성, 영호, 한암, 자운을 중심으로 (Threefold Training of Vinaya, Mindfulness, and Wisdom in the Jogye Order: An Examination of Yongsŏng, Yŏngho, Hanam, and Chaun). *Pulgyo hakpo* 70 (2015): 171–202.

Ko Yŏngsŏp 고영섭. *Taehan sidae Ilbon yuhaksaeng tŭrŭi Pulgyo yŏn'gu tonghyang: Ilche kangjŏmgi Chaeil Pulgyo yugaksaeng ŭl chungsim ŭro* 대한시대 일본유학생들의 불교연구동향-일제강점기 재일 불교유학생을 중심으로 (A Study on the Buddhist Research Trends of Japanese Students in the Korean Period—Focused on Japanese Students in Japan during the Japanese Colonial Period). Tongguk Taehakkyo Pulgyo taehak, *Tongyang taehak kukje chŏrhak yŏn'gu sentŏ che 1 hoe kukche kongdong yŏn'gu charyojip* (2014): 145–67.

Kŭmgang 금강. "Hyŏndae sahoe sŭngga chŏnggyu nŭn ŏttŏn naeyong ŭro chejŏng toeŏya hanŭn'ga" 현대 사회 승가청규는 어떤 내용으로 제정되어야 하는가? (How Should the Monastic Pure Rules Be Reenacted in Modern Society?). Paper presented at Hyŏndae sahoe sŭngga chŏnggyu. Chogyesa, 2015.

"Kŭn'go" 謹告 (Announcement). *Tonga ilbo*, February 8, 1934.

Kwŏn Oyŏng 권오영. "Ŭihyŏn chŏn ch'ongmuwŏnjang 21-nyŏn mane 'myŏlbin kullae' pŏsŏ" 의현 전 총무원장 21년만에 멸빈굴래 벗어 (Previous Administrative Head, Ŭihyŏn, Takes Off the Shackles of Expulsion after 21 Years). *Pŏppo sinmun*, June 18, 2015. http://www.beopbo.com/news/articleView.html?reply_page=1&total=13&idxno=87533&replyAll=Y&reply_sc_order_by=C.

Kwon, Nayoung Aimee. *Intimate Empire: Collaboration & Colonial Modernity in Korea & Japan*. Durham: Duke University Press, 2015.

Kyŏnghŏ Sŏngu 鏡虛惺牛. *Kyŏnghŏ chip* 鏡虛集 (Collected Writings of Kyŏnghŏ). Korea: Kŭngak sŏnwŏn, 1990/1991.

Kyŏnghŏ Sŏngu 鏡虛惺牛. *Kyŏnghŏ chip*鏡虛集 (Collected Writings of Kyŏnghŏ). *Han'guk Pulgyo Chŏnsŏ* 韓國佛教全書 (Collected Works of Korean Buddhism). Seoul: Tongguk Taehakkyo Ch'ulp'anbu, 1989, vol. 11, 587b–701b.

Kyŏnghyang sinmun 京鄉新聞 (1946–present). Seoul: Kyŏnghyang Sinmunsa.

Larsen, Kirk W. *Tradition, Treaties, and Trade: Qing Imperialism and Chosŏn Korea, 1850–1910*. Cambridge: Harvard University Press, 2008.

Lee Chŏlgyo 이철교. "Pak Pongsŏk ŭi saengae wa chŏjak e taehaesŏ" 朴奉石의 생애와 저작에 대해서 (On the Life and Work of Pak Pongsŏk). *Tosŏgwan* 56, no. 3 (2001): 101–18.

Lee Songu. "The Exemplar Wife: The Life of Lady Chang of Andong in Historical Context." In *Women and Confucianism in Chosŏn Korea: New Perspectives*, coedited by Youngmin Kim and Michael J. Pettid, 29–48. Albany: State University of New York Press, 2011.

Lee, Haiyan. *Revolution of the Heart: A Genealogy of Love in China, 1900–1950*. Stanford, CA: Stanford University Press, 2007.
Lee, Jungshim. "A Doubtful National Hero: Han Yongun's Buddhist Nationalism Revisited." *Korean Histories* 3, no. 1 (2012): 35–52.
Li Qinpu. *Tuo jie, lama, Jin Jiujing* 脫解, 喇嘛, 金九经 (Nirvana, Lama, Kim Kugyŏng). Shenyang Shi: Liaoning jiao yu chu ban she, 2016.
Linji 臨濟. *Linji lu* 臨濟錄 (Recorded Sayings of Linji). *Taishō shinshū daizōkyō* 大正新脩大藏經, 47n1985, 496b–596c. Tokyo: Taishō issaikyō kankōkai, 1924–1932.
Linji. *Linji lu* 臨濟錄T. 47.1985.466b–506c.
Lua Zhenyu 羅振玉. *Liaoling shikejilu* 遼陵石刻集 (Records on the Collection of the Stone Carving in Liaoling). Taren: Youwenge, 1934.
Maeil sinbo 每日申報 (1910–1945). Keijō: Maeil sinbosa.
"Magoksa chuji huim chaengt'al chŏn" 麻谷寺住持後任爭奪戰 (Struggle for New Head Monk at Magoksa Monastery). *Tonga ilbo*, February 6, 1927.
"Magoksa sinim chuji yussi pandae undong" 麻谷寺信任住持 兪氏反對運動 (Magok Monastery's Movement against New Head Monk Yu). *Tonga ilbo*, December 19, 1926.
MBC PD Notebook. "Kŭn sŭnimkke mutsŭmnida I" 큰스님께 묻습니다 I (Could We Ask Questions, Venerable Monk? Part I). May 1, 2018. https://www.youtube.com/watch?v=jXFsbMYv4IA.
MBC PD Notebook. "Kŭn sŭnimkke mutsŭmnida II" 큰스님께 묻습니다 II (Could We Ask Questions, Venerable Monk? Part II). May 29, 2018. https://www.youtube.com/watch?v=4wb6j-qvP1c.
McBride, Richard. "Watch Yourself! (Jagyeongmun 自警文), by Yaun." In *The Collected Works of Korean Buddhism*. Vol. 6, edited by A. Charles Muller, 501–26. Seoul: The Jogye Order of Korean Buddhism, 2012.
McBride, Richard. "Wŏnhyo's Pure Land Thought on Buddhānusmṛti in Its Sinitic Buddhist Context. *Acta Koreana* 18, no. 1 (June 2015): 45–94.
McBride, Richard D., II. "The Complex Origins of the Vinaya in Early Korean Buddhism." *The Eastern Buddhist*, New Series, 45, nos. 1–2 (2016): 151–77.
McBride, Richard D., II. "Dhāraṇī and Mantra in Contemporary Korean Buddhism: A Textual Ethnography of Spell Materials for Popular Consumption." *Journal of the International Association of Buddhist Studies* 42 (2019): 361–403.
McBride, Richard D., II. "Wŏnhyo." In *Brill's Encyclopedia of Buddhism*. Vol. II: Lives, ed. Richard Bowring, Vincent Eltschinger, and Michael Radich, 913–17. Leiden: Brill, 2019.
McDaniel, Justin Thomas. *Gathering Leaves and Lifting Words: Histories of Buddhist Monastic Education in Laos and Thailand*. Seattle: University of Washington Press, 2008.
McMahan, David L. *The Making of Buddhist Modernism*. Oxford: Oxford University Press, 2008.

Mignolo, Walter D. "Coloniality: The Darker Side of Modernity." http://www.macba.cat/PDFs/walter_mignolo_modernologies_eng.pdf.

Mignolo, Walter D. *The Darker Side of Western Modernity: Global Futures, Decolonial Options*. Durham: Duke University Press, 2011. http://site.ebrary.com/lib/unsw/reader.action?docID=10516146.

"Mobŏmjŏk Pulgyo sinja: yumyŏnghan Chŏn Ilchŏng yŏsa" 모범적 불교신자: 유명한 千一清女史 (An Exemplary Buddhist: Famous Madame Chŏn Ilchŏng). *Maeil sinbo*, February 13, 1915.

"Monkey Business: Buddhism in South Korea." *The Economist*, October 3, 2013. https://www.economist.com/asia/2013/10/03/monkey-business.

Mori Eisuke 毛利英介. Manshū shi to tōhoku shi no aida—Inaba Iwakichi to Jin Yufu no kōryū yori 満洲史と東北史のあいだ—稲葉岩吉と金毓黻の交流より (Between the History of Manchuria and That of Dongbei: The Relationship between Inaba Iwakichi and Jin Yufu). *Kansai daigaku tozai gakushutsu kenkyū kiyo* 4 (2015): 343–63.

Muller, A. Charles, ed. *Wŏnhyo: Selected Works*. Collected Works of Korean Buddhism. Vol. 1. Paju, Korea: Chun-il Munhwasa, 2012.

Muller, A. Charles. "Awaken Your Mind and Practice (Balsim suhaeng jang) 發心修行章." In *The Collected Works of Korean Buddhism*. Vol. 1, edited by Charles Muller, 261–68. Seoul: The Jogye Order of Korean Buddhism, 2012.

Mun Kwang 문광. "Hyeam Sŏnsa ŭi chasŏng samhak ŭi Sŏn suhaeng koch'al" 慧菴禪師의 自性三學의 禪修行 考察 (Studies on Sŏn Master Hyeam's Sŏn Practice of Three Disciplines of Self Nature). In *Hyeam Sŏnsa ŭi sam kwa sasang* 혜암선사의 삶과 사상 (Life and Thoughts of Sŏn Master Hyeam), edited by Hyeam Sŏnsa Munhwa Chinhŭnghoe, 23–55. Seoul: Sihwaŭm, 2019.

Mun, Chanju. *Ha Dongsan and Colonial Korean Buddhism: Balancing Sectarianism and Ecumenism*. Honolulu: Blue Pine Books, 2009.

Mun, Chanju. *Purification Buddhist Movement 1954–1970: The Struggle to Restore Celibacy in the Jogye Order of Korean Buddhism*. New York: Blue Pine Books, 2011.

Mun'gwang 문광. "Milleniŏm sidae ŭi sŭngga wa suhaeng: Kyeyul kwa chŏnggyu chŏngsin ŭi pokkich'o rŭl parwŏn hamyŏ" 밀레니엄 시대의 승가와 수행: 계율과 청규 정신의 복기처를 발원하며 (The Sangha and Buddhist Practice in the Millennial Age: Praying for the Revival of the Spirit of the Vinaya and the Pure Rules). *Munhak sahak chŏrhak* 9 (2007): 110–25.

"Naeji hŭibo" 內地彙報 (Miscellaneous News from Japan). *Taehan hyŏphoe hoebo*, February 25, 1909.

Nam Kwŏnhŭi 남권희. Chŭngdogaja ŭi palgyŏn kwa Nammyŏngch'ŏn hwasang song Chŭngdoga ŭi yŏn'gu 證道歌字의 발견과 南明泉和尚頌證道歌의 연구 (Discovery of the "*Song of Enlightenment*" Movable Metal Type and the Study of *The Song of Enlightenment* Praised by Nammyŏng). *Sŏji hakpo* 36 (2010): 5–84.

"Namjangsa kwanŭm kangwŏn ŭi nisŭng kangwŏnsaeng suryosik" 南長寺觀音講院의尼僧講院生修了式 (Bhiksuni Students' Graduation Ceremony of Kwanŭm Seminary at Namjang Monastery). *Pulgyo shibo* 96. July 15, 1943.

Nathan, Mark A. *From the Mountains to the Cities: A History of Buddhist Propagation in Modern Korea.* Honolulu: University of Hawai'i Press, 2018.

Nathan, Mark Andrew. "Buddhist Propagation and Modernization: The Significance of P'ogyo in Twentieth-Century Korean Buddhism." PhD diss., University of California, Los Angeles, 2010.

Nattier, Jan. "Sex." In *Critical Terms for the Study of Buddhism*, edited by Donald Lopez Jr., 271–90. Chicago: University of Chicago Press, 2005.

Numrich, Paul. *Old Wisdom in the New World: Americanization in Two Immigrant Theravada Buddhist Temples.* Knoxville: University of Tennessee Press, 1996.

O Kyŏnghu 오경후. "Ilche singminji chŏngch'aek kwa Chosŏn Pulgyo ŭi Ilbonhwa e taehan chaegŏmt'o 일제 식민지 정책과 조선 불교의 일본화에 대한 재검토 (Reexamination of Japanese Colonial Policies and Japanization of Korean Buddhism). *Yŏksa minsokhak* 49 (2015): 37–57.

O Yŏngsŏk 오영석. "Hyeam Sŏnsa ŭi Kanhwa Sŏn e taehan koch'al" 慧菴禪師의 간화선에 대한 고찰 (Studies on Sŏn Master Hyeam's Kanhwa Sŏn). In *Hyeam Sŏnsa ŭi salm kwa sasang* 혜암선사의 삶과 사상 (Life and Thoughts of Sŏn Master Hyeam), edited by Hyeam Sŏnsa Munhwa Chinhŭnghoe 혜암선사문화진흥회, 69–94. Seoul: Sihwaŭm, 2019.

Okamura Keiji 岡村敬二. "Ryōneishō toshokan hōmonki" 遼寧省圖書館訪問記 (A Record on the Visit to the Liaoning Library). *Senzenki Chūgoku tōhokubu kankō nihongo siryō no shoshi teki kenkyū* (2007): 188–92.

Okamura Keiji 岡村敬二. *Nichi-Man Bunka Kyōkai no rekishi: sōsōki o chūshin ni* 日滿文化協會の歷史「草創期を中心に (History of the Cultural Association of Japan and Manchuria: Focusing on the Early Stage). Kyōto-shi: Okamura keiji, 2006.

Olson, Carl. "Celibacy and Human Body: An Introduction." In Celibacy and Religious Traditions, edited by Carl Olson, 3–20. New York: Oxford University Press, 2008.

"Paegin paekhwa" 百人百話 (Hundred People and Hundred Stories). Kaebyŏk 1 (November 1934): 116–17.

Paek Soa 백소아. "Sŏlchŏng Sŭnim ŭi sumŭn ttal ŭihok ŭn hŏui . . . ibyanghaetta" 설정스님의 숨은 딸 의혹은 허위 . . . 입양했다 (The Chief Monk Sŏlchŏng's Accusation Is Untrue . . . He Adopted Her). *Hankyoreh sinmun*, May 24, 2018. http://www.hani.co.kr/arti/society/society_general/846109.html.

Paek Yongsŏng. *Chosŏn'gŭl Hwaŏmgyŏng* 조선글 화엄경 (A Korean Translation of the *Avatamsaka Sutra*), advertisement, back cover of *Pulgyo* (Buddhism, 佛教) 49 (1928).

Paek Yongsŏng. *Kwiwŏn chŏngjong* 歸源正宗 (Correct Doctrines That Return to the Source). Keijo (Seoul): Chung'ang p'ogyodang, 1913.

Pak Chaehyeon 박재현. "Chogyejong chongdan kaehyŏk pulsa" 조계종 종단개혁불사 (Reformation of the Jogye Order). *Sŏnu toryang* 6 (1994): 39–55.

Pak Chaehyeon 박재현. "Kyŏnghŏ pŏmmaek ŭi chŏnsŭng e kwanhan sŏjihakjŏk kŏmt'o" 경허 법맥의 전승에 관한 서지학적 검토 (Bibliographical Examination of Kyŏnghŏ's Dharman Lineage and Transmission). *Pojo sasang* 37 (2012, 2): 295–330.

Pak Chaehyeon 박재현. *Han'guk kŭndae Pulgyo ŭi t'ajadŭl* 한국근대불교의 타자들 (Outsiders of Modern Korean Buddhism). Seoul: P'urŭn yŏksa, 2009.

Pak Chaehyeon박재현. "KuHanmal Han'guk Sŏn Pulgyo ŭi Kanhwa Sŏn e taehan han ihae: Song Kyŏnghŏ ŭi Sŏn sasang ŭl chungsim ŭro" 구한말 한국 선불교의 간화선에 대한 한 이해: 송경허의 선사상을 중심으로 (An Understanding of Kanhua Sŏn in Modern Korean Buddhism—Regarding Yen Song Gyeongheo (1846–1912). *Ch'ŏrhak* 83 (2009): 1–24.

Pak Chaehyŏn 박재현. "Kŭndae Pulgyo ŭi taech'o shikuk munje e kwanhan yunlijŏk koch'al" 근대 불교의 대처식육 문제에 관한 윤리적 고찰 (Ethical Dimensions on the Issue of Taking a Wife and Eating Meat in Modern Buddhism). *Han'guk Ch'ŏrhak hokhoe* 93 (2007): 47–70.

Pak Chaehyŏn 박재현. "Han'guk kŭndae Pulgyo ŭi t'ajadŭl: sap'ansŭng kwa taech'ŏsŭng ŭi t'oejo" 사판승과 대처승의 퇴조 (The Others in Modern Korean Buddhism: The Decline of the Administrative Monks and Married Monks). *Ch'ŏrhak sasang* 28 (May 2008): 131–59.

Pak Chaehyŏn 박재현. "Sŏngin chŏn iron kwa Han'guk Pulgyo ŭi kŭn sŭnim mandŭlgi e taehan goch'al" 성인전 (聖人傳)이론과 한국 불교의 큰스님 만들기에 대한 고찰 (Theory of Hagiography and Studies on Korean Buddhism's Creation of Great Masters). In *Hyeam Sŏnsa ŭi salm kwa sasang* 혜암선사의 삶과 사상 (Life and Thoughts of Sŏn Master Hyeam), edited by Hyeam Sŏnsa Munhwa Chinhŭnghoe 혜암선사문화진흥회, 151–70. Seoul: Sihwaŭm, 2019.

Pak Chŏngho. "Sŭnim kuin kwanggo sidae" 스님 구인 광고시대 (The Age of Advertisement for Recruiting Monastics). *Chungang ilbo*, November 14, 2017.

Pak Haedang 박해당. "Chogyejong pŏpt'ongsŏl ŭi hyŏngsŏng kwajŏng kwa munjejŏm" 조계종 법통설의 형성과정과 문제점 (Formation of the Dharma Lineage Discourses of the Jogye Order and Their Problems). *The Buddhist Review* 3 (June 2000). http://www.budreview.com/news/articleView.html?idxno=306.

Pak Sangjin 박상진. *Kungnyŏ ŭi haru: Yŏindŭl i ssŭn sumgyŏjin sillok* 궁녀의 하루: 여인들이 쓴 숨겨진 실록 (Court Ladies' Day: True Hidden Stories Written by Women). Kyŏnggi-do P'aju-si: Kimyŏngs, 2013.

Pak Yŏnggyu 박영규. *Hwan'gwan kwa kungnyŏ* 환관과 궁녀 (Eunuch and Court Lady). Kyŏnggi-do P'aju-si: Kimyŏngsa, 2004.

Pak Sŏkhong 박석홍. "Ppuri hŭndŭnŭn Pulgyo hyŏndaehwa param" 뿌리 흔든 불교현대화 바람 (A Radical Modernization Movement in Buddhism). *Kyonghyang sinmun*, August 19, 1982. http://newslibrary.naver.com/viewer/

index.nhn?articleId=1982081900329211001&editNo=2&printCount=1&-publishDate=1982-08-19&officeId=00032&pageNo=11&printNo=11351&-publishType=00020.
Pak Suho 박수호. "Sahoe undong ŭrosŏŭi Chogyejong chongdan kyehŏk undong" 사회운동으로서의 조계종 종단개혁운동 (The Reformation of the Jogye Order as a Social Movement). *Tongyang sahoe sasang* 11 (2005): 59–90.
Park, Jeongeun. "Clerical Marriage and Buddhist Modernity in Early Twentieth-Century Korea." PhD diss., University of British Columbia, 2016.
Park, Jin Y, ed. *Makers of Modern Korean Buddhism*. Albany: State University of New York Press, 2010.
Park, Jin Y, trans. *Reflections of a Zen Buddhist Nun: Essays by Zen Master Kim Iryŏp*. Honolulu: University of Hawai'i Press, 2014.
Park, Jin Y. "A Crazy Drunken Monk: Kyŏnghŏ and Modern Buddhist Meditation Practice." In *Korean Religion in Practice*, edited by Robert E. Buswell Jr., 130–43. Princeton, NJ: Princeton University Press, 2007.
Park, Jin Y. "Kyŏnghŏ Sŏngu and the Existential Dimensions of Modern Korean Buddhism." *Journal of Korean Religions* 10, no. 2 (October 2019): 247–74.
Park, Jin Y. "Zen and Zen Philosophy of Language: A Soteriological Approach." *Dao: A Journal of Comparative Philosophy* 1, no. 2 (June 2002): 209–28.
Park, Jin Y. "Zen Language in Our Time: The Case of Pojo Chinul's Huatou Meditation." *Philosophy East & West* 50, no. 1 (January 2005): 80–98.
Park, Jin Y. *Buddhism and Postmodernity: Zen, Huayan, and the Possibility of Buddhist-Postmodern Ethics*. Lanham, MD: Lexington Books, 2008.
Park, Jin Y. *Women and Buddhist Philosophy: Engaging Zen Master Kim Iryŏp*. Honolulu: University of Hawai'i Press, 2017.
Park, Pori. "A Korean Buddhist Response to Modernity: Manhae Han Yongun's Doctrinal Reinterpretation for His Reformist Thought." In *Makers of Modern Korean Buddhism*, edited by Jin Park, 41–60. Albany: State University of New York Press, 2010.
Park, Pori. "Korean Buddhist Reforms and Problems in the Adoption of Modernity during the Colonial Period." *Korea Journal* 45, no. 1 (2005): 87–113.
Park, Pori. "The Buddhist Purification Movement in Postcolonial South Korea." In *Identity Conflicts: Can Violence be Regulated?*, coedited by J. Craig Jenkins and Esther E. Gottlieb, 131–48. New Brunswick, NJ: Transaction Publishers, 2007.
Park, Pori. *Trial and Error in Modernist Reforms: Korean Buddhism under Colonial Rule*. Berkeley: Institute of East Asian Studies, University of California, 2009.
Park, Sojin. "Mother's Anxious Management of the Private After-School Education Market." In *No Alternative? Experiments in South Korean Education*, edited by Nancy Abelman, Jung-Ah Choi, and So-Jin Park. Berkeley: University of California Press, 2012.

Petley, Julian, ed. *Media and Public Shaming: Drawing the Boundaries of Disclosure*. London: I.B. Tauris, 2013.

Poceski, Mario. "Xuefeng's Code and the Chan School's Participation in the Development of Monastic Regulations." *Asia Major* 14 (2003): 33–56.

Pŏppo sinmun (1988–present). Seoul: Pŏppo sinmunsa.

Powers, John. "Celibacy in Indian and Tibetan Buddhism." In *Celibacy and Religious Traditions*, edited by Carl Olson, 201–24. New York: Oxford University Press, 2008.

Prebish, Charles S, ed. *Buddhist Monastic Discipline: The Sanskrit Prātimokṣa Sūtras of the Mahāsāṃghikas and Mūlasarvāstivādins*. University Park: Pennsylvania State University Press, 1996 (1975).

Prebish, Charles S. "Varying the Vinaya: Creative Responses to Modernity." In *Buddhism in the Modern World: Adaptations of an Ancient Tradition*, edited by Steven Heine and Charles Prebish, 45–74. Oxford: Oxford University Press, 2003.

Pulgyo sinmun 佛『新聞 (1951–present). Seoul: Pulgyo sinmunsa.

"Raichō no Kankoku san jōkan" 『朝の韓國三女官 (Three Korean Court Ladies Visiting Japan). *Asahi sinbun*, February 19, 1909.

Rainichi jokan danppen 渡日女官ノ談片 (A Short Story of a Court Lady Who Visited Japan (196)." *Sōkanfu bunsho* 6 (March 22, 1909). http://db.history.go.kr/id/jh_096_0010_1960.

Reader, Ian, and George J. Tanabe Jr. *Practically Religious: Worldly Benefits and the Common Religion of Japan*. Honolulu: University of Hawai'i Press, 1998.

Ruppert, Brian. "Buddhism and Law in Japan." In *Buddhism and Law: An Introduction*, edited by Rebecca Redwood French and Mark A. Nathan, 273–87. New York: Cambridge University Press, 2014.

Sagaster, Klaus. "The History of Buddhism among the Mongols." In *The Spread of Buddhism*, edited by Ann Heirman and Stephan Peter Bumbacher, 379–432. Leiden: Brill, 2007.

Sakayori Masashi 酒寄雅志. "Bokkaishi kenkyū to kindai nihon" 渤海史研究と近代日本. (Research on Bohai History and Modern Japan). *Sundai shigaku* 108 (1999): 1–21.

Samchŏlli (1929–1943). Keijō: Samchŏllisa.

"Samgyo ilhang" 三校一行 (Three Schools' Trip). *Chosŏn Pulgyo wŏlbo* 10 (December 1912): 65.

"*Sanggung Chŏn Ilchŏng t'anwŏnsŏ*" 상궁 천일청 탄원서 (Court Lady Chŏn Ilchŏng's Petition). http://yoksa.aks.ac.kr.

"Sangsisawŏn yŏgwan dŭng samsip'yŏmyŏng ch'ong haejik" 掌侍司員女官等三十餘名總解職 (Dismissal of Thirty High-Ranking Court Ladies and Others). *Tonga ilbo*, August 23, 1928.

Sasaki, Shizuka. "Bukkyō ni okeru kai to ritsu no imi" 仏教における戒と律の意味 (The Meaning of Precepts and Discipline in Buddhism). *Han'guk Pulgyohak* 45 (2006): 73–97.

"Sasŭng chosap'yo" 寺僧調査票 (Survey of the Number of Buddhist Monks and Nuns). *Hwangsŏng sinmun*, December 25, 1909.
Schonthal, Ben. "Guest Editor's Introduction: Buddhist Legal Pluralism? Looking Again at Monastic Governance in Modern South and Southeast Asia." *Buddhism, Law & Society* 3 (2017–2018): vii–xxx.
Schopen, Gregory. "Doing Business for the Lord: Lending on Interest and Written Loan Contracts in the Mulasarvastivada-Vinaya." *Journal of the American Oriental Society* 114, no. 4 (1994): 527–54.
Schopen, Gregory. "Monastic Law Meets the Real World: A Monk's Continuing Right to Inherit Family Property in Classical India." *History of Religions* 35, no. 2 (1995): 101–23.
Schopen, Gregory. "The Good Monk and His Money in Buddhist Monasticism of 'The Mahayana Period.'" *The Eastern Buddhist* 32, no. 1 (2000): 85–105.
Séguy, Jean. "Une Sociologie Des Sociétés Imaginées: Monachisme et Utopie" (Sociology of Imaginary Societies: Monasticism and Utopia). *Annales* 2 (1971): 328–54.
Shimada Tōsui 嶋田東水. "Kakunōji no nyūbusshiki" 覺皇寺の入佛式 (Kakhwang Temple and the Enshrinement Ceremony of the Buddha). *Chūgai nippō*, November 11, 1910.
Shinma Susumu 新馬晉. "Aru hi no kenryūtei" 或る日の乾隆帝 (One Day, Emperor Qianlon). *Shūsho keppō* 60 (1941).
Shinma Susumu 新馬晉. "Kamioshi shinjuzō koraiban nameisen shōdōka nitsuite" 神尾氏眞珠莊藏高麗板南明泉頌證道歌について (On *Nanmingquan song zheng dao ge* in the Koryŏ Dynasty's Tripitaka-Woodblock of Mr. Kamio shinjuzō's Collection). *Shiryō kōhō* 3, no. 8 (1942): 13–21.
Sidae ilbo 時代日報 (1924–1926). Keijō: Sidae ilbosa.
Sifen lu 四分律 (Dharamguptaka Vinaya). 60 vols. *Taishō shinshū daizōkyō* 大正新脩大藏経 (T 1428).
Sim Chaegwan 심재관. "Kŭndae Pulgyo ŭi han jingyŏng: Gogi mŏkgi wa manura kkwech'agi" 근대 불교의 한 진경: 고기 먹기와 마누라 꿰차기 (An Exotic Scene of Modern Buddhism: Eating Meat and Taking a Wife). *Pulgyo p'yŏngnon* 22 (2005): 58–74.
Sim Chaeryong 심재룡. "Hanguk Pulgyo nŭn hoet'ong Pulgyo inga?" 한국불교는 회통 불교인가? (Is Korean Buddhism hoet'ong Pulgyo?). *Pulgyo p'yŏngnon* 3 (2000): 176–90.
Sin Hoejŏng 신회정. "Ch'imun kyŏnghunju ŭi kyoyukchŏk kach'i e kwanhan yŏn'gu" 치문 경훈주의 교육적 가치에 관한연구 (Research on the Educational Value of the Commentary to the Admonitions to the Gray-Robed Monks). Master's thesis, Dongguk University, 2007.
Sin Kyut'ak, ed. 신규탁. *Kongbu hada chugŏra: Hyeam Taejongsa sangdang pŏbŏjip* 공부하다 죽어라: 혜암대종사 상당 법어집 (Practice until Die: Collection of Great Master Hyeam's Dharma Talks). Vol. 1. Seoul: Sihwaŭm, 2019.

Sin Myŏngho 신명호. *Kungnyŏ: Kunggwŏl ŭi kkott* 궁녀: 궁궐의 꽃 (Court Ladies: Flowers of the Palace). Sŏul: Sogongsa, 2004.

"Singyo puingye e iron ŭro kyŏngoham" 信敎婦人界에一言으로警告 (A Word of Warning for [Buddhist] Female Believers). *Chosŏn pulgyo wŏlbo* 3 (April 1911): 44–47.

"Sirŏp sŏnp'ung un 'Nain' egedo, Andong Pyŏlgung to hŏllyŏ" 失業旋風은 '나인'에 게도, 安洞別宮도헐려 (A Sweeping Unemployment Hits the Court Ladies, and Even the Andong Royal Palace Faces Demolition). *Tonga ilbo*, June 3, 1936.

Sŏ Chaeyŏng 서재영. "Pongamsa kyŏlsa ŭi chŏngsin kwa T'woeong Sŏngch'ŏl ŭi yŏkhal" 범어사 결사의 정신과 퇴옹 성철의 역할 (The Spirit of the Community of Bongam Monastery and the Role of T'woeong Sŏngch'ŏl). *Hang'uk sŏn hak* 18, no. Décembre (2007): 11–64.

Sŏ Chŏngju 서정주. "Sŏkchŏn Pak Hanyŏng sŭnim 4" 석전 박한영 스님 (Master Sŏkchŏn Pak Hanyŏng). *Haein* 120 (February 1992). http://haein.or.kr/contents/?pgv=v&wno=93&cno=1064.

Sŏ Hwadong 서화동. "Tobak ŭnch'ŏsŭng chingye ch'ŏt kŏron" 도박 은처승 징계 첫 거론 (The First Attempt to Taking a Disciplinary Action against Those Monks Who Have a Wife or Monks Who Gamble). *Kyŏnghyang sinmun*, August 3, 1996. http://newslibrary.naver.com/viewer/index.nhn?articleId=1996080300329115003&editNo=40&printCount=1&publishDate=1996-08-03&officeId=00032&pageNo=15&printNo=15842&publishType=00010.

"Sō Naishō no kien" 宋内相の氣焔 (Internal Minister Song's Spirit). *Asahi shinbun*, February 17, 1909.

Soloves, Daniel J. *Understanding Privacy*. Cambridge: Harvard University Press, 2008.

Son Chihye 孫知慧. "Wasurerareta kindai no chishikijin Kim Kyūkei ni kansuru chōsa" 忘れられた近代の知識人「金九経」に関する調査 (Study of Forgotten Modern Intellectual Kim Kugyŏng). *Ōtani gakuhō* 94, no. 2 (2015): 91–119.

Song gooseng zhuan 宋高僧傳. T 2061.50.709a–900a.

Song Hyŏnju 송현주. "Chogyejong chŏnt'ong ŭi ch'angjo wa honjongjŏk kŭndaesŏng: Sŏgu kŭndae Pulgyo waŭi pigyo rŭl chungshim ŭro" 조계종 전통의 창조 와 혼종적 근대성: 서구 근대불교와의 비교를 중심으로 (The Invention of the Jogye Order and Hybrid Modernity: In Comparison with the Modern Buddhism in the West). *Chonggyo munhwa pipyŏng* 30 (2016): 14–49.

Sŏnwudoryang Han'guk Pulgyo Kŭnhyŏndaesa yŏn'guhoe, ed. *22-in ŭi chŭngŏn ŭl t'onghae pon kŭnhyŏndae Pulgyosa* 22인의 증언을 통해 본 근현대 불교사 (Modern and Contemporary Buddhist History through the Testimonies of 22 People). Seoul: Sŏnwu Toryang Publishing, 2002.

Sørensen, Henrik H. "Buddhism and Secular Power in Twentieth-Century Korea." In *Buddhism and Politics in Twentieth Century Asia*, edited by Ian Harris, 157–252. New York: Continuum, 1999.

Sørensen, Henrik H. "Korean Buddhist Journals during Early Japanese Colonial Rule." *Korea Journal* 30, no. 1 (January 1990): 17–27.

Sørensen, Henrik H. "Mirror of Emptiness: The Life and Times of the Sŏn Master Kyŏnghŏ Sŏngu." In *Makers of Modern Korean Buddhism*, edited by Jin Y. Park, 131–55. Albany: State University of New York Press, 2010.
Sponberg, Alan. "Attitudes toward Women and the Feminine in Early Buddhism." In *Buddhism, Sexuality, and Gender*, edited by José Ignacio Cabezón, 3–36. Albany: State University of New York Press, 1992.
Statistics Korea. "2015 in'gu chut'aek ch'ongjosa p'yobon chipkye kyŏlgwa" 2015 인구 주택 총조사 표본 집계 결과 (The Result of the Sample Survey on the 2015's Population and Housing Census). December 19, 2016. https://kostat.go.kr/portal/korea/kor_nw/1/1/index.board?bmode=read&aSeq=358170.
Sū Sōsō 鄒双双. *Sanjū nendai no Pekin ni okeru Sen Tōson-zō no—Nihonjin ryūgakusei no me wo tōshite* 30年代の北京における銭稲孫像「日本人留学生の目を通して (The Image of Qian Daosun in Beijing in 1930s: Through the Eyes of Japanese Oversea Students). *Higashi Ajia bunka kōryū kenkyū* 5 (2012): 89–101.
Sugyŏng 수경. "Samsŏn kangwŏn ŭi paltalsa" 삼선 강원의 발달사 (The History of the Development of Samsŏn Buddhist College). In *Piguni sŭngga taehak ŭi yŏksa wa munhwa*, edited by Taehan Pulgyo Chogyejong Kyoyugwŏn, 205–83. Seoul: Chogyejong Ch'ulpansa, 2009.
Suh, Sharon A. *Being Buddhist in a Christian World. Gender and Community in a Korean American Temple*. Seattle: University of Washington Press, 2004.
Sunjong sillok 4 3/38/B (August 21, 1910). http://sillok.history.go.kr/id/wzb_10308021_001.
"Sŭt'ori t'elling inmul yŏlchŏn" 스토리 텔링 인물열전 (Storytelling Biographies). *Yŏngnam ilbo*, October 19, 2011. https://www.yeongnam.com/web/view.php?key=20111019.010070750470001.
Suzuki Hiromune 鈴木宏宗. Toshokan fugō (Toshokan chizu kigō) to (ku ni kamae ni to) 図書館符号（図書館の地図記号）と卜（くにかまえにト）(Library Symbols [Library Map Symbols] and to). *Bunkei keishō* 17 (2010): 1–7.
Suzuki, Daisetsu Teitarō. *Studies in the Lankavatara Sutra*. Oxfordshire, UK: Routledge & K. Paul, 1930.
T'ak Hyojŏng 탁효정. "Chosŏn sidae wangsil yŏin tŭrŭn sach'al ŭi 'taehwaju' yŏtta" 조선시대 왕실여인들은 사찰의 '대화주(大貨主)'였다 (Royal Women during the Chosŏn Dynasty Were the Great Financial Resources for Buddhist Temples). *Pulgyo p'yŏngnon* 28 (December 10, 2006). http://www.budreview.com/news/articleView.html?idxno=152.
T'oeong Sŏngch'ŏl 퇴옹성철. *Sŏnmun Chŏngno* 禪門正路 (The Orthodox Path of the Sŏn School). Seoul: P'yŏnghwa dang, 1981.
T'woeong Sŏngch'ŏl 退翁性徹. *Han'guk pulkyo ŭi pŏpmaek* 韓國佛教의 法脈 (The Dharma Lineage of Korean Buddhism). Kyŏngnam, Korea: Changkyŏnggak, 1976.
Taehan hŭnghakpo 大韓興學報 (1909–1910). Tokyo: Taehan hŭnghakhoe.
Taehan hyŏphoe hoebo 大韓協會會報 (1908–1909). Seoul: Taehan hyŏphoe.

Taehan Maeil sinbo 大韓每日申報 (1904–1910).
Taehan Pulgyo Chogyejong Chʻongmuwŏn 대한불교 조계종 총무원, ed. *Chogyejong-sa kŭnhyŏndaepʻyŏn* 조계종사 근현대편 (History of the Jogye Order: Contemporary Times). Seoul: Chogyejong Chʻulpʻansa, 2005.
Taehan Pulgyo Chogyejong Chʻongmuwŏn 대한불교 조계종 총무원, ed. *Ilche sidae pulgyo chŏngchʻaek kwa hyŏnhwang: Chosŏn chʻongdokbu kwanbo Pulgyo kwallyŏn charyojip* 일제 시대 불교 정책과 현황: 조선총독부 관보 불교 관련 자료집 (Buddhist Policy and Circumstance during the Japanese Colonial Period: Source Book of the Official Gazette of the Government General about Korean Buddhism). Seoul: Sŏnu Toryang Chʻulpʻanbu, 2001.
Taehan Pulgyo Chogyejong Kyoyugwŏn Purhak Yŏnʼguso, ed. 대한불교조계종 교육원 불학연구소. *Pongamsa kyŏlsa wa hyŏndae hanʼguk pulgyo* 봉암사 결사와 현대 한국불교 (The Community of Bongamsa and Contemporary Korean Buddhism). Seoul: Chogyejong Chʻulpʻansa, 2008.
Taehan Pulgyo Chogyejong Kyoyugwŏn, ed. *Chogyejong-sa: Kŭnhyŏndaepʻyŏn* 조계종사: 근현대편 (History of the Jogye Order. Contemporary Times). Seoul: Chogyejong Chʻulpʻansa, 2001.
Taehan Pulgyo Chogyejong Kyoyugwŏn Purhak Yŏnʼguso 대한불교조계종 교육원 불학연구소, ed. *Pongʼamsa kyŏlsa wa hyŏndae hanʼguk Pulgyo* 봉암사 결사와 현대한국불교 (The Pongam Monastery Compact Community and Contemporary Korean Buddhism). Seoul: Chogyejong Chʻulpʻansa, 2008.
Taehan Pulgyo Chogyejong 대한불교조계종. *Chonggyejongbŏp ŭi ihae* 조계종법의 이해 (Understanding the Jogye Order Laws). Seoul: Taehan Pulgyo Chogyejong, 2011.
Taehan Pulgyo Chogyejong 대한불교조계종. *Sŏnwŏn chʻongnam* 선원총람 (A Comprehensive Survey of Chan Halls). Seoul: Taehan Pulgyo Chogyejong, 2000.
Taehan Pulgyo Chogyejong 대한불교조계종. *Chonghŏn* 종헌 (Order Constitution). Seoul: Taehan Pulgyo Chogyejong, 1962.
Taehan Pulgyo Chogyejong 대한불교조계종. *Hogyewŏnbŏp* 호계원법 (The Precepts-Court Law). Seoul: Taehan Pulgyo Chogyejong, 2015.
Taehan Pulgyo Chogyejong 대한불교조계종. *Kyŏlgye mit pʻosal e kwanhan pŏp* 결제 및 포살에 관한 법 (Law Regarding Habitation and Uposatha Sites). Seoul: Taehan Pulgyo Chogyejong, 2010.
Taehan Pulgyo Chogyejong 대한불교조계종. *Sŏnwŏn chŏnggyu* 선원청규 (Pure Rules for the Chan Halls). Seoul: Taehan Pulgyo Chogyejong, 2010, 2013, 2015.
Taehan Pulgyo Chogyejong 대한불교조계종. *Sŭngnyŏpŏp* 승려법 (Law of the Monastics). Seoul: Taehan Pulgyo Chogyejong, 2015.
Taishō Shinshū Daizōkyō 大正新修大蔵経 (Tripitaka Compiled during the Taishō Period). Edited by Takakusu Junjirō et al. Tokyo: Taishō Issaikyō Kankōkai, 1924–1935.
Takahashi Tōru 高橋亨. *Richo Bukkyō* 李朝佛「 (Buddhism in the Chosŏn Dynasty). Tokyo: Tokyo Kokusho Kankōkai, 1973 (1929).

Takeda Hanshi 武田範之. *Kōchū iseki* 洪疇遺績 (Collection of Takeda's Writings) (microfilm). Vol. 10. Compiled by Kawakami Zenbē 川上善兵衛, 1928.

Tanaka Ryōshō 田中良昭. *Tonkō Zenshū siryō bunrui mokuroku shoko* 敦煌禅宗資料分類目錄初稿 (A Draft of the Classified Catalogue of the Zen Buddhist Texts from Tunhuang). *Komazawa daigaksu bukkyogaku kenkyū kiyo* 27–29 (1969–1971): 1–18.

Tang, Xiaobing. *Global Space and the Nationalist Discourse of Modernity: The Historical Thinking of Liang Qichao*. Stanford, CA: Stanford University Press, 1996.

Tarocco, Francesca. *The Cultural Practices of Modern Chinese Buddhism: Attuning the Dharma*. New York: Routledge, 2007.

Taussig, Michael. *Defacement: Public Secrecy and the Labor of the Negative*. Stanford, CA: Stanford University Press, 1999.

Tedesco, Frank M. "Social Engagement in South Korean Buddhism." In *Action Dharma: New Studies in Engaged Buddhism*, edited by Christopher Queen, Charles Prebish, and Damien Keown, 152–80. London: Routledge Curzon, 2003.

Teltscher, Kate. *The High Road to China: George Bogle, the Panchen Lama, and the First British Expedition to Tibet*. London: Bloomsbury, 2006.

Thich Nhat Hanh. "Dharma Talk: History of Engaged Buddhism." *The Mindful Bell* (Autumn 2003): 1–8.

Tikhonov, Vladimir, and Miller Owen, trans. *Selected Writings of Han Yong'un: From Social Darwinism to Socialism with a Buddhist Face*. Kent, UK: Global Oriental Ltd., 2008.

Tōa Kogo Gakkai. *Tokyojo* 東京城 (Tokyo Castle). Tokyo: Tōa Kogo Gakkai, 1939.

"Toman palsimnyŏn ŭi kyŏlchŏng!" 渡滿八十年의 結晶! (The Fruit of the Eighty Years of Korean Immigration to Manchuria). *Tonga ilbo*, December 3, 1937.

Tonga ilbo 東亞日報 (1920–present). Keijō: Tonga ilbosa. Chosŏn ilbosa.

Tongguk Taehakkyo Han'guk Pulgyo Chŏnsŏ P'yŏnch'an Wiwŏn 동국대학교 한국불교 전서 편찬 위원, ed. *Han'guk pulgyo chŏnsŏ* 韓國佛敎全書 (Collected Works of Korean Buddhism). 14 vols. Seoul: Tongguk Taehakkyo Ch'ulp'anbu, 1979–2004.

Tŏngmun 덕문. "Yulchang ŭi chinggye kalma wa hogyewŏnbŏp" 율장의 징계 갈마와 호계법 (The Penal Proceedings in the Vinaya and the Precepts-Court Law). *Taegak sasang* 19 (2013): 43–77.

Translation of the Rastrapalapariprccha-sutra. Honolulu: University of Hawai'i Press, 2008.

Tuladhar-Douglas, Will. *Remaking Buddhism for Medieval Nepal: The Fifteenth-Century Reformation of Newar Buddhism*. London: Routledge, 2006.

Turner, Alicia, Laurence Cox, and Brian Bocking. "A Buddhist Crossroads: Pioneer European Buddhists and Globalizing Asian Networks 1860–1960." *Contemporary Buddhism: An Interdisciplinary Journal* 14, no. 1 (2013): 1–16.

Tweed, Thomas A. "Theory and Method in the Study of Buddhism: Toward 'Translocative' Analysis." *Journal of Global Buddhism* 12 (2011): 17–32.

Tweed, Thomas A. *Crossing and Dwelling: A Theory of Religion*. Cambridge: Harvard University Press, 2006.

"Ujadong e paekgŭisu" 愚者動에 百鬼隨 (A Foolish Person Moves, Numerous Ghosts Follow). *Sidae ilbo*, May 21, 1925.

Unsan 운산. "Unmun sŭngga taehak ŭi chŏnťong kwa hyŏnjaesŏng" 운문승가 대학의 전통과 현재성 (The Traditional and Present Character of Unmunsa's Sangha University). In *Piguni sŭngga taehak ŭi yŏksa wa munhwa*, edited by Taehan Pulgyo Chogyejong Kyoyugwŏn, 11–52. Seoul: Chogyejong Ch'ulpansa, 2009.

Vásquez, Manuel A. *More Than Belief: A Materialist Theory of Religion*. New York: Oxford University Press, 2011.

Vermeersch, Sem. "Views on Buddhist Precepts and Morality in Late Koryŏ." *Journal of Korean Religions* 7, no. 1 (2016): 35–65.

Vermeersch, Sem. 2012. "Wŏnhyo the Unbridled." In *Wŏnhyo: Selected Works*, edited by A. Charles Muller, 285–93. Paju, Korea: Chun-il Munhwasa.

Walraven, Boudewijn. "A Re-examination of the Social Basis of Buddhism in Late Chosŏn Korea." *Seoul Journal of Korean Studies* 20, no. 1 (2007): 1–20.

Wang Shifu 王實甫. *Sŏn-Han Ssangmu*. *Sŏsang-gi* 西廂記 (鮮漢雙文) (The Story of the Western Wing) (with Korean and Chinese parallel texts), 1916. Accessed through National Library of Korea, January 18, 2016. http:// www.nl.go.kr/nl/search/search_wonmun.jsp?img=n&hanja=&sort=&desc=desc&topF1=title&kwd=%EC%84%9C %EC%83%81%EA%B8%B0&x=40&y=27#none.

Wang Shifu. *Hyŏnťo chuhae* 懸吐註解. *Sŏsang-gi* 西廂記 (The Story of the Western Wing) [with a Korean vernacular gloss], ca. 1920). Accessed through National Library of Korea, January 18, 2016. http://www.nl.go.kr/nl/search/search_wonmun.jsp?img=n&hanja=&sort=&desc=desc&topF1=title&kwd=%EC%84%9C%EC%83%81%EA%B8%B0&x=40&y=27#none.

Wang Sŏnyŏp 왕선엽. "Yŏngnamdae tosŏgwan tongbin mun'go sojang p'yohun sap'an Ch'imun kyŏnghun ŭi Sŏji mit Kugyŏl" 영남대 도서관 동빈문고 서장 표훈 사판 치문 경훈의 서지 및 구결 (A Study of the Bibliography and Kugyŏl of Ch'imun Kyŏnghun at Yŏngnam University Central Library). *Minjok munhwa nonch'ong* 48 (2011): 147–67.

Wang, Richard G. "The Cult of Qing: Romanticism in the Late Ming Period and in the Novel *Jiao Hong Ji*." *Ming Studies* 1 (1994): 12–55.

Watson, Burton, trans. *The Lotus Sūtra*. New York: Columbia University Press, 1993.

Watson, Burton, trans. *The Zen Teachings of Master Linji*. Boston: Shambhala, 1993.

Weber, Max. *Wirtschaft und Gesellschaft: Grundriss der verstehenden Soziologie (1921–1922)*. 5., Aufl., Studienausg., Tübingen: Mohr-Siebeck, 2009.

Werner, Janelle. "'Just as the Priests Have Their Wives': Priests and Their Concubines in England, 1375–1549." PhD diss., Chapel Hill, North Carolina, 2009.

Wŏnhyo 元曉. *Palsim suhaengjang* 發心修行章. *Han'guk Pulgyo Chŏnsŏ* 韓國佛教全書 (Collected Works of Korean Buddhism). Seoul: Tongguk Taehakkyo Ch'ulp'anbu, 1979.

Wŏnyŏng 원영. "Yulchang kwa Chogyejongbŏp ŭi ihae" 율장과 조계종법의 이해 (Understanding the Vinaya and the Jogye Order Laws). *Chŏngt'ohak yŏn'gu* 20 (2013): 227–67.

Woodbine, Onaje. *Black Gods of the Asphalt: Religion, Hip-Hop, and Street Basketball*. New York: Columbia University Press, 2018.

Woodside, Alexander. "Territorial Order and Collective-Identity Tensions in Confucian Asia: China, Vietnam, Korea." *Daedalus* 127, no. 3 (1998): 191–220.

Woodside, Alexander. *Lost Modernities: China, Vietnam, Korea, and the Hazards of World History*. Cambridge: Harvard University Press, 2006.

Wumen 無門. *Wumen guan* 無門關 (Gateless Gate). *Taishō shinshū daizōkyō* 大正新脩大藏經, 48 n2005, 292a–299c. Tokyo: Taishō issaikyō kankōkai, 1924–1932.

Yanagida Seizan 柳田聖山. *Shoki no zenshi I* 初期の禪史 I (The History of Early Zen I). Tōkyō: Chikuma Shobō, 1971.

Yanagida Seizan 柳田聖山. *Shoki no zenshi II* 初期の禪史 II (The History of Early Zen II). Tōkyō: Chikuma Shobō, 1976.

Yi Chigwan 이지관. *Han'guk kosŭng pimun chŏngjip: Chosŏnjo kŭndaegi* 한국 고승 비문 전집: 조선조 근대기 (The Collection of Stele Inscriptions of Eminent Korean Buddhist Monks: Chosŏn and the Modern Periods). Seoul: Kasan Pulgyo Munhwa Yŏn'guwŏn, 2010.

Yi Chigwan 이지관. *Han'guk pulgyo kyeyul chŏnt'ong* 한국불교 계율 전통 (Vinaya and Precepts Tradition of Korean Buddhism). Seoul: Kasan Pulgyo Munhwa Yŏn'guwŏn, 2005.

Yi Chigwan, ed. *Han'guk kosŭng pimun chŏngjip—Chosŏnjo kŭnhyŏndae* 한국고승비문전집-조선조근현대 (Collection of Stela Inscriptions of Notable Korean Monks and Nuns—The Chosŏn, Modern and Contemporary Periods). Seoul: Kasan Pulgyo Munhwa Yŏnguwŏn, 2000.

Yi Chigwan. "Yangsan Naewŏnsa piguni Hwansandang Suok hwasang Pimun" (Epitaph of *Bhiksuni* Hwansandang Suok *Hwasang* of Yangsan Naewŏnsa). In *Han'guk Kosŭng Pimun Ch'ongjip—Chosŏnjo Kŭnhyŏndae* (Collection of Stela Inscriptions of Notable Korean Monks and Nuns—The Chosŏn, Modern and Contemporary Periods), edited by Yi Chigwan, 1197–98. Seoul: Kasan Pulgyo Munhwa Yŏn'guwŏn, 2000.

Yi Hanme 이한메. "10/27 pŏmnan kwa kŭ chŏngsan kwajŏng e taehan hoego wa sŏngch'al" 10/27 범난과 그 청산 과정에 대한 회고 와 성찰 (Recollection and Examination of the 10.27 Buddhist Persecution and Its Settlement Process). *Journal of Social Thoughts and Culture* 27 (March 2013): 317–50.

"Yi Hoegwang Sŏnsa changsŏ" 李晦光禪師 長逝 (Zen Master Yi Hoegwang Passes Away). *Chung'ang ilbo*, February 7, 1932.

Yi Hoegwang 李晦光. *Mirŭk sangsaenggyŏng* 彌勒上生經 (Sutra on Maitreya's Previous and Future Lives). Kyŏngnam: Haeinsa, 1913.

Yi Hŭngu 이흥우. *Kyŏnghŏ Sŏnsa: Kongsŏng ŭi p'ian* 鏡虛禪師: 空性의 彼岸 (Sŏn Master Kyŏnghŏ: The Other Shore Called Emptiness). Seoul: Minjoksa, 1995.

Yi Kidae 이기대. "Hangŭl py'ŏnji ae nat'anan Sunwŏn Wanghu ŭi ilsang kwa kajok" 한글편지에 나타난 순원왕후의 일상과 가족 (Queen Sunwon's Daily Life and Family on Hangul Letters). *Han'guk kojŏn yŏsŏng manhakhoe* 18 (2009): 315–49.

Yi Kiun 이기운. "Chosŏn sidae wangsil ŭi piguniwŏn sŏlch'i wa sinhaeng" 조선시대 왕실의 比丘尼院 설치와 신행 (The Establishment of the Bhksuni Temple by the Chosŏn Royal Family and Buddhist Belief). *Yŏksa hakpo* 178 (2003): 29–58.

Yi Kiyŏng 李箕永. "Haeinsa kihaeng" 海印寺 紀行 (A Trip to Haein Monastery). *Samch'ŏlli* 12, no. 6 (June 1, 1940): 87. http://db.history.go.kr/id/ma_016_0760_0120.

Yi Nŭnghwa 李能和. *Chosŏn Pulgyo t'ongsa: kŭndae* 조선불교통사: 근대 (A Comprehensive History of Korean Buddhism: Modern). Translated by Yi Pyŏngdu. Seoul: Hyean, 1993.

Yi Nŭnghwa 李能和. *Chosŏn Pulgyo T'ongsa* 朝鮮佛敎通史 (Comprehensive History of Korean Buddhism). 3 vols. Seoul: Sinmungwan, 1918.

Yi Sanggyun 이상균. "Hyeam Chongjŏng yeha haengjang" 혜암 종정예하 行狀 (Life of the Eminent Supreme Patriarch Hyeam). *Pulgyo sinmun*, February 15, 2002. http://www.ibulgyo.com/news/articleView.html?idxno=900.

Yi Sangha 이상하. "*Kyŏnghŏ chip* p'yŏnch'an, kanhaeng ŭi kyŏngwi wa pyŏnmo yangsang." 경허집 편찬, 간행의 경위와 변모양상 (An Account of the Creation and Publication of Collected Works of Kyŏnghŏ and Changes over Time). *Tongyanghak* 50 (August 2011): 1–19.

Yi Sŏngtak 이성탁. "Kyŏnhŏ ŭi Sŏn sasang" 鏡虛의 禪思想 (Kyŏnghŏ's Sŏn). In *Han'guk pulgyo sasangsa: Sungsan Pak Kilchin paksa hwagap kiyŏm* 韓國佛敎思想史: 숭산 박길진박사 화갑기념 (A History of Korean Buddhist Thought: In Honor of Dr. Sungsan Pak Kilchin's 60th Birthday), edited by Sungsan Pak Kiljin Paksa Hwagap Kinyŏm Saŏp Ch'onghoe, 1103–20. Chŏnbuk, Korea: Wŏnbulgyo Sasang Yŏn'guwŏn, 1975.

Yi Taehwa 이대화. "Ch'angssi kaemyŏng chŏngch'aek kwa chosŏnin ŭi taeŭng" 창씨개명 정책과 조선인의 대응 (The Name-Changing Program and the Response of Koreans). *Sungsil sahak* 26 (2011): 179–223.

Yi Tŏkchin 이덕진. "Ilche ha inmul ŭi saeng ae wa sasang" 일제하 인물의 생애와 사상 (The Life and the Thought of Buddhist Figures during the Colonial Period). Unpublished paper presented at the conference "Han'guk kŭnhyŏndae pulgyosa yŏn'gu ŭi tonghyang kwa kwaje," Seoul, November 2, 2006, 43–72.

Yi Tŏkchin 이덕진. "Yongsŏng Chinjong ŭi Sŏn sasang e kwanhan ilgoch'al" 龍城震鐘의 선사상에 관한 일고찰 (A Study of Yongsŏng Chinjong's Sŏn Thought). *Hanguk Pulgyohak* 48 (2007): 481–513.

Yi Ŭnjŏng 이은정. "Ch'ima Pulgyo poda sangŏpchuŭi ka pip'andoeya" 치마불교보다 상업주의가 비판되야 (Commercialized Buddhism Should Be Criticized More Than Skirt Buddhism). *Hyŏndae Pulgyo*, December 7, 2011. https://cdn.hyunbulnews.com/news/articleView.html?idxno=270698.

Yi, Charang 이자랑. "Yulchang e kŭn'gŏhan Chogyejongdan chinggye chedo ŭi kaesŏn panghyang: Sŭngnyŏbŏp, Hogyewŏnbŏp ŭl chungsim ŭro" 율장에 근거한 조계종단 징계제도의 개선 방향: 승녀법, 호계원법을 중심으로 (Reforming the Penal System of the Jogye Order Based on the Vinaya: Focusing on the Law of the Monkhood and the Precepts-Court Law). *Pulgyo hakpo* 54 (2010): 223–53.

Yi, Charang. "Yulchang ŭi kŭnbon inyŏm e ipkakhan Chogyejong chŏnggyu chejŏng ŭi pangyang: chegyesimni lŭl chungsimŭro" 율장의 근본 이념에 입각한 조계종 청규 제정의 방양: 제계십리를 중심으로 (The Creation of Jogye Order Pure Rules Based on the Fundamental Principles of the Vinaya with Focus on the "Ten Benefits of Keeping the Precepts"). *Taegak sasang* 19 (2013): 9–42.

Yi, Charang. "Yulchang ŭl t'ongae pon sŭngdan kwa hyŏndae sahoe ŭi chohwa" 율장을 통해 본 승단과 현대 사회의 조화 (The Monastic Order Seen through the Vinaya and Its Agreement with Contemporary Society). Paper presented at the conference of "Kyeyul kwa hyŏndae sahoe" (The Vinaya and Modern Society) held at Naesŏsa Temple in Puan, Chŏlla Province, 2006.

Yi, Chongsu 이종수. "Pong'amsa kyŏlsa wa kŭ Pulgyosa chŏk ŭimi" 봉암사 결사와 그 불교사적 의미 (Pong'amsa Association and Its Historical Significances). *Sŏnhak* 48 (2007): 95–122.

Yifa. *The Origins of Buddhist Monastic Codes in China*. Honolulu: University of Hawai'i Press, 2002.

Yŏ Suryŏng 여수령. "Hobŏp pun'gwaŭi t'ŭkpyŏl samyŏn taesangja 52myŏng kŏmt'o" 호법분과의 특별사면 대상자 52명 검토 (The Precepts Department Examines Special Amnesties for 52 Monastics). *Pulgyo p'ok'ŏsŭ*. March 13, 2009. http://www.bulgyofocus.net/news/articleView.html?idxno=56619.

Yŏ T'aedong 여태동. "Chosŏn sanggung tŭri Pulgyo chik'yŏ watta" 조선 상궁들이 불교 지켜왔다 (The Court Ladies of Choson Had Preserved Buddhism). *Pulgyo sinmun*, December 19, 2003. http://www.ibulgyo.com/news/articleView.html?idxno=56860.

Yŏ Yŏn 여연. "Kayasan ŭi taetchok: Hyeam Sŏnggwan ŭi saengae wa sasang" 가야산의 대쪽: 혜암성관 대종사의 생애와 사상 (A Piece of Bamboo on Mountain Kaya: The Life and Thoughts of Great Master Hyeam Songgwan). In *Haksul taehoe* 학술대회 (*Conference Proceedings*), edited by Hyeam Sŏnsa munhwa chinhŭnghoe, 22–50. 2014.

Yogyŏng. "Piguni kyoyuk toryang Pongnyŏngsa sŭngga taehak e taehan koch'al" 비구니 교육도량 봉녕사 승과대학에 대한 고찰 (Inquiry into the Nun Education at Pongnyŏngsa's Sangha University). In *Piguni sŭngga taehak ŭi yŏksa wa munhwa*, edited by Taehan Pulgyo Chogyejong Kyoyugwŏn, 83–136. Seoul: Chogyejong Ch'ulpansa, 2009.

Yŏm Chungsŏp 염중섭. "Han'guk Pulgyo kyeyulgwan ŭi kŭnbon munje koch'al: Chungguk munhwa kwŏn ŭi t'ŭksusŏng ŭl chungsim ŭro" 한국불교 계율관의 근본문제 고찰: 중국문화권의 특수성을 중심으로 (An Examination of the Fundamental Problem for Vinaya Tradition of Korean Buddhism). *Chonggyo yŏn'gu* 72 (2013): 55–88.

Yomiuri shinbun 読売新聞 (1913–present). Tokyo: Yomiuri shinbunsha.

Yŏngnam ilbo 嶺南日報 (1945–present).

Yoon, Yee-Heum. "The Contemporary Religious Situation in Korea." In *Religion and Society in Contemporary Korea*, edited by Lewis R. Lancaster and Richard K. Payne, 1–18. Korea Research Monograph. Berkeley: Institute of East Asian Studies, University of California, 1997.

"Yu chuji pandae undong" 兪住持反對運動 (Movement Against Head Monk Yu). *Tonga ilbo*, December 21, 1926.

Yu Kyŏnghŭi 유경희. "Kojongdae Sunhŏnhwanggŭibi Ŏmssi parwŏn pulhwa" 高宗代 純獻皇貴妃 嚴氏 發願 불화 (Buddhist Paintings Sponsored by Empress Ŏm during the Reign of King Gojong). *Misul charyo* 86 (2014): 111–36.

Yun Ch'ŏnggwang 윤청광. *Kyŏnghŏ Kŭn Sŭnim: ch'akhan il mani hage, kŭdae ka puch'ŏ ilse* 경허 큰스님: 착한 일 많이 하게, 그대가 부처일세 (Great Master Kyŏnghŏ: Do Many Good Deeds, You Are the Buddha). Seoul: Uri Ch'ulp'ansa, 2002.

Yu Hosŏn 유호선. "Han'guk pulgyo-ŭi sinhaeng kaenyŏm e kwanhan yŏn'gu" 한국불교의 신행 개념에 대한 연구 (Study on the Meaning of 'Sin-Haeng' in Korean Buddhism). *Hanguk Pulgyohak* 50 (2008): 689–713.

Yun Kŭmsŏn 윤금선. *Yuwŏl hangjaeng kwa Pulgyo* 유월항쟁과 불교 (The June Resistance and Buddhism). Kyŏnggi, Korea: Korea Democracy Foundation, 2018.

"Yunghŭi Hwangche rŭl mosi nŭn saramdŭl 1" 隆熙皇帝를 모시는 사람들 (1) (Those Serving Emperor Yunghŭi]). *Maeil sinbo* (May 8, 1926).

Contributors

Eun-su Cho is a professor of Buddhist Philosophy in the Department of Philosophy at Seoul National University in Korea. She earned her PhD in Buddhist Studies at the University of California, Berkeley. Cho has published on a wide range of topics, from Indian Abhidharma Buddhism to Korean Buddhist thought. Her published works include *Language and Meaning: Buddhist Interpretations of "The Buddha's Word" in Indian and East Asian Perspectives*; "Repentance as a Bodhisattva Practice—Wŏnhyo on Guilt and Moral Responsibility"; and an edited volume, *Korean Buddhist Nuns and Laywomen*.

Gregory N. Evon is a senior lecturer in the School of Humanities and Languages at UNSW Sydney. He publishes widely on the literary and intellectual history of premodern and modern Korea, and he is currently researching the role that Buddhism played in the writings of Kim Manjung (1637–1692).

Florence Galmiche is an associate professor (maîtresse de conférences) at Paris 7 University (now Université de Paris). She received her PhD in sociology from the EHESS in 2011. Her research is centered on religious phenomena in Korean society, studied through ethnographic fieldwork. She is focusing on the contemporary transformations of Buddhism, the relations between lay and monastic practices, and the social and cultural aspects of the relations with invisible beings (ancestors, gods, and spirits).

Uri Kaplan is a lecturer at the University of Haifa. He is author of *Buddhist Apologetics in East Asia* (Brill, 2019) and *Monastic Education in Korea* (University of Hawai'i Press, 2020). For a complete list of his publications, see https://telaviv.academia.edu/UriKaplan.

Cheonhak Kim is a professor in the Humanities Korea Project, Academy of Buddhist Studies; and professor in the Department of Interdisciplinary Studies of Korean Buddhism at Dongguk University. He studied Korea Huayan Buddhism at the Academy of Korean Studies and Huayan Buddhism at Tokyo University. He is currently working on Fazang's *Dasheng qixinlun yiji* 大乘起信論義記 (Commentary on the *Awakening of Faith*). His monographs include Hwaŏmgyŏng mundab e Pŏpchang ŭi yŏnghyang ŭn poinŭn'ga? 華嚴經問答에 法藏의 영향은 보이는가? (Did Fazang Influence *Questions and Answers on the Avataṃsaka Sūtra*?) (2019); *Haidong huayan sixiang de diyu tezheng* 海东华严思想的地域特征 (The Local Characteristics of Korean Huayan Thought) (2016); and "The Cult of the Hwaŏm Pure Land of the Koryŏ Period as Seen Through Self-Power and Other-Power" (2015).

Hwansoo Kim is an associate professor of Korean Buddhism in the Department of Religious Studies at Yale University. His research concerns colonial, modern, and contemporary Korean Buddhism from a transnational perspective. He is the author of *Empire of the Dharma: Korean and Japanese Buddhism, 1877–1912* (Harvard University Asia Center, 2013) and *The Korean Buddhist Empire: A Transnational History, 1910–1945* (Harvard University Asia Center, 2018). Currently he is working on a book project about clerical marriage issues in Buddhism.

Su Jung Kim is an associate professor of religious studies at DePauw University. Her broad, interdisciplinary research covers both Japanese and Korean Buddhism. After her first monograph, *Shinra Myojin and Buddhist Networks of the East Asian "Mediterranean"* (University of Hawai'i Press, 2019), she is working on her second book, titled *Korean Magical Medicine: Healing Talismans in Korean Buddhism*, which explores sociocultural, religious, and medicinal roles talismans played in the life of ordinary people in premodern Korea.

Mark A. Nathan is an associate professor in the Department of History and the director of the Asian Studies Program at the University at Buffalo, State University of New York. He is the author of *From the Mountains to the Cities: A History of Buddhist Propagation in Modern Korea* (University of Hawai'i Press, 2018) and coeditor of *Buddhism and Law: An Introduction* (Cambridge University Press, 2014).

Contributors | 315

Jeongeun Park is a lecturer at St. Thomas More College in Canada. She completed a PhD in clerical marriage and Buddhist modernity in colonial Korea at the University of British Columbia in 2016. She worked as a limited-term assistant professor at the University of Prince Edward Island. Her recent research focuses on women and monastic families in modern Korean Buddhism, based on an in-depth analysis of household registers of nuns and monks' wives and the documents produced by the colonial government

Jin Y. Park is a professor and department chair of philosophy and religion at American University in Washington, DC. Park specializes in Korean Buddhism, Buddhist ethics, East-West cross-cultural philosophy, and modern East Asian philosophy on the topics of gender, violence, and politics. Her books include *Women and Buddhist Philosophy* (2017); *Reflections of a Zen Buddhist Nun* (2014); *Makers of Modern Korean Buddhism* (2010); *Merleau-Ponty and Buddhism* (coedited, 2009); *Buddhism and Postmodernity* (2008), *Buddhisms and Deconstructions* (2006).

Index

Page references with a *t* denote a table.
Temple and *monastery* are used interchangeably in the text;
they were indexed as they appeared in the text.

abbots, 10; branch temple abbots, 133–134, 146, 148; and Jogye Order, 188, 189t, 192, 193; and secret marriage, 182; and temple laws, 48, 54, 142–143, 149
academic scholarship. *See* scholarship
admonitions collections, 123–124, 184, 185–186, 195
Admonitions for Beginners (Ch'obalsim chagyŏngmun) (Wŏnhyo, Chinul, Yaun), 185
"Admonitions for Beginning Students" *(Kyech'o simhak inmun)* (Chinul), 123, 150n13
Admonitions to the Gray-Robed Monks (Zimen jingxun) (Rujin), 124, 150n13, 185–186
Affairs of the Internal Court (K. *naemyŏngbu*), 77
Alfred, Taiaiake, 216–217
An Hyangdŏk (head monk) (1869–?), 143, 144t, 147, 148
An Hyangrang (lay Buddhist), 131
anti-abortion movements, and Pure Rules, 199

anti-capital punishment movements, and Pure Rules, 199
anticolonialism, 171–172
anticommunism, 171–172
anti-Japanese Buddhist movement, 171–172
appropriation, 3, 62, 122, 148, 149–150
aquatic metaphors to analyze religion, 63–64
asceticism, 6, 252, 266, 267–268
Auerback, Micah, 163, 180n75
autonomy, 24–25, 37
Avalokiteśvara (Bodhisattva), 90
Avataṃsaka Sūtra (Paek), 227
awakening, 25–26, 131; dailiness of, 30–31, 32, 34; and doubt, 27; suddenness, 28–29; and women, 91–92
"Awaken Your Mind and Practice" *(Palsim suhaeng chang)* (Wŏnhyo), 123, 150n13

Baizhang (720–814): Pure Rules, 182, 184–185, 187t, 203n17

Batchelor, Martine (former Korean nun), 7, 118n29
Best, Jonathan, 204n24
bhikṣu, 10, 11, 54, 67; and head-monk elections, 140–141, 142–143, 145, 146–147; and marital status, 121–122, 138, 139t, 140, 140t, 143–149; ordination, 121, 125, 131–132, 149; ordination lineage, 125–126; precepts, 67, 121–122, 126–128, 131, 132, 133–134; purification movement, 113–114
bhikṣuṇī: ordination, 109; precepts, 103, 134
Bianchi, Ester, 205n44
Bibliography of Korean Society, 238–239
Biographies of Korean Masters (Tongsa yŏlchŏn) (Pŏmhae), 125, 126–127, 131, 136, 149
Blackburn, Anne, 7, 50, 59–60, 62–63, 123
Black Gods of the Asphalt (Woodbine), 45n57
Bocking, Brian, 217
bodhisattva: Avalokiteśvara, 90; ordination, 125, 132, 149; precepts, 124, 126–127, 128, 131, 132, 133–134, 184–185
boundaries: and Buddhist propagation, 62, 66
Brahmā Net Sūtra, 123, 125, 131, 151n28, 186, 187t; missing from traditional monastic curriculum, 185
British colonial rule, 59–60, 63, 220
Buddha, 28, 29, 35–36, 85–86, 90, 105, 179n70, 193, 207n61
Buddhahood, attainment of, 24, 131–132
Buddhism: and colonialism (See colonialism); contemporary (See modernization); differences between Korean and Japanese, 105–106; and globalization (See globalization); and intersectionality (See intersectionality); and modernization (See modernization); and prayers (See prayers); and propagation (See propagation of Buddhist teachings); and women (See women)
Buddhism (Pulgyo) (Buddhist journal), 104
Buddhism for the Masses movement. See Minjung Buddhist movement
Buddhist: layman or laywoman (See laypeople); monastics (See monastics); monks (See monks); nuns (See nuns). See also men; women
Buddhist Persecution, October 27 (K. Sibich'il pŏmnan), 33, 37–38, 43n30
Buddhist reform movements, 5; educational programs, 257–258, 259, 260, 261; p'ogyo (Yongsŏng), 48–49, 57, 61–62, 67
Buddhist sangha, 11, 12; reform of, 35–36; reputation, 166–167, 182–183, 188, 201–202. See also *Pure Rules for the Sangha*
Buddhist scandals, 157–158, 178n54, 181, 182
Buddhist scholarship. See scholarship
Buddhist Times (monthly periodical), 104, 109
Buswell, Robert, 122

canon (Buddhist), 123, 185, 186, 194, 242; Taishō, 244, 245
Canon Hall (K. *Changgyŏng-gak*) at Haein Monastery, 82
"Can we ask questions, venerable monk?" (*PD Notebook* episode), 158
Caplan, Jane, 223

Catholicism, 15, 262, 274n33
celibacy. See *bhikṣu*
cell phones, and Pure Rules, 199
centralization of Korean Buddhism, 4
Central Preaching Hall, 94
Central Propagation Hall *(Chungang p'ogyoso)*, 88
Central Propagation Temple (Imje Order), 53
Chae Pyŏgam (1924–2005), 167
Chahaeng (monk) (1781–1862), 128, 129t
Chajang (Silla monk) (590–658), 175n22, 204n24, 205n44
Chan. See Sŏn
Ch'angdŏk Palace, 77, 89
change (adaptation): and Buddhist propagation, 62
Chang Il (lay partner of Yi Hoegwang), 88
changjwa purwa (staying-sitting-in-meditation-without-lying-down), 21, 23
Chang Pomyŏng (preceptor), 135t, 141, 144t
Chasŭng (executive administrative director, Jogye Order), 157
Chasuwŏn (palace nunnery), 76
Chihŏ (monk, preceptor), 129t
Ch'ilbul Hermitage, 125
child of a secret relationship *(ŭnch'ŏja)*, 160
Ch'immyŏng (monk, preceptor) (1801–1876), 129t
Ch'imsan. See Yi Tonghwan
Ch'imsong (monk, preceptor), 129t
China: identity, 222–223, 224
Chinese Buddhism: Neo-Confucianism, 215; Pure Rules, 195–196
Chinhak (teacher), 129t
Chinul, Pojo (Koryŏ monk) (1158–1210), 25, 31, 38–39, 123, 168, 185

Cho, Eun-su, 7, 8–9, 95
Ch'oe Namsŏn (historian) (1890–1957), 171
Ch'oe Songsŏltang (court lady) (1855–1939), 85, 95
Chogye Order. See Jogye Order
Choi, Hyaeweol, 74
Ch'oi Pyŏnghŏn (scholar), 180n74
Cho Kiryong (Buddhist scholar), 34, 35–36
Chŏkkwang (novice), 182
Chŏlsŏn (monk, preceptor), 129t
Chŏndŭng Monastery, 155n84
Chŏngbong (monk) (1855–?), 129t
Chŏng Ch'anju (journalist/novelist), 22, 32
Chŏngdam (1902–1971), 22
Chŏnge (teacher), 129t
Chongjŏng (Supreme Patriarch), 22
Ch'ongo (teacher), 130t
Chŏng Suok. See Suok Sŭnim (nun) (1902–1966)
Chŏn Ilch'ŏng (1848–1934?): and Yi Hoegwang, 75, 80–81, 84–85, 87–89, 93–94
Chŏn Ilch'ŏng (1848–1934?) (court lady), 8, 73–74; on Buddhism, 89–92; death of, 92–93; diplomatic visit to Japan, 79–80, 97n32, 97n33; influence on royal family, 77–78; philanthropy, 85–86; and Takeda Hanshi, 83–84, 98n49
Chŏnt'ae Order: and clerical marriage, 161
Chŏpcham (teacher), 130t
Cho Podam (preceptor), 139t
Cho Rangŭng (preceptor), 135t
Chosŏn dynasty (1392–1910), 8, 9; and Buddhism, 76, 81, 91, 106, 108, 109, 125, 162–163; and court ladies, 73, 77; and Korean Buddhist literature, 224–226; and

Chosŏn dynasty *(continued)*
Neo-Confucianism, 2–3, 75–76, 81, 90, 215–216, 223–224; and ordination requirements, 131–132
Ch'oŭi (monk, preceptor) (1786–1866), 126, 127, 128, 129t, 130t, 131, 149, 151n19
Christianity, 3, 26, 37, 50, 53, 159, 220–221, 255, 256, 272n19; Catholicism, 15, 262, 274n33; Protestantism, 15, 49, 62, 256, 260–262, 274n33
Ch'unp'a (preceptor), 129t
Ch'wiun (monk) (1866–?), 128, 151n27
civilization and enlightenment movement (K. *munmyŏng kaehwa*), 91
Clarke, Shane, 161
clerical marriage, 9–12, 48; purification movement, 113–114, 165, 268; recognition of, 160–161; rise of, 121–122, 132, 148, 153n68, 164; temple laws, 124, 136–137, 145–146
"clerical marriage and meat eating" (K. *taechŏ sigyuk*), 132, 136, 137
colonialism, 2–3; and clerical marriage, 9–10, 11, 121–122, 145–146, 148, 164; impact on Buddhism, 59–60, 62, 66; and modernity, 213–214, 219–220; responses to, 63, 229; and writings of Buddhist figures, 224–228. *See also* Japan colonial rule
community. *See* Buddhist sangha
Community Regulation (K. *kongju kyuyak*) (compact community rules), 267
compassion (Buddhism), 202, 229
Complete School. *See* Wŏnjong

Complete School, The (Wŏnjong) (journal of Korean Buddhism), 99n72
Comprehensive History of Korean Buddhism *(Chosŏn Pulgyo T'ongsa)* (Yi), 43n37, 178n64
Conference on World Buddhism (1987), 122–123, 194
Confucianism, 74, 90, 217, 218, 220, 222, 223. *See also* Neo-Confucianism
contemporary Buddhism. *See* modernization
Corntassel, Jeff, 216–217
Courant, Maurice, 255
court Buddhism (K. *kungjung pulgyo*), 75–76
court ladies, 73, 74, 76, 89; diplomatic visit to Japan, 79, 97n32; influence of, 78, 94–95; ranks of, 77
Court Lady Buddhism (K. *sanggung Pulgyo*), 76, 95
Cox, Laurence, 217
"cult of feeling *[quing]*" (Ming), 226
cultural identity, 222–223
curriculum: monastic, 185–186, 187t, 204n28

Daehang (nun, Sŏn master) (1927–2012), 7
Daoxuan (Chinese monk) (596–667), 126
Darker Side of Western Modernity (Mignolo), 212–214
decolonization, 160
decrease in religiosity of Buddhist followers, 158–159, 174n4, 256
democratization, 24, 37, 38, 43n30, 168, 188, 193
Derrida, Jacques (French philosopher) (1930–2004), 24, 28

Index | 321

dharma age, 142
Dharmaguptaka prātimokṣa, 188. See also *prātimokṣa* rules
Dharmaguptaka Vinaya (K. Sabunyul), 162, 175n22, 184, 185, 186, 187t; compared to Jogye Order penal system, 188, 189t-191t
dharma lineage, 38-39, 44n53, 54, 68n12, 125-126, 133, 151n19; nuns', 115-116
doubt, and *hwadu* meditation, 26-28
Dreyfus, Georges, 203n19
driving, and Pure Rules, 198-199

East Asia: and Buddhism, 162, 182; and "indigenousness," 216; and Kim Kugyŏng, 13, 238, 243; and modernity, 213
"eating meat and having a wife" law (J. *nikujiki saitai*), 137
ecumenical approach to Buddhism, 58, 106
educational programs (Buddhist institutions), 257-258, 259, 260-261, 263-265
Eight Chief Rules (K. *p'algyŏnggye*) (in the Vinaya), 109
Eihei Dōgen (Japanese Zen master) (1200-1253), 30-31
Elders Council, 34-35
enlightenment. See awakening
environmentalism, 33
epoché (suspension), 28
Evon, Gregory, 12-13
existentialism, 25-26, 40-41, 45n57

Fate (K. *Pangmyŏng*) (Han), 13
Fayuan Monastery, 126
female Buddhism (K. *posal Pulgyo*), 95
Fengtian: National Library, 236; *stūpas*, 240-241

Fogel, Joshua A, 215-216
founding patriarch, 38-39, 105
four grave offences (*pārājika*), 168-169, 178n60
Four-Part Vinaya (Dharmaguptaka Vinaya), 123, 146, 151n28
freedom, concept of, 24-25
Fukuzawa Yukichi (1835-1901), 13, 213-214, 215, 216; on Western democracies, 220-221, 223

Galmiche, Florence, 14
Gateless Gate (Wumen guan), 30
Ginger Garden Collection, 238, 239-240, 243-245
globalization, 217-218, 227-228
Godō Zuigan (Rinzaishū missionary) (1879-1965), 87
Gondō Shirōsuke (palace advisor), 79
Gooseart, Vincent, 5
gradualism, 28-29
Great Awakening Religion *(Taegakkyo)*, 49, 55, 58
Great Code for Managing the State (Kyŏngguk taejŏn), 77
Guillemoz, Alexandre, 256

Haein Monastery, 52, 81-82, 85, 88, 102, 125-126
Haemyŏng (monk), 131
hagiography, 39, 41
Hall, David, 45n57
Hammyŏng (monk) (1824-1902), 129t
Hanam (disciple of Kyŏnghŏ), 39-40
Han'am (1876-1951), 22
Hanpai (Chinese preceptor), 126
Han Pogwang (scholar), 52, 56, 68n8
Han Yongun (Manhae) (1879-1944), 5, 12-13, 49, 53-54, 57, 58, 87, 95, 176n37; on clerical marriage, 163-164, 176n35; and Fukuzawa,

Han Yongun (Manhae) *(continued)* 215–217; *Miserable Fate, A,* 212, 228–229; propagation of Buddhist teachings, 219–220, 226; on renunciation (monastic withdrawal), 254; scholarship, 211–212, 227; *Silence of Love,* 225; *Story of the Western Wing, The,* 218–219
Haŭi (monk) (1779–1852), 128, 129t
Haŭi (teacher), 129t
head-branch temple laws, 121, 132. *See also* temple laws (K. *Sabŏp*)
head-monk elections, 140–141, 142–143, 145, 146–147
Heine, Steven (scholar of Japanese Zen Buddhism), 30–31
Hervieu-Léger, Danièle, 262
Hīnayāna Buddhist practice: precepts, 131
Hodong Hakkyo (private school), 85
Hoeam (monk) (1808–1887), 129t
Hogi (teacher), 129t
Holcombe, Charles, 223
Hong (descendant of Three Scholars), 236
Hong Sunmin, 77
Honhŏ (monk) (1826–?), 129t
Honsŏng (monk), 131
Hoŭi (monk) (1778–1868), 129t, 130t
householder (K. *chaega*), 263
Howŏl (monk) (?–?), 129t
Huh, Woosung (scholar), 57, 227
Hŭimun (teacher), 130t
Hŭngguk Monastery, 136
hwadu meditation, 22–23, 32, 45n57; and doubt, 25–26; Hyeam's life as a *hwadu*, 40–41; and suddenness (K. *ton*), 28–29
Hwang Chin'gyŏng (chief of the Jogye Order) (1936–), 166–167

Hwaŏm Monastery, 125–126
Hwasŏn (monk) (1827–?), 129t
Hwaun (monk, preceptor) (?–1864), 129t
Hwawŏl (monk) (1820–1886), 129t
Hyeam Sŏnggwan (Sŏn Master) (1920–2001), 6; on doubt, 25–26; Jogye Order crises (1994, 1998), 34–35; legacy, 40–41; on practice, 31–32; rigorous practice, 22–23; sangha reform, 35–36; Sŏn thought, 23–24; on suddenness (K. *ton*), 28–29
Hyebong (1874–1956), 111, 117n20
Hyebong (monk) (1816–1881), 129t
Hyegŏ (monk), 257–258
Hyein Monastery, 22
Hyŏngjong, King, 76

ilchongsik (one-meal-per-day), 21
Im (court lady), 80, 82
Imjejong. *See* Imje Order
Imje Order *(Imjejong chung'ang p'ogyodang)*, 53, 68n12, 68n13, 85, 87
imperialism, 2, 3, 213, 214
Inaba Iwakichi (historian) (1876–1940), 237
Indian Buddhism, 188; "ten benefits of keeping the precepts," 183, 203n13; *uposatha* ritual (K. *p'osal*), 193; Vinaya, 128, 161, 182, 185, 186, 187t, 189t, 192
Insuwŏn (palace nunnery), 76
intersectionality, 15–16, 50, 59–60
Iryŏp. *See* Kim Wŏnju
Itō Hirobumi (Japanese resident-general), 78, 79, 83

Jaffe, Richard, 5, 203n19, 217

Japan: cultural identity, 222–223, 224; modern household register system, 138; opening up of Korea, 5, 10, 222
Japan colonial rule, 2–4, 9, 10, 47–50, 60, 105; censorship, 212; clerical marriage, 121–122, 145–146, 148, 153n68, 163, 171–172; and court ladies, 77–78; name-change policy, 237; and temple laws, 132–134, 137, 142–143
Japanese Buddhism, 3; and clerical marriage, 9, 11, 137, 161, 163, 215; and nuns, 107; and Paek Yongsŏng, 48, 49–50, 52–55, 58, 62; and Suok Sŭnim, 8, 103–107, 110–111
Jogye Order, 4, 6, 173n1, 184, 187t; and celibacy, 161, 172; crises (1994, 1998), 33–35, 38; founding patriarch, 38–39, 177n45; and Hyeam Sŏnggwan, 22; laity education programs, 14; *Law of the Monastics* (penal system), 168–169, 178n59, 185, 186, 188, 189t–191t; and nuns, 113, 114, 173; Pongam Monastery Compact Community, 266–267, 268; Precepts-Court (K. *Hogyewŏn*), 192–193, 202; *Pure Rules for the Sangha*, 196, 196t, 197–200; purification movement, 165, 177n46; recruitment campaign, 159; reformation of the order, 36–37, 193–194; scandals, 157–158, 178n54, 181, 182; and secret wives, 165–169; supreme patriarch, 22, 35, 37, 167, 188; and T'aego Order, 167, 177n47; *uposatha* ritual (K. *p'osal*), 193; and Vinaya rules, 11–12, 162

Jogye Temple, 4, 94, 181
Journal of Korean Buddhism (*Chosŏn Pulgyo Ch'ŏngbo*), 85
Jung Ji-Young, 90

Kabo Reforms, 5, 78
Kagan. *See* Pŏmhae (monk, preceptor) (1820–1896)
Kakhwang Temple, 84, 85–86, 87, 92, 93–94
Kamio Kazuharu (1893–?), 241–242
Kanhwa Sŏn, 25, 40, 195. *See also hwadu* meditation
Kant, Immanuel (philosopher) (1724–1804), 25
Kaplan, Uri, 11–12, 123, 269
Kendall, Laurel, 256
Kibong (monk, preceptor) (?–?), 130t
Kim, Hwansoo, 8, 58–59, 163, 255
Kim, Sujung, 11
Kim Cheonhak, 13–14
Kim Chŏnghae (1887–?), 148
Kim Chŏngsŏp (head monk), 155n84
Kim Ch'ungyŏn (court lady) (1848–1936), 89, 96n5, 99n70
Kim Hobok (preceptor), 135t
Kim Hwanŭng (preceptor), 135t
Kim Kugyŏng (1899–1950?), 13–14, 223, 246–247, 247n3, 248n14; Beijing, 235; collation method, 244–245; disappearance of, 239; *Ginger Garden Collection*, 238, 239–240, 243; Kamio edition of *Nanming's Ode to the Song...*, 242–243; name change, 14, 237; scholarly works by, 237–238, 239–241, 247n1; study in Japan, 234; Three Scholars, 236
Kim Kuha (first head monk of T'ongdo Monastery) (1872–1965), 126, 137–138, 139t, 140

Kim Sunsŏk, 122
Kim Suok (1902–1966) (Buddhist nun), 74
Kim T'aehŭp, 104
Kim T'aejun (Korean scholar) (1905–1949), 238
Kim Wŏnju (Buddhist nun, Sŏn master) (1896–1971), 6, 7, 8, 25, 26, 40–41, 74
Ko (court lady), 85
Ko Chaesŏk, 225
Kogyŏng (nun), 102
Kojong, King (r. 1897–1907), 73, 78, 79, 82
Kŏnbong Temple, 81
Korea: Buddhist literature, 224–227; and Christianity, 3, 15, 26, 37, 49–50, 53, 62, 220–221, 255, 256; cultural identity, 222–223, 224; invasion by Manchuria (1636), 236; opening of by Japan, 5, 222
Korean Buddhism Monthly (Chosŏn Pulgyo wŏlbo), 57, 69n24, 89
Korean Declaration of Independence, 47, 49
Koryŏ Canon, 82
Koryŏ dynasty (918–1392), 52, 75, 77, 108, 162, 241
Ko Taesu (member of reform party, court lady), 77–78, 94
Ko Yŏngsŏp, 122
Kŭmdam (master monk) (1765–1848), 125, 126, 151n18, 151n19
Kŭmhŏ (monk) (1824–?), 128, 129t
Kŭmp'a (monk) (1833–?), 128, 129t
Kŭmsŏng (monk) (1825–1893), 129t
Kŭmwŏl (monk) (1811–1888), 129t
Kwangju Democratization Movement, 43n30
Kwangsik, Kim (scholar), 56–57, 58, 84
Kwangu (nun) (1925–2019), 111–112, 117n20
Kwansim Non ("Treatise on Contemplating Mind"), 244, 245
Kwanŭmjŏn (residential hall at Haein Monastery), 82
Kwanŭm Seminary, 111–112
Kwiju Monastery, 134, 141
Kwŏnmin (teacher), 129t
Kwŏn Sangno, 69n24
Kyeyul (precepts and Vinayas), 131
Kyŏngbok Palace, 77, 78
Kyŏnggwan (teacher), 129t
Kyŏnghŏ Sŏngu (Sŏn master) (1849–1912), 6, 11, 23, 39–40, 170
Kyŏngwŏl (monk) (1775–1857), 129t
Kyŏnhyang (teacher), 129t
Kyŏnsŏng Hermitage, 102, 103, 112
Kyunghyang Newspaper (Kyŏnghyang), 166

laity. *See* laypeople
Law of the Monastics. See Jogye Order
laymen. *See* men
laypeople: accessible Buddhist teachings, 14, 53, 55, 255–256, 258, 260–261, 263–265; bodhisattva precepts, 131; expectations of monastics, 198, 263–264; ordination of, 134; and urban temples, 252, 262–263. *See also* men; women
laywomen. *See* women
Liang Qichao (Chinese modernizer) (1873–1929), 215
Liao dynasty, 240, 241
life, as a dream, 24
Li Hongzhang (1823–1901), 213–214
lineage. *See* dharma lineage
"List of Married Monks Among T'ongdo Monastery Monks" (Akira), 140
lived experiences: of women, 41

Index | 325

Lived Religion in America: Toward a History of Practice (Hall), 45n57
Locations of Buddhism (Blackburn), 59–60
locative pluralism, 7, 59
love (K. *yŏnae*), as a concept, 225–226
Lu Xiangshan (1139–1192), 215–216
Lu Xun (Chinese writer) (1881–1936), 235–236

macrohistorical studies of Korean Buddhist tradition, 60–61, 65
Maeil sinbo (national daily newspaper): article about Chŏn, 86
Magok Monastery, 122, 141–148
Mahāyāna Buddhist practice, 105, 106, 169; and nonduality, 170–171; precepts, 131, 187t
Makers of Modern Korean Buddhism (Park), 1, 7
Manchuria, 55, 222–223; invasion of Korea (1636), 236
Mangwŏl Temple, 80, 81, 82, 86
Manha (monk). *See* Pak Manha
Manhae. *See* Han Yongun
Manhyu (preceptor), 130t
March First Independence movement, 47, 48, 49, 54, 87
marginalization, 41
marriage. *See* clerical marriage
"married *bhikṣu*" (K. *taechŏsŭng*), 10, 138, 139t, 140t, 149; head-monk elections, 140–141, 142–143, 145
Mass Saving Buddhist Clinic *(Pulgyo chejungwŏn)*, 88
McBride, Richard, 204n24
meat eating, 9, 48, 54, 122, 124, 136–137, 185
meditation: *hwadu*, 22, 25–26, 28–29
mega churches, 262
mega temples, 269, 270

Meiji government (Japan): on clerical marriage and meat eating, 137
men, 181; bodhisattva precepts, 131; ordination of, 11, 134
microhistorical studies of Korean Buddhist tradition, 50–51, 60–61, 65
Mignolo, Walter D., 212–214
Mihwangsa Temple, 129t, 130t
"Mind is the Buddha" (K. *sim chŭk Pul*), 31
Minjung Buddhist movement (1970s–1980s), 5, 37, 57
Min Pyŏngsŏk, Envoy (1858–1940), 79
Mirhong (teacher), 129t
Miserable Fate, A (K. *Pangmyŏng*) (Han), 212, 228–229
misogyny and Buddhism, 91–92, 108–109
modern household register system, 138
modernity: and colonialism, 62–63, 213–214, 219–220; and Korean Buddhist writings, 226–227; sources of, 5
modernization: challenges facing contemporary Buddhism, 251–252; and Chŏn Ilchŏng, 8; events leading to, 5, 137; and *Pure Rules for the Sangha*, 198–200
monasteries: Chŏndŭng, 155n84; Fayuan, 126; Haein, 52, 81–82, 85, 88, 102; Hŭngguk, 136; Hwaŏm, 125–126; Hyein, 22; Jogye (T'aegosa), 4; Kwiju, 134, 141; Magok, 122, 141–148; Myoshin (Japan), 107; Naewŏn, 7, 114, 115, 118n29; Namjang, 111–112; Paegyang, 11, 181–182; Podŏk, 113; Pohyŏn, 141; Pŏmŏ, 126; Pomun, 113; Pongam, 266–

monasteries *(continued)*
  267; Pongŭn, 147, 154n83, 159, 253; Pŏpchu, 141; P'yoch'ung, 126; Sŏgwang, 134; Songgwang, 125–126; Sudŏk, 102; Taedun (was Taehŭng), 125, 127, 134, 150n13, 151n27; Taewŏn, 114; T'ongdo, 52, 122, 126, 137–141; Unmun *(bhikṣuṇī* seminary), 114, 118n30; urban, 269–270; Wŏlchŏng, 126; Wŏn'gak, 84; Wŏnhŭng, 134; Yŏnggam (was Sago Hermitage), 22; Yongju, 158; Yongyŏn, 136. See also temples
monastic codes, 123, 124, 159, 161, 162
monastic community. See Buddhist sangha
monastic curriculum. See curriculum
monastic marriage. See clerical marriage
monastics: aging population, 15; and court ladies, 94–95; education of laity, 264–265; as face of Buddhism, 183, 202n5; proposed dual structure for, 166; role of, 262–263, 266; social status, 255, 267–268, 274n34; tourist programs, 195, 206n57; women, 7, 8, 15, 17n28, 41. See also monks; nuns
money, and Pure Rules, 200
Mongolian Buddhism: and clerical marriage, 161
monks: eccentric, 169–170; head monks, 133–134, 140–141, 142–143; Japanese Buddhist, 107; ordination requirements, 131–132; of principle or of worldly affairs, 34, 43n37; prohibition on access to capital, 5, 253; purification movement, 165; rise in ordinations, 132–137, 148, 149; secret wives, 159–160; treatment of nuns, 108–109, 114, 116
morality, 25, 39–40
Mori Arinori (1847–1889), 213–214
mountain Buddhism, 91, 95, 114, 254, 268–270
movement: and Buddhist propagation, 62
Muha (monk, preceptor), 130t
Mun, Chanju (scholar), 58
Muwi (monk) (1826–1886), 130t
Myŏngjin (former abbot), 159
Myŏngsŏng, Queen *(bhikṣuṇī)* (1851–1895), 78, 115–116, 118n30
Myori Pŏphŭi (Sŏn master) (1887–1975), 102
Myoshin Monastery (Japan), 107

Na Chŏngho, 154n83
Naewŏn Monastery, 7, 114, 115, 118n29
name-change policy, 237
Namjang Monastery, 111–112
"Namo Amit'abul" ("Homage to the Buddha Amitābha") (Chŏn), 85
Nango. See Taeŭn (monk) (1780–1841)
Nanming's Ode to the Song about Realizing the Truth (Kamio edition), 242–243, 246
Nathan, Mark, 6–7, 254
nationalism, 3–4, 227, 229
Nattier, Jan, 161
Neo-Confucianism, 2–3, 75–76, 81, 90, 215. See also Confucianism
Newari Buddhism: and clerical marriage, 161
"new women," 74
New Women's Movement (1920s colonial Korea), 74

Nichiren Buddhism, 8, 105, 106
no-meal-in-the-afternoon (K. *ohu pulsik*), 21, 23
nonduality, 170–171
novices: decline in women, 15, 17n28; and Pure Rules, 198–199; recruitment of, 159; training, 123–124, 150n13, 187t, 204n28
Numrich, Paul, 183
Nŭnggasa Temple, 129t
nunneries, 76, 96n14
nuns, 7–9; and court Buddhism, 76; education, 115, 117n20; Eight Chief Rules (K. *p'algyŏnggye*) (Vinaya), 109; Japanese Buddhist, 107; Kwanŭm seminary, 111–112; purification movement, 113; rebuilding of monasteries, 114–115; reformation, 37; rise in ordinations, 149; treatment by monks, 108–109, 114, 116

O (descendant of Three Scholars), 236
"Observations from a Tour of Japanese Buddhism" (Naeji Pulgyo Kyŏnhakki) (Suok), 103–104
Office of the Coalition of the Thirty Head Temples (K. *Samsip ponsan yŏnhap samuso*), 87
ohu pulsik (no-meal-in-the-afternoon), 21, 23
Okamura Keiji (scholar) (1947–), 241
Olson, Carl, 172
Ŏm, Queen (former court lady) (1854–1911), 73, 78, 79, 80, 82
one-meal-per-day (K. *ilchongsik*), 21
On'gok (teacher), 129t
On the Restoration of Korean Buddhism (Chosŏn Pulgyo yusillon) (Han Yongun), 53, 58

oppression: of Korean women, 89–90, 108
ordinations, 10; installation of ordination platforms, 134, 135t; ordination lineage, 125–127, 132, 149, 151n18; records, 127–128; requirements, 131–132; rise of, 132–137, 148, 149; self-ordination (K. *chasŏ sugye*), 125, 151n18. See also *bhikṣu*; *bhikṣuṇī*; bodhisattva
orthodox dharma lineage. See dharma lineage
Orthodox Path of the Sŏn School, The (Sŏnmun chŏngno), 38
Outline of a Theory of Civilization, An (Fukuzawa), 214, 221
Ownby, David, 5

Pacific War, 3, 112
Paegam (preceptor), 130t
Paegnyŏn (monk) (1737–1807), 130t
Paegyang Monastery: 2012 incident, 11, 181–182
Paegyangsa Temple, 130t
Paek Changgong (ancestor of Paek Yongsŏng), 52
Paek Namhyŏn (father of Paek Yongsŏng), 51–52
Paek Yongsŏng (1864–1940), 5, 6–7, 47, 103; and clerical marriage, 164; and court ladies, 94–95; March First movement, 48, 54; microhistorical study of, 51, 61; *p'ogyo* (propagation), 48–49, 53, 57, 61–62, 67; pursuit of one's own enlightenment (K. *sanggu pori*), 51–52; studies of, 55–58, 66, 68n8, 227; teaching and saving others (K. *hahwa chungsaeng*), 52–55; and Yi Hoegwang, 81–82, 85, 86–87

Paengnyŏn (teacher), 129t
Paengnyŏnsa Temple, 129t
Pak, Kyŏnghun, 84
Pak Hŏŭn (preceptor), 135t
Pak Hyedang (scholar), 44n53
Pak Isŏng (fifteenth century), 244
Pak Manha (monk, preceptor) (1890s), 125, 126, 134, 135t, 136, 139t, 149
Pak Pongsŏk (1905–?), 239
Pak Suho (sociologist), 37
palace nunneries, 76, 96n14
Palace style penmanship (K. *kunch'e*), 85
Pali Canon, 186
Pang Hanam (1876–1951), 95
pārājikas (four grave offences), 168–169, 178n60, 189t, 192
Park, Jeongeun, 10
Park, Jin Y., 1, 6, 7, 74, 96n8
Park, Pori, 7, 122
Park Hanyŏng (1870–1948), 95
Park Jae-Hyun (Buddhist scholar), 40
Park Kijong (chief administrative director) (1907–1987), 166
patriarch, founding, 38–39, 105
patriarchy, 90, 172–173
PD Notebook (K. *PD Such'ŏp*) (television program), 158
penal system. *See* Jogye Order
"People's Coalition for Purging the Jogye Order's Corruptions," 168
Podŏk Monastery, 113
Pogam (preceptor), 129t
p'ogyo. *See* propagation of Buddhist teachings (*p'ogyo*)
Pohae (teacher), 129t
Pohyŏn Monastery, 141
Poje (monk) (1828–1875), 130t
Pŏkbong (teacher), 151n19
Pŏmhae (monk, preceptor) (1820–1896), 125, 126, 127, 128, 129t, 130t, 136, 149

Pŏmŏ Monastery, 126
Pomun (monk) (1816–1892), 130t
Pomun Monastery, 113
Pomun Order, 161
Pongam Monastery, 266–267
Pongam Monastery Compact Community (K. *Pongamsa kyŏlsa*), 266–267, 268
Pongnyŏgwan (nun) (?–1938), 17n20
Pongŭn Monastery, 147, 154n83, 159, 253
Pongŭn Temple, 257, 259, 260, 261
Pŏpchu Monastery, 141
Popular National Sovereignty, On (Fukuzawa), 221
P'oun (monk) (1806–1867), 128, 130t
prātimokṣa rules, 123, 161, 184, 200
prayers, 256–257, 258
Prebish, Charles, 122–123
preceptors, 126, 129t, 130t, 131–132, 135t
precepts, 54; *bhikṣu*, 67, 121–122, 126–128; *bhikṣuṇī*, 103; bodhisattva, 124, 126–128; receiving of, 22, 38; and temple laws, 124, 145–146; and Vinayas (*Kyeyul*), 131, 132; violation of, 39, 88, 163
Precepts-Court (K. *Hogyewŏn*), 192–193, 202. *See also* Jogye Order
Promotion of Buddhism (*Pulgyo Chinhŭnghoe*), 87
propagation of Buddhist teachings (*p'ogyo*), 43n37, 84, 199–200, 220, 258; Jogye Order, 12, 14, 273n25; and Paek Yongsŏng, 48–49, 53, 57, 61–62, 67; propagation centers, 88, 254–255; urban centers, 262–263, 265–266, 269–270
propitiatory rites, 257, 258

proselytizing. *See* propagation of
Buddhist teachings *(p'ogyo)*
Protestantism. *See* Christianity
public secrecy, concept of, 159; and
secret wives, 160–161
P'unggok (teacher), 129t
Pure Land Sect, 106, 228
Pure Rules for the Sangha (K. *Sŭngga chŏnggyu*), 12, 182–184, 186, 193, 197; and driving, 198–199; ecological behaviors, 199; missing from curriculum, 185; and personal money, 200; Sŏn Halls, 194–196, 196t
purification movement, 11, 113, 165, 177n46, 268
P'yoch'ung Monastery, 126
Pyŏkp'a (monk) (1807–1887), 128, 130t
P'yŏngch'ŏl (teacher), 129t

Qianlong (emperor) (1735–1796), 223

"Radical Attempt to Modernize Buddhism, The" (1982), 166
Record of the Masters and Disciples of the Laṇkāvatāra School, 239, 246
"Reformation of the Order" (Jogye), 36–37, 193–194
relationality model, 64–65
religiosity: decrease in Buddhist followers, 158–159, 174n4, 256
renouncer (K. *ch'ulga*), 263, 265
renunciation, 253
"Report on T'ongdo Monastery's Head Monk . . ." (Watanabe), 138
Restoration. *See Treatise on the Restoration of Korean Buddhism* (Han)
Rhi Kiyong (scholar) (1922–1996), 171
rigorous practice (Sŏn), 21–23
Rinzai Buddhism, 8, 87, 106, 107

Ritzinger, Justin, 5
Rujin (Chinese monk) (1425–?), 124

Sago Hermitage, 22
sangha. *See* Buddhist sangha
Sangun (monk) (1827–?), 130t
Sasaki, Shizuka, 194
scandals, Buddhist, 11, 95, 157–158, 178n54, 181, 182
Schmithausen, Lambert, 183
scholarship: approaches to understand modern Buddhism, 62–64, 180n76; conventional Korean Buddhist, 5, 9–10, 13–14, 15–16, 55–57, 60, 66, 74
Schopen, Gregory, 200
secret wives *(ŭnch'ŏ)*, 11, 160, 161–162; Jogye Order, 166–169, 172–173. *See also* clerical marriage
secularization, 15, 24–25, 159. *See also* religiosity
Séguy, Jean (sociologist), 267
self, 25, 31
"Self-Admonitions" *(Chagyŏngmun)* (Yuan), 123, 150n13
Self-Admonitions for Beginning Practitioners (Ch'obalsim chagyŏngmun), 124
self-ordination (K. *chasŏ sugye*), 125
Seminary for the Study of Sŏn (*Sŏnhagwŏn*), 54, 58, 67
Seminary Pure Rules, 194–195
Seoul: reintroduction of Buddhism, 7, 8, 54, 75, 81, 83–84, 94–95
sex scandals, 11, 95
Shinba Susumu. *See* Kim Kugyŏng (1906–1950?)
Shinran (founder of Jōdo Shinshū sect) (1173–1263), 174n13
Silence of Love (Han), 225
Silla period (57 BCE–935 CE), 162
Sinhŭng Temple, 80

skirt Buddhism (K. *ch'ima Pulgyo*), 95
Sŏam (monk) (1812–1876), 130t
Sŏgwang Monastery, 134
Sŏ Haedam (preceptor), 135t
Sŏ Hŭisun (court lady), 77
Sŏil (monk), 127
Sŏju (preceptor), 129t, 130t
Sŏkho (teacher), 129t
Sŏlchŏng (chief monk) (1942–), 158, 159
Sŏl Ch'ong (660–720), 170
Sŏldu (monk) (1824–1889), 130t
Soloves, Daniel, 169
Sŏn: antinomianism, 169–170; and doubt, 26–27; *hwadu* meditation, 22, 25–26, 28–29; and Hyeam Sŏnggwan, 6, 23–24; masters, 6, 7, 21; orthodox dharma lineage, 38–39; rigorous practice, 21–23
Sŏn and Kyo Dual Orders (*Chosŏn Pulgyo Sŏn-Kyo yangjong*), 68n13
Song about Realizing the Truth. See *Nanming's Ode to the Song about Realizing the Truth*
Sŏngchŏl (Sŏn master) (1912–1993), 6, 22, 23, 38, 57–58, 267–268, 274n43
Songgwang Monastery, 125–126
Songgwangsa Temple, 130t
Song Man'gong (Sŏn master) (1871–1946), 95, 102
Sŏngmuk (teacher), 129t
Sŏng Ogyŏm (last court lady) (1920–2001), 78, 95
Song Sŏru (head monk) (1871–?), 139t, 140–141
Sŏngwŏl (abbot) (1954–), 157–158
Song Wŏlchu (Jogye Order) (b. 1935), 33, 35, 43n32, 167
Sŏn'gyŏng (nun, Sŏn master), 7
Song Yongp'il (lay Buddhist working for Yi Hoegwang), 88

Sŏn Hall Elders Committee (K. *Sŏnwŏn sujwahoe*), 195
Sŏn Halls Pure Rules (K. *Sŏnwŏn chŏnggyu*), 194–196, 196t
Sŏn school, 38, 104–105, 106
Sørensen, Henrik (scholar), 56–57, 69n22, 69n24, 122
Sŏrhŏ (preceptor), 129t
Sŏru (monk) (1830–1868), 130t
So Sego (preceptor), 135t
Sōtō Sect (Japan), 53
Sōtōshū Sect (Japan), 83, 84
Sŏ Ŭihyŏn (Jogye Order) (b. 1936), 33, 34–35, 43n31, 167, 178n54, 181, 201–202
Southeast Asia, 188, 200
South Korea: religion, Gallup census data, 274n33; religion, national census data (2015), 15, 174n4, 261, 275n52; role of urban temples, 252–253
Sŏ Wŏrhwa (preceptor), 135t
spatial metaphors to analyze religion, 63–64
Sri Lanka: Buddhism changes under British colonial rule, 59–60
Ssangnyŏn (monk, preceptor), 129t
Statistics Korea, 15
staying-sitting-in-meditation-without-lying-down (K. *changjwa purwa*), 21, 23
Story of the Western Wing, The, 218–219
studies. See scholarship
stūpas in Fengtian, 240–241
subitism. See suddenness
suddenness (K. *ton*), 6, 28–29
Sudŏk Monastery, 102
Sŭngga chŏnggyu. See *Pure Rules for the Sangha*
Sŭngil (teacher), 130t
Sŭngnim. See Pak Manha (monk, preceptor) (1890s)

Sungsan (1927–2004), 177n46
Sunjong, King (r. 1907–1910), 74, 78, 89
Sunyŏng (protagonist in *A Miserable Fate*), 228–229
Suok Sŭnim (nun) (1902–1966), 8–9, 101–102; and Buddhist nuns, 107–109; as dharma instructor, 111–112; dharma lineage, 115–116; and Japanese Buddhism, 103–104, 110–111; and Korean Buddhism, 105–107; and Moyri Pŏphŭi, 102; purification movement, 113; rebuilding Naewŏn Monastery, 114–115; study of Buddhist practice, 102–103; travelogue, 8–9, 101–102, 103, 109–110
supreme patriarch (K. *Chongjŏng*), 22, 35, 37, 167, 188
Susŏng (monk) (?–1885), 130t
suspension *(epoché)*, 28
Sūtra of Maitreya Bodhisattva's Attainment of Buddhahood, The (Yi), 92
Sūtra on the Descent of Maitreya, The (Mirŭk sangaeng kyŏng) (Yi), 92
Syngman Rhee (president), 165
systems approach to Korean Buddhist tradition, 65

Taedun Monastery, 125, 127, 134, 150n13, 151n27
Taedunsa Temple, 129t, 130t
Taegakkyo (Great Enlightenment Teaching), 5. *See also* Paek Yongsŏng
Taegak Kyodang (Buddhist temple), 54–55
Taegaksa (Great Awakening Temple), 49, 67n5, 85, 94–95

T'aego Order, 268; and clerical marriage, 161, 162, 165; and Jogye Order, 167, 177n47
T'aego Pou (1301–1382), 38
T'aegosa (Jogye Monastery), 4
Taehŭng Monastery. *See* Taedun Monastery
Taeŭn (monk) (1780–1841), 125–126, 130t, 149, 151n18
Taeŭn Kim T'aehŭp (scholar monk) (1899–1989), 103
Taewŏn Monastery, 114
Taixu (1890–1947), 5
Takahashi Tōru (Japanese historian) (1878–1967), 171
Takeda Hanshi (Sōtōshū priest) (1864–1911), 83, 98n49
Tasan Chŏng Yagyong (1762–1836), 108
Taussig, Michael, 157, 159, 173
tea ceremonies, 195–196
Teachings of Great Awakening (Taegakkyo), 95
Teltscher, Kate, 223
temple laws (K. *Sabŏp*), 151n14; and building a temple, 87; and celibacy, 9–10, 48, 54, 122, 141; and head-monk elections, 138, 140–141, 142–143; and meat eating, 48, 54, 122; rise in *bhikṣu* and bodhisattva ordinations, 132–133, 136–137; and Vinaya, 124, 149
Temple Ordinance (K. *Sach'allyŏng*), 132, 133
temples, 251; Central Propagation Temple (Imje Order), 53; education programs, 257–258, 259, 263–265; Jogye Temple, 94, 181; Kŏnbong Temple, 81; Mangwŏl Temple, 80, 81, 82, 86; Mihwangsa Temple,

temples *(continued)*
129t, 130t; and modernization, 252; Nŭnggasa Temple, 129t; Paegyangsa Temple, 130t; Pongŭn Temple, 257, 259, 260, 261; Sinhŭng Temple, 80; Songgwangsa Temple, 130t; Taedunsa Temple, 129t, 130t; Taegaksa (Great Awakening Temple), 49, 67n5, 85, 94–95; Taegak Temple, 54–55; Togapsa Temple, 129t, 130t; Unhŭungsa Temple, 130t; urban, 262–263, 269–270. *See also* monasteries

Temple Stay (monastic touristic program), 206n57, 269

"ten benefits of keeping the precepts," 183, 203n13

Thich Nhat Hanh (Vietnamese Buddhist monk/thinker), 27

Three Scholars (K. *Samhaksa*), 236

Tibetan Buddhism, 203n19; and clerical marriage, 161

Togapsa Temple, 129t, 130t

ton. *See* suddenness

T'ongdo Monastery, 52, 122, 126, 137–141

Training School for Nuns (Japan), 104, 107, 111

translation of Buddhist scriptures, 54

"Treatise on Contemplating Mind" (K. *Kwansim Non*), 244, 245

Treatise on the Reformation of Korean Buddhism (Han), 13, 163–164, 254

Treatise on the Restoration of Korean Buddhism (Han), 53, 58, 215, 216, 220

Tripitaka Translation Association *(Samjang yŏkhoe)* (Yongsŏng), 54

True Doctrines that Return to the Source, The (Kwiwŏn chŏngjong) (Paek), 53

True Pure Land Sect, 106, 228

Turner, Alicia, 217

Tweed, Thomas, 7, 63–64, 217

Ŭisun. *See* Ch'oŭi (monk) (1786–1866)

Ŭnam (teacher), 130t

Ŭngam (monk) (1829–1886), 130t

Ŭnghŏ (teacher), 129t

Unhŏ (1892–1980), 112

Unhŭungsa Temple, 130t

Unmun Monastery *(bhikṣuṇī* seminary), 114, 118n30

Unp'a (preceptor), 134

uposatha ritual (K. *p'osal*), 193, 205n44

urban Buddhism, 252–255, 262–263, 265–266, 269–270

Vásquez, Manuel, 64

"venerable" (as a respectful title), 268

Vermeersch, Sem, 204n24

views (rejecting or being attached to), 27

Vinaya, 10, 161, 175n22; classification of texts, 123–124; Eight Chief Rules (K. *p'algyŏnggye*), 109; enforcement of, 188; *Four-Part Vinaya*, 123, 146, 151n28; missing from traditional monastic curriculum, 185; and precepts *(Kyeyul)*, 131, 132, 145–146; and temple laws, 124, 149; updating of rules, 11–12, 182–183, 193–194

Vinaya School of China, 126

Vinaya Schools of Korea, 187t

visionary ordination (K. *sŏsang sugye*), 125, 151n18

Wang Yangming (1472–1529), 215–216
Wanho (monk, preceptor) (1758–1826), 127–128, 129t, 151n19
Watanabe Akira (official of Department of Religion), 137–138, 140, 142, 152n35
wealth, and Pure Rules, 200
Weber, Max, 263
West, the: Christianity, 221, 262; colonialism, 2–3, 213–214
wives (secret). *See* secret wives (ŭnch'ŏ)
Wŏlchŏng Monastery, 126
Wŏlsong (Sŏn master), 34, 130t
women: and awakening (enlightenment), 91–92; and Buddhism, 7–8, 99n83, 101, 134, 259–260; conditions faced by Korean women, 89–90, 108, 112; lived experiences of, 41; ordination of, 134. *See also* monastics; nuns
Women in Korean Zen: Lives and Practices (Bachelor), 7
Wŏn'gak Monastery, 84
Wŏnhae (monk) (?–?), 130t
Wŏnhŭng Monastery, 134
Wŏnhyo (Silla monk) (617–686), 11, 123, 163, 175n27, 185; veneration of, 170–171, 179n70
Wŏnjong (Complete School), 83–84, 87, 93
Wŏn Order *(Wŏnjong)*, 53, 68n13, 105. *See also* Jogye Order
Wŏnŭng (monk) (1855–?), 130t
Woodbine, Onaje, 45n57
"Word of Warning for [Buddhist] Female Believers, A" (Chŏn), 85, 89
Wŏrhwa (monk) (1836–?), 130t

Wŏryŏ (monk) (1824–?), 130t
written or textual propagation (K. *munsŏ p'ogyo*), 57

Yangjŏng Yŏhakkyo (private school), 85
Yang Kŏnsik (aka Paekhwa) (1889–1944), 225
Yaun (monk) (late Koryŏ period), 123, 185
Yeam (monk) (1834–1894), 130t
Yi, Prince, 78–79, 89
Yi Charang, 183
Yi Han-meh (sociologist), 37–38
Yi Hoegwang (1862–1932), 8, 53, 57, 69n24, 75, 92; alliance with the Rinzaishū, 87; building the Wŏnjong (Complete School), 83–84; and Chŏn Ilchŏng, 75, 80–81, 84, 86, 93–94; financial difficulties, 88–89; and Paek Yongsŏng, 81–82, 85, 86–87; as preceptor, 134, 135t, 136, 144t, 147
Yi Nŭnghwa (scholar) (1869–1943), 5, 34, 43n37, 178n64
Yi Pŏpch'ŏl (senior leader of Jogye Order), 167
Yi Royal Household, 73, 78, 88, 89, 92–93, 95, 96n2
Yi Sŏnghae (head monk-elect) (1874–?), 141–142, 143, 144t
Yi Sŭnguk (department head of Yi Royal Household Office), 92–93
Yi Tŏkchin (scholar), 56
Yi Tonghwan (lay Buddhist) (1827–?), 131
Yi Ŭngun (treasurer of Yi Royal Household Office), 92–93
Yŏngbong (preceptor), 135t
Yŏngdam (preceptor), 130t

Yŏnggam Monastery (was Sago Hermitage), 22
Yonghŏ (monk), 134
Yŏngho (preceptor), 130t
Yongju Monastery, 158
Yongun (monk) (1813–1888), 130t
Yongyŏn Monastery, 136
Yŏnha (monk, preceptor), 127, 128
Yŏnju (monk) (1827–?), 130t
Yŏnp'a (monk) (1772–1811), 130t
Yoon, Yee-Heum, 256
Yosŏk (Silla princess), 170, 179n70

Yu Inmyŏng (head monk), 141, 143, 145, 147
Yun (descendant of Three Scholars), 236

Zen. *See* Sŏn
Zen Monastic Experience, The (Buswell), 122
Zhaozhou, 26–27, 30
Zhou Zuoren (1885–1967), 235–236
Zongze's (died c. 1107) Pure Rules, 193, 205n44

www.ingramcontent.com/pod-product-compliance
Lightning Source LLC
Chambersburg PA
CBHW031433230426
43668CB00007B/524